1987

YUMAN TRIBES
OF THE GILA RIVER

YUMAN TRIBES
of
THE GILA RIVER

By LESLIE SPIER

COOPER SQUARE PUBLISHERS, INC.
NEW YORK
1970

Originally Published 1933
Published by Cooper Square Publishers, Inc.
59 Fourth Avenue, New York, N. Y. 10003
Standard Book No. 8154-0333-X
Library of Congress Catalog Card No. 74-118641

Printed in the United States of America

This study is based on fieldwork jointly sponsored by
YALE UNIVERSITY
AND
THE UNIVERSITY OF CHICAGO

PREFACE

The Yuman tribes on the Gila River were originally the Maricopa and Kaveltcadom alone. Prior to 1800, the Maricopa occupied the river above Gila Bend; the Kaveltcadom, a hitherto-unrecorded Halchidhoma speaking group, lay from the Bend downstream halfway to the Colorado. These are the Cocomaricopa and Opa of early Spanish records. About the opening of the nineteenth century the Maricopa shifted a few miles eastward to the middle Gila, where they established themselves in close proximity to the Pima. Here they were joined between 1825 and 1830 by the Halchidhoma fleeing from the Colorado. A decade later (1838–39) the remnant of Kohuana and Halyikwamai followed the Halchidhoma from the Colorado, and about the same time the Kaveltcadom were absorbed from the lower Gila. Since all these movements took place under wholly aboriginal conditions, it seems legitimate to refer to them now in the aggregate as tribes of the Gila River.

It must be understood that the descriptions of the present account apply to the Maricopa unless specifically ascribed to the other tribes. The mixed community has been Maricopa in speech and essentially Maricopa in custom since its formation a century ago. My impression is that in material culture the Maricopa, Kaveltcadom, and Halchidhoma were essentially alike in the days before their commingling, so that in this respect the description of the Maricopa must also apply to the others. It proved possible to get specific information on most of Halchidhoma non-material culture, so that in the second instance, this paper embodies a description of that people. Notes on the Kaveltcadom, Kohuana and Halyikwamai are incidental.

Maricopa and Halchidhoma spoke barely separable dialects. Yuma was intelligible to them; Mohave and Walapai-Havasupai-Yavapai were closely related, but unintelligible. The other lower Colorado Yuman tribes, Cocopa, Kohuana, and Halykwamai spoke tongues similar or identical with each other, but set off from Maricopa-Halchidhoma.

The Maricopa have been historically linked with the adjacent Pima. For this reason they have been invariably dismissed as merely Pima-like by earlier writers who uniformly approached from the side of the historically more important, and more numerous, Pima. Their culture was, however, not that of the Pima. It was rather a lower Colorado culture resembling the Pima to no greater degree than the Pima themselves resembled the lower Colorado peoples.

There are today two Maricopa communities; one in the confluence of the Gila and Salt Rivers, the other, smaller, on the south bank of the Salt at Lehi, a few miles north of Mesa. To the local whites, all the members of these communities are "Maricopa." Actually they consist of the five Yuman tribes mentioned above, intermarried through several generations. It would be difficult to say whether Maricopa or Halchidhoma blood is now preponderant: the Kohuana, Halykwamai, Pima, and lesser ingredients, such as Yuma, are small. Today they form tribally unsegmented communities of Maricopa speech.

The larger Maricopa community in the Gila-Salt confluence numbers somewhat under three hundred individuals. Their scattered houses lie on the extreme western end of the Gila River Indian Reservation, a few miles west of Laveen and about fifteen southwest of Phoenix. There is little contact with the Pima villages, the nearest of which is now ten miles southeast near Gila Crossing. All the notes on which this paper is based were obtained from this community. That at Lehi was not visited. The Lehi group was said to consist of a half dozen families, primarily Halchidhoma. The earlier location of these mixed groups was on both sides of the Gila from Gila Crossing for ten miles upstream to Pima Butte. This area was abandoned in favor of the present locations a half century ago. There is now no Yuman-speaking person in their former territory, nor on the so-called Maricopa Indian Reservation twenty-five miles south, and none in the Gila Bend district.

Little of the ancient culture remains, the "Maricopa" having happily effected the change to modern rural conditions. Every household still has its metate and mortar in daily use; mesquite and other wild plants are sometimes gathered; grain is still stored in basket granaries; cookery is not entirely transformed; occasionally a cradle-board is constructed and its binding band woven; a few gourd rattles survive, and at least one calendar stick. Quantities of pottery are yet made by the ancient process; the bulk is modified to suit tourist tastes, but the common cooking pots of former days are to be found at every hearth. On the other hand the ancient dress, houses, and implements have gone completely. Native varieties of corn, beans, pumpkins, cotton, and tobacco have disappeared. Non-material elements have survived to some degree. To be sure, dances have long been forbidden, with shamanism, and the songs have disappeared with these. I was told that no living person has had dreams of the ancient type. There is one possible exception, a man with some pretensions to shamanistic knowledge, but I was unable to make contact with him. Only a few know fragments of the old song series, although the knowledge of their names and functions is well preserved. On the whole though, the old religious outlook persists: few of them are Christians. The younger people incline to agnosticism; older ones will call in a Pima shaman, or did so until a few years ago. Chiefs are a thing of the past and were probably never of much moment. The sib system and its attendant naming habits is undoubtedly the most flourishing part of the old thought system, although it too is beginning to disintegrate. But the old culture persists best in everyday behavior: mannerisms, sayings, personal relations, and speech. Although all the younger people and many of middle age speak English as well after a fashion, Spanish is little known.

On the whole, the Maricopa today are as much deculturated as the Yuma and Mohave and perhaps as much so as the Pima. Far less is open to direct observation than among the Papago and Western Apache. All items of non-material culture in the present account are the result of inquiry. Some fragments of material culture are still extant, and I found it quite possible to have

informants manufacture most of the implements as they had
seen them in their youth.

My principal informant was Kutŏ′x (also known as uwȧ′nyᵃ),
an Halchidhoma, eighty-three years old in 1929–30. He was born
near Maricopa Wells before that place became a way-station for
California-bound Americans in the 1850s. He died in the summer
of 1930. I thought it would be possible to get a complete picture of
Halchidhoma culture from him, as he knew it from his father,
who was one of the original migrants from the Colorado. He had,
however, grown up speaking the nearly identical Maricopa di-
alect and in predominantly Maricopa communities. It was possible to get a partial picture of life on the Colorado. He proved a
thoroughly useful informant for both Maricopa and Halchidhoma. My other principal informant was Last Star (xomȧce′-
kupa′Rȧ; also known as Thomas Sak O Par), a man of about
sixty-five, essentially Maricopa, but with Kaveltcadom and
Kohuana affiliations. On the whole his information was more
trustworthy than Kutox's. Some use was made of Josepha Juan
(tŭksa′vȧ), a woman of about the same age, an Halchidhoma; her
daughter Mary, aged about thirty; Hoot Somegustava (ᵃxuⁿt),
an Halchidhoma-Maricopa woman about sixty-five; her daughter-in-law, aged thirty; Charlie Redbird (matȧkwĭsnunyĕ′), a
Maricopa-Halchidhoma in his late forties; his son Claude; and
Manyan (maiⁱnyȧ′n), a Kaveltcadom-Kohuana man who was
born, by his own calendar record, in 1859–60. In addition a number of anonymous informants were interviewed incidentally by
myself, or on her own account by Mrs. Redbird, my interpreter.
It must be understood that these informants cannot really be
separated by tribes; the ascriptions given indicate only the pre-
dominant strains in their mixed lineage. Their information was
essentially Maricopa, except as they happened to remember
otherwise.

My interpreter throughout was Mrs. Ida Redbird, now in her
late thirties. She is a granddaughter of Kutox, daughter of Hoot,
and wife of Charlie Redbird above. Altogether an exceptional
woman, much of my success was due to her understanding and
sympathy with my purpose, and to her enterprise in voluntarily

ferreting out information. Although she had had little formal schooling, her English vocabulary was very wide and her understanding of modern American culture as full as that of her own people. To only one characteristic could I take exception; none of the good humored obscenity, so characteristic of Yuman speech, was ever translated without being toned down. I visited the Maricopa community in the winter of 1929–30 (November–March) on field funds supplied by the University of Chicago, and again in October 1931 and January 1932 on those of Yale University. My thanks for these opportunities must go to Dr. Edward Sapir and Dr. Fay-Cooper Cole. Collections were made for the Washington State Museum (University of Washington, Seattle), and for the Peabody Museum (Yale University) on which I have drawn for illustrations. During part of my stay in the field, I had the good fortune to have the companionship of Dr. A. L. Kroeber and Mr. E. W. Gifford, who drew freely on their wide acquaintance with the Yuman field for my benefit. Later they generously put in my hands their manuscripts on the ethnology of the Walapai, Southeastern Yavapai, Kamia, and Cocopa, as did Dr. Ralph Beals a summary on northern Mexico and his Cahita manuscript.

With characteristic kindness Dr. George Herzog transcribed the set of songs which I recorded on a phonograph. He has permitted me to include his remarks on the music verbatim with the metrical notation of the songs.

Edward S. Curtis has published a very brief account of the Maricopa, in which cultural borrowings from the Pima are stressed.[1] These seem inferences rather than native assertions.

The phonetic scheme used in this paper is the simpler system described in *Phonetic Transcription of Indian Languages* ("Smithsonian Miscellaneous Collections," LXVI [1916], No. 6) with some use of the fuller system described there. I diverge only in using R for a strongly trilled r-sound; even more strongly trilled than Spanish rr.

LESLIE SPIER

August, 1932

[1] Curtis, Vol. II.

TABLE OF CONTENTS

LIST OF ILLUSTRATIONS

LIST OF ILLUSTRATIONS

CHAPTER I

TRIBAL DISTRIBUTION AND INTERTRIBAL RELATIONS

THE TRIBES OF SOUTHERN ARIZONA

The Maricopa lived on the southern side of the vast plain in central southern Arizona through which flow the Gila and Salt Rivers. West of their country the rivers join, sweep by mountain barriers in a great arc (Gila Bend), and continue westward through a hundred miles of wide basin to join the Colorado River at Yuma. Immediately north of the Salt and the lower Gila the country rises in a succession of broken mountain ridges to the heights of the plateau that constitutes northern Arizona. The eastern end of the Salt-Gila valley is blocked by the same mountains sweeping southeasterly to the Sierra Madre of Mexico. From the Gila the country rises gradually to the south; a slope broken by many small sharply rising mountain ranges whose trend is northwest to southeast.

The habitat of the Maricopa was on the middle Gila, from its junction with the Salt River for thirty miles eastward to Pima Butte. The Maricopa have no tradition of ever having lived anywhere else. East of them on the Gila were the allied Pima, some of whom lived until the opening of the nineteenth century somewhat further east in the Santa Cruz valley. West of the Maricopa were an Halchidhoma speaking group, the Kaveltcadom, hitherto unrecorded. They occupied the Gila from Gila Bend downstream halfway to the Colorado. The highlands south of the Gila from the eastern mountains westward to the Colorado were occupied by Papago. The mountains of eastern Arizona were held by various bands of Apache. Those rising north of the Salt and lower Gila contained Yavapai bands, whose territory extended from near Globe westward to the Colorado. In the valley of the lower Colorado were the Yuma at the Gila confluence, the Cocopa nearer the Gulf of California, and upstream, south of the Colorado gorge, the Mohave. Various smaller tribes (Halchidhoma, Kohuana, Halyikwamai, Chemehuevi, Kamia, and perhaps others) had shifting loci in the historic period, now between Yuma and Cocopa, again between Yuma and Mohave.

The current notion is that in early Spanish days the people we now call Maricopa were living on the lower Gila, from Gila Bend downstream, and that they left there before 1850 to join the Pima on the middle Gila. This is the region occupied, according to my information, by the Kaveltcadom. It is generally assumed that the Spanish writers made no mention of Maricopa settlements above Gila Bend. They described the inhabitants of the district downstream from Gila Bend as Cocomaricopa and Opa, both Yuman in speech; sometimes distinguishing between them, sometimes asserting their identity. With the exception of Garcés they ignored the settlements on the great sweep of the river north and east of Gila Bend.

I believe it can be shown that there was at most but a slight shift of Maricopa from perhaps as far as Gila Bend to the middle Gila, but more probably from above the Bend and the vicinity of the Salt-Gila junction to the home they ascribe to themselves a few miles to the east. Whether the Cocomaricopa and Opa of the Spanish writers can be distinguished may never be known. If the Cocomaricopa are to be identified with the present-day Maricopa, of which I am none too sure, the Opa must be by distinction the Kaveltcadom. The best explanation would seem to be that the Spaniards were aware of a tribal distinction, now represented in native parlance by the terms Maricopa and Kaveltcadom, but confusedly applied it in only part of the territory, namely the district from Gila Bend downstream.

The sections which follow give native testimony and documentary evidence on these points in some detail.

The slight shift suggested here is a far cry from the current idea of a Maricopa migration from far down the Gila. Perhaps one reason for this erroneous view is that the traditions of the Halchidhoma, Kohuana, and Halyikwamai of their own migrations from the Colorado have been mistaken for those of the

Maricopa. The reason is intelligible, since these Yuman remnants have been thoroughly incorporated in the Maricopa community for the better part of a century. The Halchidhoma fled the Colorado about 1825–30, going to Sonora, and shortly after joining the Maricopa near the Pima. Ten years later the linked Kohuana and Halyikwamai followed them eastward. The Kaveltcadom joined the Maricopa community at about the same time.

Population estimates are available from the late eighteenth and middle nineteenth centuries. In a tabular statement in 1776, Garcés set the number of Halchidhoma and Cocomaricopa each at 2500. These Cocomaricopa include the Opa of those days, together being the Maricopa and Kaveltcadom of the present paper. Previously (May 1774) he had written of the Cocomaricopa-Opa that "it appears to me that they number no less than 2500 souls between Agua Caliente and the villages of La Pasión de Tucavi [near Hassayampa Creek]," the whole span of their territory. He repeated this (November 1775), "It appears to me that this nation will number some 30 hundred souls," evidently again including those both above and below Gila Bend. This total for the combined Maricopa-Kaveltcadom is inferentially confirmed by Anza (November 1775), who gives a careful estimate of those below Gila Bend: "For, most of this tribe having come before me with the intention of not living hidden now, because of the peace which they enjoy, as well as to receive the presents . . . . for which purpose I have convoked them, there have assembled on the way from San Simón y Judas de Opasoitac [Gila Bend] to here [San Bernardino, above the Mohawk Mountains] scarcely fifteen hundred persons." It is palpable that he omits the population north of the Bend, where Garcés noted that the settlements were very populous. In his complete diary Anza offers direct confirmation: "The Opa or Cocomaricopa tribe . . . . apparently does not reach three thousand persons." The numbers seen at various villages are cited by these gentry, but they are not significant because there is no way of knowing how many had flocked to see the strangers. However, Anza (December 8, 1775) abruptly revised his estimates downward, reporting that the inhabitants of the Colorado, and the "Cocomaricopas, including the Opas," must be a third less than he had previously reported.[1]

Fifteen hundred to two thousand is not an impossible number for the Maricopa and Kaveltcadom jointly in the third quarter of the eighteenth century. On the other hand, the same number for the Halchidhoma may well be too large. Garcés' opportunities for observation were poor. Kroeber believes that Garcés overestimated all the smaller groups on the Colorado and prefers to believe the Halchidhoma about one thousand at that time.[2]

In 1852 Bartlett credited the Pima and Maricopa jointly with not above two thousand and quoted approvingly Johnston, who estimated them as over this number. "Of the number stated by me, I was told that two thirds were Pimos,"[3] a proportion that seems to hold from the century before. By this time the Maricopa had received accessions of Halchidhoma, Kohuana, Halyikwamai, and Kaveltcadom, who collectively may have comprised half the number of these "Maricopa."

They are reported to have dwindled to 386 in 1910.[4] Today Maricopa and Halchidhoma constitute the bulk of the population, being represented in about equal numbers.

TRIBAL DISTRIBUTION FROM NATIVE ACCOUNTS

The ethnic configuration at the opening of the nineteenth century was described by the Maricopa as follows. The Maricopa settlements clustered on both sides of the middle Gila near Secate (at the foot of Pima Butte). They called themselves pipai' or pipa's, "men." Since their languages are identical, this was also the name the Halchidhoma applied to themselves; for distinction, they called each other respectively païnya', "eastern men," or pa'ïnyaxa'na, "true eastern people," and xaltcaðŏ'm.

[1] Coues, I, 123; II, 442; Bolton, *Anza's California Expeditions*, II, 375, 388; III, 31; IV, 63; V, 304–5.

[2] Kroeber, *Handbook*, pp. 796, 799, 883.

[3] Bartlett, *Personal Narrative*, II, 263.

[4] Dixon, *Indian Population*, p. 18.

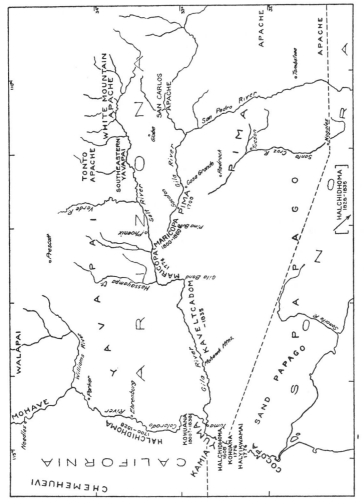

Fig. 1.—Map of tribal distribution in southern Arizona

According to Mrs. Redbird, the name xaltcȧϑŏ'm is derived from xalya-
ϑŏ'mbȧg, "people with queer ways."⁵ (A man who acts queerly is called pipax-
alyaϑŏ'mbȧg). Less certainly she suggested at another time that kavĕltcȧϑŏ'm
(see below) meant "western (or downriver) queer people." On the other hand
Kroeber recorded the divisions of the Mohave as Mat-halyadhoma and Kavilya-
dhoma, northern and southern (up- and downstream) respectively. Similarly
Forde recorded the names of two outlying settlements of the Yuma as kavēlt-
caϑum, "south (i.e., downriver) dwellers," and metvaltcaϑum, "north dwellers."
He writes, "The term altcaϑum, according to my informants meant 'pushed out
to a distance.' "⁶ The etymologies are not incompatible.

The names Maricopa, and its antique form Cocomaricopa, have no meaning
according to Mrs. Redbird and others, but are recognized only as "Spanish"
names. One old man offered what I believe a folk-etymology: the Spaniards
called them "mariposa" (butterfly), because they were in the habit of painting
stripes on their faces and hair, which the Indians transposed to "maricopa."
Opa, the name given by the Spanish writers of the eighteenth century to the
people of Gila Bend, was not recognized. (It may be an abbreviation of the full
name, as Supai is in common use for Havasupai, or it may be related to their
town at Gila Bend in Spanish days, Upasoitac or Opasoitac.) The element coco—
(koko—) has no meaning. Harrington translates Maricopa (Maríkapa') "bean
people,"⁷ but Mrs. Redbird, with whom this was discussed, said the form would
not be maʀi'kȧpa but maʀi'kpipa. There is yet another possibility; that Maricopa is a Yuma designation for them. Font remarked (1775), "Among the
[Yuma] women I saw some men dressed like women, with whom they go about
regularly, never joining the men. The commander [Anza] called them *amari-
cados*, perhaps because the Yumas called effeminate men *maricas*."⁸ While this is
not the regular Yuma word for berdache (male transvestite, elxa'; female,
kwe'rhame:⁹ cf. Maricopa ĭlₐȧxai' and kwĭʀaxamĕ'), it may be an alternative or
the jocular application of a name given the Maricopa.¹⁰ The embattled Yuma and
Maricopa were in the habit of hurling insults at each other, styling their opponents women or berdaches. Their respective mountain champions were supposed
to transform the opponents into berdaches. The word may thus be a Yuma
designation for effeminate men in general. On the other hand, this is certainly
not the Maricopa expression: an effeminate man, or one so mocked, would be
called cĭlₐȧxai'g, "girlish" (from mȧcȧxai', "girl"). Maricopa informants did not
recognize Font's words.

---

⁵ Kroeber (*Handbook*, p. 759) translates Mohave halyadhompa, "odd" or
"crooked."

⁶ Kroeber, *Handbook*, p. 746; Forde, *Yuma Ethnography*, p. 102.

⁷ Harrington, *Yuma Account of Origins*, p. 324.

⁸ Bolton, *Anza's California Expeditions*, IV, 105.

⁹ Forde, *Yuma Ethnography*, p. 157.

¹⁰ *Amaricado* and *marica* are both good Spanish, meaning effeminate man,
sodomite. The latter is known from at least the seventeenth century in the form
maricon. According to the context *marica* is by a coincidence also the Yuma
word and Anza was evidently indulging in a pun.

The Yumans to the west (Kaveltcadom, Yuma) also called the Maricopa tŏxpaĭnya', "east Pima," but the informants could see no reason for this, since the Maricopa lay west of the Pima. (Tŏxpaĭnya' is the Maricopa rendering: the River Yumans used the form hatpainya.) The Pima (tŏxpa')[11] lived principally on the Santa Cruz River in the vicinity of Tucson and Red Rock, with a division on the Gila about Sacaton. Apache, east of them in the mountains, drove the Santa Cruz group west to join their relatives in the Sacaton district. A Piman speaking group, called tŏxpa àxa't, "dog Pima," had a village a little distance south or southeast of San Xavier Mission. Their tongue was somewhat distinct from that of the Pima and Papago.

Their name derives from the following tale. Following the cremation of the culture hero two brothers went there to live. They had a little female dog for a pet. Every evening, when they returned from hunting, they had to cook for themselves. The little dog decided to cook for them. When the men left, she changed herself into a girl. Then she ground wild seeds, preparing several kinds, and put them in a bowl. When the men came home they wondered who had cooked it. They looked around the house for tracks, but could find only their own. This went on for some time, until they determined to find out who did the cooking. They went off some distance. The dog climbed on top of the house to see if they had gone far enough. She came down and changed into a girl again. While she was grinding, the men crept back to the house. They stepped right in. The little dog screamed in fright. The men sat down and asked the little dog why she could not remain as a girl. They said it was too bad that they had not fed her properly, but had given her only bones. As they said this, the girl transformed herself into a dog again. Then the two set off again to hunt. Then she made up her mind to change into a girl permanently. She lived with the two brothers. Some time after she bore children. They said these children would intermarry: this was the origin of this tribe.

The Papago (tŏxpa àmai', "high Pima") lived in all the mountains from the Yuma desert eastward to Tucson. A group called xapu'k, said to be "a kind of Papago" and friendly with the Yuma, lived in the Yuma desert region, probably in the mountains south and east of the true desert.

[11] The word tŏxpa' was said to be meaningless in Maricopa, as was also the Mohave form, hatpa (Kroeber, *Handbook*, p. 800). They may be the same word phonetically transposed. Other tribal names were also said to be meaningless: kwĭtca'n, kwapa', koxwa'n, xalyĭkwàmai'.

The Cocopa also describe a small band of "Pima" (hatbas) living near Somerton who were exterminated by the Mexicans. They traded with the Yuma. These are undoubtedly the Sand Papago of Lumholtz, who occupied the desert tract east of the Colorado and at the head of the Gulf of California southward to the Rio de Sonoita. Their principal camps were at the waterholes in the Gila and Pinacate Ranges east and south of the desert.[12]

South of the Papago in general in Mexico were Indians today called indiscriminately Yaqui (yaks). This may not be an ancient designation but derive from Yaqui now living at Nogales and Phoenix.

Yavapai and Apache, the dwellers of the mountains north and east, were alike called yăvipai'. The unfriendly Apache who drove the Pima westward were called yăvipai' ĭnya', "eastern Yavapai." Another Apache group living eastward of the Pima and south into Mexico was described as friendly with the Pima and Maricopa and in enmity with the present San Carlos Apache. These were called yăvipai' xastàu'lĭc, "washed Yavapai." The Apache of the Globe district, now the San Carlos Apache, were yăvipai' àhuadj, "Apache Yavapai" (àhua, "fierce [person]," "enemy"). The subdivisions of Yavapai recognized by themselves were not known to the Maricopa; a clear indication of their lack of contact other than through bitter warfare. The Maricopa classed them only roughly by their position: yăvipai' àxa'n, "true Yavapai," were the eastern people, inhabitants of the Verde River and the headwaters of the Salt; yăvipai' kàve', "west Yavapai," those occupying the mountains from Hassayampa Creek to the Colorado. (Corbusier's term Tulkepaia, which Gifford found applies to the western Yavapai, was unknown, and has no meaning in the Maricopa language.[13]) These mountain dwellers were known as a roving people, cave dwellers, who sometimes came down to the low country on the Salt River to stay for some weeks gathering the ripened fruit of the giant cactus.

Beyond the screen of mountain tribes, through which there was no penetrating, were known to live the Walapai (huàlàpai) and Hopi (muk, i.e. Moqui). The Walapai were known as friendly to

[12] Gifford, Cocopa MS; Lumholtz, *New Trails in Mexico*, pp. 329, 394, map.
[13] Corbusier, p. 276; Gifford, *Southeastern Yavapai*, p. 177.

PLATE I

KOTUX, HALCHIDHOMA INFORMANT

the Halchidhoma while the latter were still on the Colorado. The Paiute (paiu'tc) were known to be somewhere to the north. Havasupai, Navaho, Zuñi, and Ute were wholly unknown.[14]

Indians called pase'ĭndj (possibly "man ———") were said to live north of and close to the Apache proper.[15] They wove blankets and owned many sheep. When Kutox was a small boy (1850–55) they passed through Maricopa Wells several times driving sheep to California. Possibly they were Navaho, Zuñi, or eastern Pueblo.

A hitherto unrecorded people were described as living west of the Maricopa, the Kaveltcadom (kavĕltcàϑŏ'm, "west or down-river dwellers"). Their settlements were on the south side of the Gila from Gila Bend westward to the Mohawk Mountains. They were said to be Halchidhoma who had left the Colorado long prior to the main body because of dissension among themselves. To the Maricopa they were xaḷtcàϑŏ'm as frequently as kavĕltcà-ϑŏ'm, but distinguished by the name of their home about Gila Bend, kwa'akàma't. They numbered as many as the Halchidhoma proper, at least at the time of the latter's exodus. Where their orginal location on the Colorado may have been is unknown.

That the lower Colorado tribes were well known is attested by the following sequence given by Kutox, my aged Halchidhoma informant. In the north were the Mohave (maxa'vas) holding the river bottom from Fort Mohave downstream. Northeast of them in the mountains were the Walapai. The Chemehuevi (tcŭmàwo'và), a people of wholly incomprehensible speech, lived northwest of the Mohave. In the same direction were "Mission Indians" (xatcĭ'tc), undoubtedly Cahuilla, since they are called "Hakwicha by the Mohave, and a dialectic equivalent of Hakwicha by the other Yuman groups that know them."[16] (This

[14] Names for these people known to the Havasupai (coconino, hua'àmu"u, sà'u'u', and yu'ta) were not recognized.

[15] Russell mentions the Päsĭnâ allies of the Apache "from the north" (*Pima Indians*, p. 43). Bartlett in 1852 mentioned the droves of sheep driven along this route from New Mexico, Chihuahua, and Sonora to California (*Personal Narrative*, II, 177, 293).

[16] Kroeber, *Handbook*, p. 693; Garcés recorded it as Gecuiches (Coues, p. 423 *passim*).

agrees with a statement about their language: that it in no way
resembled Maricopa but was not like Chemehuevi. Cahuilla and
Chemehuevi do indeed belong to quite different branches of the
Shoshonean stock.)[17]
The Halchidhoma (xaltcáðŏ'm) were two or three days journey down river from the Mohave at the opening of the nineteenth century, that is, below Parker.
Next downstream, according to Maricopa information, were
the yăvipai' kăve', "western Yavapai," who, however, did not
live directly on the Colorado but in the mountains to the east.

Inquiry was made of two tribal names recorded by Oñate in 1605. At or below Parker he encountered the Bahacechas, allied with the Mohave and of the
same speech. This was prior to Halchidhoma occupation of this territory. The
name is clearly Yuman, but as Kroeber remarks is unidentifiable.[18] The Maricopa did not recognize it, but Mrs. Redbird suggested it might be the sib name
pakï't mistaken for a tribal designation. She pointed out that "people would tell
their sib names first, being proud of them." Collectively the people of this sib
would be pakï'tcïc. At the same time we must recognize that while the Halchidhoma and Maricopa have the sib pakï't, the Mohave do not. Oñate also reported
the Ozaras on the lower Gila, extending to the shores of the sea. Kroeber's suggested possible identification with a Pima or Papago division seems plausible,
since it is known that isolated bands of Piman speech were in this general locality in later times. Again Maricopa informants failed to recognize the name.
Mrs. Redbird's suggestion was that it might be ose'ʀăm, "I am freezing," mistaken for a tribal name,[19] hence the group may have been of Yuman speech. This
is not impossible since Oñate reached this group in midwinter.

The Yuma (kwĭtca'n) were three days below the Halchidhoma
at the mouth of the Gila River. (The mouth was called hŏmkwĭ-
táva'vă.) The informant had never heard that the Yuma lived
in any location other than this. A days' journey south of the
Yuma were the Kohuana (koxwa'n; singular k'wĭn), probably on
the west side of the Colorado, west or northwest of the Cocopa.
They had already incorporated the Halyikwamai (xalᵧikámai'),
a people of identical speech, so that koxwa'n and xalᵧikámai' are
sometimes considered interchangeable names.

[17] Kroeber, *Handbook*, p. 577.

[18] Kroeber, *Handbook*, p. 802.

[19] As the tribal name Pima is derived in error from the Piman words pia, piate,
"none" (Russell, *Pima Indians*, p. 19).

The Cocopa (kwapa') were three days' journey up from the mouth of the Colorado and two days below the Yuma. The Akwa'ala (kwàa'xl) were principally west of the Cocopa, but also lived among them. People of the mountains west of the Imperial Valley were kumàθa', that is Kamia or Southern (Eastern) Diegueño or both.[20] Other Californian tribes were unknown.

THE EASTWARD MOVEMENT

The Yuman scene was not static. Though the foregoing presents the picture in the year 1800, it was different both before and after that date. The river tribes were caught up in a great swirling movement, wherein the lesser peoples, shifting their loci along the river under the hammering of Yuma and Mohave, were finally pinched off and fled to the east. The information obtained from the Halchidhoma and Maricopa informants accords fully with that marshaled by Kroeber from Spanish sources and Mohave information,[21] and amplifies its detail.

Constant and devastating warfare had marked lower Colorado life from ancient times. Centuries of conflict may well have preceded Alarcon's comment in 1540 of "warre and that very great, and upon exceedingly small occasions; for when they had no cause to make warre, they assembled together and some of them said let us go to make warre in such a place and then all of them set forward with their weapons." From that time forward, the Spanish writers and the Americans of the nineteenth century record nearly incessant warfare.

There can be little doubt that the Maricopa once resided on the lower Colorado. This in face of the fact that they have no tradition of ever having lived elsewhere than on the middle Gila. Yet it seems quite credible that they set the habit of eastward movement across the desert in which they were followed successively by the Kaveltcadom band of Halchidhoma, the Halchid-

---

[20] This is the familiar confusion which Gifford has discussed (*Kamia*, pp. 1–9). A Mohave tradition places the Alakwisa, long extinct, between Cocopa and Kamia. Kroeber suggests this a possible synonym for Halyikwamai. My informants failed to recognize the name.

[21] Kroeber, *Yuman Tribes; Handbook*, pp. 796 f.

homa proper, Kohuana and Halyikwamai. Where they may
have lived on the Colorado we can only conjecture, but as their
language is still identical with Halchidhoma after centuries of
separation (as early as Alarcon they were not numbered among
the river tribes), we may assume it was somewhere near the
Halchidhoma country north of the Cocopa. Their culture as well
was that of the lower Colorado, but this is not thoroughly con-
vincing evidence, for they may have acquired it in their eastern
home. The date of the separation is also uncertain: it was at
least before the sixteenth century, and the veriest guess would
place it not many centuries earlier.[22]

Similarly, the Kaveltcadom had left the Colorado to occupy
the Gila Bend district prior to the historic period. If they were
indeed the Opa-Cocomaricopa of the eighteenth century, the
movement occurred at least two centuries ago. Halchidhoma
and Maricopa informants describe them as Halchidhoma, a
branch that left the main stream so long ago that tradition no
longer preserves precise mention of it. They are looked on as one
with the Halchidhoma in speech and blood, but distinct in culture and habitat. Today their descendants are reckoned wholly
Halchidhoma: for instance, it was only at the end of my first extended stay that I learned from the informant Last Star that
other Halchidhoma referred to his family as Kaveltcadom.

The earliest location of the Halchidhoma known to living
Halchidhoma and Maricopa was the Colorado below Parker,
from which the tribe fled just a century ago. This was in the day
of parents and grandparents of these aged informants. The
country as a whole was known as xaltcáðŏm nyĭma't, "the Halchidhoma's land"; the only specific locality remembered was
matkwaxwĕ'lc, at or near Parker. They lived sometimes on one
or the other side of the Colorado, planting in the bottom land on
levels annually inundated by the river. They made no ditches
and practiced no artificial irrigation in any form (like others on

[22] There is no warrant whatever for Kroeber's dogmatic statement: "It seems
unlikely that they left the Colorado more than about a hundred years earlier"
than Kino's advent just before 1700 (*Seri*, p. 50). Yet neither Oñate (1605) nor
Alarcon (1540) mention them on the Colorado, as Kroeber elsewhere recognizes.

PLATE II

Last Star and Mrs. Ida Redbird, Maricopa-Halchidhoma
Informant and Interpreter

the river). "The Halchidhoma were more numerous than any other tribe on the Colorado;" a doubtful statement. But they had a number of villages along the river. "A single village of houses close together might cover this farm [forty acres]. If one visited from village to village, it would take three days." At any rate their number was considerable; the 2,500 numbered by Garcés in 1776 may be an overestimate, but not an impossible one.

The location of the Halchidhoma in the summer of 1776 was recorded by Garcés.[23] Fourteen leagues south of a stream identifiable as Williams River he arrived at the northernmost group of their rancherías on the left bank, styling them San Antonio. Two leagues below were the Rancherías de Santa Coleta, "much abounding in crops." Two and a half leagues more brought him to the Laguna de la Trinidad, where he was "detained to talk with the old men," presumably at a settlement at this place. Crossing to the right bank, after half a league he found the Rancherías de la Asumpcion. Two and a half leagues below on the same side were several rancherías (Lagrimas de San Pedro). In the next five and a half leagues he passed "two rancherías and some ranchos" and crossing again to the Arizona side, found another ranchería. A final step of a league and a half brought him to the most southerly of the Halchidhoma settlements. This was, by his reckoning, sixteen and a half leagues (about forty-five miles) above the mouth of the Gila. None of the points in Halchidhoma territory is easily identified, but the span of their holdings is clear. It stretched on both sides of the Colorado for some forty miles (fourteen and a half leagues) from a point about that distance below Williams River to forty-five miles above the Gila. Making due allowance for both his circuitous route and the winding of the Colorado, we can place this middle third roughly from somewhat below Parker to above the Trigo Mountains. This is the region cited by my informants for the half century following.

His earlier route of May 1774 is even more difficult to trace, but leaves clearly the impression that he found the Halchidhoma in the same district. Some of the place names are duplicated in the two accounts. Leaving Agua Caliente, he reached the Colorado at a point which Bolton plausibly suggests was in the vicinity of Ehrenburg. Two leagues southwest was the home of the chief, "where assembled many Jalchedunes who lived down the river." He found these Indians through a district of ten leagues north of this point, all on the Arizona side.[24]

Attacked by both Yuma and Mohave, the Halchidhoma were constantly forced to shift their position. There is some recollection of having lived at first nearer the Yuma.

When the Yuma killed some of our men, we moved a little farther up the river each time and settled again. When we moved closer to the Mohave, they came

[23] Coues, II, 423–30.

[24] Bolton, *Anza's California Expeditions*, II, 376–87.

down and fought. Then, when some were killed, the Halchidhoma moved downstream a little. If only one tribe had fought us, we might still be on the river.

There is no recollection of any earlier location. Yet Oñate in 1605 found them the first tribe on the river below the mouth of the Gila. Kino, a century later, found them above the Gila. Garcés (1776) found them occupying some forty miles of the Colorado from somewhat below Parker to above the Trigo Mountains. This is the locale of their earliest recollections, with which Mohave memories agree. Presumably they had shifted northward of the Yuma to escape them, only to subject themselves to double peril from Mohave above as well as Yuma below.

The uneven conflict became too much for the dwindling Halchidhoma, despite the accession of Kohuana and Halyikwamai. A peace arranged by Garcés proved only temporary. The Mohave tell that they drove the joint tribes south from Parker, the Halchidhoma settling "at Aha-kw-atho'ilya, a long salty 'lake' or slough, that stretched for a day's walk west of the river at the foot of the mountains. The Kohuana removed less far, to Avi-nya-kutapaiva and Hapuvesa, but remained only a year, and then settled farther south, although still north of the Halchidhoma."[25] The Mohave further relate that again attacking the Halchidhoma, the latter withdrew, fleeing east across the Colorado to Ava-chuhaya, and thence east across the desert to the Maricopa. Of these details, my informants have no recollection.

Their own accounts, which follow, fix the flight from the Parker district in 1825–30. They stopped for two days with their relatives, the Kaveltcadom, at Gila Bend, before continuing the flight. They reached their objective in northern Sonora, having traversed some four hundred miles of desert, where they took refuge with an unidentified friendly tribe, with whom they were living in 1833. Gradually they began to drift back to the Gila to join the Maricopa; the remnant urged to this action by an epidemic. By 1838, when the first Kohuana-Halyikwamai arrived

[25] Kroeber, *Handbook*, p. 800. My own Mohave information is that the place from which the Mohave drove the Halchidhoma was located about two miles northeast of Blythe, near the river.

among the Maricopa, all the Halchidhoma that remained had reassembled on the Gila.

The Yuma, when intending to fight, would send word to the Mohave, and the two tribes would surround our villages. So a great many of our people were killed. They became so few that only a few villages remained on the river. Finally they decided to leave for safety, to remain away for a while, but not permanently. One night they gathered to discuss it. Some time before three families had left together and had disappeared. Their supposed fate decided the issue. But that very night, a man of the lost families returned. He told them that they had gone to Mexico, where they had been treated with great respect.[26] Then the whole tribe determined to follow them.

Next day they dug holes under their houses; stored their beans, corn, black-eyed peas, and everything they had in pots; and buried them deep in the ground. Long after, the Mohave told how they had discovered this hoard.

No one knows just when or where they started. The returned wanderer guided them, the whole tribe. Camping all the way in the desert, it must have taken a long time. They reached the Gila Bend Mountains (vixalgwa'a'mpàs, "lying on its breast mountain") where they stayed at kwa'akàma't with the Halchidhoma [Kaveltcadom] who lived there. They remained two days while women of the local group prepared provisions. On the third day, those from the Colorado went on; the local people remaining. It took some time to reach Mexico. When they reached there, they were received and fed. Who were the hosts is not known, but they were Indians and sometime referred to as Yaqui. The Halchidhoma lived in a village apart. The men worked for their hosts and the women sold pottery to the Mexicans. [The name of the Mexican settlement is given as tamalĕ'n or lamalĕ'n, an unidentified place in northern Sonora, which seems to have lain much south and east of Nogales.[27]] They had made up their minds to return to the Colorado if they were unfavorably received. But they were well cared for, and stayed there for some years. The great meteoric shower [November 13, 1833] occurred while they were there.

Maricopa men from the Gila visited them there: Halchidhoma visited the Maricopa and Kaveltcadom. Some Halchidhoma families left for the Sacate district on the Gila to be near the Maricopa, but many stayed in Mexico. Finally there was general sickness there; nearly the whole tribe died. The few families who escaped it, came away to settle with these others among the Maricopa. Kutox's father came at this time. This was before the arrival of the first group of Kohuana and Halyikwamai [in 1838].

The dates given above were fixed inferentially on the basis of the following information. Kutox, the Halchidhoma from whom the body of the foregoing account was received, was eighty-three in 1929–30, born at Maricopa Wells in

[26] Some acquaintance with Mexican localities is evidenced by Velasco (*Sonora*, p. 147) who states that in 1801 Cavorca (Caborca) was visited by "an Indian of the tribe called Tadchidume, to the north of the Colorado." (I am indebted to Dr. Ralph Beals for this reference.)

[27] Last Star fixed its location by repute as three days' foot journey southeast from Tucson. Near by was a mission. The name has no meaning in Maricopa and does not sound like a Maricopa word to this informant.

1847. He was born, according to his account, fourteen years after the meteoric shower. (Thanks to the existence of calendar records,[28] many of the older individuals know precisely when they were born.) His father was born on the Colorado, and was a young man, perhaps thirty years old, when they fled from the river. His father died when Kutox was about twenty, the elder being then about seventy. Hence the father was born about 1797; the flight took place about 1827. The several informants volunteered that the Halchidhoma were in Mexico "when the stars fell" (1833). Last Star thinks it was about four or five years after this event that the first group of Kohuana joined them. Kutox fixed it six years after the stars fell (1839) and at another time two years before he was born (i.e., 1845). The calendar stick records their advent in 1838. All the dates are harmonious and agree substantially with Kroeber's inference that the Halchidhoma and Kohuana abandoned the Colorado between 1820 and 1840, the Kohuana following the former by ten years. This accords with his doubt that the Kohuana left "at least as early as 1820."[29]

The movements of the Kohuana and Halyikwamai somewhat later are known with greater precision. According to my informants, they were neighbors of the Yuma, first south and later north of the Yuma villages. It was from the latter point that they fled the river following the Halchidhoma by a decade. Nothing was said of their sojourn with the Halchidhoma in the Parker district or with the Mohave in Mohave Valley, but Kroeber's Mohave information on this point is explicit and undoubtedly correct. Maricopa information is that in 1838 half the Kohuana, with the Halyikwamai of identical speech already incorporated, fled to the Maricopa, followed the next year by the remainder of the linked tribes.

The Halyikwamai were first known to Alarcon in 1540. They occupied the east bank of the Colorado next to the Cocopa in 1605, according to Oñate, and the west bank above the Cocopa and below the Kohuana, according to Garcés in 1776. The Mohave knew them as non-agricultural hill-dwellers, west of the river, north of the Akwa'ala and near the Yuma. Kroeber interprets this to mean that they were once a river people, who dispossessed, abandoned agriculture. Some may still remain among the Akwa'ala or maintain a separate existence north of them.

The Kohuana were found by Alarcon and Oñate; the latter recording their position above the Halyikwamai. Garcés noted their presence on the east side of the Colorado, above the Hal-

[28] See p. 138.   [29] Kroeber, *Handbook*, p. 801.

yikwamai, and makes them the next tribe below the Kamia and Yuma. Mohave information places them with the Halchidhoma at Parker, presumably subsequent to 1776. From this position, the Mohave drove them southward with the Halchidhoma, but not so far. They remained for a year, then moved still farther south but not quite to the Halchidhoma. In the conflict that followed, in which the Halchidhoma fled the river, the Mohave guarded the Kohuana against participation and subsequently removed them under compulsion northward to Mohave Valley. They lived there for five years, then went south to live with the Yuma. Some remained among the Mohave. After a five-year sojourn with the Yuma, they fled the river to join the Maricopa. So much for the Mohave view:[30] the accounts which follow mention only their association with the Yuma.

The Kohuana and Halyikwamai were distinct tribes of identical speech, who originally lived below the Yuma. The Kohuana, like the Halchidhoma, were constantly moving. They sometimes lived with the Cocopa, the Yuma, and Halchidhoma, helping each in turn in warfare.

The Kohuana had been living north of the Cocopa, when the Yuma invited them to live close to their village so that they could help each other in war. The Yuma had discovered that the Kohuana were friendly with the Halchidhoma. When the Yuma arrived one morning, the Kohuana thought they were being attacked. But the former told them not to run away, that they had only come to talk with them. The meeting was held in the Kohuana village. The Yuma invited them to come live with them. They took the Kohuana that very day, establishing them north of the Yuma village. The Kohuana were kept a good deal as prisoners, not as true friends. Sometimes two or three of them caught away from home would be killed by the Yuma. They decided to leave the river and join the Maricopa. They started from Yuma at night. [From another account: When the Maricopa went to fight the Yuma many years before Kutox was born, some of the Kohuana decided to return with them.] This was the first group of Kohuana to come. They captured and brought with them some Yuma children. They were more than two hundred [in another account, a hundred families], leaving as many behind. The Yuma tried to get their chief to make war on this remnant. This chief's daughter was among the captives. He [undoubtedly fearing reprisal on the captives] said, "Well, they are not going to kill my daughter. They took her over there. There she will have some cotton blankets to cover her." [The Yuma wove few or none.] A year later [1839] the remainder of the Kohuana, fewer in number, also joined the Maricopa and Halchidhoma. The Halikwamai came with the Kohuana; by that time they were one people.[31]

[30] Kroeber, op. cit., 799.

[31] Bartlett in 1852 noted the presence of ten surviving Cawinas among the Pima-Maricopa (Personal Narrative, II, 251). Today there remains only a sol-

By 1840 the Yuman scene had changed materially from that of the century preceding. The lower Colorado was in the hands of the Mohave upstream, the Yuma at the mouth of the Gila, and the Cocopa nearer the Gulf. But the Halchidhoma, Kohuana, and Halyikwamai, tired of being battered about and unable to secure freedom from attack on the river, had gone to join the Maricopa and their Pima allies. Some remnants of the Halyikwamai and Kohuana perhaps remained: the former in the mountains southwest of the Yuma, the latter resident among the Mohave.

MARICOPA AND KAVELTCADOM SETTLEMENTS

The Maricopa have lived on the Gila above its junction with the Salt since at least 1800. Their settlements were on both sides of the river from Sacate and Pima Butte to Gila Crossing as the western limit. On mesquite gathering and fishing expeditions, they were accustomed to camp along the slough (Santa Cruz River) at the northeastern foot of the Sierra Estrella, in the Gila-Salt confluence, and on the Salt as far upstream as Phoenix, but they had no settlements there. No one lived permanently on the Salt River below the point where it emerged from the mountains. In fact, the whole of the open plain north of the Gila to the mountains was unoccupied as too exposed to Yavapai and Apache attacks.

The principal settlements were on both sides of the Gila below Sacate.[32] When the Halchidhoma came from Mexico, they established themselves below the Maricopa at Sacate, i.e., nearer Pima Butte. The Kohuana-Halyikwamai, on coming from the Colorado, settled about the sandhills on the north side two miles southeast of St. John's Mission in the direction of Gila Crossing. This mixed group was still quite large in 1850: it was said that

itary aged Kohuana woman and two Halyikwamai speaking families of young people.

[32] Lumholtz's Papago annals imply that the Maricopa were living in 1850 at Red Rock in the Santa Cruz valley. It is doubtful that this can mean a permanent settlement so far east and in Pima territory (*New Trails in Mexico*, p. 74).

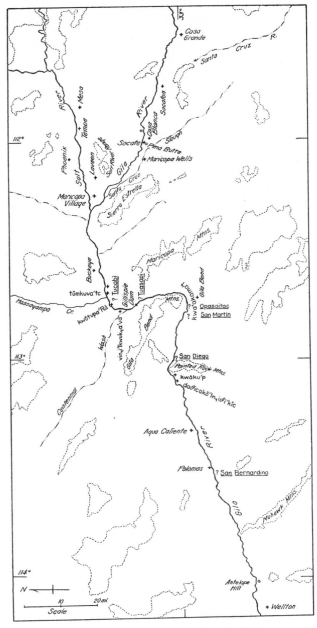

FIG. 2.—Map of Maricopa and Kaveltcadom Territory

there were so many that a small pond a mile and a half east of Gila Crossing was crowded with bathing children.[33]

The settlements of the combined "Maricopa" community about the middle of the last century were the following (Fig. 3):

1. cĭlyáai'kwĭtĭta'lĭc, "more than a few sandhills" (lit. "sand higher"), was the most westerly village. It lay close to the sandhills on the north bank of the Gila. Beyond this to the west was mesquite gathering ground.
2. tĭlpo"pĭlyámĭn, "scorched roadrunner," east of the above on the same bank.
3. axa'gua'lyà, "water showing," was by a slough to the east of the last.
4. kwuckĭ'tkwàxau'ĭc, "potsherds," on the north bank to the east.
5. utcĭ'ϑau'ĭc, "coals lying around," lay on the south bank almost opposite No. 2.
6. xiko"tokĭ'tŏv'au'ĭc, "Mexican cut down something standing" (xiko', "Mexican, white man"; tokĭ't, "to cut down") was somewhat farther from the river than the preceding.
7. ax'atwota'ʀà, "thick cottonwood," on the south bank perhaps a mile above No. 4.
8. ax'akwaxo't, "good cottonwood," lay close to the river south of the last.
9. ca'kŏv'ᵃau', "standing bone" (àca'k, "bone"), was just below Maricopa Wells, close to Santa Cruz slough. This was the most important village in Mexican days;[34] that in which the chief lived. No one lived directly at Maricopa Wells until after the coming of the Americans in the decade 1850–60.
10. kwatu'lxalyapŏ'mĭc, "lizard fell into the water," was on the north bank, seemingly due east of No. 8.
11. kusi'lydj, "rough dirt," perhaps a mile or more above the last on the north bank.
12. iu'xnyĭvai'ĭs, "living there with colds" (iu'x, "colds"), on the south side west of No. 11.
13. xapi'vĭc, "cattails" (? grow in the slough at this place), on the south side four miles west of Sacate.
14. axta"sĭl, "reedy place," a village at a long sloughy place east of Maricopa Wells. (The same name was given to the locality west of No. 12.)
15. xulnyinivàau'ĭc, "cactus standing,"[35] on the south side of the Gila two miles west of Sacate.
16. mĭse'kwĭni'ly, "black muddy slough" (mĭse', "muddy slough"), was located where the present settlement Sacate now stands. This was the last village to the east.

[33] Bartlett in 1852 stated that only ten Cawinas survived (*Personal Narrative*, II, 251).

[34] It was known to the Mexicans by the literal translation Huesa Parada, according to my informant. This is listed as El Juez Tarado (!), the residence of the chief Juan Chevereah, in the *Report of the Commissioner of Indian Affairs for 1858*, p. 207.

[35] A cactus resembling cholla, but very thorny; thorns white; grows in the mountains.

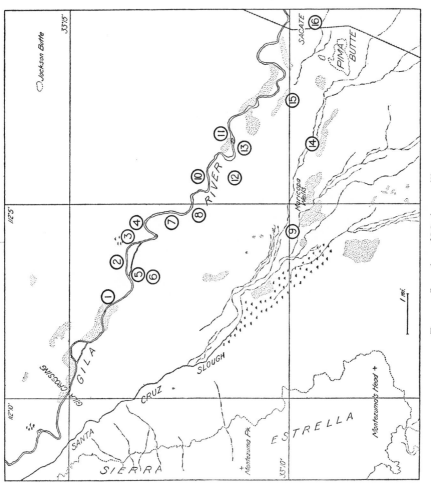

FIG. 3.—Location of Maricopa villages

The settlements were scattering and constantly shifting within this area. Houses were scattered, not in compact clusters. The Maricopa-Halchidhoma settlement near Maricopa Wells about 1850, for instance, contained houses one hundred and fifty to two hundred feet apart, and extended perhaps for two miles. By the middle of the last century, the accumulated losses from Yuma-Mohave attacks had become so great, that for protection communities were settled more compactly.

In 1852 Bartlett described these groups. "The villages consist of groups of from twenty to thirty habitations, surrounded by gardens and cultivated fields, intersected in every direction by acequias, which lead the water from the Gila."[36]

The shifting locus of the settlement seems based on an old habit. When someone died, his residence was burned, and the family reestablished themselves elsewhere. In fact, several related families would commonly decide to relocate. They might go but a mile or so, but this would furnish a nucleus for a new community. Other families would soon follow. Because of this, practically every inch of the valley from Sacate to Gila Crossing had at one time or another been the site of dwellings. The practice is ancient: it was tremendously accelerated in recent times by the rapid decimation under attack and epidemic.

Some of the shifting was due to seasonal residence. The villages were on higher land away from the river, beyond the reach of winter and spring floods. The fields, in the bottom land subject to inundation, contained scattered summer residences:[37] the regular earth-covered houses, needed against rain. In winter, the Maricopa gathered in more compact communities on higher ground.

A few names of topographic features and place names were recorded. The Gila had no name: it is merely àxa', "water," "river." The Salt was àxacĕ'nd, "one river," so named, Mrs. Redbird thought, because, unlike the Gila, it has no affluents in the plain. (Its modern name is àxasåï'l, "salty water.") Hassayampa Creek was xataikuve'ʀà, "hard canyon." The Colorado was xa'kwĭtàs, "red water." The country about Sacate, and perhaps the river itself have "always" been called xil. The district farther down the Gila toward the Salt River junction was ⁱic'ĭlyàmu'c (ⁱic', "screw bean mesquite"), from the quantity of mesquite

---

[36] Bartlett, *Personal Narrative*, II, 233.

[37] Where Bartlett saw them in the summer of 1852 (*loc. cit.*).

growing there. The Santa Cruz slough and the country about it at the foot of the Sierra Estrella was axasǎi′lyᵃ, "salty water." A place east of Sacate, beyond Blackwater, was called i′ivᵃau′, "standing stick." It is said that some Pima are still called by this place name.

Four nearby heights were named: Pima Butte (viva′vǎ, "solitary mountain"), Sierra Estrella (vialyxa′, "berdache mountain"), Salt River Range (vikwaxa′s, "greasy mountain"), and a butte, probably a northwesterly outlyer of the Sierra Estrella, south of the Gila and just below the Salt junction (xagǎvǐcǎϑo′, "water divider").³⁸ Sierra Estrella as seen from Sacate appeared to the Maricopa as a person lying on his back covered with a blanket, hence it was also called pipakwatkǐ′ʀᵃ, "man lying on his back." A peak at the eastern end was called mago′rokǎxavǐ′g, "two heads."³⁹ A butte at the northeastern foot of the Sierra was called "the mortar." A high hill on the north side of the Gila opposite Pima Butte, said to look like house ruins, was matǎu′lgwǐsiϑe′ʳc, "high dirt that is a shaman," (mat, "dirt"; ǎu′l, "high"). Painted Rock Mountains were kukupu′ʀǎnyiva′c, "Kukupura's house," named for a spirit living in a cave in these mountains. In the mountains to the north of the Salt River were "willow mountain" (vi′iϑo′) south of Prescott, possibly Crown King; "ridge pole mountain" (viakǎvǎnau′), a little north or northeast (so called because its top is level); and "dancing with horn" ('ikwǐmkwima′tc), a mountain east of the last.

The country of the Kaveltcadom was on the lower Gila from Gila Bend for fifty miles downstream to the Mohawk Mountains, that is, halfway to the Colorado.⁴⁰ The Mohawk Mountains, their western limit, were called ᵃvikatcǎkwi′nyᵃ, "granary basket mountain." The Yuma came upstream as far as Antelope Hill, fifteen miles west of this. It was called axpě″, "metate," a name recorded by Garcés and Font in 1775. (Forde writes that the Yuma travelled there for stones from which to manufacture metates.⁴¹) Between the two was a little cleared space, perhaps a barren wash, or the line of sandhills known to be there, which was regarded as the actual boundary.⁴² The Kaveltcadom were

³⁸ For the reason for these names, see p. 252.

³⁹ Hence the peaks of this range on modern maps, "Montezuma Sleeping," "Montezuma Peak," and "Montezuma's Head." The Maricopa also refer to the Sierra in connection with the xanǎvʀe′, "king" (Spanish *general*), whom they may associate with the "Montezuma" of their tradition.

⁴⁰ There are none in this country now, the reservation at Gila Bend containing only Papago.

⁴¹ Forde, *Yuma Ethnography*, p. 102.

⁴² It seems strange that an actual line should figure as a boundary, but it must be remembered that both peoples were in the habit of drawing lines on the ground before commencing their highly formalized battles.

said to be wholly on the south side of the river, scattered at considerable intervals. They farmed the bottom land on the river, without dams or ditches, planting only after the seasonal floods. The Kaveltcadom were also known by the name of their most important district, kwa'akáma't, the wide fertile lowlands about Gila Bend (kwa'ak, a mesquite-like tree growing everywhere through the farm lands there; áma't, "farm"). Strictly speaking, the name applies only to the slope from just south of the present town of Gila Bend to the river after it turns westward. Settlements stretched continuously through the length of this district, as Anza also noted in 1775. Although the settlements extended westward to Mohawk, the bulk of the population was said to have been nearer Gila Bend. This is in agreement with Spanish evidence from the eighteenth century, given below.

Kaveltcadom settlements known to Last Star as occupied in his father's day or earlier were as follows:

kwáku'p, "hole" (i.e., a hollow spot) was the largest community. It lay on the south side of the Gila immediately west of the Painted Rock Mountains.
daθicakŏ'ln_yiϑi'kĭc, "the place of long corn," was half a mile or more west of kwáku'p. It was so called because between the two villages lay a long level stretch on which corn was planted.

Three nameless villages lay on the south side to the west, evidently at no great distance. They were designated as opposite the following places on the north bank (in order westward):

gwĭlxo'n_yiϑi'kĭc, "where the old 'board' lay."
vituʀu'tc, "rocks around in a ring."
vivàϑi'l_yc, "mescal drink mountain"; a little black hill.

The following place names were recorded; all were west of the Painted Rock Mountains on the south side of the Gila: ana.uϑau'ĭc, "standing boiled black mesquite sap"; xuma'ʀ⁴unyĭ'kwĭca'm, "a child looking for the road"; vulpo'-àvàau'ĭc, "standing post." The last was supposed to be the western boundary established by the Mexicans. Agua Caliente (xakupĭ'nc, "hot water"), although occupied in Spanish days, had no settlement within the memory of informants.

Other Kaveltcadom settlements of the middle of the last century lay on the Gila in the northern section of the great bend. A village called vin_yi'lkwuk_ya'va, "where the black mountains meet," stood on the west bank above Gillispie Dam at or near Centennial Wash. Three temporary sites, occupied only when gathering mesquite in the vicinity, were on the south side of the river opposite the mouth of Hassayampa Creek. They took their names from three small hills near which they lay (probably Powers Butte, Robbins Butte, and another): kwŭtupa'Rả, "the last," was the most westerly; tŭmkuva'tc, "the middle one"; the easternmost had no name. The people using these three sites about the middle of the last century were Kaveltcadom, not Maricopa, according to Last Star, himself of Kaveltcadom descent.

DOCUMENTARY EVIDENCE ON MARICOPA AND KAVELTCADOM TERRITORY

It seems to have been taken for granted by many writers on Arizona tribes that within the historic period the Maricopa lived on the lower Gila below the great bend. It is assumed that they are the Cocomaricopa of Spanish record and that they moved eastward to join and become absorbed by the Pima well within our own day. The foregoing record of the native view of the matter is so much at odds with this that it is necessary to examine here the early documentary evidence.

The anthropological question involved is whether Piman contacts and Pima ingredients of Maricopa culture are ancient or recent. An answer will mean much for our conception of the rapidity of cultural assimilation.

The view that the Maricopa have moved from the lower Gila seems to be wholly mistaken. This inference seems to have arisen because (1) the Spanish explorers of the eighteenth century found Cocomaricopa and Opa at Gila Bend and below; (2) they met no inhabitants in nineteenth century Maricopa territory between Gila Crossing and Pima Butte; (3) the existence of the Kaveltcadom in the very territory assigned the Cocomaricopa was hitherto unknown; (4) Emory (1846) and Bartlett (1852), who found the Maricopa in the Gila Crossing-Pima Butte district, asserted that the Maricopa had moved from the lower Gila.

Are the Maricopa to be identified with the Cocomaricopa of the lower Gila? If not, where were they during the eighteenth century?

The argument of these questions will take the following form. I will try to show that the identification is uncertain; that the Spanish Cocomaricopa-Opa jointly are the Kaveltcadom, or at best Kaveltcadom and Maricopa collectively. It appears to me that the Spaniards did not know how to apply these two names; did not know whether they were alternative terms for the people at Gila Bend or referred to two tribes. It would seem that finally they decided arbitrarily on the latter alternative. It is true that they found no one living in the Gila Crossing–Pima Butte region. They did find natives in the northern part of the great bend of the Gila (the Hassayampa district) and near the mouth of the Salt River. Since this is above the territory of the Kaveltcadom as described by my informants, it may be that these natives were Maricopa. This then might mean that about 1775 the Maricopa were living from the Salt-Gila confluence down to Gila Bend and that about the beginning of the nineteenth century they moved eastward to Gila Crossing–Pima Butte. This is a shift of only thirty or forty miles; not at all the supposed major dislocation from a lower Gila home.

The matter cannot be wholly resolved. We must reckon with the unanimous opinion of the Maricopa that they have always lived in the general vicinity of Gila Crossing–Pima Butte. Since their memories are demonstrably correct on events back to 1825–30, there is no reason why they should not be aware of a shift of location fifty years earlier or less. The region of the Salt-Gila confluence and downstream to Hassayampa is declared to have been Maricopa hunting grounds in the first half of the nineteenth century. It may well be that, when stating that they have always lived in their present location, a shift from the lower part of their territory was ignored as of no consequence.

The statements of Emory and Bartlett, that the Maricopa moved from the lower Gila, are demonstrably confused references to the eastward movement of the Colorado tribes (Halchidhoma, Kohuana, and Halyikwamai) in 1825–30 and 1838–39.

The minor eastward shift of the Maricopa suggested here has, of course, no direct bearing on the inference that at some time in the indefinite past they were living on the lower Colorado (p. 11).

This is based solely on their close linguistic affinity to Yuma, Halchidhoma, and Mohave.

Our first question then concerns the identification of the Maricopa and Kaveltcadom with the Cocomaricopa and Opa of the Spanish records. Fortunately we have illuminating sets of data at intervals covering three centuries: Kino and Manje in 1694–1700, Anza, Garcés, Font, and Diaz in 1774–75, and Bartlett in 1852. It seems advisable to present this documentary evidence in some detail.[43]

In Kino's day (1694–1700) the occupation of this region was somewhat different from that described by native testimony as of 1850. Northern Sonora and the interior south of the Gila River were occupied by Pima. The modern division into Papago and Pima was not recognized, but the Pima of the San Pedro and Santa Cruz Rivers were set off from those to the south as Sobaipuris or Pimas Sobaipuris. They occupied the San Pedro from roughly the vicinity of the present Tombstone northward to the Gila, and the Santa Cruz valley from Tucson to about Red Rock.[44] But most significantly for our present purpose, the middle Gila from Casa Grande to Gila Crossing, in its western part the traditional home of the Maricopa, seems to have contained Sobaipuris Pima villages alone. The Cocomaricopas and Opas, who were by inference from Kino's memoir linked tribes, were placed on the Gila from Gila Bend westward to the Mohawk Mountains. This is precisely the territory assigned by my native informants to the Kaveltcadom and to them alone. The inference from Kino's record alone would be that since the opening of the eighteenth century the Maricopa shifted from below and about Gila Bend to the district above, settling with the Pima in the direction of Casa Grande, leaving the Kaveltcadom behind or being replaced by them.

The details are worth pursuing. It must be borne in mind that while Kino traversed the Gila from Casa Grande downstream several times, he is nowhere explicit as to tribal occupation. Fur-

---

[43] These are by no means all the records from the eighteenth and early nineteenth centuries, but are by far the most complete and significant.

[44] Bolton, *Kino's Historical Memoir*, I, 170, n. 193, 173.

ther, his point of view was that of the Pima, as is borne out by the names of the Cocomaricopa settlements, which appear in general to be Piman in form, not Yuman.[45]

Kino reached Casa Grande for the first time in November 1694. He found two rancherías beyond: El Tusonimo, four leagues to the west, and four leagues still farther west, El Coatoydag (San Andres). He does not name the occupants, merely implies that they were Pima, and remarks of two nations farther on (i.e., to the west, to the northwest on Salt River [Rio Azul], and on the Colorado), that "they speak a language very different." He designates them Cocomaricopas and Opas. In November 1697 he observed that six or seven rancherías of Pimas Sobaipuris lay near Casa Grande. At San Andres he spoke with some Cocomaricopas and "even sent them messages," implying that they were not residents of this village which lay in the general vicinity of Sacaton. In September (?) of the following year there came to San Andres Opas and Cocomaricopas, "who are a people of very distinct dress, features, and language, though connected by marriage with the Pimas." So far there is nothing in the evidence to prove that the Maricopa did not live on the Gila between Sacaton and the Salt River junction; on the contrary, since they are mentioned as on the lower Salt, part of their habitat according to native information, they may well have lived in the Sacate–Gila Crossing district. But according to Manje's account, a Pima village (San Bartolomé) was found three leagues above the junction of the Gila and Salt (in this account called the Rio Verde). This point would be Gila Crossing or somewhat to the west; that is, in historic Maricopa territory. We are confronted with two alternatives: either this was an isolated Piman village among the Maricopa (although no other villages are mentioned) or it was not then Maricopa territory. The best interpretation would be that the Maricopa were at the time chiefly resident in the general vicinity of Gila Bend, and near or on the

---

[45] All the place names given by Kino, Sedelmair, and the Anza party were discussed with Maricopa informants. Beyond suggesting that Kino's Tutto was kwáku'p and Sedelmair's Caborh was kukupu'ʀányiva'c, none of the names were recognized. They, too, thought the words Piman in origin.

lower Salt River, but later moved into the Gila Crossing–Sacate district. This is partially confirmed by the entries of October 1700. At the ranchería El Tutto, somewhere near Gila Bend, his party was visited by Indians "from farther up and farther down" who by the context were Cocomaricopa.[46]

The distribution of villages on the lower Gila below Gila Bend coincides exactly with our information. A list of villages and the distances separating them is given twice in the journals.[47] In order downstream they were:

1699	1700
Oyadoibuise (San Felipe y Santiago), west of Salt River	Oyadoibuise, east and up river from El Tutto
	El Tutto, near Gila Bend
Two unnamed villages noted by Manje below Gila Bend	Guoydag, 6 leagues west
Tucsani (San Simón)	
Vaqui (San Tadeo)	Batki (San Mateo), 7 leagues west
Cuat (San Mateo)	Three unnamed rancherías
Tutumagoidad or Tutum (San Matías), 4 leagues west of Cuat	Tutumagoydag (San Matías), 13 leagues west of Batki

Beyond San Matías "we would be entering the Yuma nation, with whom they were on unfriendly terms." "Various rancherías which had been deserted during the preceding months" were seen in the succeeding fifteen leagues. The first Yumas were now encountered at San Pedro y San Pablo, twenty-seven leagues below San Matías (Manje makes it thirty). From here to the junction with the Colorado was about eighteen leagues.

This gives twenty-six leagues of Cocomaricopa territory from Tutto to San Matías, an interval (partly unoccupied) of twenty-seven or thirty leagues to the nearest Yuma, with the Yuma extending to the Colorado for about eighteen leagues; a total of about seventy-one leagues from Gila Bend to the Colorado. The recorded traverse is too great to assume a direct course: the distance is about 120 miles in an air line. But the proportions 41 $(26+15$ [the deserted villages]): 12 $(27$ [or 30] $-15)$:18 fits very

---

[46] Bolton, *op. cit.*, I, 128, 172–73, 186, 196, n. 262, 202, 246.

[47] *Op. cit.*, I, 196–97, n. 262, 246–53; cf. II, 207.

well with our information. If Tutto was at or near Gila Bend, more than half the distance downstream takes us to the Mohawk Mountains; then comes the unoccupied territory extending slightly less than halfway to the Colorado, that is, to between Wellton and Dome, the known upper limit of the Yuma. The villages cannot be identified beyond this. Tutto seems to have been the principal village and may therefore be our kwȧku'p, situated immediately west of the Painted Rock Mountains. The implication of the itinerary of 1700 is that all the Cocomaricopa villages were south of the Gila, which agrees with our information.

It is noteworthy that Kino ceased to mention the Opas in the later part of his record. It is also clearly implied that under Piman tutelage he designated the Cocomaricopas and Opas separately. Further, the languages of the Opas, Cocomaricopas, and Yuma are said to be one,[48] that is not only Yuman, but specifically of the Yuma-Maricopa division. A possible implication is that the Opas, if they really formed a separate group, may have been the Kaveltcadom.

Sedelmair's information (1744) is brief and vague. He lists a score of Cocomaricopa rancherías within a span of thirty-six leagues downstream from what was apparently Gila Bend, beyond which by forty-five leagues lay the Colorado.

The distribution given by Kino is confirmed and our inferences augmented by the information given seventy-five years after him by Garcés, Anza, Font, and Diaz. In May 1774 Anza and Diaz traversed the Gila from its mouth eastward nearly to Casa Grande. In June of the same year Garcés made a detour from Gila Bend to the north and east along the course of the Gila to the same terminal point near Casa Grande. As all other Spanish chroniclers cut off this segment of the river by taking the direct route from the Bend to the Pima villages, his excursion proves of the utmost significance for our purpose. The following year, in November, Anza, Font, and Garcés made the reverse traverse from near Casa Grande to the Colorado.

On the upstream journey in 1774 Anza reached the first village of the Cocomaricopa six leagues above the easily identifiable Mo-

[48] Bolton, *op. cit.*, I, 195.

hawk Range, itself seventeen or eighteen leagues east of the Colorado. This village, San Bernardino, was located on the south bank. Here he remarks "Some of them [Cocomaricopa] live on this river, but most of them dwell in the mountains between the Colorado and the Gila." This may refer only to their absence at the time gathering foodstuffs in the back country. But Garcés came through this hinterland at this time and found it deserted. Five leagues east brought Anza to an abandoned settlement on the north bank at Agua Caliente, still so named. Passing the Painted Rock Mountains after six leagues, he reached in three more San Simón y Judas de Upasoitac (Opasoitac). This was clearly in the vicinity of Gila Bend. "This place is well peopled by these Cocomaricopas, and others who really are the same, although they call them Opas, to which are added now some Págagos or Pimas who have deserted their country on account of the great drought and the still greater famine which is experienced in it." His gloss on his tabulated distances remarks on this as the "last village of the Cocomaricopa on the same Gila River." He now moved directly east, "in order to cut off the bend which the river makes to the north, which is entirely uninhabited": so he remarks, but note below that Garcés found villages there. Thirteen leagues from Gila Bend he reached "the Pima village of Sutaquison, which is maintained permanently on the river." In two leagues more he arrived at Juturitucan (San Juan Capistrano), "the last Pimas on the Gila River." He left the Gila after another two leagues, at a point the same distance below Casa Grande.[49]

Diaz's account of the same journey is but a replica of Anza's. He notes the Cocomaricopa village San Bernardino (seven leagues above the Mohawk Range) as "the first village of the tribe upstream." The region up to this point was uninhabited because of continuous war with the Yuma. A village of the Opas was reached fourteen leagues east and another at eighteen. A league beyond was San Simón y Judas de Upasoitac, "which is a village of the same tribe, although some Pimas ordinarily live in it." "Between the village of San Bernardino and this one of

[49] Bolton, *Anza's California Expeditions*, II, 122–27, 235–40.

Upasoitac, this river and its adjacent watering places are inhabited by Opas, Tutumaopas, and Cocomaricopas, none of
which are different from the Yumas in anything, either in language or in any of their native qualities." After fifteen leagues
he arrived at "the first pueblo of the heathen Pimas, called
Sutaquison," and at the last Pima village in three leagues more.
The Pima were confined to a space of three leagues on both
banks of the river, with six villages within this span. Diaz's observations differ from Anza's only in noting the presence of two
Opa villages a short distance below Gila Bend.[50]

Three parallel accounts are given for the westward journey
down the Gila in November 1775, which followed the route of the
previous year. All three set the distance from Casa Grande to
the easterly Piman village, Uturituc, at seven leagues. From here
to Sutaquison was four leagues (or two), with "two large villages
of Pimas" between, or as Font wrote, "two smaller pueblos."
Font wrote on Pima occupation of this tract, that "in the district
of some six leagues there are five towns, the four above mentioned on this [south] side of the river, and one on the other side
which Father Garcés called San Serafino de Nabcúb." It is noteworthy that, unlike Kino, none of these chroniclers leave the implication that Maricopa were living among these Pima. It is of
further importance to note that the party spent several days at
certain rain pools two leagues to the west of Sutaquison, that is
in the vicinity of Pima Butte. In the middle of the nineteenth
century this was in the heart of Maricopa territory, but none of
the three chroniclers mention any settlements in the vicinity.
Sixteen or seventeen leagues after leaving Sutaquison, they
reached Opasoitac (Uparsoytac, "the settlement of the Opas")
at Gila Bend by the direct route, without noting any signs of occupations in all the intervening territory. "Some villages of
Opas," which Anza called Rancherías de San Martín, were
reached two short leagues west of Opasoitac, and in four or five
more some ranchos (San Diego) at the eastern foot of the Painted
Rock Mountains. Anza remarks that from Opasoitac to this
place "we have come through continuous villages and signs of

[50] *Ibid.*, pp. 300–305.

cultivation." Agua Caliente, on the north bank, was reached in another eight leagues: this year the place held two hundred people. Garcés wrote, "Immediately in this position are the rancherías called San Bernardino, and they are of the same nation" as those above at Gila Bend, or as Font had it, "This place and its district were named San Bernardino del Agua Caliente." The point is that this cannot be the San Bernardino of the eastward journey of 1774, because that was explicitly on the south bank and five leagues downstream. In fact at their next halt seven leagues down from Agua Caliente, Anza wrote, "A little above this place is San Bernardino, last of the habitations of the Opas or Cocomaricopas, who are one and the same." Further, at Agua Caliente Garcés had written, "Here is where ends this Opa or Cocomaricopa nation, which is all one; though nevertheless some of them are found further down river," presumably at or near the San Bernardino of the previous year. Evidently there were settlements both at Agua Caliente and here five leagues below. Confirming Garcés' remark on this as the western end of Opa-Cocomaricopa territory, Anza remarks at the lower San Bernardino, "all the country from here as far as the Yumas is unpopulated."

Localities from here westward to the Colorado are easily identified. The Mohawk Mountains were eleven and a half leagues below Agua Caliente (Anza) or fifteen (Font and Garcés). Five or six leagues westward was Antelope Hill. Both Font and Garcés note that this was called "metate hill" by the Indians, precisely the name given it by my Maricopa informants. The mouth of the Gila was fifteen to seventeen leagues beyond.[51]

To marshal all the evidence for the position of the Pima and Opa-Cocomaricopa settlements on the river, I present Table I giving the distances traversed in leagues. Obviously the travellers differed in their conception of each day's march or of the length of the league. How far they diverged is exemplified by the total distance from Uturituc (the eastern Pima pueblo) to the Mohawk Mountains: from thirty-five to fifty-one leagues. Font and Garcés either collaborated or copied one another's itinerary. Anza's record of the westward journey of 1775 appeals to me as the most precise: figuring two and two-thirds English statute miles to the Spanish league, it yields admirable results between fixed points when scaled on a map.

[51] *Ibid.*, III, 15–41, 214–24; IV, 34–71; Coues, I, 65–130.

Important information on the occupation of the Gila above Gila Bend can be derived from Garcés' account of a detour he made in June 1774.[52] Instead of taking a direct course due eastward from Gila Bend to the Pima villages below Casa Grande as

TABLE I

DISTANCES FROM CASA GRANDE TO THE COLORADO RIVER

	EASTWARD, 1774		WESTWARD, 1775		
	Anza	Diaz	Anza	Font	Garcés
Casa Grande to Uturituc................	4	.....	7	7	7
Uturituc to Sutaquison (Casa Blanca)....	2	3	2	4	4
Sutaquison to Opasoitac (Gila Bend)....	13	15	16	17	17
Opasoitac to San Martín................	.....	1	1½±	2—	2
San Martín to San Diego (east of Painted Rock).................................	.....	4	4	5	5
Opasoitac to Painted Rock.............	3	.....	.....	.....	.....
San Diego to Aritoac (river crossing)....	.....	4	.....	.....	.....
San Diego to Agua Caliente.............	.....	.....	8	8	8
Painted Rock to Agua Caliente.........	6	.....	.....	.....	.....
Aritoac to San Bernardino.............	.....	10	.....	.....	.....
Agua Caliente to San Bernardino........	5	.....	.....	.....	.....
Agua Caliente to below San Bernardino..	.....	.....	7	.....	.....
Agua Caliente to Mohawk Mountains...	.....	.....	.....	15	15
San Bernardino to Mohawk Mountains..	6	7	.....	.....	.....
Below San Bernardino to Mohawk Mountains................................	.....	.....	4½	.....	.....
Mohawk Mountains to Antelope Hill....	.....	.....	5	6+	6
Mohawk Mountains to Colorado River...	17(18)	19	.....	.....	.....
Antelope Hill to Colorado River........	.....	.....	15	16	17
Uturituc to Mohawk Mountains........	35	44	43	51	51
Gila Bend to Colorado River..........	37(38)	45	45	52	53

all others had done, he followed the river north from the Bend, east to the Salt River junction, and up its course nearly to Casa Grande. Leaving Uparsoytac (Gila Bend), he found a village called Tugsapi six leagues north, presumably below the present Gillispie Dam. Two leagues north was Tucabi (Tugabi), which by his statement must have been a straggling settlement two and

[52] Bolton, *Anza's California Expeditions*, II, 388–89.

a half leagues in extent. This was presumably in the general vicinity of Hassayampa Creek. Both these places were evidently on the left bank of the Gila. Since he does not state that the people occupying these settlements differed from those of Gila Bend, we may plausibly infer that they were Opa-Cocomaricopa.[53] Still following the south bank, after seven and a half leagues Garcés met people of Sutaquison (the Pima village) gathering sahuaro fruit, and five leagues beyond he reached the Pima villages named below ("three pueblos with many people"). If Sutaquison was in the vicinity of Casa Blanca, as all other records indicate, he met these Pima on Santa Cruz slough midway of Sierra Estrella, that is, in what was later Maricopa territory. Garcés then adds to our knowledge of Pima occupation: on the north side of the Gila a league east of Sutaquison he found a large pueblo called Nacub and in a little more than another league, but on the south side, a "very populous" settlement, Tuburs Cabors. Uturituc was reached a little more than a league beyond. Now he adds an easternmost Pima village (Pitac) three leagues east, which none of the others mention.

To bring this long consideration of observations in 1774–75 to a head, they may be summarized as follows. Pima villages occupied both sides of the Gila from some distance below Casa Grande westward to Casa Blanca and perhaps beyond. There is no mention of encountering Yuman speaking peoples in the district, and more significantly, the region west of Pima Butte, that is, the heart of Maricopa territory in 1850, was unoccupied. Opa and Cocomaricopa held the Gila from below the Salt River junction downstream to San Bernardino, sixteen to nineteen miles above the Mohawk Mountains. Their villages were all on the left bank, with the exception of Agua Caliente, and were concentrated in the fifteen or twenty mile stretch from Gila Bend down to the Painted Rock Mountains. Below the Mohawk Mountains the country was uninhabited until the Yuma were reached near the mouth of the Gila.

All this is as closely confirmatory of Kino's information as one should reasonably expect. The accounts of 1694–1700 and of

53 Bolton also assumes this.

1774–75 agree rather precisely for the Gila below Gila Bend. Kino's reference to Yumans "to the northwest on the Rio Azul" (that is from the direction of the Pima villages) should perhaps now be interpreted to mean on the Gila below the Salt junction where Garcés found them. But since Garcés did not traverse the Salt River, it may well be that they were also on its extreme lower course. In any event the Maricopa could have been but a short distance west of their position of the following century.

To return to the identification of the names Cocomaricopa and Opa. The chroniclers of 1774–75 used the terms as though synonymous or at least implied that there was no distinction of moment between them. At Opasoitac (Gila Bend) Anza wrote in 1774, "This place is well peopled by these Cocomaricopa, and others who really are the same, although they call them Opas," and again in 1775, "the tribe of the Opas and Cocomaricopas," in the singular. At the other end of his march he spoke of "San Bernardino, last of the habitations of Opas or Cocomaricopas, who are one and the same." Diaz alone wrote that the district between Opasoitac and San Bernardino was "inhabited by Opas, Tutumaopas, and Cocomaricopas," mentioning a third people, but Diaz was the most casual of the four chroniclers.

Garcés' manner of reference is especially significant. Twice he wrote, "the Opa nation, or Cocomaricopa, which is the same" and "this Opa or Cocomaricopa nation, which is all one," as though these were synonyms. But he may have meant to distinguish two divisions of one people, or at least linked groups. Later in his diary he ignores the Opa, referring regularly to the Cocomaricopa.[54] There is, however, an important exception to this: on his return journey (1776) through their settlements he speaks of arriving among "the Cocomaricopas of the Agua Caliente" and later "continued my journey, visiting the rancherias of the Opas." This would seem to make a distinction, with the Opa upstream of the Cocomaricopa. This may also be inferred from Font's statements: he wrote of Opasoitac as a "settlement of the Opas" and of "some villages of Opas" just below.

---

[54] Note that he refers only to Cocomaricopa in his tabular summary of tribal populations (Coues, II, 443).

But at Agua Caliente, "Many Cocomaricopa Indians assembled
to see us. They are the same as the Opas, but are distinguished
in name by the district they inhabit." Again he remarked, "I may
note that the Opas and Cocomaricopas are one and the same
tribe." Anza writing in retrospect also makes the distinction:
"Ascending the Gila from the junction [with the Colorado], we
have a desert for about fifteen leagues, till we come to the first
village of the Cocomaricopas, after which come the Opas and
Pimas, whose last pueblo must be about fifty leagues from the
junction."[55]

Here is conflicting testimony: either the Opa and Cocomaricopa were a single people or they were two tribes identical in
language and customs and perhaps occupying somewhat distinct
territories. My interpretation is that the natives recognized a
distinction between two peoples who may have occupied joint
territory (as the Maricopa and their guest tribes did in the following century), and that the Spanish, failing to see how the
distinction applied, came finally to state that the Cocomaricopa
were below and the Opa above, which may not have been the
geographic relation at all. If then there was truly a distinction
between the two, and the Cocomaricopa are to be identified with
the Maricopa of our day, I do not see that we can avoid the implication that the Opa were the Kaveltcadom.[56]

By the middle of the nineteenth century the lower Gila was
abandoned and the Maricopa were found in the position assigned
them by native testimony. Emory in 1846 and Bartlett in 1852
found the Gila unoccupied for two hundred miles above its
mouth. Emory's testimony is that the Maricopa occupied the
Gila valley from a point identifiable as the Maricopa Wells–Sacate district to north of the Salt River.[57] Bartlett found the
most westerly Maricopa village a mile or more east of a point

[55] Bolton, *Anza's California Expeditions*, II, 124, 238, 301; III, 23, 31; IV, 46,
57; V, 391; Coues, I, 113, 123; II, 436.

[56] The name Opa may be simply the common Yuman stem apa', "man." If
it is permissible to identify it in the name of their village Opasoitac, as commonly
Upasoitac, this would be confirmation, since the latter (upa) more closely resembles the Yuman pronunciation.

[57] Emory, p. 86.

later to be known as Maricopa Wells; that is, in the neighborhood of Pima Butte or Sacate. From this point eastward Maricopa and Pima occupation was continuous for twelve or fifteen miles along the south side of the Gila.[58]

"The valley or bottom-land occupied by the Pimos and Coco-Maricopas extends about fifteen miles along the south side of the Gila, and is from two to four miles in width, nearly the whole being occupied by the villages and cultivated fields. The Pimos occupy the eastern portion. There is no dividing line between them, nor anything to distinguish the villages of one from the other. The whole of this plain is intersected by irrigating canals from the Gila, by which they are enabled to control the waters, and raise the most luxuriant crops. At the western end of the valley is a rich tract of grass, where we had our encampment [Maricopa Wells]. This is a mile or more [west] from the nearest village of the Coco-Maricopas. On the northern side of the river there is less bottom-land, and the irrigation is more difficult. There are a few cultivated spots here; but it is too much exposed to the attacks of their enemies for either tribe to reside upon it."

Several unoccupied houses were found on the Salt River about twelve miles above its mouth, i.e., just below Phoenix.

"Francisco [a Maricopa] told us they were used by his people and the Pimos when they came here to fish. He also told us that two years before, when the cholera appeared among them, they abandoned their dwellings on the Gila and came here to escape the pestilence."

This agrees precisely with my information on the location of settlements and fishing stations in the 1850s.

The Kaveltcadom had left the lower Gila and Gila Bend before this day. Emory found at Gila Bend signs of "modern Indian tenements" but the place was unoccupied, as indeed was the whole span to the Colorado River. He wrote:

"We know the Maricopas have moved gradually from the gulf of California to their present location in juxta position with the Pimas. Carson found them, so late as the year 1826, at the mouth of the Gila; and Dr. Anderson, who passed from Sonora to California in 1828, found them, as near as we could reckon from his notes, about the place we are now encamped in [Gila Bend]. The shells we found today were, in my opinion, evidently brought by the Maricopas from the sea. They differ from those we found among the ruins."[59]

[58] *Personal Narrative*, II, 179, 210, 215, 232, 241. Bartlett had excellent opportunity for observation. He followed the Gila closely from its mouth to above Casa Grande, leaving it only between Gila Bend and Maricopa Wells. He also made a circuit from Maricopa Wells north to the Salt River, reaching it at a point about twelve miles above its mouth, thence up the Salt to the mountains, and south to the Pima villages.

[59] Emory, p. 89. Carson was a member of his party. Incidentally, Emory is notorious as a careless observer.

The testimony is that the lower Gila was occupied until at least 1828, but there is nothing to show with certainty that its inhabitants were Maricopa rather than Kaveltcadom or some other Yuman speaking group. Emory's assertion that the Maricopa moved from the Gulf is pure inference. The evidence of the shells, of course, certifies nothing.

Bartlett also found no settlements on the lower Gila. He was told by a Maricopa that

"the Cocomaricopas came here not many years before, to escape from the Yumas, with whom they were constantly at war, and by whom they had been greatly reduced in numbers. Their former range was along the valley of the Gila, on the opposite side of the Jornada and toward the Colorado. [The Jornada here referred to is the desert stretch between Gila Bend and Maricopa Wells.] Their present position adjoining the Pimos, was chosen for the benefit of mutual protection. . . . . The Coco-Maricopas took up their abode in the valley immediately adjoining the Pimos about thirty years since [1820–25], from a point lower down the Gila, where they were exposed to the constant attacks of the Yumas and the Apaches, which tribes, in consequence of their greater numbers, had nearly annihilated them. They came hither for protection, and formed an alliance, offensive and defensive, with the Pimos."[60]

These "Coco-Maricopa" must be the Kaveltcadom. Bartlett must have been confusing their abandonment of the lower Gila with traditions of the Halchidhoma flight from the Colorado about 1825. It is of course quite possible that the Kaveltcadom abandoned their settlements at the time of the Halchidhoma hegira, or immediately after, being then exposed to the Yuma attacks, but they were certainly at Gila Bend about 1835 when Halchidhoma visitors were slain there by the Mohave. The final abandonment of Kaveltcadom territory must therefore have occurred after 1835 and before 1846.

Apparently we have here the origin of the current but erroneous notion that the Maricopa have traditional knowledge of their own former position on the Colorado. There is of course solid linguistic evidence connecting them with the Colorado Yumans, but there is no traditional knowledge that the Maricopa themselves migrated thence. The Kaveltcadom, Halchidhoma, Kohuana, and Halyikwamai have been indiscriminately called Cocomaricopa with their Maricopa hosts, and their movements

[60] Bartlett, *Personal Narrative*, II, 221, 262.

from the lower Gila and the Colorado assigned to the latter.[61] Bartlett himself asserts no more than that the Maricopa lived on the lower Gila, and places the blame for assigning their earlier habitat to the Colorado on Emory. He quotes the latter's affirmation that the Maricopa moved gradually from the Gulf of California, adding "I cannot learn that they ever were on the Gulf."[62] The former position of the Maricopa on the Colorado must remain an inference.

To summarize, after this long excursion into the documentary evidence, we can assert with some confidence that during the eighteenth century the Maricopa were occupying the Gila from the Salt River junction down toward Gila Bend, with the Kaveltcadom below them from Gila Bend to within twenty miles of the Mohawk Range. There may have been Maricopa settled on the extreme lower course of the Salt and even on the Gila immediately above the junction with the Salt, although this is frankly a supposition. At any rate the region of the junction may well have been their fishing and mesquite gathering territory. Some such use may also have been made of the Gila bottoms eastward to Pima Butte. From Gila Bend downstream the two tribes may have occupied the river bottom jointly. By 1825–30 the Maricopa had shifted their locus upstream thirty or forty miles to the Gila Crossing–Pima Butte district. Here they were joined by the Halchidhoma between 1833 and 1838, with the Kohuana and Halyikwamai following in 1838 and 1839. More or less simultaneously with Maricopa occupation of the middle Gila near the Pima, the latter received increments of their own people from the Santa Cruz valley, abandoned by reason of Apache pressure. In 1835–38 the Kaveltcadom were still at Gila Bend, although they may by that time have left the river below Painted Rock. By 1852 all the Kaveltcadom had joined the Maricopa in the Sacate district.

It was the fact that the existence of the Kaveltcadom was

---

[61] For example, Curtis (II, 81) states that vague Maricopa, Yuma, and Mohave tradition relates that the Maricopa once lived on the Colorado between the Mohave and Yuma, making their way up the Gila in a series of movements. There is nothing to show that the reference is not to the allied tribes rather than to the Maricopa.

[62] Bartlett, *Personal Narrative*, II, 269.

hitherto unknown, as much as the name Cocomaricopa, that made possible the assumption that the residents of the lower Gila were Maricopa alone.

We must assume from the Spanish references from the end of the seventeenth century on, that the relations of the Pima and Maricopa were close. There is therefore no reason for assuming that their reciprocal cultural influence dates only from their close proximity in the nineteenth century. In fact, I am very doubtful that there was any great accession of novelties from the Pima in the later days of their association, since my informants implied that most of the traits they had in common were old traits among the Maricopa. This means much for our interpretation of the period and the rapidity with which the Maricopa acquired a Piman gloss. But it must also be borne in mind that the Pima were at least as heavily infiltrated by Maricopa culture, as I shall demonstrate elsewhere.[63]

INTERTRIBAL RELATIONS

The greatest friendships of the Halchidhoma while on the Colorado were with the Pima, the "Mission" Indians (i.e. Cahuilla), Walapai, Cocopa, and of course the Maricopa and Kaveltcadom, according to Kutox. We know from other sources of their friendship with the Kohuana and Halyikwamai. Why the Papago were not mentioned is not clear; possibly because they were seen only infrequently when the Halchidhoma were visiting the Gila River peoples. The case of the Walapai is not clear. To be sure, they had an enemy in common, the Mohave,[64] yet the Halchidhoma may not have known the Walapai until they moved northward to Parker. It is difficult to know whether Kutox was not generalizing from a particular case; his own paternal greatgrandfather was Walapai or part Walapai. At any rate, this remote ancestor must have lived among the Halchidhoma, since Kutox carries his sib name.

[63] I have in preparation a paper, entitled "Cultural Relations of the Gila River and lower Colorado Tribes," demonstrating that all the lowland Arizona tribes shared a single culture.

[64] Although the Walapai were not persistently unfriendly to the Mohave (Spier, *Havasupai Ethnography*, pp. 238, 244).

Maricopa friendships differed only by reason of their eastern position: they might be weighted as Pima and Papago, Halchidhoma and Kaveltcadom, and Cocopa. Despite the fact that the Pima were their allies and immediate neighbors, especially so in more recent times, the Maricopa had relatively little to do with them. To this day, they know little and care little about the Pima. Nevertheless, they readily speak of the Piman culture as richer than their own, at least in material arts. The fact is, that despite their proximity the Maricopa have absorbed relatively little from the Pima, having had much less to do with them than their constant coupling in the early accounts implies. The Papago were known largely as friends of the Pima and were not often seen.

Maricopa and Halchidhoma shared unremitting warfare with the Yuma, Mohave, Yavapai, and Western Apache. The foci of attack were more properly Yuma and Yavapai. Against the Yuma, the Halchidhoma joined or were joined by the Cocopa, the Maricopa by the Pima. The Yuma attacks in return were participated in by Mohave and Yavapai. Maricopa and Pima made common assault on the Yavapai, and suffered alike from Yavapai and Apache marauders. The shift of the Halchidhoma base to Maricopa territory did not alter the situation. The position of the lesser tribes on the Colorado seems always to have been equivocal; sometimes friendly perforce to Yuma, Mohave, Cocopa, or Halchidhoma; sometimes hostile.

Garcés, who was keenly alive to intertribal relations, summarizes the situation in the late eighteenth century as follows:

"The Jalchidunes [Halchidhoma] have always been well disposed toward the Cocomaricopas, the Pima Gileños, and all the nations that there are from the Yumas downward, as also toward the Papagos of the north, toward all the Yabipais [the Yumans of upland Arizona collectively] excepting the Yabipais Tejua [the Yavapai proper], and likewise toward the Jequiches and Jenigueches of the sierra who extend to the sea [Cahuilla and Serrano]; being unable ever to reconcile themselves with their enemies, the Jamajabs [Mohave], the Yabipais Tejua, the Chemeguet [Chemehuevi], and the Yumas. . . . . Those of the Rio Gila [Maricopa, Kaveltcadom, and Pima] are all friends of one another and of the Jalchedunes, but enemies of the Tejua [Yavapai] and Apaches."[65]

[65] Coues, II, 450–53.

Little could be learned regarding trade relations. The Maricopa traded cotton blankets with the Papago for horses; from them they also procured a red pigment for coloring pottery. They obtained coiled tray baskets, used for winnowing and parching seeds, from the Pima, and tobacco seed, at least, from the Halchidhoma on the Colorado. The last also provided the red paint used for facial decoration, which they in turn had obtained from the Walapai.

A little information can be gleaned from Spanish sources. Font wrote (1775) that the Opa of Opasoitac (Gila Bend) had some blankets of "black wool, with white stripes, which they obtain from El Moqui [Hopi]." Among the Yuma he saw some of the same, "which the Jalchedunes and other friends obtain from the Moquinos" and again "which they have been able to acquire through the Cocomaricopas and Jalchedunes." The Halchidhoma as source of this supply was again noted: "In virtue of this peace some Jalchedunes came down to the junction of the rivers, bringing their Moqui blankets and other things."[66] That the Halchidhoma should have these is intelligible enough, since there was a well defined trade from the Hopi pueblos to at least the Walapai and Mohave.[67] But surely the Maricopa had no direct contact with any of the Pueblos, hence we must assume that they also obtained them from their Halchidhoma visitors from the Colorado.

Maricopa contact with the Halchidhoma was by way of the direct route cross-country from the lower Gila to the Ehrenberg–Parker district on the Colorado. Garcés wrote (1774) at Tugsapi, an Opa-Cocomaricopa settlement near Gillispie Dam above Gila Bend: "Here they said that the best road to the Jalchedunes led out from there, and that they went in three or four days according to their pace." He had himself just previously accompanied some Halchidhoma from Agua Caliente by a more southerly route northwestward to their home in the vicinity of Ehrenberg.[68] My information is in agreement. But they did not ordinarily take the route northwest from the Gillispie Dam–Hassayampa Creek region, because Yavapai lived on the lower course of that stream. It was preferable to leave the Gila at the Mohawk Mountains or even as far downstream as Dome, since the coun-

[66] Bolton, *Anza's California Expeditions*, IV, 52, 73, 103, 109.

[67] Spier, *Havasupai Ethnography*, p. 244.

[68] Bolton, *op. cit.*, II, 376-88.

try they would then traverse was uninhabited, probably for lack of water.

Visits of the Maricopa to the Cocopa were by way of the Gila to the Mohawk Mountains (the limit of friendly Kaveltcadom territory), thence directly across the desert southwestward to avoid the Yuma. It took six or seven days afoot from Sacate to Yuma and two days longer to the Cocopa. This means thirty or more miles a day.

From the Mohawk Mountains the course was southward across a big mountain containing a spring, called kuhwĭ'tc, thence southwestward across a sandy desert. In this desert was a second spring, called xamĭlkwĭɵau', "lofty water" (Tinajas Altas?),[69] distant from the first by a day, a night, and the morning of the second day. From there they went westward to another spring, xacàpa'-kwĭnɣàko'ʀàc, "little wells"; thence west to the Cocopa, who lay two days journey downstream from the Yuma.

A visit to the Indians of Sonora, among whom the Halchidhoma were living in 1833, was by way of the desert east of Sacaton. It was always a year before travelers returned to the Gila, although the place was said to lie only three days foot journey southeast of Tucson.

The Maricopa seem to have been markedly conservative in the matter of marriage with other tribes. For one thing, they objected strenuously to having their girls marry into sibless tribes. After 1839 and the appearance of the mixed community, the Maricopa, Halchidhoma, Kohuana, and Halyikwamai married almost wholly among themselves and with the Kaveltcadom. It seems reasonably clear that marriages with the Pima were wholly or almost wholly confined to the last century: the immediate·

---

[69] Tinajas Altas is almost certain to have been the objective since it was the principal camping place in the region. From Kino's day (ca. 1700) on, it was the pivotal point on the route from Caborca in Sonora to the Yuma. Kino was, of course, following an aboriginal line of march. From Tinajas Altas the Maricopa must have used the only practicable route to the Cocopa, that followed by Lumholtz (*New Trails in Mexico*, p. 245, map), westward to Laguna Prieta in the desert, thence southwesterly to the vicinity of Colonia Lerdo. Gifford learned from the Cocopa that their route to the Maricopa brought them first to near the Fortuna mine in the Gila Mountains, that is, somewhat north of the Maricopa route, thence to the Mohawk Mountains and Gila Bend (Cocopa Ms). It is more probable that Tinajas Altas was meant than Fortuna, since Lumholtz records no Papago camp at the latter place.

Pima ancestors of those credited with Pima blood are remembered. "The Pima were too far from the Maricopa to intermarry with them much: they did not see much of them." They did not marry the Papago to the south. A few Papago living in the mountains nearer the Colorado, however, married with the Kaveltcadom at Gila Bend. Some of the present-day population are descended from a Yavapai woman captive; it is barely possible from more than one.

Contacts with Spaniards and Mexicans before the American occupation of the territory are little remembered. Their settlements were at a considerable distance, at Tucson and southward, and with these there was slight trade. Chiefs may not have existed or been of much importance until they were appointed, or received documents of authority from Spanish and Mexican officials. Two Mexicans are known to have accompanied the Maricopa on a raid against the Yuma before Kutox was born (in 1847).

An incident of uncertain meaning was reported by Kutox. When he was about four years old (1851 or 1852), "the first Spaniard" came and went on to the coast (?). He brought back with him from the Colorado the head chief of the Kamia, named kwĭcĭnyă'tȧo'ʀȧ. They went "on top" of Pima Butte, calling all the local Indians together, and said they were going to talk to them. The Maricopa and Kohuana crowded around this chief and killed him. The Spaniards and Americans who were there fled the same night. "We were proud of scaring away the Americans." The Americans acquired this territory at that time.

Americans were first seen in the Halchidhoma village when Kutox was three (1850). (They began to come in numbers following the discovery of gold in California in 1849.) Actually individual trappers and parties had been passing throughout the quarter century preceding. One trapper, a friend of the Maricopa, was killed by Yavapai at his home west of the Gila Bend Mountains. The best known was a beaver trapper living nearby, who brought the Mohave to them to make peace in 1863. He was known only as pĕngwĭtcsa', "beaver eater." Kutox gave a circumstantial account of the massacre of the Oatman family when he was about six (1853). The actual date is 1851.[70] He also remembered a body of American soldiery coming through "a year after" the Yuma raid of 1857. This may have been the California column of 1862.[71] Episodes of the Civil War period were remembered: in 1862–63 a white trader at Casa Blanca was captured by Texans, and the soldiers fought near Tucson.

Mexicans and Americans were called xiko'[72] or more literally ipahama'l,

[70] Stratton, *Captivity of the Oatman Girls.*

[71] Russell, *Pima Indians,* p. 47.

[72] A folk-etymology was offered, deriving the word from the cooing of doves which the whites' language was said to resemble. The word occurs in other Yuman tongues: Mohave hiko, hiiko, haiko (Kroeber, *Handbook,* p. 770); Southeastern Yavapai hako (Gifford, *Southeastern Yavapai,* p. 182); Havasupai hai'ku. Font (1776) recorded the Yuma form as Jéco (Assende Jéco, "one white man")

"white man." Today, following the solecism of uneducated whites, x̥iko' is reserved for Americans, but nevertheless a Mexican is called x̥iko'x̥an, "real white
man." They may also be called, like members of a foreign tribe, pipakwa'm,
"foreign man" (as differentiated from áhua, "enemy").

The Maricopa attitude toward the Halchidhoma was one of
amuṣed tolerance. The Maricopa thought them a queer lot: any
unusual action was explained, "Oh, he is an Halchidhoma."
From this the latter took their name, derived, according to Mrs.
Redbird, from xalyaᴅŏ'mbàg, "people with queer ways." This
may, of course, be a folk-etymology. A number of tales were told
to illustrate the point, which, by the way, serve also to indicate
the character of their humor.

When the Halchidhoma lived on the Colorado, they would not protect themselves. If an enemy arrived and someone gave the alarm, they would remain in
their houses, saying, "Well, it is not right to fight just one or two." So they were
easily killed.

The Halchidhoma would never protect themselves by gathering their forces
at once. That is why they were killed off.

One of them stole into the Yuma meeting house unrecognized, and heard
them planning to fight. A second night he went in but fell asleep. When he went
in he put mud all over his hair [like the Yuma]. He slept until mid-morning.
When he rose, he did not know what to do, for it was broad daylight. A family
was eating outside, so he went back, and arranged his hair to fall over his face.
Then he walked out of the house slowly. They thought he was a Yuma, but
when he had almost reached the nearby bushes, they realized he was a foreigner.
They called to each other, "An enemy!" But he ran off as fast as he could. This
man always did such funny things.

Two young Halchidhoma went to war against the Yuma. A little before sunset, the Yuma were eating. There was a willow tree standing near them. One of
the Halchidhoma climbed into it and imitated a screech owl. The other hid in the
arrowweeds close by. One of the Yuma said, "I am going to hit that baby screech
owl," and threw a big stone at the man in the tree. It hit him on the head, and
down he crashed. The man in hiding heard him fall and burst out laughing instead of running away. The man who fell ran as fast as he could, but his companion laughed so hard that the Yuma overtook and killed him.

An Halchidhoma was hiding in the bushes near the Yuma. He overheard two
Yuma who were playing hoop and pole. One had bet a horse. The other announced he had won it and had already put beads around its neck and a rope
halter. He described precisely where it was. So the Halchidhoma stole away and
ran to the horse, got it, and circling around, rode home with it.

The Maricopa say the Halchidhoma had such queer ways. One of them might

(Bolton, *Anza's California Expeditions*, IV, 497). It appears in the languages of
Shoshoneans adjacent to the Yumans: Chemehuevi haiku, Kitanemuk aiaikik-
am, Vanyume haiko-y-am (Kroeber, *Shoshonean Dialects*, p. 73).

be dying of thirst, and yet, passing a river, say "I am not a bird to stoop down to drink," and die right there. Queer in fighting too. They might outnumber the enemy and be winning, when they would stop, saying, "Let us put away our bows and arrows," and run off.

They say that if an Halchidhoma, while they were still living on the Colorado, found a strange horse in his cornfield, the horse having a white face and hocks, he would immediately cut these off, wearing the white boots around his wrists.

CHAPTER II

BASIS OF SUBSISTENCE

Since the basis of subsistence of the Maricopa and their allies has changed greatly since aboriginal days it is by no means easy to draw a picture of the original food quest. Even before white settlers appeared, Maricopa acquisition of wheat from Mexico had almost entirely displaced the cultivation of corn, and since that day dependence on traders' products has almost obliterated what remained of their original habits.

The staples of the Maricopa and of the Halchidhoma while still on the Colorado seem to have been identical and used in much the same proportion. There is a possibility, however, that the Halchidhoma cultivated corn somewhat more than their Gila relatives and had access to more fish. In contrast, then, they depended less on mesquite and rabbits. This must remain an inference based on what is known of other lower California peoples, since Halchidhoma informants no longer know precisely what ancestral life on the Colorado was like.

The Maricopa seem to have depended largely on gathering mesquite beans, hunting jackrabbits, and on fishing. Relatively little corn was cultivated. The picture of the food quest drawn by informants shows that women were occupied every day gathering mesquite beans during the season, while the men hunted hard by for rabbits or fished. The quest was unceasing: "people starved in those days unless men and women kept at it all day long." Kutox maintained that in those days children were undernourished: "a child of two or more might not be able to stand because it lacked food." On the other hand, Bartlett (1852) makes it appear that Pima and Maricopa cultivation was so great as to allow long periods of inactivity.[1]

Yet mesquite was abundant in the valley, especially in the

[1] Bartlett, *Personal Narrative*, II, 264.

TABLE II

CALENDAR OF THE FOOD QUEST

	WILD PLANTS GATHERED	CULTIVATION		HUNTING AND FISHING
		Planting	Harvesting	
January...	Trees bud Floods	Corn		
February...		Beans, black-eyed peas, pumpkins		
March...	Cholla beans	Watermelons Cotton		Mountain sheep Caterpillars
April.... } Rainy				
May.....	Berries		Beans, peas	
June......	Crucifixion thorn berries Giant cactus fruit		Corn, water-melons, pumpkins	
July......	Excessive heat	Mesquite	Pumpkins Watermelons Cotton Beans Peas Corn		Jackrabbits Fish
August....	Floods				
September.	Rainy	Opuntia fruit Ironwood nuts			
October...		àgwa'và leaves			Caterpillars
November.				Pumpkins Watermel-ons Corn	Deer
December.	Floods, ex-cessive cold*	Wild seeds			

* The climatological conditions are those of a desert. Temperatures range between the extremes of 120°F. and 18° F., with means in January 51°, July 91°. The temperature is one or two degrees lower above Gila Bend than in the low country downstream. The growing season is 260 to 300 days in length. Variations in rainfall are extreme along the river. The annual precipitation ranges from seven to nine inches in the Casa Grande-Sacaton region down to three and less in the vicinity of Mohawk on the lower river. Rains fall mostly in January, March, and August (*Climatological Data*). Flood stages of the river, affected perhaps more by rain and melting snow along the higher tributaries, occur in March (February to April), secondarily about August and in December (Ross, *The Gila Region*, pp. 106-7). The climatic observations in the table above are those of the Indians.

country included within the juncture of the Gila and Salt Rivers. Indeed, this region was so choked with mesquite and other bushes as to be nearly impenetrable. For that reason, being at the same time relatively near the Yavapai, it was dangerous territory. This was also the best region for fishing and abounded in rabbits. Fish were taken mostly in Santa Cruz slough at the northern foot of the Sierra Estrella and at the Salt-Gila confluence. From there the Maricopa drifted up the Salt fishing and gathering to a point just above Phoenix, beyond which it was not safe to go. They did not fish much in the Gila. Family parties went together, camping under the bushes. As the women went out gathering mesquite beans, men would accompany them for protection and to hunt jackrabbits. Camp was frequently shifted as the bushes were stripped clean. It was also their habit to move back and forth between the Gila and Salt to foil any lurking enemies. It was customary to include the whole family on such expeditions, although younger children were ordinarily left home in the care of friends when women went out on a day's excursion.

The chief interest in wild plant products lay in the mesquite beans and giant cactus (sahuaro) fruit. Other wild plants were more casually used: the following description includes the principal but is not exhaustive.

Mesquite furnished the plant staple. Two or three varieties of the bush grew in this region: screw and straight bean mesquite, and a subvariety of the latter, differing from the common variety in its large thorns. (It is of interest that the straight bean and its bush bore separate names, iya' and ana'l$_y$: this was not true of the screw bean, i'i'c, nor the long thorned bean, tŏtxaĕ'tk.) The straight bean variety was most plentiful. These bean pods were said to be softer than those growing in the old Halchidhoma country on the Colorado. Mesquite was gathered from early July to the end of August. Certain trees were known for large or sweet beans, but these were not private property. A group of women would go gathering together for fear of the enemy; several men might be within reach. Mesquite was picked day after day until the bushes held no more, even after they thought they had enough, because mesquite was their staple.

On returning home late in the afternoon, the beans were sorted. The dry beans were put on the roof of the house to dry more thoroughly. These were piled, load upon load, until the last load had remained for three or four days. Should it be cloudy or wet, they were taken off the roof and covered. The thoroughly dry beans were then stowed away in huge basket granaries. An average family would have one large granary filled, with a surplus stored in the house in large pots.

The green beans sorted out at the end of each day's gleaning were prepared at once. Mesquite beans resemble our string beans, but while the pods can be readily pulverized in a mortar, it is practically impossible to crack the seeds. These greener pods were pounded up and, without removing the hard seeds, were mixed in water for a drink. Or this was boiled and used as a liquor to mix with other ground seeds.

After the storage receptacles were filled, the beans that were discarded as not good enough for storing were ground to be made into cakes. The ground bean meal was sifted in a Pima tray-basket by shaking it over the edge onto a cloth. An elliptical hole (eighteen inches long, twelve wide, by ten deep) was dug in the ground and sprinkled with water until its surface was firm. The sifted flour was poured into this, sprinkled, another layer of flour added, sprinkled, and so on. Finally it was sprinkled and covered with dirt. The following morning they would remove the hard cake of mesquite flour. A woman kept busily at this until twenty or more were prepared. These cakes (hapa'ndj) were intended for use on damp days when the stored pods could not be ground because they were damp. (Mesquite beans absorb the slightest moisture in the atmosphere.) A bit of the cake would be broken off, soaked in water to be used as a drink, or boiled and mixed with other ground seeds.

Mesquite was ordinarily used only after pounding in a mortar and grinding on a metate. This was a daily task of the women. The ground meal formed the basis of most food preparations.

Occasionally a quantity was ground and stored in a pot to be eaten dry by the pinch, with a swallow of water. Sometimes the dry pods were boiled without grinding, the liquor to be added to other ground seeds. Mesquite juice was not fermented.

Screw beans, which when picked are bitter or sour, were rotted in a pit for ten days or more, until they became soft and sweet. The pit was lined above and below the beans with green arrow-weeds and the whole covered with dirt. Such pits were made near the dwelling.

A number of varieties of wild seeds were gathered, all in the same fashion by stripping the seeds from the plants with the fingers into a basket held beneath. Seed beaters were not used. None of these served for more than to give variety to the meals. The plant used more than others was ĭkse'vȧ, which furnished tiny red seeds.[2] The seeds were so tiny that a large quantity was needed. They were pounded in a mortar and the chaff blown out as they were shaken in a shallow basket. They were next parched and ground on a metate. Their use was principally for a drink. It was said to feel cool, so that men hunting for jackrabbits liked to drink this. Another low bush, ᵃ'tŏ'n, had tiny black seeds gathered in December. These were also prepared by pounding, parching, and grinding, and were eaten dry by pinches or mixed with water for a drink. Two other seeds were prepared different-ly. These were ȧvȧa'c, a low bush,[3] and kȧvȧsω, a common bush three to four feet tall, both gathered in December. The seeds of the latter were tiny and black. These were pounded in the mor-tar, but not parched. A fire was built in a hole, the coals raked out, and the ashes soaked or damp dirt placed over them. The seeds put in the hole were covered with green leaves, followed by a layer of coals. The whole was plastered over with soaked hot ashes to retain the heat. The following morning they were ground on the metate, then mixed with water to a stiff dough which was eaten raw. Another wild seed plant, ĭkca'mac, differed

[2] This was a low bush, two feet high, with sparse leaves standing out from the stem two inches apart.

[3] Possibly from ȧvᵘa'k, "I am walking," referring to stripping the bushes as one walked along.

from these in that it was sometimes cultivated. This was a weed resembling tall Bermuda grass. The seeds were pounded in a mortar to remove the hulls, sprinkled with water, and ground on a metate. The meal was mixed into a dough with a little salt. It was baked in the ashes, which were later washed off, and eaten with mesquite bean soup and the like. The seeds of àgwa'và, probably pigweed, were also eaten.

While seeds appear to have been gathered in the late fall, i.e., December, berries were gathered in May and June. A bush about four feet tall, axtŏ'tàxa'n, bore little sweet red berries. The berries were washed and thrown into hot water to boil. They cooked quickly. This was strained through a cloth, the berries mashed, and replaced in the liquor. This was used as a drink. Sometimes ground wheat (not mesquite) was cooked in this for a mush. If they wished to store the boiled berries, they were spread on a cloth in the shade, and stored in pots when thoroughly dry. Similar berries, axtŏ'tàvi' (so called because they were bitter?), were prepared in exactly the same way. Mistletoe (kamu'c) grew plentifully on the mesquite bushes. Sprigs of this were gathered, the berries stripped off and boiled to furnish a juice which was sticky but tasteless. This was used as a liquor for wheat mush. Somewhat later than these, in June, the little blueblack berries of Crucifixion thorn (? uwe') were gathered. They were mashed in a basket to make a foamy liquid which was eaten without cooking. Sometimes the berries were dried and stored: when wanted they were soaked in hot water.

A sifter (caxaRa'c) was used with the axtŏ't berries. This was elliptical, like those of the Pima,[4] shallow, and about a foot long. Thin willow twigs were laid transversely and longitudinally, and bound to the willow hoop.

When a young girl had gathered axtŏ't and uwe'berries for the first time, it was customary for some older woman to mash and rub them on the girl's arms so she would be industrious.

The nuts of the abundant ironwood tree were ground and leached after the fashion in which California Indians prepare acorns. By the end of the season, October, they are said to lie

[4] Russell, *Pima Indians*, p. 146.

thickly under the trees. Gathered in piles, they were beaten until broken, winnowed in baskets, and the meats taken home. Several women together parched them by tumbling with coals; then they were finally ground on the metate and again winnowed in baskets. This occupied a morning. At noon the ground meal was taken to the river bank, where it was put in a big hole, prepared by firmly patting down the sand. One woman alone proceeded to leach the bitter meal; one who was specially versed in the technique. She was called "a woman with dry hands" (ica'lᵧàsŭtk, "dry hands"). She alone fetched water to pour through the meal, repeating the soaking as it drained away. All afternoon was required for this task. So long as the nuts remained bitter, the water poured on them continued foamy. When the liquid was finally clear, all the women cut the meal cake with sharp sticks, lifted out their portions, carefully scraped the sand from the bottom, and carried them home in baskets. This was eaten dry.

The little sour beans of the cholla cactus (? àtŏ't; also the beans), ripening in March or early April (?), were pit roasted. These were placed on a flat rock in the mountains to be rolled about with a stick to remove the spines. The pit in which they were roasted was small (up to two feet in diameter, one foot deep), since the beans were only about the size of peanuts, and it was hard work to fill the hole. Flat stones were heated in the pit. Late in the evening the beans were put in the hole on a layer of branches of a certain green bush covering the hot stones. They were heaped higher than the surface of the ground, covered with another layer of the same bush, then more hot stones, and banked with a little dirt. A small fire was started over this to keep the stones hot. They were ready in the morning, when they were taken out to dry, while the women went off to gather more.

Opuntia cactus fruit, which was rare in this locality, was gathered in September. It was eaten only fresh, and was said to give the eater chills.[5] The prickly pear was rolled on the ground with a stick to remove the fine spines or brushed with a bit of sage bush. Tongs were unknown. It was split, peeled, and the flesh eaten raw. (Sometimes the juice was squeezed on a white

[5] Lloyd (p. 123) notes identical Pima opinion.

horse to make decorative spots.) Both the fruit and the plant were called kǎlyǎ'p, "flat," for the flat leaf-like stems.

Yucca baccata grew in the desert to the north. The banana-like fruit was eaten fresh; also stored by splitting and drying. Plant and fruit were ĭtcakwa'tc.

Some stems and leaves of plants were eaten. A plant growing in the mountains (hence called àvi', "mountain") looked like asparagus and was bitter. The stems were roasted in ashes. A little plant, called mŭckwo', was washed and boiled. When tender this was squeezed out between the hands and eaten with salt. The leaves of àgwa'và, probably pigweed, larger than spinach leaves, were boiled and eaten with salt. This was gathered in the fall.

Mescal, the agave plant (maϑĭ'l), was not much eaten because it did not grow in this locality. A few plants grew on the higher parts of the mountains to the south and more plentifully beyond in that direction. It was gathered by men because it grew too far away for the women to go. Most that they used was brought from the Papago country in cooked form. The growing plant was severed from its root by the customary chisel (nᵧĭmtakĭ't or maϑilᵧyĭmtàkĭ'tĭc, "mescal–to cut off with"). This was a stick twenty inches long, two in diameter, flattened near one end to provide a chisel edge at one side. (The chisel edge was not at the end, as with other tribes.) This was held against the base of the mescal and hammered with a convenient stone or stick. The long leaves were trimmed short with a knife; the mescal hatchet of other tribes being unknown. One leaf was left long so that the heads might be tied in pairs, or they were fastened in pairs by a stick thrust through them. A man would bring home only six or eight, not a full load, because they were scarce.

The mescal heads were baked in a pit. A fire was built in it, but the usual stones omitted. The coals were raked out, the ashes sprinkled a little, the heads laid on this, covered with dirt, then ashes and a little fire. If prepared late in the morning, they were allowed to bake all the following night. The short leaves remaining on the baked head were stripped off to be chopped up and mashed in a mortar. This mass was spread to dry on peeled

sticks laid side by side or on a cloth, and when dry was rolled in a
bundle. This was called mĭl̜ypŏk, "spread," or hama'n̩k,
"pruned; trimmed off." The head proper was eaten without
mashing. The prepared mescal could be soaked in water and
chewed on, or the foamy sweet liquor drunk.

Tule pollen and roots formed a most minor food. A child playing or a hunter would pause to strip the pollen off in his hand and
swallow it. Women gathered it occasionally. They broke the
heads off gently so as not to shake out the light pollen, holding a
basket beneath to catch the heads. Using a large pot placed on
its side for protection against the wind, the heads were shaken out
inside it. The pollen was poured into the basket, which was
rocked from side to side to bring the chaff to the top. A sweet
mush was made of this pollen mixed with a little ground wheat.
When they wanted to preserve it, a hole was made, sprinkled and
patted, the pollen poured in layer by layer, each being sprinkled,
and the whole covered with dirt. A little fire on top baked it
cake-like by the next day. Sometimes the large roots of older
tules were chewed. They might also be dried and ground to make
a gruel. Tules are at'ȧpi'l.

Sunflowers grew wild, but were not a foodstuff.

Travellers sometimes boiled the water-filled pulp of the barrel
cactus (mĭltŏ't) with a little alkali.

The time when the giant cactus (sahuaro) fruit ripened, the
middle of June, was eagerly welcomed, not because the fruit
formed any considerable portion of the dietary but as an occasion for celebration and debauch. The plant was not common in
Maricopa territory proper, growing rather on the lower hill
slopes north of the Salt River. Hence the desire to collect the
fruit was spiced with the dangers incident to treading so close to
Yavapai country. The Yavapai themselves descended from
their mountains to gather it in the same area.

The fruit is ripe when it is red at the bud end. The few long
spines it bears are at this end: these were readily plucked off
with the fingers. The fruit was gathered with a long hook: a pole
(presumably a rib of this tree-like cactus) crossed obliquely near
one end by a short stick to provide both a hook and crotch to

work with.[6] Fruits that were fully ripe and open were allowed to remain until on drying the flesh dropped to the ground, when it might be gathered. Those that had not reached this stage were pulled from the plant. These were torn in two and eaten as they were. The fully ripened fruit sours in the summer heat. These were in consequence split and the flesh put into pots. As soon as they reached the river these were placed over a little fire so that the potful was brought nearly to the boiling point. The fruit would then keep; otherwise it soured in half a day. The unripe fruit, on the other hand, if carried about in a pot in this fashion, would simply become a watery mass. The fruit might be stored in this manner until winter, when it was dissolved in water for a drink, said to be very sweet, or strained through a cloth and boiled to syrup.

By preference however, the sahuaro harvest formed the basis of a jollification. If this was their intention, they forbade anyone gathering it until it ripened on the plant: nevertheless some did steal off to get it. They would boil it as above and set as many as one hundred large pots away in the meeting house to ferment. The boiling was done under a shade conveniently near. It was stored in the house while still hot, a little fire being maintained there to keep it warm. A man who was adept watched it for the two days required to ferment. When one potful fermented, he poured some of the contents into others, so that all would finish fermenting at the same time. Each family owned one to three of these potfuls, which they were called to carry home when ready.

Friends in other tribes were invited to dance at this time, saying that "Our store house is ripe." The guests came in a group slowly, camping at some distance from the village. The messenger who bore the invitations now walked out to the camp where he named those invited by each Maricopa, pointing out where he lived.

The method of handing out the drinks was stereotyped. The men invited would bring three or four friends. The host would send his wife into the house to bring out a cupful (a small pot or

---

[6] Curtis' description (II, 82) of a pole provided with a wooden blade was specifically denied by my informants.

gourd), which he gave to his guest. He continued plying him with liquor until he was drunk. Then he himself drank and after that furnished it to the friends of the man invited.

The song for this dance was xatca', "wine"; sung at no other time. "When they were drunk they thought of war." The song told of "red water," i.e., blood, and how it was made.[7] It told how the enemy had come to drink with them: they had joined in battle, now they would drink together. The intoxication and the incitement of song commonly ended in a decision to go on a raid. At the time the sahuaro was harvested, the Yavapai were camping in the mountains not far distant, not, as in winter, in isolated caves.

The drink is said to have been only mildly intoxicating. Neither the flower stalk of the mescal nor sprouted corn were used for fermented drinks, as by the White Mountain Apache.

The celebration was called xatca'poŭm, "water mixing" (a folk etymology?); the fruit, a'a'; the dried fruit hamă'nyᵃ; its syrup, a'anyàxa' (sahuaro's water"?); the drink xatca' or xatca'csiu'm, "wine drink."

CULTIVATION

Some field crops were planted by the Maricopa: corn, beans, black-eyed peas, pumpkins, watermelons, cotton, and ïkca'mac seeds. Relatively to the lower Colorado tribes and certainly to the Pueblos, comparatively little planting was done. It is not altogether certain how much corn was cultivated since corn seems to have been almost entirely supplanted by wheat at an early date, even before whites settled in the immediate district. Even then my informants were certain that mesquite, rather than wheat, was the staple in their childhood (the middle of the last century).

The fields lay in the bottom lands of the Gila River, on flood plains subject to inundation, where planting took place immediately on the subsidence of the waters. According to native informants, the principal floods were those of December and Janu-

---

[7] The drink is blood-red in color (Davis, *Papago Ceremony of Vikita*, p. 176), but my Maricopa informants said that xatca' meant neither "blood" (nyihwï't) nor "red water."

ary, with rains again in April and September. They depended wholly on the inundations and on sub-surface seepage, true irrigation being unknown. Irrigation ditches first came into use, according to Kutox, only when he was a small boy (1850–55).

This late date for the introduction of ditch irrigation among the Maricopa may not be correct, although there is nothing flatly contradictory in the documentary record. An extensive system of ditches was observed by Font and Garcés among the Pima of the Casa Grande–Casa Blanca district as early as November, 1775. They describe the fields divided by fences of poles, a main ditch surrounding the whole with laterals to individual fields, and a rudimentary dam of logs and branches to raise the Gila to the ditch level. Bartlett's observations in 1852 may apply only to the Pima, although it is unlikely, or may record the Maricopa use soon after the introduction of ditches. He wrote, "The whole of this plain [occupied by the Pima and Maricopa] is intersected with irrigating canals from the Gila, by which they are enabled to control the waters, and raise the most luxuriant crops." On the other hand, inundations alone were relied on at Gila Bend (Opasoitac, the Kaveltcadom-Maricopa settlement). Font wrote, "These Opas Indians support themselves from their fields of wheat, maize, and calabashes, and apparently they do not eat so much pechita and tornillo [mesquite] as the Gileños [Pima]. Because they live near their fields, the settlement or rancherías embrace a stretch about a league long on the bank of the river. From it they do not run irrigating ditches, because from near the end of the Sierra de Comars [Sierra Estrella], near the Laguna del Hospital, the Gila river and the Assumpción [Salt River] come united; and since the channel is very wide and carries a large amount of water now, and more during the time of the floods, for then it spreads out a long distance and waters a large area of level land, by means of this irrigation they obtain their harvests." At the same time and place Garcés observed, "Here the Indians raise all sorts of grain, and regularly two crops each year, whether the season be good or bad; but apparently an acequia can be brought from the river," implying that none were in use there. The greater volume of water below the mouth of the Salt made it possible to rely on inundation alone. It may be that the Maricopa preserved this traditional type of farming for a time after moving eastward to the neighborhood of the Pima.[8]

An individual's land holdings were in a continuous strip, not in scattered patches. Only when he was living away from home temporarily, did he clear and plant a small field elsewhere. The land he occupied was of his own choosing or inherited from his father. There was no distribution by allotment, as recorded for the Pima,[9] nor had the chief any voice in the matter. "He did not

[8] Bolton, *Anza's California Expeditions*, IV, 43, 51; Coues, I, 107, 116; Bartlett, *Personal Narrative*, II, 232.

[9] Russell, *Pima Indians*, p. 82. We may suspect that this is not an aboriginal custom of the Pima, but dates, like a similar Maricopa usage, from the day when these tribes were located on their reservations.

own the land: we all owned it, so that a man could choose what land he pleased." Women also owned fields, that is, normally only widows who had no male members of their families to plant for them.

Since floods were slow and mild on the Gila, a stream with low gradient and wide flood plains, there were no difficulties caused by a marauding stream necessitating relocation of the fields.

Boundaries came into dispute: such quarreling had its special name, xamĭltŏ'tà ak_ye'vàm, "[boundaries] bristling side by side." This was one of the rare occasions when the dead were named, not in insult, but as warrant of ownership. "My father had his land over to there, but when you took it you pushed it [the boundary] over to here"; to which the other would reply, "No, my land extended farther to your side." Exasperating and drawn-out quarrels arose over minute pieces of land. If they finally reached the fighting stage, a third man was called on to decide. He might say, "Your land is good enough to that place, so give up this little piece for his benefit, so he will not have any more to say," or he would divide the disputed patch equally. There were, however, no pushing contests or stick fights over disputed boundaries in the manner of the Mohave.[10]

Cultivation in all its stages was man's work, but gathering the harvest was woman's alone. At that time men were busy making the store houses for pumpkins and watermelons. An old woman, with no men to help her, would, of course, plant for herself.

It is now difficult, with the old fields long done away with, to discover what the ownership of field tracts may have been. But it seems to have followed on this male occupation with cultivation that fields were, on the whole, regarded as the personal possessions of men. Inheritance was specifically said to be in the male line. Normally when a man died, the land was inherited by his immediate family: his widow, sons and daughters. Ultimately it came into the possession of the children. A daughter would get some one to plant for her. It may well be that daughters did not transmit their claim.

During the period of mourning, the survivors made no use of

[10] Kroeber, *Handbook*, p. 744.

the land, allowing it to lie fallow for a year, provided they were able to live by gathering wild products. But if a widow had young children dependent on the crops, they would plant the season following (half a year later). On the owner's death they invited others to turn horses into his tract to clear it off as quickly as possible. If the crop was ripe the widow might tell relatives or neighbors to take it, "because while her husband was dying they had stayed night and day with her when they might have been planting for their own use." However should someone other than the male owner die, they might destroy the crops in this fashion, but usually not. This reinforces the conviction that title to the land was vested in men, but that all members of the family had some presumptive right to its use.

Two crops a year were obtained, as today by the white farmers of the Gila-Salt valleys, by planting in the early spring and again in midsummer. This biannual cropping system was coördinate with a biannual calendar, the series of month names opening with the planting of the first crop in early February and repeated with the second crop of late July or early August. Since the month names were also those of the sibs, there has derived a triple association of sib, month, and plant as totem. This does not imply that the association was historically primary with the Maricopa, since the lower Colorado tribes share it. Only one cultivated plant was so associated; corn with xavàtca'c sib, the other totem plants being wild. Xavàtca'c was the name given the lunation during which corn was planted: January–February and again July–August.

Corn was planted when the trees budded in early February, following the drying off of the floods of the preceding month which left the fields soft and moist. Pumpkins, beans, and black-eyed peas were planted at the same time, watermelons and cotton a month later. The beans and peas ripened about May, corn and watermelons in June, and pumpkins during the summer. A second crop of all these was obtained by planting again during July and the first half of August. Pumpkins and watermelons planted early in July and corn in early August would be ripe when the frost came in November. Cotton was planted in a separate patch at the same time as watermelons. The Maricopa and some of the Yumans of the lower Colorado planted seeds which grew wild locally. Here ïkca'mac, a grass seed, alone was cultivated (see above).[11]

Six varieties or colors of corn were named: light red corn (daði'cahwï't), dark red (daði'caka'k̟), white (daði'cxama'l), yellow (daði'càkwě's), blue (daði'caxavàcu'c), light pink (daði'-ckaly ă'p), and corn with streaked kernels (daði'caʀuwa'). It was impossible to secure specimens of these, since they are said to be no longer cultivated, with the exception of a single small ear, which I am not sure was a local product. This is similar to the small ears grown by the Havasupai and known to them as Mohave corn.

Corn was planted in little holes scratched with a planting stick, five or six kernels together in a hole, at a depth of about six inches. It grew rapidly, pushing through the earth in three or four days. The grain was not previously prepared, as by soaking, but an old man creeping along would hold kernels in his mouth where they absorbed some moisture, but solely because he would not want to go back for seed. After the stalks came up, hills were hoed up around them with the same stick.

Corn was the totem of the xavàtca'c sib. Hence they would say, as the first kernels were planted, "You [xavàtca'c] are known all over the world, are famous. Come up strong like that and feed everybody, so that no one will go hungry." I was also told that a man or woman of this sib would be got to repeat the formula, "Put me down in your field; bury me. I will be glad to come up."

The planting stick (i'i'xamiï'ɬ or i'i'nyĭmàxwě'lyĭc, "stick for digging") was of cottonwood, about four feet long, two and a half inches in diameter, and flattened chiselwise for twelve inches at the lower end. It lacked the footrest of the Zuñi. My informant insisted on several occasions that they did not have the side-

---

[11] My informants maintained that modern cultivation has wholly wiped out this plant. Kroeber (*ibid.*, p. 736) mentions four normally wild plants cultivated by the Mohave, among them aksamta which may be the same plant.

scraper hoe of the Mohave,[12] but used the same planting stick as a shovel, cultivating while standing.

Corn was almost always prepared on the metate before it was used. If green the kernels were mashed; when dry they were thoroughly ground. It was almost always eaten in the form of mush. Green corn was mashed, wrapped in the husks, and either boiled or placed on a spot previously heated by the fire, covered further with husks, then ashes and a little fire until baked into a loaf. Green corn was sometimes lye-hulled: half-boiled, ashes added, and stirred until the hull came free of the kernel. It was also cut from the ears, mashed on the metate and boiled with salt. The flavor of roasted corn was preferred to boiled. Kernels of roasted corn were plucked from the ear with the thumb nail and the handful poured into the mouth.

Corn for storage was dried on the house roof and placed in the basket granary either on the ear or shelled. Sometimes ears were roasted on a pile of brush or coals and also dried on the roof. Or the kernels were removed to dry on a cloth. Roasted ears were not ordinarily prepared for storage, but if so, they too went into the granary. Dry corn might be soaked in water and gently pounded in a mortar to remove the hulls.

Wafer bread, corresponding to that of the Pueblos and Havasupai, was made, but instead of a stone gridle, a lenticular pottery plate (maði'l) was used. This was about a foot in diameter, and less than half an inch thick (Pl. VI, i). It was made very hot on the coals, when the thin corn batter could be rapidly spread over its concave side to form immediately as a wafer-thin cake called havàri'k or maði'lyàm. Corn of any color was used. This hot plate was in constant use in earlier days, since tortillas of parched wheat or seeds were made on it, the dough being patted out into cakes about the size of the hand.

Wheat, which displaced corn, was treated in much the same fashion. The ears were fastened in bundles of an inch diameter, roasted on coals, and thrown on the roof to dry. These were stored in large pots, and when wanted the grain was beaten out.

[12] *Ibid.*, p. 736.

Parched ground wheat became a common article of food in the form of gruel (the Mexican pinole). It was always carried when travelling, when it might be mixed to a dough in a cavity hollowed in the top of a barrel cactus if nothing else was available, then roasted on the coals.

Beans came in two varieties: a little white bean (maʀi'k xama'l, "bean white") and a brown (maʀi'k gwĭs, "bean yellow"). They were prepared alike. After being shelled they were spread on the ground for three or four days until dry, then stored in the basket granary. They were boiled, not baked. Parched and ground, they were also added to ground wheat, with salt, to make a gruel. Boiled beans might be drained, then fried in a vessel having the shape of a parching pan.

Black-eyed peas (axma') are not aboriginal but like wheat have been cultivated for a long time. Green pods were broken up like our string beans and boiled. Like beans they might further be fried with fat. For storage they were broken, half-boiled in large pots, spread out to dry and stored in similar vessels. Later green food might be had by boiling them further.

Pumpkins (xama't) and squash were kept in the storehouses. The rind of the pumpkin was hacked off and the seeds scooped from the interior. After these had dried on the roof overnight, the vegetable was cut spirally in long strips which dried thoroughly while hung from a beam slung under a shade. The strips were looped into bundles, fastened by a turn of one end, for storage. The usual preparation was chopped bits of pumpkin boiled, with ground wheat stirred in. Pumpkins were also roasted whole, after the stem end was removed, the seeds scooped out, and this plug replaced. They warmed them, turning each side to the fire, then baking them in the ground after the coals were raked away. Pumpkin blossoms were also cooked. After boiling them, they stirred in ground mesquite beans, which had been soaked and strained, and ground wheat. Squash was also cooked like beans: pieces were dropped into plenty of fat and stirred until thoroughly amalgamated, then salt was added.

Watermelons (kwiðu'i) were known in two varieties, with pink and black seeds, as on the lower Colorado. Beside being eaten fresh, the pulp might be squeezed between the hands, the liquor strained through a cloth, and boiled to a syrup which was used on corn bread or wheat tortillas. The melons were of some importance in providing a fresh food during the winter. They were stored in the storage houses adjacent to the dwellings, where they may have been covered with sand to keep through the winter. They were not ordinarily stored by burial in sand in the fashion of the lower Colorado tribes, but this was resorted to if they were to be hidden from the enemy.

The semi-desert environment of the Maricopa provided only a meagre range of animals for food. Rabbits and other rodents were relatively abundant, but large game was scarce in the immediate vicinity. The larger mammals, such as deer and mountain sheep, could be hunted in the mountains to the south and west, but even there were by no means plentiful. A secondary source of flesh food was nearer home in the form of fish, with which the streams were well stocked at certain seasons. Consequently the Maricopa were primarily hunters of small game, chiefly rabbits, and were also fishermen. They had little interest in ranging far from home for larger game.

Rabbits, especially jackrabbits, bulked as large as mesquite in the food supply. In addition they took deer, mountain sheep, antelope, peccary, beaver, prairie dogs, doves, turkey, quail, and even made use of turtles, honey, and caterpillars, but none of these were regular foodstuffs. They stopped at nothing except outright carnivores, as well as dogs, badgers, gophers, ground squirrels, and porcupines, nor did they eat bird eggs.

Possibly because of a general indifference to hunting, tabus and rites were few. There was no notion here, as among the Havasupai, that wasting game made the hunter ill. A lad was prohibited from eating his kill, however, and mountain sheep hunting was something altogether special. Deer hunting was less restricted, but was preceded by a rite.

A lad dared not eat any animal, bird, or fish he caught. He brought it home and butchered it, but he had to give it away to older people. This tabu applied not only to his first kill, but continued until he was full grown, twenty-five or thirty. Should he eat it blood might run from his mouth until he died, or at least he would never kill anything more. There was no ceremonial termination of the tabu. This prohibition is not an unfamiliar provision but usually extends only to the first kill.[13]

All three local varieties of rabbits were eaten: jackrabbits (ȧkȧu'ly^ȧ), cottontail (xaly^ȧau'), and the little chamissa or blue rabbit (xaly^ȧau' ĭnyamtackωeʀᵃ, "made slender by the sun rabbit"). Cottontails could be eaten by any one, but the others were held "poisonous." Chamissa was dangerous to little children, who therefore might not eat it. Jackrabbits were also somewhat "poisonous" for adults, but they nevertheless ate them.

There is a confusion here, because according to myth the cottontail was considered poisonous, the others derivatively from the cottontail. In handling the raw flesh of jackrabbits they carefully avoided letting the least drop of blood splash on them, else they would sicken. And if a hair of this rabbit got into one's eye, he would be stricken blind.

Jackrabbits were sought rather than the smaller species. They were hunted chiefly in summer, when they were fattest, near where the women were at work gathering mesquite. They were exceptionally plentiful in the valley: a hunter returned from a day's hunt with at least four or five, sometimes as many as ten. The excess beyond the day's needs were skinned, opened, and hung to dry on the house beams.

There was a saying (but it was regarded as no more than a saying) that when a man had set a day for hunting jackrabbits and it turned out cloudy, it was a sign he had been incontinent.

Although rabbit hunting was for the most part individual, organized drives were sometimes decided on at evening meetings. One man was chosen as leader (xalyȧaui'ck, "planner of rabbit killing"), who assigned men to their positions. Nets were set in

[13] Pima, Havasupai, Kaibab, Paviotso, Shasta, Klamath (Russell, *Pima Indians*, p. 191; Spier, *Havasupai Ethnography*, p. 324; *Klamath Ethnography*, p. 168). The Maricopa extended tabu holds for the Kaibab Paiute: boys are forbidden to eat jackrabbits they themselves kill (Sapir, *Paiute Song Recitative*, p. 466).

the rabbit runways, guarded by appointed men. When directed by the leader, men armed with bows moved forward toward the nets, others on the flanks driving the game in. Other nets were set in the rear of the advancing line to catch those rabbits which doubled back.[14]

The rabbit net (ca'a'k) was a purse net about a yard square. A stout cord was threaded through the periphery and both ends tied to a stake. If necessary the upper edge was laid over a stick lying horizontally from one bush to another. The rabbit dashing into the net pursed it and was held fast to the stake (Pl. XI).

A twitch-up trap (xalyȧau' axe'ʀum, "rabbit tied in") was used for rabbits, quail, or other small game. Two stakes were planted in a rabbit runway (Fig. 4). At their upper ends a horizontal stick (*A*) was tied. Another stick (*B*), parallel to this and nearer the ground, was held in place by a little trigger stick (*C*), itself under tension of a cord attached to a springy sapling planted near by. The end of the same cord formed a slip noose which lay on a series of sticks (*D–D*), which in turn rested on the loose horizontal bar (*B*). When the rabbit stepped on the grid (*D–D*) the stick B was forced down, releasing the trigger *C*. The spring of the bent sapling jerked the animal, caught in the noose, into the air. Wings of arrowweeds stuck into the ground on each side forced the rabbit to step into the trap. When a fence of such weeds was erected, several traps were placed at as many openings.

Rabbits were also dug from their burrows, first stopping up the entrance by treading down the dirt. Digging began a foot and a half from the opening. Or they thrust an arrow down the burrow and twisted it in the animal's fur to pull it out. (A notched or crooked stick was not prepared for this.)

A charm for jackrabbits was made of ground-up yellow lichens, obtained in the mountains, mixed with the leaves of a redolent medicinal plant. This was carried in a tiny sack into which the finger was dipped and the powder rubbed on the bow string. The jackrabbit would not run off when it smelled this. It was also

---

[14] The curved rabbit club of the Mohave (Kroeber, *Handbook*, p. 632) was absent.

useful to attract girls! For cottontail rabbits, the hunter bit a strong smelling tiny pod. The rabbit smelling this, hopped toward him. But it was dangerous, because it ruined the hunter's stomach.

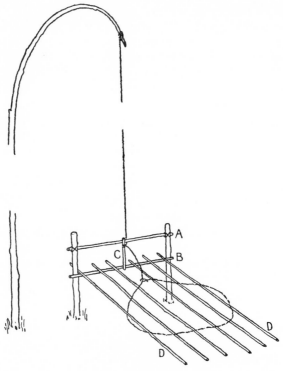

FIG. 4.—Rabbit trap

Deer were quite scarce. They had to hunt hard for them and shared the flesh if any were obtained. If they were exceptionally fortunate two deer might be killed. Deer were found in the canyons of the Sierra Estrella, where they were ambushed at the springs. There were none in the Salt River range and they never came down to the thickets along the rivers. They were hunted when the cottonwood leaves turned yellow (November), when they were fattest.

Deer hunting was undertaken by the few who understood
tracking them. This was wholly practical knowledge, for one did
not dream such power. A man who knew how to hunt them was
looked up to: they waited for him to set the day for hunting and
always expected him to succeed.

There was a ritual preliminary to the hunt called tculoiⁿg
(meaningless). The hunters never told of their intention, but the
night before the hunt met in secrecy away from the settlement.
There they talked of that most beautiful (axo'tk) woman or girl
they would meet, by beautiful meaning fat, and having in mind
the deer. One of their number then took the part of a deer,
standing on hands and feet. Each contributed a cotton blanket
in which to swathe the "deer's" head and shoulders. While they
sat in a circle singing, the swaddled man in their midst acted like
a deer. One of their number then shot and the "deer" must drop
right down. Another then pretended to butcher him, stripping
off the blankets to distribute to the company as so much meat
and hide. Throughout the performance "they must be sober
minded; they must not smile or laugh." They then returned to
bed and in the morning set out to hunt. There were no special
qualifications for the actors in this rite. A special song was used
at this time, which Last Star thought may have been called
tculoiⁿg like the rite.

Continence was not prescribed for deer hunters; no charms
were known, as with rabbits; and while deer calculi were known to
exist, there was no notion that their possession gave luck as with
the Havasupai.

Occasionally a deer head disguise was worn by a hunter, who
imitated the browsing animal. The deer head with horns attached was used, the skin hiding the wearer's body. This sort of
deer stalking was called ăkwe'g. A similar disguise was used in
taking antelope but not mountain sheep.

Antelope (ma.u'l) were found in the mountains southeast of
Maricopa territory.

Mountain sheep hunting was hedged about by special observances, for the animal was regarded as sacred. Hunters must talk
softly, they must not mention the mountain sheep at all, for they

held that the night would tell the sheep, the two being cousins (ĕstcuma'và, mother's sister's child). The hunters must be continent before they set off. The reason for all this is anything but clear, for so far as I could discover the beliefs were not integrated with the body of religious attitudes and practices. The connection of night with the sheep may rest on the fact that Orion's Belt was, as usual in this area, called "mountain sheep."

The best time to go for the sheep was when the palo verde was in bloom, that is, in the spring. They were hunted in the Gila Bend Mountains (and northwestward?) where they were by no means plentiful. Before they set out, the hunters prayed. (The special prayer was unknown to my informant, Kutox.) They had to be very quiet, speaking softly, and they would not tell even their own families they were going. On the way to the mountains they rested at night if necessary in order to arrive there at midday. There they were very quiet, never laughing. They would sit up all night, smoking, and talking of very fat animals (other animals). If a deer was being described, they would say they wished for a deer when the leaves turned yellow (i.e., when deer were fattest). If they spoke of a horse, they would wish they had the fattest horse; or if a rabbit, the hunter described how he had killed a fat one. They began hunting before dawn and continued only until noon. They were thought always to be successful in killing at least one sheep. Five or six men always went together, and even a single sheep would be sufficient for all of them. When the sheep was killed, the hunter must not describe any part of it as he approached. If he should say what an ugly thing it was, rain would pour down. If they failed to kill one the first day, they returned home, because they believed some one of their number had made some sort of disturbance to scare the sheep.

When a mountain sheep was killed, a long time was required to skin it because only one man worked at it and that leisurely. He took four puffs of smoke before commencing. He would cut down the breast, but only a little way, and then stop to smoke with the others sitting around him. This was repeated so that by the fourth smoke he had completed the skinning operation. The carcass would be left lying on the hide while they went to one side to talk of happy things. When they had finished smoking four cigarettes, the same man would butcher and divide it among those present. They were careful to lift the flesh slowly from the ground. If it were jerked up, rain would pour down and it would thunder hard. Even when carrying it home, they would walk their horses slowly all the way. When they neared home, those on horses dismounted slowly and carefully lifted off the meat. These men would divide the meat among their friends and relatives, or after it was cooked invite them to eat. Those to whom it was given must thank the giver, else in winter it would rain hard or be very cold, or if summer, become so hot as to scorch the plants and sand storms blow. Similarly if one should beat or shake the mountain sheep skin or horns, the weather would be frightful. (The horns were not carried home.)[15] They had to be careful at all points in handling the sheep. Women cooked its flesh. It was not thrown into the pot, but put in slowly. Sticks had to be thrust into the fire slowly, too. Even when eating it, they chewed slowly, for fear of choking.

Peccaries were sometimes seen in the desert east of Sacaton; they were hardly ever found in Maricopa territory. Hence while the Pima hunted them, the Maricopa killed them only when passing eastward, as on a war party. The meat was divided, roasted and eaten on the spot. The tusks were not used. While the peccary is now known as kyω'chǐlyuvacàϑŏ'm, "wild pig," and the domestic pig as kyω'c, obviously the latter was the original name for the peccary.

Beavers (pĕm) were eaten, especially the fat tail. There were a great many beaver in the neighborhood. The entrances of the beaver house were stopped up, while they dug through its top, using their digging sticks to kill the inmates.

No one would eat ground squirrels (aϑi'c) for fear of deafness.

Birds were not important in the diet and their eggs were never eaten. Quail, mourning doves, and whitewing doves could be

[15] Pima hunters also never brought home the horns. "Each man had a place set apart where he deposited them in order that they might exert no evil influence upon the winds or rains." The Papago deposited mountain sheep tails with feathers at springs during rain ceremonies (Russell, *Pima Indians*, p. 82).

taken locally, and turkeys in the mountains north of Salt River.[16]
Birds were shot, especially at their roosting places after sun-
down. They did not use a jacklight like the White Mountain
Apache. A quail trap was also used. This was a basket-like contrivance of arrowweed propped on a split stick and baited with
seed (Fig. 5). The prop had a scarf-joint at its middle, unbound,
and simply stuck together to stand in unstable equilibrium. A
string, fastened to the lower corners of the basket, looped around
the stick to hold it taut. When the birds struck the string the

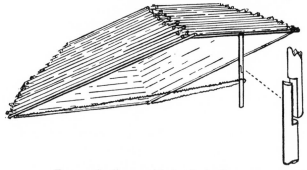

Fig. 5.—Quail trap, with detail of split prop

prop was upset and the trap dropped. The mechanical inefficiency
of this contrivance nicely illustrates Maricopa indifference to
things material. This trap was called 'aʀikŭ'm ("to trap" was
tapĕ'tŭm); the split stick, kȧca.u'n. Quail were aχma'; mourning doves, kuavȧta'; and turkeys, ωʀo'tĭc.

Meat was more commonly broiled than boiled. Small birds
were plucked and drawn, and spitted in rows on sticks. A great
number of such spits might be set up around the fire. To roast
small birds and rabbits, they brushed the ashes aside, placed the
eviscerated animals or birds, still with fur or feathers, on the hot
ground, covered them with ashes, and heaped coals over this.
This method was called pa'vŭg; broiling was cil. The informants
had never heard of pit-roasting small game. All small game and

[16] Quail were not tabu for women as among the Pima (*ibid.*, p. 80).

fish was cooked by men; women, however, cooked deer and mountain sheep flesh. The reason is not apparent.

Large mountain turtles (kapĕ't), about a foot across, were eaten; also by Papago and Yavapai according to my informant. These were usually baked in ashes; sometimes boiled. The shells were not used for any purpose.

Honey was occasionally obtained from the flower stalks of mescal, but these contain very little. This was the product of large bees (mŭspo'kwĭni'lyà, "black bee"). The classification of "bees" is rather interesting: working bees were called flies (xǎlyàsmo''kwĭlyàvi'na); another bee with a yellow back (not a hornet) was mŭspo'cĭlyàmŏ'kkàkwĭ'sĭc; a fourth variety, resembling a wasp, was mŭspo'kwĭsĭ'c, "yellow bee." The nests of working bees were found and the insects killed individually, but their honey was not eaten.

A worm, called àmĕ' (more probably a caterpillar, since it was said to have a horn on each end) was caught, boiled, dried, and eaten.[17] They caught them in their hands in the spring and late autumn. There was a peculiar way of catching them: with one hand they caught the beast, broke off the end with the thumb nail, squeezed it out, and inserted it between the other fingers of the same hand. In some fashion they braided long strings of these, perhaps because the "worm" coiled around its fellows. Then they boiled and dried them. They were eaten dry or boiled. Dried "worms" were also heated in warm water and fried. The finger tips got sore gathering them.

Pets (nyàxa'tk, "my dog," any pet) may be conveniently described here. These were dogs and various birds. The chicken hawk was perhaps the sole bird deliberately excluded, because one who handled it would "get sick in the lungs." Turkeys were not pets.

Dogs (xatk) were said to be like present-day dogs; some black, others spotted. They were called by whistling or by calling their names. Several expressions were recorded: kàθi'k, kàθi'k, "come, come," govŭna'lyŭm, "get out, go away," sĭkiyĭ'mdĭk, "go

---

[17] Said to travel rapidly. These are undoubtedly the same as the Pima ma'kŭm (*ibid.*, p. 81).

away," and more emphatically gĕcpa'm, "go away!" Pups were trained for hunting, but since they were not used to hunt deer, this was most casual. Objects were thrown for them to fetch, so that they would catch rabbits and bring them on call. Horse meat was eaten but not dog, "because the dog is a person."[18]

Dogs were named for their appearance. A dog with a gray nose was called aucăki'n, "fire poker," because he resembled the burnt end of a poker. A dog with a white patch around his neck was xama'lgwexa'nŏk, "white collar"; a woolly little dog was mule'l, "bushy"; a black one with white spots over the eyes was hiϑa'kgwĭcåmpŏ'p, "four eyes."

Doves were kept as pets. They were brought by the Papago and were kept in long, cylindrical cages made of tules. The cage was about three feet long by one in diameter; the tules were mounted on a willow hoop at each end, with other tules woven through them at intervals along the side. This sort of cage was called åkwi'k, "woven, twined." Mocking birds (kwĭcila') were also kept as pets, because they woke their owners in the morning and because they were dreamed of.

Young birds were caught and reared, so that each year their feathers might be plucked. These were mostly hawks; rarely buzzards and crows. A cage, about four feet high, was made of willow limbs thrust into the ground close together and bent over to be tied at the top. This lacked horizontal ribs. No nest was made inside, but simply a stick for a perch. Such a cage was gacωla'nᵧĭva' tciwŭ'm, "built for [a particular species of large] hawks."

FISHING

Both Maricopa and Halchidhoma gave more attention to fishing than might have been expected. This is especially astonishing in the case of the Maricopa since their semi-desert habitat with its seasonally variable streams, containing at best little water, would seem most unprofitable for fishermen. There is no question, however, that even for them fish held second place beside jackrabbits in providing flesh. As between Halchidhoma and

[18] See p. 254.

Maricopa, the former, situated on the banks of the Colorado, were undoubtedly greater fishermen.[19] The information which follows relates specifically to the Halchidhoma in their Colorado River home. Maricopa habits were identical.

Native statements of the amount of fishing are borne out by Kino, who wrote of the middle Gila (February, 1699): "All its inhabitants are fishermen, and have many nets and other tackle with which they fish all the year, sustaining themselves with abundant fish and with their maize, beans, and calabashes, etc. . . . . In some places they gave us so much and so very good fish that we gave it as a ration to the men, just as beef is given where it is plentiful."[20]

The Maricopa took fish mostly in the Santa Cruz slough at the northern foot of the Sierra Estrella. They also fished about the confluence of the Gila and Salt, and up the Salt to the vicinity of Phoenix. This point was, of course, close to enemy territory, hence many men were killed while fishing. Fish were few in the Gila except in times of flood. The fish of these streams were chiefly chub, a soft fleshed, bony fish. The Halchidhoma on the Colorado also caught a very large fish, which may have been the "Colorado salmon."

Three methods were commonly employed for fishing on the Colorado. A small net like a rabbit net (and like it called ca'a'k) was used when the river was high and muddy so that one could not see fish in it. It was held spread out between the hands, aided by a little stick at each side threaded through the meshes, so that the fisherman might reach down and catch at a chance. Another method was by diving to look into beaver holes and the like under the bank where fishes took refuge when it was cold. One man after another dove down, catching the fish in his hands. A third was with large nets (called davi'tc), six to eight feet long and a yard deep. These were very valuable since it was hard to spin so much cotton cord. A pole was fastened at each end, so that it could be held vertically by two men who dragged it through shallow water. Several such nets might be dragged side by side. Other men would walk through the water scaring the

[19] The Mohave also fished more than they hunted (Kroeber, *Preliminary Sketch of the Mohave*, p. 276).

[20] Bolton, *Kino's Historical Memoir*, I, 195, 197.

fish into the nets. The Maricopa used nets like these in the Salt River. There can be little doubt that the Halchidhoma used fish scoops like Mohave and Maricopa.

The fish scoop of the Maricopa was like that of the Mohave[21] but smaller (Pl. IV, e). An elliptical hoop of willow, three feet by eighteen inches, was provided with a series of longitudinal willow twigs bound to it. A long handle was fastened transversely to the hoop. A mate to this was a conical basket of willow twigs slung on the fisherman's back by a forehead band of rolled willow bark (Pl. IV, d). In form and construction it resembled the travelling mortar (Pl. XIV, c), having a willow hoop to which the twigs were bound. These were also bound together at the point and fastened on the side by several rows of twining. The small fish caught with the scoop were thrown over the shoulder into this basket. The scoop was called kwisŏ'tc; the basket kŭ-pàʀω'c.

Spearing was unknown to the Halchidhoma and shooting fish not regularly employed. When the large "salmon" were caught, the net was almost torn to pieces. Then all the men joined in capturing it. It might be shot when driven into shallow water. Maricopa also shot fish in the shallow sloughs of their country. Such arrows did not have retrieving lines attached.

Young boys fished with cotton lines attached to the ends of long poles. Their hooks were the curved spines of the barrel cactus, heated and bent. A hole was drilled in the butt to take the line. These were baited with worms. The lines were further furnished with floats of wood or pumice, said usually to have been crescentic, like one collected (Pl. XII, b). This, which had been found in a local ruin, was of a light vesicular stone and had been drilled through the middle so that the points stood vertically.[22]

Such boats as they had on the Colorado for fishing and ferryage were merely rafts formed of bundles of dry tules. My informant did not know how they were shaped. Such rafts might hold ten men and their nets. Sometimes an unshaped log was used: the Maricopa also used this. Catamarans (kopŏ'p) were

---

[21] Kroeber, *Handbook*, p. 737.   [22] Washington State Museum, No. 2–11926.

also made for use in high water: these were two logs side by side with sticks tied across them. They used their hands for paddling and long punt poles. The Halchidhoma, like the Mohave, also ferried babies across the Colorado in large pots. These people were good swimmers; the Maricopa were not.

Fish were usually eaten fresh. The excess of a day's catch might be half broiled and hung to dry from the house beams. But no attempt was made to keep them longer than a week. Whether this was because such soft-fleshed fish cannot be successfully dried, or for want of knowledge or interest, I do not know.

Fish were either broiled or boiled with corn. In any event, they were always cooked by men, who served their wives before themselves. No reason was assigned for this, other than that it was so strongly customary as to be obligatory. Men never ate fish before their wives; when the wives had had enough they called their husbands.

Broiling was done by two methods. In one, the fish was always cut open along its right side near the backbone. If a man cut it on the opposite side, they made fun of him; told him to go back and grind his wheat (that is, that he was womanly, for he did not know how). The intestines cleaned away, the fish was spread open on the hot ground. Burning sticks were then propped over stones set around the fish so as to broil the upper side. All fish were treated in this fashion. They were broiled in this way very quickly. The other method consisted of cutting the fish along the belly, but not spreading the flanks. Again the coals were raked away, the fish laid side by side, and covered with ashes on which coals were heaped. It took all morning to cook them in this fashion.

They were boiled with salt. This took half a day. When done, finely ground corn, mixed with water to a thin gruel, was added to the pot of fish. The cook, always a man, stirred this, not round and round, but by inserting his stirrer down close to the sides of the vessel and lifting the fish. After the corn was added, another half hour was required to complete cooking. The stirrer used was a stick eighteen inches long, one and a half inches in diameter, and wedge-shaped at one end. It will be noted that scales, skin, bones and all went into the mess. In fact, the enormous number of small bones these fish contained gave them no concern at all.

Shellfish and crayfish were probably not eaten, if they occur in these waters at all. My informants knew of no mollusks nearby and professed ignorance of the Colorado.

MEALS AND DOMESTIC HABITS

Domestic duties began before sunrise. A woman rose and immediately began her preparations for the morning meal, the cooking utensils being conveniently at hand near her head. (They slept with their heads to the east: these articles were kept near the doorway which was on the east side of the house.) She then went to fetch water sufficient for the day's supply, carrying a large pot on her head balanced on a cloth ring. Each family had several large vessels for storing water, mounted on branching posts erected under the shade. Fetching water was a feminine task alone: they always made a point of having the storage jars filled before the sun rose.

Cooking was done under the shade, with which each house was provided, in the summer, but in winter anywhere in the open. If need be they erected a little screen of arrowweed stalks thrust into the ground to keep off wind and dust. They only cooked inside the dwelling if forced to by bitter cold. There, as outdoors, the fire was not confined, as in a pit nor walled in. Cooking pots were supported on three stones. Today, a little trench is dug for the fire, the pot being supported on several iron rods or even green sticks set across, but I was assured this was not aboriginal. Clay cooking pots and bowls, ladles of clay and wood, mush stirrers, and baskets were the utensils. For a people primarily pottery using, they put an exaggerated value on the convenience of baskets (the shallow bowl baskets obtained from the Pima) and held it highly awkward to have to do without. Stone boiling was unknown. The mush stirrer was three or four arrowweeds twined together near one end (Pl. XIV, *d*).

Mesquite branches were considered the best firewood; of these the supply was abundant. Men would go out to burn down and break up wood, but they would not carry it home; that was a woman's task. Nor would they fetch water, grind seeds, nor ordinarily cook. Men, however, would kindle the fire to warm the house in the evening. A fire to cook by was built of several large chunks of wood at the sides with sticks between. The common palm drill was used to light it.

The preparation of meals was laborious rather than complicated. With mesquite as the staple, a large part of a woman's daily routine had to be given over to pounding it in a mortar and grinding it on the metate. The metate was also requisitioned for corn in all its stages and many of the wild seeds. Ability to labor long and rapidly at it was reckoned the chief of a housewife's accomplishments; so much so that every prospective bride was set to work grinding by her mother-in-law to prove her proficiency. The wooden mortar came in for far less use. In it they broke up the mesquite beans preparatory to grinding on the metate, hulled various seeds and shelled corn. The principles of cooking were simple and few. Mesquite flour and tule pollen were preserved in cakes made by packing layer after layer into a hole. Other foods, vegetal and flesh, were half-broiled, roasted, or boiled to be dried for storage. In the final preparations for the meal, great use was made of baking in the ashes: seeds, stems, corn, and small grain were treated in this fashion.[23] For this the ground was heated, and the ashes with a few live coals raked back over the article. Boiling was, however, the mainstay in cooking, at least for vegetal products: mesquite, corn, seeds, pumpkins, squash, and beans regularly went into the pot. Mesquite gruel, and in later days wheat gruel (pinole), was commonly mixed with other foods: in fact, ground wild seeds were used for little more than to give variety to the flavor of the gruel. Pit roasting was rare, since mescal and cholla beans were obtained only infrequently. Parching with live coals in shallow bowls

[23] The Papago also roast rabbits in ashes (Lumholtz, *New Trails in Mexico*, p. 334).

probably came into common use only after the introduction of wheat. Previously its use was primarily to prepare seeds and beans for grinding. Salt (ĕs'i') was little used in cooking. In fact, they had no true salt but scraped up saline or alkaline deposits found near certain sloughs.[24] (Curiously enough, they say that commercial salt is bitter!)

Only two meals a day were served: morning and evening. The morning meal was usually prepared at dawn, and when all had risen at sunrise, the family would eat. If a woman was seen preparing it after the sun had risen, they would call her lazy. Women were ordinarily away from home all day gathering foodstuffs. Children who were left at home were expected to keep up the fire in order to have plenty of ashes on hand to roast with. Women had to spend a large part of their time grinding on the metate. They began preparing the evening meal in the middle of the afternoon: as soon as it was ready, they would eat it, that is, quite early, before sunset. This was the big meal of the day. (Breakfast and dinner had no special designations like ours.) There was no sort of grace before eating.

Women shared food. A woman would cook a large vessel full of pumpkin, then go about the village gathering bowls from other women, and share out the pumpkin in these until all was gone. She then carried them to the owners, who in turn brought her something.

Men ordinarily ate first, morning or evening; then the women and children of the household. But if there were present visitors of either sex, friends and relatives, of whatever status, they were served even before the men. It happened to be the general rule that women served their husbands first, but this was because most foodstuffs were vegetal. Actually whoever cooked served the others first. Thus, men prepared the small game they killed —rabbits, fish, quail—and served their wives first. That is, "they treated each other alike."

[24] The salt gathering expeditions of Papago and Pima, with self-purification, were not made by the Maricopa (Lumholtz, *New Trails*, p. 269; Russell, *Pima Indians*, p. 94).

Food was served in large bowls. The housewife would set out a dish of pumpkin, e.g., and another of mush. The men would sit around them fishing around the sides with their fingers or with bits of bread. When the pumpkin dish was emptied, they passed it aside to the women and began on the other.

Those who were fastidious washed out their mouths before and after the morning meal. Some would bathe before coming to breakfast.

CHAPTER III

HOUSES

The Maricopa dwelling was dome-shaped, markedly flattened on top, and earth-covered. It was built on a central rectangular frame of posts linked by rafters, surrounded by a circular wall of poles bent over to be tied to the rafters, thatched, and dirt-covered. The construction was identical with that of the Pima and Papago and different from the earth-covered, but rectangular, hip-roofed houses of Mohave and Yuma. Halchidhoma houses, and possibly those of the two other remnant groups, Kohuana and Halyikwamai, were identical with the Maricopa, at least since they joined the last on the Gila. Kutox insisted that he had been told that still earlier the Halchidhoma houses on the Colorado River had been of the same form. (He knew the rectangular Mohave house.) But it is more than probable that he was mistaken since the known house forms of the lower Colorado (Mohave, Kamia, and Yuma) were all rectangular. Garcés in May 1774 remarked that the Halchidhoma "have better and larger houses than any I have seen" among the Yuma and on the Gila.[1]

The modern houses in the Maricopa community are for the most part of the Mexican jacal type: a rectangular structure having walls formed of posts at short intervals, with adobe between, held in place and protected against the wash of rain by horizontal ribs of the inner wood of the giant cactus nailed in place. The roof is flat, consisting of beams, sticks, brush and dirt (Pl. III, *A, C*). A solitary house of different construction was the home of the last surviving Kohuana in 1930 (Pl. III, *B*). It has the same wall posts and roof. The walls are thatched, however, with thick layers of arrowweed, held in place by horizontal willow branches inside and out, tied together through the thatch at intervals. This was said to be in imitation of the Mexicans, but the form is known to Pima and Papago.[2] There are now no houses of the ancient type.

Anciently house constructions included the flat-domed, earth-covered dwelling; the meeting house, which was but a larger

[1] Bolton, *Anza's California Expeditions*, II, 386.

[2] Kissell, *Basketry of the Papago and Pima*, p. 147.

PLATE III

A

B

C

Modern Maricopa Houses and Woman Grinding

edition of the dwelling; an open-sided, flat-roofed shade; a small structure resembling a gable roof set directly on the ground, built as needed for a storage house, for purification rites, for a girl's puberty rite, and as a menstrual hut. A small hemispherical sweat lodge was also built. Sometimes a temporary kitchen was made by erecting a screen of weeds to windward of the cooking place.

Housebuilding was man's work alone, whether a dwelling, storehouse, or meeting house: the women did not assist. A man was helped by his male friends and relatives in the construction of his dwelling. In building a meeting house, all the men of the village were engaged and built it in a day.

Dwellings stood indefinitely, until some one of the inmates died, when they were torn down and burned. This also happened on the infrequent occasions when relatives who had married were mourned as dead. A new house was erected elsewhere, so that the community was constantly crawling away from its original location. So great was the decimation from disease and warfare during the past century, that the shifting went on with some rapidity despite the localizing ties of available water supply and tillage. The movement may have been somewhat less in earlier times, but there is no doubt that the habit of shifting the locus is old and ingrained. Houses did not suffer much from the elements; rainfall is slight and confined largely to the spring, snow practically never falls. The dirt covering of the house needs no renewal; at most, it must be patched here and there.

The size of the dwelling naturally depended on the number of inmates it was intended to house. An average dwelling was about eighteen to twenty feet in diameter, larger houses perhaps twenty-five feet: Bartlett (1852) says fifteen to twenty-five feet.[3] It was built on level ground, no excavation being made.

For the ordinary dwelling, four cottonwood posts were set in the ground at the corners of a square, measuring nine or ten feet. These stood as high as a man could reach, about seven or eight feet, so that he could work at the ridge. (It must be remembered that these people are quite tall.) Yet Bartlett wrote, "These

[3] Bartlett, *Personal Narrative*, II, 234.

habitations vary in height from five to seven feet; so that in many of them one cannot stand erect." The four main posts were stout, about a foot in diameter, because of the weight of the dirt covering, and were provided at the upper end with a crotch

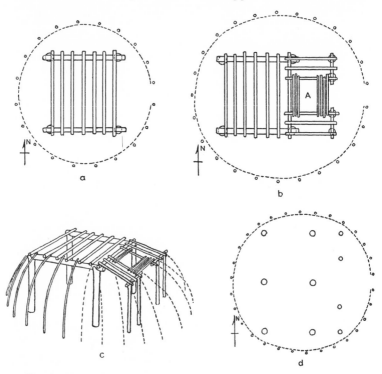

FIG. 6.—Diagrams of house frames (*a*, dwelling; *b*, *c*, larger dwelling; *d*, meeting house).

formed by short branches or a notch cut into the top. The posts were connected in pairs by longitudinal stringers of almost the same diameter placed in their crotches. Transverse rafters were laid in those to complete a rectangular grid supported on the tops of the posts (Fig. 6, *a*). Around this central frame a row of flexible poles was set in a circle to form the wall. These were willows, four or five inches in diameter where they were set into the ground, with their tips bent over to the rectangle formed by the roof beams, where they were lashed in place. Bartlett adds that they were further united at the center.[4] A space for entrance was left on the eastern side. The wall had a clearance of about three feet from the corner posts, five feet at the mid-points between them.

Larger houses were sometimes made by setting the circular wall at a greater distance from the central frame and using longer willow poles. They were more commonly made by increasing the size of the frame, keeping the wall at the same distance from it. For this purpose, four auxiliary posts were placed in front of the central four (i.e., to the east), arranged in pairs on either hand as viewed from the doorway (Figs. 6, *b*, *c*). These four were somewhat shorter than the central four, about five feet high, and stood perhaps six feet in front of the easterly pair of main posts. They were connected in pairs by short beams in their crotches; short rafters were laid longitudinally between these beams and the eastern transverse beam of the main frame, and the grid completed with sticks laid transversely between these rafters, leaving, however, an opening (*A*) for a smoke vent. The wall was said to pass three feet in front of these auxiliary posts. Since the frame was thus longer than wide, it appears that the house may have been oval in ground plan, but the information is not decisive. At any rate, these houses always approached circles and were never squarish with rounded corners.

The Halchidhoma informant Kutox gave a somewhat different picture of the framework. In the first place, the ordinary dwelling, according to him, was somewhat larger than that described above; the central frame measuring sixteen feet on the side. It was built of nine main posts, set in parallel rows of three; the posts spaced about a fathom from each other in both directions. The middle row was slightly higher than those to north and south: seven or eight feet for the middle row, six feet for the sides. Longitudinal stringers were placed on each row of posts so as to lie east and west, like those already described. The transverse rafters were twenty-four in number, twelve to the side, reaching from the central line of stringers to those at the side. This resulted in a very low gable at the center of the roof; so low as to be scarcely recognizable. He was contradicted by three individuals as well-informed on house building as he. (Such houses were in use within the present century.) None of them had ever seen a dwelling with nine

4 *Ibid.*, p. 233.

main posts nor even a meeting house, which, being larger, might have called for such an arrangement. It was suggested that he had confused the construction with that of the shade. This is quite likely, for he was, in fact, using a shade with its conventional nine posts for demonstration. There is also a possibility, though slight, that the Maricopa and Halchidhoma houses may have differed in this particular. Further, the gable roof he described resembled that of Mohave-Yuma houses. Bartlett stated that for the small houses four posts were used, nine for "larger dwellings"; the latter may have been the meeting houses.

The ground plan of a house was never laid out by accurate measurement, neither the distance between posts nor the circumference. At most one of the long posts was laid on its side to give the distance between the corner posts.

Before the house was thatched, willow poles were bound horizontally around the wall poles on the outside. These could not have been more than a foot or a foot and a half apart, since a high house was said to have six or eight such ribs. The walls were thatched with green arrowweeds placed in two rows. The lower row was of shorter weeds than the upper. Both rows were placed so that the butt ends were uppermost. Horizontal willow ribs were tied outside of this thatch to hold it in place, the withes passing through the thatch to the inner ribs and vertical wall poles. For the roof, lengths of arrowweed stem were laid longitudinally on the transversely set rafters. (These were broken to length under the foot.) The green leafy parts of the arrowweeds were then piled over these, but lying transversely. These had the stem-end in (in Kutox's house, nearest the ridge) so that the tips protruding beyond the "eaves" would hang over the upper part of the wall. The arrowweed layer in all was six inches deep. The roof was then covered with dirt to as much again, so that the whole covering was a good foot thick. Dirt was banked all around the periphery of the house and as far up the wall as its curvature would permit. It was patted firmly in place. To hold the dirt on the upper slope, bundles of arrowweed were tied horizontally over the thatch all the way around to give a footing for the dirt cover. These were not only tied with willow twigs, but were propped on bundles of arrowweeds set vertically to help support the great weight. The dirt available at most house sites was adobe, which from its clayey nature was admirably adapted to set on the sloping walls. In localities where sand blew about, the houses soon became drifted over and resembled sand dunes.

The entrance invariably faced the east. It made no difference what was the nature of the terrain about the house site, this was its invariable orientation. This, rationalization had it, was because the culture hero had built the first house in this fashion. As a matter of fact, as Russell remarks of the Pima living but a few miles away in the same sandy waste:

> A more practical motive for placing the doors on the east side is to avoid the southwest winds which blow in the afternoon during nearly the entire year and which are especially strong during the month of March. The wind usually begins to blow at about 10 in the morning and increases to a velocity of 10 miles an hour by mid-afternoon, after which it decreases until midnight.[5]

So strong is the old habit of orientation that of sixteen present-day houses counted on the reservation (mostly of the jacal type), only four faced other than due east, and of these four, three are modern frame houses.

The doorway was narrow and low; so low that one had to stoop to enter (about three feet high or little more). As most houses, at least the smaller ones, had no smoke-hole, this was the only egress for smoke. They must have been densely filled with smoke except for a few feet above the floor.

The doorway of most houses was left unprotected, but those who were more particular built a sort of porch. Two forked posts were erected immediately in front of the entrance but on either side, and a stringer was laid between them. Bundles of arrow-weeds were placed from this stringer to the sloping wall above the entrance and others were set upright on each side between post and wall. Dirt was spread on top of this entry.

A door was made by hanging a thick willow bark or rabbit skin blanket in the opening. It was let down at night and in the morning thrown back over the house. More recently a door was made of parallel bundles of wheat straw lashed to willow poles at each end and in the middle. Not every house had a door.

The interior arrangement of the house was simple: there were neither partitions nor furniture. The fire was in the center, un-

[5] *Pima Indians*, p. 154.

confined by any sort of built fireplace. Sleeping places were on each side, marked by bundles of coarsely woven blankets of cotton to serve as mattress and covering. The parents of the household slept together at one side, with their smaller children between them to prevent them getting in the fire. Older children and other relatives slept on the opposite side. It was said that parents always slept on the north side, but in at least one household described in detail, they occupied the opposite side. Guests were placed in the best sleeping place, the rear of the house (the west side), so that they might have the fire between them and the doorway.[6] A big fire was built late in the afternoon to warm up the house for the night. The beds were arranged so that they always slept with their heads to the east. Men kept their bows and arrows at their heads on stormy nights for then the enemy could be expected. Men slept with their breechclouts on; women took off their willow skirts and wore only the little under-aprons.

They tell as a joke of a man who ran out at a false alarm of the enemy. His wife grabbed for her skirt in the dark, but caught hold of the fringe of his breechclout by mistake, and tore it from him. He ran out naked with his bow.

The several parts of the interior were not named. Someone sent to find something in the house would be told he could locate it in "the middle" (vuto") or "east wall," "south wall," etc. The names of parts of the construction are not altogether peculiar to a house:

ava', house
wŭlpo", post (wŭlpo" tŭkuvω', middle post; wŭlpo" kwĭnĭpaʀĭ's, side post, of a house having three rows of posts)
wucwe'ʀĭ, wall (of a house only); cŭvi'k, vertical wall pole; itcàmi'sĭs, horizontal rib; tcăpĕtu'm, thatch
mai', "top, high," roof
de'ᵃvàm, dirt layer (but dirt is àma't)
vuya', doorway; vuya'pŭk, entry (There is no specific name for the door-flap itself)

Probably every house was provided with a flat-roofed shade (matᵃk_yiă'lᵃ): every existing house has one. This was sometimes built against the front (east side) of the dwelling, where two posts supported the outer edge like a porch roof, but it was usu-

[6] For the arrangements of an actual family, see p. 226.

ally at a little distance to the southeast. This resembled the
central frame of the dwelling, was of the same height but perhaps
greater area, and invariably was framed on nine posts, set three
in a row. The roof was covered with arrowweeds but not dirt.
Sometimes willow branches were placed vertically on the west
side against the sunshine, but all the sides were never enclosed.
This structure furnished shade in summer: it never served as a
dwelling.

Beneath the shade stood several mesquite posts supporting
large jars for the storage of water. These stood about thirty
inches high and, like those of the Pima and Papago,[7] had three
short branches to hold the jar. The mouths of these jars were
usually unprotected but sometimes covered by Pima baskets.

Travelling parties never built houses of any description, perhaps because they were never far from home and even then within the enemy's striking distance. Further, families ordinarily left
home to gather mesquite, etc., only in the summer when shade,
rather than any other protection, was needed. They camped
under the overhanging boughs of big trees. The White Mountain
Apache custom of enclosing the camp in a ring of brush to keep
out flying sand was unknown.

Each dwelling was also provided with a single storehouse
(va'na'ʀà). There was no conventional place for its location: it
stood in front, rear, or at the side of the house indifferently. In
form it was simply a gable roof set over a pit. This pit was oval,
six to eight feet long, and almost knee deep. A post was set up in
the pit near each end, a ridge pole connecting the pair. Willow
branches were stuck into the ground around the brink of the pit
so that they would lean against the ridge. (They were not tied
to it.) Other willows were lashed horizontally to these to form two
ribs around sides and end, one above the other. Arrowweeds
were then placed over the frame as carefully as the thatch of the
dwelling. There were three rows of thatch; the first, stem end up,
all around at the base; another, also stem up, at a higher level;
the third row, stem end down, lapped over the ridge. No outer
ribs were needed to hold this thatch in place, since the house was

[7] Russell, *Pima Indians*, p. 127; Dorsey, *Indians of the Southwest*, p. 203.

so low (only three or four feet above the ground level at the ridge) that the dirt, now banked around it and spread over the whole, held it firmly. The ridge pole ran east and west; the tiny entrance, through which one could just creep, was in the eastern gable-end. Logs piled one on another closed the opening. A man working alone took a month to build such a storehouse, but friends or relatives usually helped. They were fed by him but not otherwise paid. Melons, pumpkins, and similar foodstuffs were stored in these houses.

Modern storage houses are like those described by Bartlett in 1852. These are small rectangular houses, the walls consisting of stakes set close together and provided with a dirt-covered roof. The space between the wall stakes usually allows free circulation of air, but Bartlett remarks, "They are wattled with straw and rushes, and are sometimes covered with a thick layer of mud."[8] This has become the modern residential type.

While basket granaries were quite unlike these structures in construction, they stood so invariably as part of the house group that they should be described here. The granaries (såkwi'n) were huge nest-like affairs crudely coiled of bunches of arrowweed, one or more of which stood near every house. They were three to five feet in diameter, three to four feet high, depending, of course, on the amount of material to be stored. These were, strictly speaking, not baskets at all, since they lacked a bottom, but thick-walled, coiled cylinders. The process of their manufacture was exactly that described by Kissell for the Pima.[9] Mrs. Redbird, who made a small granary for me as a model, used a base ring taken from an old granary, and wove counter-clockwise working on the outside of the near edge. They were woven by both men and women; those who did not know how, employed experts. These granaries lasted for years.

The granaries rested on a low platform or were half-buried: they were not placed on the roof as by the Pima. A crib-work was built to raise them off the ground a foot or more to keep the contents dry and away from rodents. This consisted of two short

[8] Bartlett, *Personal Narrative*, II, 234.

[9] Kissell, *Papago and Pima Basketry*, p. 178; see also Russell, *Pima Indians*, p. 144.

logs with small sticks across, covered with a layer of arrowweed. The basket was set on this and in turn covered with a layer of arrowweeds crossed by another laid at right angles. Arrowweed base and cover extended considerably beyond the edges of the basket. To protect them more adequately from foxes and gophers, they were sometimes half-buried. A hole was dug, waist-deep and far larger than the basket. A deep layer of brush was rammed into this by treading it down, so as to cover the bottom and the sides in part. The basket was set in this. Willow branches were thrust into the periphery of the pit, brought over the top of the basket and covered thickly with dirt.

Huts that were practically identical with the storehouse were built for a girl's puberty rite, for menstrual lodges and childbirth, and for warriors undergoing purification. They differed primarily in the absence of the pit; other differences were inconsequential. These, like the storehouse, were called va'na'ʀà. The puberty hut was built with more slender willow poles, so tall that they lapped considerably over the ridge. Dirt was banked only halfway up the weed-covered sides. The menstrual-childbirth hut was described as circular in plan, the willows bent over to reach the ridge, and entirely (?) covered with dirt.

Each village had its meeting house standing in the middle of the sprawling community. The decision to build one was made by an old man, a chief, who appealed to the younger men to work on it. All the men of the village participated. Several women cooked for the workmen. The structure stood for four or five years without renewal. If the village moved, and it seems they were always slowly moving as dwellings were burned down and erected elsewhere, the meeting house was taken apart to be reconstructed in a new location.

The meeting house differed from the dwelling only in its greater size. It was thirty to thirty-five feet in diameter, but no higher than the dwelling, and provided with the same small doorway to the east. Kutox described the central frame as having nine posts (three rows of three), both posts and rafters being stouter than in the ordinary house. Other informants again disagreed and are undoubtedly right. According to them, there were six main posts, in two rows north and south, with four auxiliary posts nearer the doorway (Fig. 6, *d*). Nine main posts would be used only if three additional were needed when they thought the original six were rotted. The whole was thatched and dirt covered like the dwelling. A meeting house was called matàluwe'vàs (said to be from àma't, "dirt"; luwe'và, "meeting," but this is doubtful; compare the words for councillors, matàsǐ'nyŭk, "those who agree" and matàwi'kǐk, "helpers").

The meeting house was essentially a man's club house and sweat house like those of central California and the Pueblo estufa-kiva. Like the southern Californian forms, it was not a dance house. Its appearance here is significant, because as Kroeber has pointed out, this structure was lacking among the Colorado River tribes.[10]

The eastern sweat house was also in use; the true miniature sweat lodge, not an assembly house. (Whether the Halchidhoma also had them is unknown, but it is not likely.) This was hemispherical, three and a half feet high, just big enough for a single person, and covered with arrowweed (?) and mud. A fire was built inside as in the Californian sweat house of the assembly type; heated stones were not used, as in the western plateaus and the Plains.[11] When the fire had burned to coals, these were spread, and covered with dirt: one sat on this. Bathing followed sweating. The little lodge was built near the dwelling of the owner; others, including women, used it without pay. Sweating was to rid one's self of illness, not for pleasure. The lodge was called matǐl_yàci'l_yᵃ, "flesh roaster."

[10] Kroeber, *Handbook*, pp. 365, 810.

[11] Cf. Spier, *Havasupai Ethnography*. p. 343.

CHAPTER IV

DRESS AND ADORNMENT

Everyday clothing for both sexes was quite scanty. A man wore a breechclout, a woman a fringed skirt with brief aprons beneath; young children went naked. A cape of rabbit-skin or a cotton blanket was thrown over the shoulders against the cold. Hats were unknown, and sandals used only on journeys. So far as is known Maricopa and Halchidhoma had identical clothing and adornment. Scanty clothing and the bare foot habit aligns these tribes with Californian and Basin peoples. On the other hand, while the woman's fringed skirt is Californian, the breechclout is not, but aligns with other Southwestern peoples and the east.

Garcés stated of the Halchidhoma in 1776, "It must be observed that these Jalchedun Indians are the best dressed [of the Colorado River tribes], not only in such goods as they themselves possess, but also in such as they trade with the Jamajabs [Mohave], Genigueches [Serrano], Cocomaricopas, Yabipais [Yumans of upland Arizona generally], and Moquis, obtaining from these last mantas, girdles, and a coarse kind of cloth (sayal), in exchange for cotton, of which they raise much." Previously (1774) he had written, "The majority of them go dressed with blankets and blue cloth from Moqui and the Pimería."[1]

In 1744 Sedelmair simply observed of the Cocomaricopa, "The women all go honestly garbed, some with petticoats of cotton or deerskin; most covered from the waist to the knees with inner bark of the willow, of which, pounded and prepared, they make a sort of petticoat."[2]

The people of Gila Bend (Kaveltcadom, Maricopa, or both) were described by Font in November 1775 as going "dressed in their blankets of cotton and likewise others of black wool, with white stripes, which they obtain from El Moqui [Hopi]." Very significantly he added, "Here we began to see the women with little skirts such as the Yumas wear, which they make from the inner bark of cottonwood and willows. This, with a deerskin which they tied and wear from the waist down, is their attire. The men go somewhat covered with blankets." Just previously he had observed of the Pima below Casa Grande: "Of the sayal they make their cotton breeches, and those who did not have breeches supply their place with a blanket gathered up and tied, while the women cover themselves

[1] Coues, II, 423; Bolton, *Anza's California Expeditions*, II, 386.

[2] Sedelmair, p. 851.

with deerskin." The same substitute for breechclouts was observed by Bartlett, who in the summer of 1852 remarked that "the dress of the Coco-Maricopa and Pimos is the same. . . . . The men in general go naked, except the breechclout. A few, however, are provided with their native blankets of large size, which they fold and throw over their shoulders in the manner of the Mexicans. Some fasten them around their waists in graceful folds, letting the ends fall to their knees; then drawing a cord between their legs and attaching it to their waists, their garment resembles a capacious pair of pantaloons. I suppose that all are provided with cotton blankets; but, owing to the almost incessant heat of the day, they seldom wear them. At night, when cool, these constitute their sole covering."[3]

It is doubtful that the men ever went wholly naked.[4] While none of my informants had witnessed truly aboriginal conditions, Last Star believed that in earlier times, say in his father's day, men never went without at least a breechclout, not even old men.

It must be borne in mind that mid-winter on the Gila is quite cold. Yet the Maricopa did not carry torches to warm themselves in the manner of the lower Colorado tribes, as attested by Alarcon and other Spanish writers.[5] When travelling, the Maricopa would scrape ashes into a hole, covering these with dirt, to lie on for warmth.

The man's breechclout was a woven strip of willow bark, less than a foot wide, hung fore and aft over a belt. The pendent flaps hung to the knees in front, to the upper calf behind. Some had only the central portion woven, that which passes between the legs, and the ends hanging in fringes. According to Kutox the clout was woven on a horizontal loom: a continuous warp passed to and fro over the loom bars, with willow strings as wefts twined across at intervals of one and a half inches. Last Star's information is rather to be trusted: that the strip was woven of bark strands in checkerboard weave, without the use of a loom. A specimen he made illustrates this (Plate IV, a).[6] The belt was

[3] Bolton, *Anza's California Expeditions*, IV, 49, 52, 53; Bartlett, *Personal Narrative*, II, 229; cf. I, 452.

[4] Cf. the Yuma (Forde, *Yuma Ethnography*, p. 92).

[5] Sedelmair implied that the custom was in vogue on the several rivers he traversed in 1744, among them the Gila, but one cannot be certain that he was not generalizing from what he saw on the Colorado River (Sedelmair, p. 851).

[6] Peabody Museum, Yale University, No. 19077.

PLATE IV

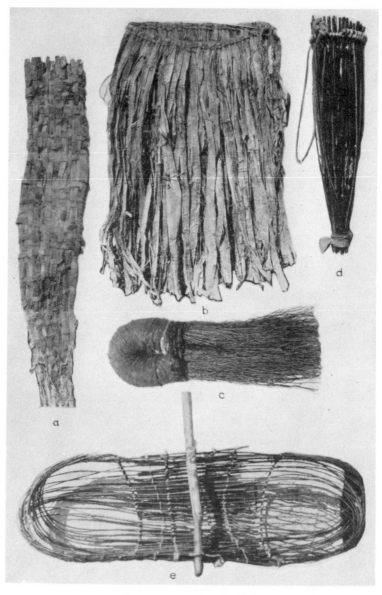

DRESS AND FISHING BASKETS

(*a*, Man's breechclout of willowbark; *b*, woman's skirt; *c*, hairbrush;
d, fisherman's basket; *e*, fishing scoop)

a stout willow bark cord rolled on the thigh. This was tied at one side at the hip. Belts of human hair, their own or enemies', known to the Yokuts and in southern California,[7] were not used.

The woman's fringed skirt was also of willow bark. It descended to mid-calf, hanging free in a thick bushy mass covering the thighs as fully as the front and buttocks. In other words it was in no sense two aprons as among the generality of Basin and Californian peoples. The thighs were covered at all times.[8] A belt, a cord of this bark rolled on the thigh, formed a foundation over which one end of each strand was doubled. In a specimen[9] made by Last Star (Pl. IV, *b*) these strands are held in place by two willow bark cords twined through them immediately below the belt or foundation cord. At each end the twined cords are crossed and tied to the belt-foundation in a square knot. By this twining the bark strands are pulled together as closely as possible. Kutox described an alternative method for fastening them: a cord sewed through them close to the belt cord. Since informants spoke of the skirt as woven on a belt-foundation, it may well be that several such strands were placed close to the belt. At least, the fringes hung free in a bushy mass, neither twisted, rolled, nor knotted together. These strips of willow bark were narrow, string-like, not broad like those seen among the lower Colorado tribes. Women did not use an additional belt to secure their skirts.

Under the skirt was worn a little apron in front and another behind. These were fabrics of cottontail rabbit skin or fine willow bark closely woven, about ten inches wide, sixteen or more inches long. These correspond to the small under-apron worn by the Havasupai women.[10]

Bartlett, on the other hand, mentioned only skirts of cotton cloth. "The women fold the smaller blankets or other cloths, and pass them around their loins, letting them hang to their knees. They are sometimes fastened with one of the

[7] Kroeber, *Handbook*, p. 840.

[8] In contrast, I was told, Yuma women's skirts were scanty on the outside of the thighs.

[9] Peabody Museum, Yale University, No. 19078.

[10] Spier, *Havasupai Ethnography*, p. 188.

belts before mentioned [woven bands, three or four inches broad], but are generally kept in place by simply tucking one end in."[11] Font, as we noted above, saw
skin skirts in use as well.

Robes used in winter were rabbit skin capes and cotton
blankets. The latter were never cut nor woven with a slit, pon-
cho-like. Bartlett and Font mention only cotton and woolen
blankets. The rabbit skin cape (kwĭlŭ′l), made by both Maricopa and Halchidhoma, was rectangular and came only to the
waist or a little below. (When plenty of skins were available, this
was made longer and served as a blanket as well. But such blankets were seldom used; pelts never.) The rabbit skins were cut
spirally into strips, which were wound along thin sticks so as to
dry as spiral cords. Old women made these capes. The worker
tied one end of a rolled willow bark cord to her toe and the other
end around her waist, to serve as a taut foundation for the fabric.
One end of each skin strip was lapped over this cord: when the
strip was long, it was doubled back to pass over the cord again.
These strips were then fastened by a second cord, set close to the
foundation cord, which was wound once around each successive
strip and its short lapped end. At intervals of a hand's span
other cords were twined through the pendent strips parallel to
the foundation cord.

A "woven" (probably twined) willow bark robe was also worn, according to
Kutox. Last Star emphatically denied its existence. It was rectangular, not
square; a span in length, and hung almost to the ankles behind. Loose ends of the
fabric tied together in front of the breast served to hold it on, no belt being used.
Those of men and women were alike.

Little children wore nothing. When they were seven to nine
years old, the breechclout and bark skirt were adopted. Somewhat earlier a little rabbit skin blanket might be tied about their
middles, but such covering was given girls rather than boys.
Bartlett remarked, "Although the men and boys go naked, I
never saw a girl, however young, without clothes around its hips
similar to those worn by the women."[12]

Sandals were worn by both sexes only when travelling. At

[11] Bartlett, *Personal Narrative*, II, 224, 228.

[12] *Ibid.*, p. 231.

home they went barefoot, as they do today. Moccasins have never been used. Sandals were formerly woven of willow bark, but since the acquisition of cattle, rawhide has been the favored material. Woven sandals were said to have come over the top of the foot and to have looked somewhat like shoes, hence they may have resembled the slipper-like forms of the Paviotso.[13] The manner in which these were fastened is somewhat obscure: it seems that a twisted willow bark string was laced through loops all around the foot and then carried back and forth over the instep from loop to loop. The rawhide sandal was slightly larger than the sole of the foot (Pl. XIV, e).[14] A separate piece of rawhide was inserted through slits under the arch of the foot, the ends of which came up on each side to take the heel-strap. These cuts were not made vertically, but with the knife held obliquely (i.e., with its handle inclining toward the margin of the sandal), in order that the thin edges of the slits might lie flat on the inserted strip. The position of these slits was one finger length from the rear end of the sandal: this was gauged by inserting the rear end between the fingers. The sandal was held on by two thongs, knotted beneath the sole at the toes and passing, one between the big toe and the first, the other between the middle toe and the third. In the several specimens seen the first of these was a rawhide thong, the latter a rolled cord of willow bark or cloth. These passed in back of the heel where they were permanently bound into the heel strap. The latter was a cord or thong passing back and forth behind the heel between the two ends of the rawhide strip that went under the arch, and wound with the soft inner bark of the willow to prevent chafing. Sandals were moderately valuable, because one could not travel far without them. An old woman from whom I bought a pair, her only footgear, brought them, repeating somewhat humorously, "Oh, my precious feet (i.e., the sandals)! I have to part with them."

Crude leggings were also worn by men. These were broad

[13] Lowie, *Notes on Shoshonean Ethnography*, p. 218.

[14] Washington State Museum, No. 2-11878.

pieces of deerskin wrapped around the leg below the knee, bound in place by a strip of skin.

Although skin shirts and moccasins are credited to the Pima,[15] the Maricopa made no use of them.

The breechclout was called wemakxa'và; the bark skirt upu'i or upu'iavàxai (avàxai' being now a woman's skirt of any material); the under-aprons tilyuϑi'k; the belt amĕ'l; the robe atkwĭnyĕ'p; the sandal haminy'o' acika'tĭs (haminy'o' being now any shoe), a woman's sandal xamanyu' hacàgya'dĭc ("cut out"); the legging kŭm^ᵃĕ't.

Garments were made by old people; old men making breechclouts and being repaid with rabbits or whatever the recipient acquired when hunting; old women made the bark skirts. Men alone made bark or hide sandals.

Old people carried staffs (nᵧicao'ʀà, "for the old"), some four and a half feet long.

The hair was worn hanging to the waist in back and cut in a bang at the eyebrows. But while the back hair of the women fell in a loose mass over their shoulders, men arranged theirs in some twenty strands, partially braided but primarily rolled. Some men let the hair at the sides hang loose as low as the breast, braiding only that at the back. There was intense pride in its appearance: a handsome man was reckoned one whose thick, glossy hair hung in a profusion of rolls quite to his waistline. This is the habit and attitude of the lower Colorado tribes, yet there was no attempt to lengthen it artificially as there. My Halchidhoma informant Kutox had his scanty, short hair in six braids lengthened with other human hair and horse hair, but he stated that he is the only one who had ever done this. Formerly when an old man's hair got short, he bunched it at the back of the head, where it was held in place by a woven band.[16] For convenience a man wrapped one roll around the others at the back of the head to hold them out of the way.

---

[15] Russell, *Pima Indians*, p. 157.

[16] My notes are not quite clear whether this was bound about the back hair alone or worn as a head band.

Bartlett's observations on hairdress among Pima and Maricopa confirm my information. "Nothing is worn on the head [by women], nor is the hair ever tied up. In front it is cut off square across the eyebrows; the rest is suffered to hang loosely over the ears, neck, and about half way down the back, affording a protection to these parts from the intense heat of the sun. . . . . The head-band is worn by nearly all the men gracefully put on in several folds, with the braided ends hanging down on their shoulders. They also have a large woolen cord, from half an inch to an inch in diameter, of different colors, which they use as a head ornament, twining it around the hair. . . . . The men wear their hair long, never cutting it except across the eyebrows, down to which it hangs, and thus partially protects the eyes. When loosed, their hair reaches to their knees; but usually it is clubbed up in a large mass on their backs. Their earlocks either hang loose, or are braided in several strands, with little ornaments of bone, tin, or red cloth attached to them. But the decoration of their heads with the bands of which I have spoken, forms the most picturesque part of their costume. They have a singular practice of filling their hair with clay; so that when dry it resembles a great turban." He also described the hairdress of a war party: "Some had them [their head dresses] plastered with clay, so as to resemble huge turbans. Others had decorated the great club of hair which hung down their backs with bits of scarlet cloth, but more of them with the richly-figured sashes of their own manufacture. Some again wore their hair in braids tastefully wound around their heads, intermingled with pieces of scarlet cloth; while a few, less particular of their appearance, wore it clubbed up in a huge mass."[17]

Font declared the coiffure of the Kaveltcadom-Maricopa of Gila Bend the same as that of the Pima, which he described as follows: "The coiffure which the men practice with their hair is peculiar. They take a woolen cord, thin like the finger and long like a halter rope. Doubling it up they insert it in the hair. With the long end they tie it together and twist it over the head from the left side to the right, and then secure it with the loose end, giving it one or two turns around the head. In this way they carry on their heads a crest like a crown, in which they insert their feathers, little sticks, and other ornaments. The women wear their hair hanging down their backs and over their ears, banging it in front even with the eyes or the eyebrows."[18] I interpret his description of men's hairdress as a band twined into and wound around a mass of braids, themselves wound around the head.

Infants of both sexes had their hair singed all over the head with a little firebrand. This was done only by a person having nice thick hair, presumably so that the child's hair would also grow well. When a boy was two years old, a man who knew how was requested to trim it. He singed it short on the crown in a counter-clockwise spiral, leaving the forelock to be cut off at the

[17] Bartlett, *Personal Narrative*, II, 216, 228–30.

[18] Bolton, *Anza's California Expeditions*, IV, 49, 52; cf. Russell, *Pima Indians*, p. 159.

middle of the forehead, the back hair hanging to the nape, and earlocks hanging to the point of the jaw. When he was five or six, it was let grow, hanging free all around, and when he was fifteen or so, he began to form it in long braids behind. Small girls wore it trimmed short all over the head. Hair was always singed, never cut off.

The hair was frequently dressed with boiled black mesquite bark to make it glossy and presumably to rid it of vermin. The long back hair was twisted in a knot on the fore part of the crown and plastered with this concoction, which when dry looks like grey mud. This presumably is the "clay" of the early observers. This could be brushed out of the hair. Yucca root was not used for washing the hair as in the more northerly parts of the Southwest; in fact, the plant was said not to grow south of the mountains occupied by the Yavapai.

The hairbrush was a bundle of stiff fibers bent at their middles and bound together. The fresh roots of a tall grass (ŏxtci', which is also the name of the hairbrush or any brush) were laid side by side, bound for some distance at the middle, bent in two, bound again, and the ends trimmed. The inner bark of willow or mesquite was used for binding since these, being sticky, held the fibers tightly. Such brushes were five or six inches long. The open loop of these brushes (Pl. IV, c) was quite characteristic.

A well-dressed man wore eagle down attached by a short string to his back hair. In default of down, an eagle feather was used. An old man who saw a little boy without this adornment would be perturbed and would scurry about until he had procured it for the lad. Last Star thought there must have been some special significance to wearing this, but did not know what it might be. Of course, eagle feathers had first to be purified by a shaman (one who dreamed of the eagle or buzzard) before they might be worn.

Hats were not worn, nor, in all probability, did many men wear headbands. A feather bonnet (kapu'ʀ)[19] was sometimes worn by men to signify the wearer's bravery. This was a hood of

[19] Doubtfully from Spanish *capucha, capota*; compare Havasupai pŭt, "hat," "headband," kăpŭ'dïvà, "wearing a hat."

deer hide, closely covering the crown and brimless: eagle feathers projected sidewise and vertically. Strings tied under the chin held it in place.

The beard and moustache, naturally scanty, was plucked out with the finger nails. An old man, as he plucked each hair, touched his fingers to his tongue, to feel whether he succeeded. The facial hair was pulled out, not to be good looking, but because it got in the way when talking or eating (!) and also because they wanted to paint their faces.

Facial painting for decoration seems to have been limited. White, red, and black were the principal colors. Men sometimes marked a stripe of black paint across the face covering the eyes; women used it only to blacken the lids and eye-sockets. Participants in certain dances, such as that connected with Killdeer singing, were specially painted. Men also applied white paint in transverse stripes across the long hair hanging down their backs.[20] On the other hand, face paint was used by both sexes as a cosmetic. Red paint was mixed with deer grease as a vehicle for this purpose. The Halchidhoma, while on the Colorado, obtained their best red paint in little bags from the Walapai. This was brought by the Halchidhoma to relatives among the Maricopa or traded there. Other red paint, used for decorating pottery and obtained by Maricopa from the Papago, may also have served for painting the face.

Font observed of the Kaveltcadom-Maricopa at Gila Bend, "They are accustomed also to paint their faces and bodies, even though it may be with soot, as they cannot obtain red hematite. They decorate the painted parts with various stripes, and this is their gala dress."[21]

In cold weather, when hands were chapped, pumpkin seeds were parched and ground, soaked in water, and smeared on the skin.

Tattooing resembled that of the lower Colorado tribes but was more moderate. Men were tattooed (agwisk) only on the forehead, women on the chin and sometimes the arm. There was no

[20] Font stated that the Yuma were accustomed "to decorate it [their hair] with figures in other colors" (Bolton, *Anza's California Expeditions*, IV, 108).

[21] *Op. cit.*, p. 52.

tattooing at the eyes, like the Pima, nor did the men bear it on the chin, like the Mohave. Body and legs seem not to have borne this decoration. Male decoration consisted only of a series of vertical lines covering the whole forehead or a zigzag line. Women had two straight narrow lines drawn downward on the chin from each corner of the mouth. Occasionally the narrow spaces between each pair of lines was solidly filled just at the corner of the mouth. Many of the older women of the Maricopa community today bear this decoration. The lines are invariably narrow, nearly vertical, and about a half inch apart. The outer lines are not quite at the corners of the mouth. The dye spreads along the lower margin of the lips. My informant knew that Mohave women and others in the vicinity had the chin area filled in, but stated that Halchidhoma women never had this. Sometimes women bore above the elbow of one arm a double line drawn like an **S**.

The tattooing was done only at puberty: to a girl at first menstruation,[22] to a boy when his voice began to change. Any expert woman did it for either. She was not paid, nor need she be a relative nor of any particular age. The process, which took a few hours, was without ritual. Yet those who were not tattooed would not be able to enter the land of the dead.

Cactus thorns were held in a row between the fingers, eight or nine together. When blood flowed from the punctures, a black mineral from the mountains was rubbed in, the spot washed off, and puncturing begun again. It was said that when arm or forehead was tattooed, there was no soreness, but the lip became so sore and swollen that one could not eat. Yet nothing was done to salve the soreness.

Some men had the nasal septum pierced. These were brave men: "this stands for bravery." In war such men were obliged always to go forward. A boy's septum was pierced when his voice began to change. An expert man was chosen; then the septum would not get sore. He made the perforation with a sharpened twig of an unidentified bush and inserted a cotton string to keep the hole open until it healed. The nasal pendant (xamsuwĭ′n)

[22] See p. 326.

PLATE V

Potter Polishing Vessel and Stack Prepared for Firing Pottery

was hung on a short string so that it flapped over the mouth.
This was either a small fragment of sheep leg bone, ground to
disk-shape and bored, or of blue shell (kovosω, "haliotis"?) from
an unknown source. It was said that the form depended on the
shape of the nose: a man with a snub nose wore one long and
flat, hanging over his mouth; one with a Roman nose only a small
pendant close to the septum.

Of the Kaveltcadom-Maricopa at Gila Bend Font wrote, "They are very fond
of beads for collars, and for pendants which they wear in the ears and also in the
nose, whose middle cartilage they usually have pierced."[23]

The earlobes were pierced only at birth. A single hole (smal-
gàku'p, "earhole") was made in each ear and only in the lobe.
(It was known that Yuma and Mohave had more than one.) An
expert woman made the hole without ceremony at the mother's
request. (The aboriginal implement is now forgotten.) There
was no belief that a person would become deaf if his ears were not
pierced. Ear pendants (smalgĭ's) were made of shells or glass
beads. These invariably hung at least an inch below the lobe and
sometimes came down to the collar bone.

In recent times necklaces (xana'k) of glass beads were made
somewhat in the Yuma-Mohave style. Men wore them as a tight
collar, women hanging loose to the waist. In earlier days drilled
shell beads, long and white, were used. The shells were procured
somewhere to the south: "they travelled year after year for
them." Arrowheads were not attached to necklaces, as among
the Western Apache, for this would invite the lightning to strike
the wearer.

Of the same Kaveltcadom-Maricopa group, Font wrote again, "The men
go . . . . very heavily laden with beads and pendants around their necks and in
their ears; indeed I did not see a single woman with so much adornment." Bartlett observed of Maricopa and Pima, "Occasionally a fair one gets a string of
beads; but I saw more men and boys with these ornaments than women. One boy
in particular, who might pass for a dandy among them, wore some twenty or more
strings of beads. . . . . The men also wear a profusion of beads when they can
obtain them. Some have long strings of sea-shells or parts of shells, which are
highly prized."[24]

[23] Bolton, *Anza's California Expeditions*, IV, 52.

[24] *Op. cit.*, IV, 53; Bartlett, *Personal Narrative*, II, 228–30.

CHAPTER V

MANUFACTURES

POTTERY

The Maricopa were essentially a pottery using people in the sense that the central Californians were basket users. To make the contrast even more explicit, we may compare them with a people in the same general area, the Havasupai, who, like themselves, used both pots and baskets. Where the Havasupai household had a dozen baskets standing about, where baskets were used for every domestic purpose, the Maricopa substituted pottery.

Every Maricopa household held innumerable pottery utensils: jars, bowls, parching pans, ladles, etc. Even today the common cooking pots in practically every house are of their own manufacture. Quantities of pottery are now made for the tourist trade, which while differing somewhat in size, shape, decoration, and finish, are nevertheless made by the ancient technique. But despite the huge quantity they were accustomed to make, Maricopa pottery was, as a matter of fact, relatively a poor product.

Maricopa and Halchidhoma made pottery (kwǐlyȧoma't) in exactly the same way. This was wholly a woman's occupation and a year-round task. They began at the art quite early: for instance, a five-year-old girl was seen following the mannerisms of her mother. She worked up a ball of mud, beat it flat on the bottom of an old pot with a paddle, and pinched up the sides to form a tiny vessel, which she set in the sun to dry.

The forms were almost wholly wide-mouthed vessels and bowls (Pl. VI)[1]. This is generally true of hand-made pottery the world over except in such areas of pottery specialization as Peru, in

[1] Specimens shown in Pl. VI, Washington State Museum: *a*, 2–211883; *b*, 2–11893; *c*, 2–11889; *d*, 2–11896; *e*, 2–11879; *f*, 2–11891; *g*, 2–11898; *h*, 2–11897; *i*, 2–11884.

PLATE VI

UNDECORATED POTTERY
(*a*, Parching pan; *b*, cup; *c*, bowl; *d–f*, *h*, cooking pots;
g, storage jar; *i*, griddle)

contrast to that spun on the wheel which is frequently narrow-necked. The only small-mouthed vessels here were the sahuaro syrup jars and those made to hold scalps. Multiple mouthed vessels, such as are said to be found on ancient Diegu+ño sites, did not occur. They also lacked loop handles, bosses, and legs. Pottery rattles were not made.

The largest vessels were those for carrying and storing water, called kwĭl$_y$o". These were usually eighteen inches high, but sometimes as much as thirty inches (Pl. VI, g). A woman carried this full of water on her head, resting on a bark ring, and set it on a forked post in the shade. Since the vessels were porous, seepage and evaporation kept the water cool. Water jars were not covered. Old jars of this sort were used for the storage of food. Another type for water storage was cylindrical with a rounded base (two feet tall, eighteen inches in diameter), called kwĭl$_y$o' ȧvulpo", "post water jar." It is doubtful that these were used for carrying water.

Cooking pots (tackĭ'n) resembled the water jars but were ordinarily smaller, usually about ten inches high (Pl. VI, e, f, h). Others (kaxét), of the same size as the tackĭ'n, differed in having the rim extended on either side in ears to serve as handles (Pl. VI, d).

Bowls and cups were alike called kwĭski'. The bowls were of various sizes, but all shallow and with rounded bottoms. The largest were about a foot in diameter, four inches deep (Pl. VI, c). Cups were three to five inches in diameter, with rounded bases, and with sides either cylindrical or flaring at the lip (Pl. VI, b). Another cup (kwĭskixana'm, "cup drawn together") was drawn out at one side so that the mouth was oval, in shape resembling a gourd cut longitudinally.

Parching pans (kȧtĕ'l) were like large bowls with the rim drawn out into ears on opposite sides for handles (Pl. VI, a). The ears of these pans, like those of the cooking pots, were not horizontal, but followed the curvature of the sides of the vessel. Such pans were about a foot in diameter and four inches deep.

Small mouthed jars, given a special name, "suhuaro syrup container" (an$_y$ȧxa'xĭlyȧpo'vȧ), had globular bodies, twelve inches in diameter, drawn into narrow necks with everted lips, two and a half inches in diameter. These had a total height of fifteen inches.

A special jar was made to hold scalps. This ('ie'rhĭl̯y̆ătca'vĭs, "hair container") was nearly globular, had no neck or lip, but a small mouth only large enough to thrust the hand through. (I was not told the size of the vessel.) A clay plate covered the mouth.

Ladles or spoons of various sizes were made (kamota'dako''; kamota', "spoon"). Most of them must have been ladle-like (Pl. VII, a). I was told, however, that spoons had bowls the size of our soup spoons, with handles curving backward at the tip. Larger ladles were also made of wood (Pl. XIV, a, b).

A griddle (maϑi'l), on which to bake wafer bread, was made in the form of a thin, shallow bowl (about twelve inches in diameter; less than a half inch thick). This was considered difficult to manufacture because it broke easily while being fired (Pl. VI, i).

Decoration was not applied to cooking pots and parching pans since these were soon blackened in use. Water jars were painted red over the exterior, ladles in their entirety. Bowls or cups were solid red or white inside and out, with designs in black. Designs seem to have been applied relatively rarely in the old days. The combinations of red and white surface colors and the polished surfaces of modern examples did not exist.

The clay used for the body was common adobe (matgwĭnyat-cau', "dirt for making things"), available anywhere within a few yards of the house. It was dug out with a stick, spread in the sun until well dried, and pounded fine on the metate. Fine sand was mixed with it; for every double-handful of adobe a like but scant quantity of sand was used. Sherds from the ancient ruins were also pounded up in place of sand tempering. Usually the mixed ingredients were then soaked with water, although the clay might be soaked before the sand was added. The batch was kneaded to the consistency of stiff bread-dough. The moulding of the vessel might start at once, but it was preferable to set the batch aside until the next day, spreading a little dirt over it to keep it moist.

Vessels were made by the paddle-and-anvil method; the base moulded from a single lump of clay, the sides built up by coils which were paddled into shape. The base was made by forming a flattened lump over the bottom of an old pot, beating it with a wooden paddle until it was of uniform thickness, as tested between the finger tips. This basal portion was then set, concave side up, in a little hollow dug in front of the potter. For the side walls, she rolled lumps of clay between her palms to the thickness of a finger and made these adhere to the edges of the base by pressure. Such rolls need not be as long as the full circumference. A stone or pottery anvil was held inside the vessel, while the roll was beaten with the paddle until it became integral with the pot. Further rolls were added in this fashion until the neck was reached. Most of the vessels, as pointed out above, did not have true necks; the lips flared almost directly from the body. This portion was formed by pressing on bits of clay with the fingers, without using the paddle.

The vessel, after being set aside until dry enough to handle, was smoothed inside and out with a somewhat rough stone. This completed the moulding. It was then set in the sun to dry: in hot weather, this took all day. The pot when dried was gray-ish-buff in color, which on firing became dull reddish-buff. If color was desired, it was added before the firing. Red paint could be applied to a dry pot, but white must be added while it was still moist before the final drying. Several were prepared to fire at one time.

To bake the pots, a fire of mesquite wood was built in a shallow pit only a few inches deep and two feet in diameter, and allowed to burn to coals. Small stones were placed on these to support the vessels, which must not touch the ashes else they were blackened. The pots were set up on their sides to warm near the fire: if they were not gradually warmed, they would break in firing. They were then set on the stones close together, but not touching, either mouth up or on their sides. A conical heap of mesquite sticks was piled closedly over the group of pots, the sticks standing on end, and set fire (Pl. V). In two to two and a half hours it had burned sufficiently. Too much heat would burn the paint off the surface. The pots were fished out with a pair of sticks and a fine gruel of ground mesquite beans poured into them while they were still hot. This made them non-porous.[2]

Designs, which turned black on firing, were painted on the exterior (only ?) of the pots and bowls, using the chewed end of a little stick to apply a concoction of boiled black mesquite bark. The vessels were then fired a second time, being again placed on stones set in the coals. The fire was not built up for this, the vessels being only roasted. When the designs on one side had burned black, the vessels were turned over to bake the other side.

A Kohuana woman said that whenever a pregnant woman touched a pot, it would crack in firing. She would say this to the little girls in sport as she chased them away.[3]

A pot broken in firing was mended by rubbing the gum that exudes from the base of arrowweeds into the crack while the pot was still hot.

The anvil (niktadi′xkĭtco′g, "put underneath to mould") on which the vessel wall was beaten was a rounded flat stone, two to four inches in diameter, of a convenient size to hold in the left palm. Many preferred the lighter anvils made of clay, of which two types were in use. One was mushroom-shaped; its head some four inches across, the stem hollow. The edge of the head was recurved so as to avoid marring the pot. The other, like a tall narrow bowl with rounded base (about four inches high) was used in deep objects like cups (Pl. VII, d, c). The latter form is still in common use. Paddles were of three types. These were made of mesquite, a dense, heavy wood. The smaller (n$_y$ĭ-maxŏ′mac), which tapers gradually to a handle, was somewhat curved both longitudinally and transversely. It was about eight inches long by three at its broadest (Pl. VII, b). Larger paddles

[2] There was no notion of ascribing inexhaustibility to them (cf. Spier, *Havasupai Ethnography*, p. 140).

[3] The Kamia belief that a jealous woman's touch would crack it does not occur.

PLATE VII

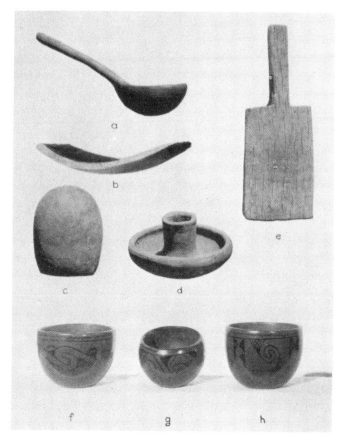

POTTERY LADLE, POTTERS' TOOLS AND DECORATED POTTERY
(a, Ladle; b, e, paddles; c, d, anvils; f, g, h, Wash. State Mus. 2-11881, 11880, 11882)

of the same shape, called kàsukǐ'', were used in making large vessels. These were about ten inches long and were not so curved longitudinally. Another type of paddle had its rectangular blade and handle in the same plane, and was heavier than the foregoing types (Pl. VII, *e*).

The surface of the vessel was colored red or white, not as with some vessels today partly red and partly white. The red was a clay procured in the mountains by the Papago: it does not occur locally. This was ground on the metate, soaked in water, and either strained through a cloth, or the liquor decanted off after the

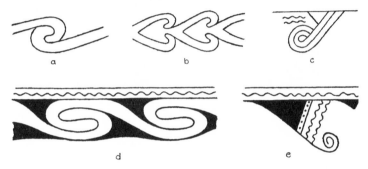

FIG. 7.—Designs on painted pottery (*a–c*, common designs from native sketches; *d, e*, from decorated vessels).

grains in suspension had settled. Only the liquor was saved. This was poured into a large porous pot so that the water would seep away. When the residue was sufficiently dry, it was formed into little rolls which were stored away. When wanted for use, these were broken up and soaked in water. The paint was smeared over the surface of the vessel with a cloth or the fingers. White paint was made from caliche (a calcareous sediment: impure sodium nitrate?) which occurs commonly in the neighborhood. It was prepared in exactly the same way. Modern pottery made for sale is polished briskly with a smooth pebble while the paint is still damp, but this was not an ancient trait.

The decoration of pottery was always by painting, never incising. The designs (hanyo'ʀàm, also writing) differed somewhat from those now in use. Figure 7, *a–c*, shows several of the old designs drawn by Mrs. Redbird (*c* was a very common design). Modern pieces bearing designs not wholly divergent from the old are shown in Plate VII, *f–h*, and Figure 7, *d*, *e*. These designs have always been copied from those on red-on-buff ware sherds taken from the ancient ruins in the vicinity. While it seems quite possible that the pottery of the Yumans and their neighbors is derived from this ancient buff ware,[4] the designs on Maricopa could not be cited to prove the case since their designs are deliberate copies, just as modern Hopi pottery is deliberately copied from that of ancient Awatobi. Designs had no names. Nor was there ownership of designs, although women had their favorites, so that who made a vessel could be told by the kind of modeling and the design. This is borne out by several examples secured; among them the pots of one woman and her daughter-in-law, who always work together, commonly have seven units of design distributed over the surface.

WEAVING

The material culture of the Maricopa differed from that of the lower Colorado tribes in the presence of weaving. This is a point they are pridefully fond of stressing. As a matter of fact, the amount of cloth woven was probably not very great, in no degree rivaling the productivity of Pueblo looms. Their fabrics were as simple as their looms were crude.

Not only the Maricopa, but the Kaveltcadom (the advance-guard Halchidhoma of Gila Bend) are credited with weaving. They learned the art from the Maricopa some years before Kutox's birth in 1847, he thought. Kutox was doubtful that the Halchidhoma proper wove cloth while still in their home on the Colorado. If they had, he should have known it, since they left there only twenty years before he was born. This agrees with what we know of other river Yumans, that they did not weave cloth.[5] The presence of the art among the Maricopa accords, on the other hand, with their proximity to the weaving Pima.

[4] Kroeber, *Handbook*, pp. 73, 823.

[5] Except the Yuma, who wove fabrics of willowbark or cotton on looms of Pima type (Forde, *Yuma Ethnography*, p. 126).

The loom products had little variety: coarse, thin cotton blankets of small size, a skirt for a girl during her puberty rite, men's belts, old men's headbands, and the binding bands for cradles were all they had. The cotton blankets served as bedding: they may sometimes have been used to draw over the shoulders but they were certainly not a part of the ordinary costume. The poncho was unknown and cloth was never deliberately cut to make a garment. All of the articles were made of cotton yarn. The blankets were plain, except such as may have had a decorated selvage; the narrow bands invariably had designs.

The weaving art is now moribund, only cradle bands being made and but few of these. Hence it is difficult to get wholly adequate information. With the aid of a make-shift loom we attempted to get a description of blanket weaving from old Kutox, but he, nearly blind and with crippled fingers, could not demonstrate at crucial points. Last Star, who had himself never seen weaving, gave what must be an essentially correct account of blanket weaving. On the other hand, thoroughly adequate information on the making of cradle bands was had from Mary Juan, a young and skillful weaver, who wove at my request.

Bartlett's information on Pima and Maricopa confirms mine.

"Cotton is raised by them, which they spin and weave. Their only manufactures consist of blankets of various textures and sizes; a heavy cloth of the same material used by the women to put around their loins; and an article from three to four inches wide, used as a band for the head, or a girdle for the waist. The blankets are woven with large threads, slightly twisted and without any nap. They are made of white cotton, and are without ornament of colors or figures, save a narrow selvage of buff. . . . . The operation, of course, progresses slowly; and from the length of time consumed in spinning and weaving, they set a high price upon their blankets, asking for these ten or twelve dollars in money, or a new woolen blanket of equal size. The weaving is generally done by the old men."

Bartlett's illustration shows the weaver sitting on the finished portion of the blanket he has under way.[6]

Loom products were considered quite valuable, especially the cotton blankets. These were about the size of our small bed

[6] Bartlett, *Personal Narrative*, II, 224-26.

blankets, just large enough barely to cover a single person. Larger ones took too long to weave. A blanket of the usual size was three weeks in the making; preparing the cotton, spinning the needed amount of yarn, and completing the weaving. Blankets were traded to the Papago for horses. According to my information the Papago did not weave, but Curtis gives evidence that they did.[7] The rate of exchange in the middle of the last century was a single blanket for a poor horse, two for a good one.[8] This furnishes some index of their high value, for the Maricopa were so poor in horses, that they still thought nothing of going long distances afoot and considered even a relatively poor horse a worthwhile acquisition. The only horses they had were those gotten by such trade. The Papago, on the other hand, were relatively rich in horses since they were situated much nearer the Mexican villages.

Weaving was properly man's work. There was, however, a division of labor such that preparing the cotton (ginning) was done by women alone, both sexes spun yarn, while weaving was solely in the hands of old men. When cloth and blankets became available from traders, the old art waned and man's part in it lapsed entirely. Nowadays only women weave, making only cradle bands as part of their construction of cradles. Only commercial yarns are now used. Some knowledge still persists among the older men, however: Kutox, who had never woven, demonstrated with a spindle, exhibiting the typical draft motion and smoothing the yarn like an accomplished spinner. Both women and men formerly wove bands, according to Hrdlička's information of 1902 and 1905.[9] While the objects he discussed in his brief account were cradle bands, it is conceivable that his informants were implying that women wove cradle bands while men made their own belts and headbands, if they were not in fact referring only to the period of transition. More serious is the implication of his statement that an old Maricopa made several blankets in

[7] Curtis, II, 6, 82, 111, 116.

[8] The same rate prevailed among the Pima (Russell, *Pima Indians*, p. 149).

[9] Hrdlička, *Maricopa Weaving*.

his youth. It was, by my evidence, an old man's art, yet this observation that a young man wove or assisted may be true.

Cotton was alone used in weaving. Such possible substitutes as mountain sheep or dog hair were not used. Nor was sheep wool used since the advent of the whites: so far as I know, the Maricopa neither own sheep now nor had them formerly. The cotton cultivated in earlier days was white, not brown; growing on bushes waist-high or little more, and not like the man-high bushes of modern varieties of cotton grown in this district. It proved impossible to obtain any specimens of ancient cotton: it has entirely disappeared. Hrdlička observed (1905):

According to information obtained from an old Maricopa, about forty years ago the people of his tribe planted native cotton, with which the men wove large decorated blankets.

They ginned the cotton by first beating it with a little stick. Then, spreading it on a flat stone, they rolled a smooth arrowweed across it to remove the seeds. This lap was layed aside; then others were similarly prepared and laid on the first. This was women's work alone. Day after day was spent in preparation until the necessary amount was accumulated.

The cleaned cotton was then spread on a smooth spot on the ground, over which clean sand had been sprinkled. A scraped arrowweed, about the size of an arrow, was strung to form a taut little bow. The bowstring was held close above the cotton and then plucked. The "tooth" of the string caught up the loose fibers; its vibration wrapped them into a compact roll around the string. This was then pulled off the string to serve as a sliver ready for spinning.[10] The first step was to roll the sliver into a loose yarn between palm and thigh.

[10] The cotton plucking bow must have had an interesting history in America: its ultimate source was Asia. My Maricopa informant ascribed its use to the Pima as well. He did not know whether the Papago had it. Doubtless they had, for, farther south Dr. Ralph Beals found it in 1931 in use among the Mayo (near the Rio Mayo and Navajoa, Sonora) for plucking wool fibers for spinning. The source for these tribes must have been the missions of northern Mexico. It occurs in South America, where Nordenskiöld records its distribution through the southern Amazon basin and southward. He writes: "We have here a cultural element that the Indians probably got from the Portuguese, presumably, as in the case of

The spindle was a smoothed arrowweed shaft about two feet long and three-eighths of an inch in thickness. For the whorl, the inner part of the giant cactus was used, a dense wood. This was a straight stick about five inches long, one inch wide, and bored in the middle to slip on the shaft about six inches from its lower end. The lower end of the spindle was rounded; the upper end somewhat more pointed.[11]

The manipulation of the spindle consists simply in twirling it with the fingers of the right hand, the lower end resting on the ground, the pull of the left hand, holding the loose roving of cotton, giving the needed draft. From time to time the spinner stopped, unwound the partially spun yarn from above the whorl, tucked the spindle under his leg to hold it fast, and worked the yarn smooth between the nails of the right hand, before spinning again to give it further twist. An alternative method of spinning was to place the spindle with its lower end uppermost and resting on the right thigh; rolling it between the right palm and thigh, while the tip was supported in the cupped left hand. The Pima method of placing the lower end directly between the toes or in a wooden cup inserted between the toes was not in use.

Yarns intended for wefts were loosely spun, perhaps a quarter inch in diameter or more. Warp yarns had a tighter twist, hence a smaller diameter, to stand the excessive strain in the loom. Russell's description of Pima yarns applies here:

The warp is smoothly and evenly spun into a thread about 1 mm. in diameter. The woof threads are softer and about 3 mm. in diameter.

the pellet-bow, from India . . . . during the times of the Missions in the 17th and 18th centuries" (*Ethnography of South America*, p. 196). Of its occurrence in Asia, Laufer writes: "The method employed by the Chinese in preparing felt is the same as that used by the Tibetans, Mongols, and Turks, with a single exception: the first step they take is to loosen the wool by means of a large bow by tightening the string and jerking it off in rapid motion. This process is derived from that of treating cotton, and the bow in either case is identical" (*The Early History of Felt*, p. 7).

[11] The Pima spindle figured by Russell (*Pima Indians*, p. 149) is much the same, except that the cactus rib crosspiece is tied on. Bartlett observes that the Pima spindle is "a slender stick about two feet long passing through a block of wood" (*Personal Narrative*, II, 225).

Cords for other purposes than weaving were always slender, perhaps one-eighth inch in diameter. The yarn was rolled into balls.

Dyed yarns were employed for bands and for the decorative selvage of blankets. For a bright red, the yarn was boiled with the root of a mountain plant, called itu'tà (now used by the Pima to dye willow twigs for baskets). It is similarly boiled with clays found in the mountains to obtain a dull red, dull black, or a faded orange. The red clay is that now used for painting pottery. No mordant was mentioned.

The Maricopa loom was horizontal, unlike that of the Pueblos and Navaho, but identical with Pima, Papago, and Opata. It consisted of four stakes driven into the ground, to which two warp bars were tied, parallel to each other and horizontal. The warp was laid directly over these bars. This was used not only for the larger fabrics, blankets, but also for the various belts and bands.

The belt loom was also known but perhaps not much used. Somewhat doubtfully I record Kutox's statement that it was used only after the advent of the Halchidhoma from the Colorado (*ca.* 1828). In this loom, the proximal end of the warps were tied to the belt of the weaver seated on the ground, the distal end to a convenient post at about the same height. This, of course, was used only for weaving narrow bands. No belt stick[12] was used.

The weaving of a cradle band on the regular horizontal type of loom was observed. Two pairs of stakes, set a foot apart, were driven into the ground at a distance equal to that desired for the length of the band. A stout arrowweed was tied horizontally on the outside of each pair, some nine inches above the ground, to serve as the warp bar. One end of the warp was tied to one warp bar at one side so that the knot lay at the bottom of the bar. The warp was carried under the opposite bar, and back over the top, thence to the first bar. It was passed over the bars always in this fashion: under the bar and back over the top. This resulted in the warps crossing each other to form a figure-eight (Pl. VIII).

[12] As at Zuñi (Spier, *Zuñi Weaving Technique*, p. 77).

Warps of several colors were used. As a warp of a new color was needed, the warp already on the loom was cut off near one of the bars, and the new warp tied to it by a double knot. The whole set of warps then merely formed one continuous cord. The warp was kept very tight, and carefully laid in order, as it was being strung on the warp bars. Great care was exercised to have the tension of each strand of warp exactly that of its fellows. Finally the end of the warp was tied to the bar opposite that from which warping was begun. This resulted in an odd number of warp strands.

Two slender arrowweed sticks (Fig. 8, *A* and *B*) were inserted in the ends of the figure-eight, worked toward the end of the loom at which the weaver desired to begin, and drawn together

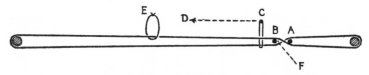

Fɪɢ. 8.—Diagrammatic sketch of the warp with healds in place

as tightly as possible, so as to arrange and lock the sheds carefully. Another arrowweed rod (*C*) to serve as a heald was tied by a loose, continuous string to every lower warp just beyond the first pair of sticks. Heald *C* was then about four inches above the warps (Pl. IX, *A*). These long loops were then loosely bound about and to the heald stick *C* with a cord, so they could be handled as a unit. The heald *C* was moved some distance away from the weaver (to point *D*, Fig. 8), and the upper and lower sheds separated between *D* and *B*. A cord (*E*) was then tied as a very loose loop around the warps comprising the upper shed. (This cord was formed by doubling a length of string, rolling the two halves separately but simultaneously up the thigh under the palm, and rolling one around the other by the return movement of the palm down the thigh. The result was a quadrupled rolled cord.) Two hours were occupied in preparing the loom.

The bands as fabrics fall in the class "warp weaving" ("warp face"); that is, the weft is only filler, almost wholly covered by

PLATE VIII

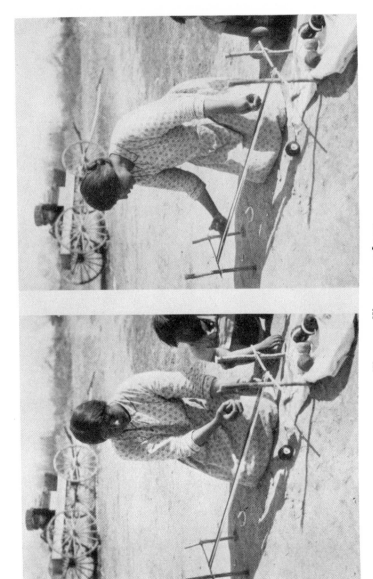

the warps. Hence the designs are in colors provided by the warp strands. On the occasion under description, the weft was common white cord. This was wound about the fingers to form little hanks, bound about by the free end, which was fastened in a slip knot (Fig. 9). Three of these were prepared, and the loose ends of the three tied in a single knot.

To begin weaving, one of these hanks was inserted between the upper and lower sets of warps as close as possible to their point of crossing (at *F*, Fig. 8), and drawn in until the knot uniting the three hanks lay at the center of the warps. It was worked close into the point of crossing by sawing it back and forth, and then ramming it home with the side of the hand. The lower set of warps was raised by the heald rod *C*, and the shed fully opened

Fɪɢ. 9.—Hank of weft yarn

by pressing into the point of crossing with the side of the hand. The sticks *A* and *B* were then removed. One of the two hanks on one side was then inserted through the open shed in the same direction as the first to form the second pick. Stick *A* was then replaced to even up the first pick. The loop *E* was used to raise the other set of warps. The second hank was then picked back. The lower shed was raised and the third hank picked in. The other shed was again raised by the loop and the first hank picked in. In this way there were always two hanks lying on one side of the warps (Pl. IX, *B* and Fig. 10). As lengths of weft were loosened from the hanks, they were temporarily tied again with a slip knot.

It was difficult to get the warps properly arranged while inserting the first few picks. Although the woman I observed was an expert weaver, and showed all the deftness of long familiarity with the process, each time a new shed was formed, the then lower set of warps had to be shaken and pulled through the upper set in a clumsy fashion.[13] Further picks were not driven home with the hand nor with a weaving sword, but simply by grasping the upper and lower sets and pulling them apart as hard as possible after a new shed was formed, to force the point of crossing down on the pick just placed and thus drive it close to the completed web. After an inch of fabric was woven, the tension on the warps

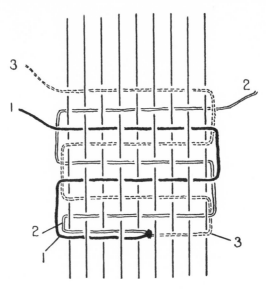

FIG. 10.—Wefting of cradle band

was lessened, to make forming the sheds easier, by resetting one warp bar inside the stakes.

Weaving was continued to about four inches of the further warp bar, just as it was begun that distance from the nearer bar. This allowed room for shedding up to that point. The band was then taken from the loom by cutting through the warps where they cross the bars. These unpicked ends were then fringes. The ends of the three wefts were not tied but allowed to lie with the

[13] Dr. L. M. O'Neale comments: "This is exactly what happens with us in working any kind of yarn the first few inches; perhaps [because of] the roughness of yarns; perhaps the not quite perfect adjustment to warp planes."

PLATE IX

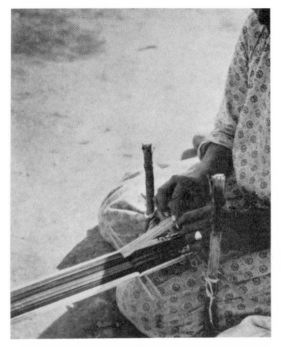

A

B

WEAVING

(*A*, Arranging the heald; *B*, pulling the wefts taut)

warps. They were cut off even with the warp-end fringes, then three or four of the outer warps were rolled with them on the thigh. Since I desired to acquire the uncompleted specimen, these final stages were not observed. In two specimens purchased, the fringes are twisted three to six together and sometimes knotted as well.

The designs on such bands were very simple: longitudinal and transverse lines. Since this is "warp weaving," in which the warps form the surface pattern, longitudinal lines predominate. Plate X shows cradle bands, which by their decoration indicate the sex of the cradled child.[14]

Blankets were woven in essentially the same way as the cradle bands. It is likely, however, that instead of warp weaving, these were in tapestry weave, i.e., with the soft fluffy weft completely concealing the warps, or in tabby weave, with the tension of the warp and weft about equal and each showing equally. At any rate they were much coarser fabrics, decorated only in the side selvages. The weaving was simple checkerboard with no twilling.

The blanket loom was the same as that described. The ground where the loom was to be erected was first prepared by spreading clean sand over it, or by sprinkling water, beating it hard and sweeping it. This was to prevent the fabric from being soiled. Four stakes, three inches in diameter and eighteen inches long, were driven six inches into the ground. Warp bars were bound near the top of the stakes with willow twigs. Both stakes and bars were prepared from the tough inner wood of the giant cactus.

The loom was warped exactly as the band loom, the warps crossing in figure-eight fashion. Normally only white yarns were used for blankets, but those who desired added several dyed warps (red and black) at each side to form decorative selvages. (This suggests that the technique was not tapestry weave, else the colored warps would not show.) Information conflicts here: Kutox, who was probably right, mentioned these colored borders, Last Star denied their existence.

The warps were fastened together at each end by a string

[14] Specimens in the Washington State Museum: *a*, 2–11913C; *b*, 2–11923; *c*, 11914D.

twined through them close to the warp bar, so that the whole set of warps could be lifted as a unit from the warp bars. The warp bars were then replaced to serve as loom bars, to which the warp was bound by a cord running about the loom bar and the previously-mentioned twined string (loom-string).

Shedding was accomplished with the aid of a weaving sword and a single heald, according to Last Star. The flat wooden sword was inserted between upper and lower sets of warps: setting it on edge raised the even warps. The sword being short, it was pushed across the warps as needed. The odd threads were raised to form the countershed by means of a simple heald: an arrowweed stick the full width of the warps laid on the even threads and bound to the odd set by a series of loose loops. (This took the place of the loop E, Fig. 8; a stick being necessitated by the wide expanse of the warps that must be lifted each time.)

According to confused information from Kutox, an arrowweed was placed on the warps near the end opposite that at which weaving was to begin, and to this the lower, odd threads were bound by loose loops. Beyond this a second arrowweed was placed on the warps and tied to each of the even threads of the upper set.

Wefting we begun where the two sets of warps crossed at the proximal end of the loom (presumably with such aids as the sticks *A* and *B*, Fig. 8). A single weft was used, carried back and forth through the sheds. It was turned once around each edge warp before returning to serve as the next pick, thus holding each pick firmly in place. (Extra warp strings beyond the edges of the warp proper, as in Zuñi weaving, were not used here.) When weaving exceptionally wide blankets, no attempt was made to place a pick across the entire width of the warp at one time: a shorter span was chosen, perhaps three before the entire width was traversed. A weaving sword of mesquite (a very hard wood) was used to ram home the picks. (It was withdrawn, not set on edge, between each new shedding, according to Kutox.) Weaving combs were unknown: instead, a pointed stick or weave dagger (six inches long) of tough ivàsĕ′ wood was inserted between the warps to move the picks into position.

The shuttle was simply a smooth arrowweed as long as the

PLATE X

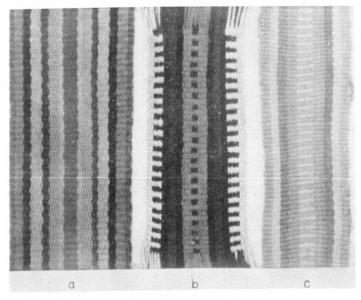

WOVEN CRADLE BANDS
(*a*, Girl's; *b*, boy's; *c*, sex unknown)

width of the blanket, flat at one end. The weft yarn was wound from one end to the other in a slightly spiral fashion, where it passed twice around the stick before returning to the first end. As more weft yarn was needed the free end of a full shuttle was tied to the end of the weft already in place. The weft was thus a single continuous strand. Two or more shuttles were never used simultaneously to deliver picks.

There was no device, such as a stretcher or temple, used to hold the warps at proper width against the narrowing pull of the weft. The informant insisted that the great tension of the warps obviated this tendency.

As weaving neared the farther warp bar, they began again at that end, leaving a narrow unpicked space between the two segments of finished fabric. The unpicked space was then filled with a weft yarn attached to a very slender, pointed, hard stick. Several men always helped at this because it was difficult to pull the weft through.

Blankets were repaired, not by sewing on a patch, but by darning the hole, as among the Pima. Sewing was wholly unknown to both these peoples.[15] The blanket was tied over the mouth of a pot so that the hole could be readily darned.

The glossary of terms employed in weaving is as follows:

atcω' or xŏtcω', cotton
hatĕ'mpk, "spreads" (i.e., along the string), the process of picking up a sliver with the cotton-plucking bow
ĭctakwe'Rĭc, spindle (from kwĭRĭ, to twirl) (the parts did not have individual names)
ackwi'R, to spin
ȧve'Rĭc, warp yarn
ȧsȧ'mc, weft
akwi'g or hĭkwi'k, weaving, also the whole loom
xŏtcω'nyĭtcami'c, warp bar

[15] Darning rather than patching may have been customary throughout the whole western American weaving area. Nordenskiöld remarks of the Choroti and Ashluslay in the Gran Chaco: "The clothes, especially the women's clothes, are often darned. On the other hand, you never see them patched. To mend a hole by putting a patch over it seems to be unknown to the Indians throughout S. America, i.e., the Indians who have still kept their original culture. The Incas, too, did not patch, but darned their clothes" (*An Ethno-geographical Analysis*, p. 108).

vaxalᵧaϑa'x, "counting the intestines," loom-string (the string by which this was
    later bound to the loom bar probably had no name)
xalyada'xk or caʀĕ'kc, heald (the latter also the name of the weaving sword?)
nᵧĭmȧkwe', shuttle
nᵧĭmai'e'kĭc, "to draw together tightly," weaving sword
cakᵧi'ʀȧ, weave dagger (also the modern name for a match)
atcω'tĭtkwĭnᵧĭ'pc, "cotton cover," cotton blanket
cuʀŏ'pa, woven belt
hapĕx, woven headband
tcuxwĭ'l or xa'a'p, woven cradle band

BASKETRY

The Maricopa manufactured only burden baskets, obtaining
from the Pima the flat bowl-like baskets needed for winnowing or
serving food. Every household had one of each, but rarely more.

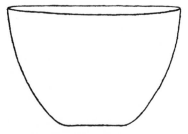

Fig. 11.—Burden basket (from native drawing)

Today a Pima basket forms part of every woman's equipment
and is highly prized. The Maricopa were a pottery using people:
where among the upland tribes of Arizona baskets were used for
every purpose, here were clay vessels in a dozen forms. This is
the lower Colorado habit, where also baskets were obtained by
trade rather than manufactured, and not much used. My informant stated at one time that neither Maricopa nor Halchidhoma made baskets, but this is surely not correct even for the
latter.

The burden basket was in coiled technique, wide-mouthed and
about as tall as wide. The base was flat, the sides flaring (Fig.
11). Unfortunately I failed to record the size, but from the manner of reference, I judge the basket about sixteen inches tall. The
foundation of the coil was a bundle of finely split tule; the sewing

element was devil claw (martynia: gwŏxtŏ'n, both plant and seed pod) on the base and split willow on the sides. The base was always made of devil claw, which, being tough, would stand dragging across the ground. The number of split tules in the foundation was ordinarily not counted, but if a finely sewn basket was desired, these were five. Naturally the slimness of the coil would depend on how thin were these tule elements. Ordinarily the width of the coil was about the same as in Pima baskets, i.e., about one-quarter inch. They preferred to weave them of such fineness because they were valuable: "they took so long to weave." A finely woven basket wore well. The attitude was that if they troubled to make them at all, pain should be taken to make a close fabric. Designs in black devil claw appeared on the sides. These were similar to some employed on Pima bowl-baskets, and were arranged in two encircling bands, one above the other.

Coiling of the base was in a clockwise direction, sewing on the edge farthest from the basket maker (the inside of the basket facing up), the free end of the foundation protruding to the right. This was continued up the sides, i.e., working on the far edge in a clockwise direction, the basket standing upright. A left-handed worker coiled in the opposite direction. The sewing was done with the aid of an awl. Basket coiling was called hapo'vŭk (or hapu'vĭc), which was an alternative name for weaving on the loom.

Such burden baskets were called iyaly̆ipai'ic, "mesquite basket," because they were primarily intended for use when gathering that fruit. When the basket was packed full of the beans, short sticks were inserted between them and the sides in order that an overload could be piled above. This was carried on the head supported, like a pot, on a ring made of the inner bark of the willow. The basket lacked loops and was not carried with a pack strap.

The netted carrying frame of the Pima and Papago was not made.[16]

[16] Bartlett stated that both Maricopa and Pima used this frame, but he was certainly mistaken (*Personal Narrative*, II, 236).

Recently a large storage basket (kwĭltŭ'n) for beans, corn, and wheat was imitated from the Pima. (In earlier days storage was in large pottery vessels.) Such baskets have rounded bases, with their sides tapering to a mouth but half the basal diameter. One specimen was thirty inches tall; its greatest diameter, near the base, the same; its mouth fourteen inches across. These were coiled on a foundation bundle of the longest wheat straws obtainable, the sewing element being strips of willow bark. The space between stitches was equal to the width of the sewing element. Since the foundation was about one half inch diameter and the bark strip nearly as broad, the result was a checkerboard pattern over the whole surface. Coiling of the base proceeded counterclockwise (looking into the basket), presumably on the near edge with the free end of the foundation to the right. When the side had been built up to a height of about a foot, the basket maker seated herself inside to work. This would bring the free end to her left. This basket was identical with those figured for the Pima by Russell and Kissell.[17]

Huge nest-like storage baskets or granaries (sȧkwi'n) were made, which were identical with those of the Pima in shape and technique of manufacture.[18] These were cylinders, three to five feet in diameter and somewhat less in height, without top or bottom, but set on a crib-work platform and covered with arrow-weeds (see p. 90). The technique was a crude coiling, the material arrowweed. They were woven counterclockwise, working at the outer face on the near edge. Such granaries were constructed by both men and women.

A sifter (caχaRa'c) was elliptical, shallow, and about a foot long. Thin willow twigs laid transversely and longitudinally were bound to a willow hoop.

Basket technique was also used in the manufacture of cradle hoods.

[17] Russell, *Pima Indians*, p. 144; Kissell, *Basketry of the Papago and Pima*, pp. 184–85.

[18] Kissell, *op. cit.*, pp. 172 f., esp. p. 178. Bartlett mentioned only the type described in the preceding paragraph for both Pima and Maricopa, not this nest-like granary (*Personal Narrative*, II, 235).

The rectangular baskets with lids in twilled, plaited weave and the sleeping mats made by the Pima[19] were not among Maricopa products.

VARIOUS TECHNIQUES AND TOOLS

Skin dressing.—Hides seem to have been but little used, not so much because deer and fur-bearing animals were rare, or that they were indifferent hunters, but because few articles were made of dressed skin. Correlatively the skin dressing process was rudimentary. Here again their habits coincide with the lower Colorado tribes. The upland tribes of Arizona were proficient workers in skins, those of the Colorado-Gila lowlands were not.

The uses of hides were few: the only uses cited were thongs, quiver, and shield. Rawhide sandals have come into use since cattle were obtained.

A deer carcass was flayed by slitting down the belly from the neck, cutting along the inside of each leg, leaving the hoofs, but taking the head skin.

To tan the hide (k'wĭlᵧȧ), the flesh side was spread with parched seeds of the giant cactus fruit (the residue after a drink was made from it) and the skin folded with the flesh side in. This was to absorb the grease (?). When opportunity came to work the skin, it was first soaked in water. It was then slung over a smooth slanting pole and the flesh side scraped with a sharpened stick, not a stone. The hair was probably removed with a split bone scraper. The hide was then pounded with a stone while lying folded on a flat rock, available only in the mountains. When it was soft, it was further worked by rubbing with the hands. My informant had heard that deer brains were sometimes used for tanning. Pumpkin seeds were not used, as by the Cocopa, nor were skins smoked or dyed. Skins were also tanned with the hair on: fox, coyote, wolf, and mountain lion. (There were no bears in Maricopa territory.) Skin dressing (k'wĭ'ltȧ-mavĭstcu'm, "hide softening") was the work of men alone.

Willow bark blankets may have been made, but it is very doubtful. Kutox described these, called xacĭlᵧě'p, as made by

[19] Russell, *op. cit.*, pp. 93, 134, 145, 147.

older women. The willow bark was stripped from the base of the tree upward, after a fire had been built near it to soften the bark so that long strips might be obtained. This bark was used for a wide variety of purposes and always prepared in the same fashion. It was soaked in water for three weeks, then the inner, finer layers could be stripped off.

My account of bark blanket weaving is very uncertain: the aged informant had never seen one made. Warps and weft were both rolled bark cords. It was said that the warps were doubled to hang over a horizontally suspended bar, the wefts being inserted first at the lower ends of the warps, and the whole closely woven. It was unknown how the lower ends of the warps were held: unless they were held, beginning at the bottom seems impossible. When the weaving reached the upper end, the bar was pulled out. It seems much more likely that the weft was twined, provided such fabrics were made at all. Last Star emphatically denied this, and it is quite possible that the foregoing is a misunderstood description of the making of a woman's bark skirt.

Woven bags (xal,ámĕ'c) were made to hold valuables, such as beads.[20] These were said to have been globular and closely woven with cotton yarn wefts and warps. Further details have been forgotten.

Carrying devices.[21]—The pack strap and the carrying net of southern California were unknown,[22] women usually carrying loads unsupported on their heads, men on their shoulders. Where need arose articles might be transported by a woman in a blanket, the corners of which were tied together and resting on her forehead, or tied around her waist so that the package rested on the small of her back. A substitute for the blanket readily made to carry home mesquite beans was a temporary mat of arrowweed, called tcuĭtcĭ'tc. The weeds were placed thickly on the ground, their stems alternately in opposite directions, and willow twigs twined through at each end, and, if the mat was large, through the middle as well. The corners were drawn together and tied as with a blanket.

Heavy ropes were also made to tie up fire wood and the like.

[20] Cf. the Mohave (Kroeber, *Handbook*, p. 738).

[21] See also p. 330 for carrying habits.

[22] Also the netted carrying frames of Pima and Mohave and the net bags of the Pima.

The strongest were of mescal fiber. Bundles of the dried leaves of this plant were brought home, pounded, the connective tissue shaken out, and the fibers rolled into rope.

Head rings (kwĭcko') were used by women to support pots and other articles carried on the head. In earlier days, these were made of the inner bark of the willow; now they are simply bound rolls of old cloth. The neighboring Pima and Papago similarly use rings of willow bark and less commonly plaited of agave (mescal) leaf,[23] but it is unlikely that the Maricopa made the latter.

Metates and mortars.—These were the principal utensils for the preparation of meals. A man must not even lay his hands on them: if he were discovered using them, he would be ridiculed as a berdache. Metates were used somewhat more than mortars even in the old days when mesquite, which required pounding in the mortar, was the primary food.

The metate was a flat slab, roughly rectangular, with one prepared face used for grinding with a hand stone or mano. The metate was of a granite-like stone; the mano of a hard, close-grained sandstone. They were considered very valuable since it required a long time to work these tough stones into shape and they were constantly needed for household tasks. Both were formed by pecking with any convenient pointed boulder. Like the Pima, stone axes found in nearby ruins were also used to dress them. One small metate seen was roughly twenty-one inches long by fourteen inches wide and two inches thick. It was perfectly flat transversely, but, on its working surface, slightly concave longitudinally. The mano in use with this was as long as the metate was wide, and had a width such as to be conveniently grasped (fifteen inches long; five and a half inches wide; two inches thick). It was of rectangular cross-section, slightly convex in a longitudinal direction on top, with a true flat surface on the bottom (i.e., the grinding surface) which rose at an angle near each end.

When the metate was to be used, the woman knelt behind it.

[23] Russell, *Pima Indians*, p. 113; Kissell, *Basketry of the Papago and Pima*, p. 159.

A pestle or other convenient stone was placed under the near end to raise it (Pl. III, *C*). A cloth was spread under the far end to catch the ground meal: the unground grain was in a basket by the side. The mano was grasped with the hands to that the fingers were over the forward edge, the thumbs over the rear. It was moved to and fro, perfectly flat for most of its stroke, but rocked, i.e., the near edge raised, at the end of the stroke toward the body to catch more grain under it. It was not rocked transversely to the metate. This motion accounts for the flat, longitudinally concave surface of the metate. When the surface became too smooth to catch the grain, it was roughened by pecking with a fragment of hard stone. They usually turned the slab face down resting on the mano when it was not in use.

Mortars were wooden. These were sections of cottonwood or mesquite logs burned to length and with a hollow burned in the end or, less commonly, in the side. Those of mesquite were said to have been as large as the cottonwood mortars; being of a much harder wood, they were more highly prized. Those that had the hollow in the upper end were sunk into the ground half a foot or so to prevent their tipping over. These measured up to sixteen inches in diameter, eighteen or twenty inches in length: one collected[24] was twelve inches in diameter with a rounded cavity in one end, nine inches across by half that depth. The pestle in use with these wooden mortars was a more or less cylindrical waterworn boulder, ten to sixteen inches in length. If the lower end was too flat, it was pecked into a proper rounded form. Infrequently stone mortars were manufactured for pulverizing mesquite and the like, but not for pigments. These were perhaps six inches in diameter, four to five high, and of a tough stone.

When camping while gathering mesquite at a distance, such bulky mortars could not be taken along. Other devices were employed. A hole, six to eight inches in diameter, was dug, carefully cleaned and sprinkled. A few hands full of mesquite pounded in the hole were sufficient to line it with fragments that adhered to the wet soil. The wooden pestle used in this was four to

[24] Washington State Museum, No. 2–11867.

six inches in diameter and breast-high, which the women used, of course, while standing. A less temporary device was a travelling mortar made of arrowweeds fastened in conical form (Pl. XIV, C).[25] A large number of peeled arrowweeds were fastened to a hoop at the mouth by twined willow bark strips. Their lower ends were pointed so that they might be bound closely together. The specimen made for me was about twenty-four inches tall, its mouth diameter about eighteen. This was set into the ground so as to stand upright. A mass of cottonwood bark jammed into the apex was soon transformed into a solid mass by the sticky mesquite. Other arrowweeds tied around the outside with willow bark prevented fragments slipping through. Again the pestle was a breast-high pole. Bed rock mortars, like those of southern California, were unknown, for the simple reason that there is no bed rock nor large boulders in the valley. Further, they dared not pound while camping in the mountains because that would announce their position to the enemy. All preparation involving pounding they tended to before they set out.

The metate was called axpĕ'; the wooden mortar, xamo". Curiously the names for mano and pestle are derived from that of the mortar: xamoči' and xamok$_y$e'r respectively. In Havasupai also the names for mano and pestle are identical (va'ha'dja"a) but differ from that for mortar.[26] The travelling mortar was isa'-vàxamo', "arrowweed mortar"; its pestle, ana'lxamuke'c, "mesquite pestle."

The *fire drill* was the simple palm drill. The hearth was made of the inner wood of the giant cactus, flattened, and provided with an indefinite number of pits on the upper face with notches to correspond cut into the side. In place of giant cactus, a cottonwood limb might be used. The drill was a peeled, straightened arrowweed some fifteen to eighteen inches long and a quarter-inch in diameter. The composite drill, used by the Navaho, was unknown here. The hearth was held by the feet while drilling. For tinder, dry rotted bark of any kind or old manure was

[25] No. 2–11863.

[26] Spier, *Havasupai Ethnography*, p. 114.

used. They did not make short travelling sets, like the Havaˊ-supai. The drill was called aun‚yĭmĭk‚yai' or a'au'giă'm, "fire shooter"; the hearth had no name; tinder was hanȧvᵃsu't.

A strike-a-light (augwĭnyata'vȧ, "fire striker") was used when travelling; striking flint against quartz. A rolled cotton cord was carried for tinder in a hollow cow horn. The use of the strike-a-light and this tinder horn was said to be ancient but I am dubious. For one thing, I was told the horn was anciently that of a mountain sheep, but it is clear that they would not use the horn of this animal under any circumstances. The slow-match for carrying fire was unknown.[27]

Of *stone knives* (ᵃxȧkwĭ', n‚yĭxakwĭ', ᵃviʀu'vᵃ, ḳwaʀȧo') all that is known is that these were made of dark obsidian (kwalacau') found near the Salt River, where it was rare. This may have been flint rather than obsidian, because it was said also to have been used for striking fire. The informant knew nothing of their handles, nor if the blade was set in the side of the handle scalpelwise.

Stone axes were not made, and those found in nearby ruins were used primarily to dress metates to shape.

Ladles were made of wood as well as clay. Wooden ladles may always have been of mesquite which is sufficiently dense to carve nicely. Several seen had small circular bowls, conical below; another an elliptical bowl, rounded below; both having long straight handles in the plane of the bowl (Pl. XIV, *a*, *b*).[28] These were about a foot to sixteen inches in length. I am inclined to agree with Russell that wooden ladles, at least those with conical bowls, were a recent acquisition. He states that they were derived from the Mexicans through the Papago.[29] The ladle with the conical bowl is certainly like old European forms. Woodworking was little developed: wooden bowls were not made.

---

[27] But Garcés' Halchidhoma travelling companion in June 1774 "carried a firebrand in one hand all the way [Ehrenberg to Agua Caliente], and it did not go out" (Bolton, *Anza's California Expeditions*, II, 387). Since it was summer, this must have been for the purpose of starting camp fires, not the torch carried for warmth by other lower Colorado Yumans.

[28] Washington State Museum, Nos. 2–11872 (or 73) and 2–11871, respectively.

[29] *Pima Indians*, p. 101.

PLATE XI

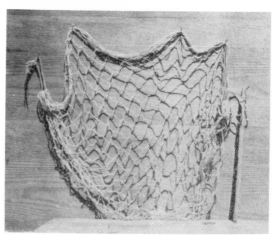

Bow Position and Rabbit-Net

The *mush stirrer* (cu.ŭ′n) was simply three or four arrow-weeds, dressed and held by loose twining at the handle end. Their lower ends were then trimmed off even (Pl. XIV, *d*).[30]

A *broom* (n$_y$imama′l) was simply a large bundle of arrowweeds bound at one end.

Temporary cups and bowls were sometimes fashioned by hollowing out small barrel cacti when travelling.

The *rabbit net* (ca′a′k) was a purse net set in the runway. It was about a yard square. A stout cord threaded through all four edges was attached to a stake. The rabbit dashing into the net, spread open on the bushes, pursed it and was held fast by the stake. The cordage for the net was rolled of the strings of black-eyed pea pods. The net was made on a loop foundation (at upper left corner, Pl. XI). Twenty-five or thirty meshes formed the first row: these tied together (?) were called an ear (smalk). No net gauge was used.

Flageolet.—This instrument was used in lovemaking, but not as an accompaniment to song. "A boy was certain to get a girl if he used it." It was a large reed, up to two feet in length, so chosen that it was formed of two internodal sections with a single node or septum between, both ends then being open. Small holes were made on each side of the node so that it could be pierced, perhaps slotted between these holes. In addition, four finger holes were made near the distal end of the flageolet. To play it, one blew into the open proximal end which was held between the lips; the forefinger of the left hand partially covered the holes at the node to serve as a reed, while the fingers of the other hand lay on the holes near the distal end. The instrument was called w'ilw'i′l or less properly taltal.

WEAPONS

Armament for the Maricopa consisted of bows, short wooden clubs, and small circular shields. A special pike was carried by the battle leader alone; rarely other men armed themselves with simple wooden pikes. Armor, pole-length clubs, and stone headed clubs, all used in this area, were unknown. The Maricopa

[30] No. 2–11874.

placed primary dependence on their bows and could make use of their very short clubs only when actually grappling with the foe. A number of war accounts I obtained make complaint of their inability to defend themselves with these short clubs in mêlées with the Yuma, whose pole-length clubs easily broke through their guard. Yet they were not prone to adopt the longer clubs for combat with the Yuma. Their preference is interesting; for while they followed the Colorado River peoples in battle formation, at least when fighting them, their dependence on shooting suggests rather that normal warfare was against the mountain bowmen, Yavapai and Apache, as indeed the accounts reveal. Even horsemen were frequently armed with bows rather than clubs.

Both self bows and sinew-backed bows were used. These were of the same length and shape, and according to my information, the sinew-backed were not considered superior. I was told that they were not harder to draw and did not give greater penetration to arrows. Self bows were more common than the others. The same bow, of course, served for hunting as well as fighting. Their bows could carry about two hundred and fifty feet, but they rarely shot at an object beyond one hundred feet. Even at this distance, the penetration of the arrow in the side of a deer was said to be not more than half an inch. It was evident that Kutox, who gave this information, had no great faith in their effectiveness. How far from deadly they were is evidenced by tales of men emerging from battle with several arrow wounds.

In fact, the bows being made of willow branches could have had no great strength. But they made up for weakness of material by their excessive length. The standard length was from the ground to the maker's forehead, but, of course, they varied. Yuma bows, they said, were the full height of a man. This agrees with the greater length of bows in the direction of Baja California which I have pointed out elsewhere.[31] There is as much a possibility that this was due to the weak bow material used there as to the greater stature of the dwellers on the lower Colorado.

All bows were straight for the greater part of their length,

[31] Spier, *Havasupai Ethnography*, p. 160.

PLATE XII

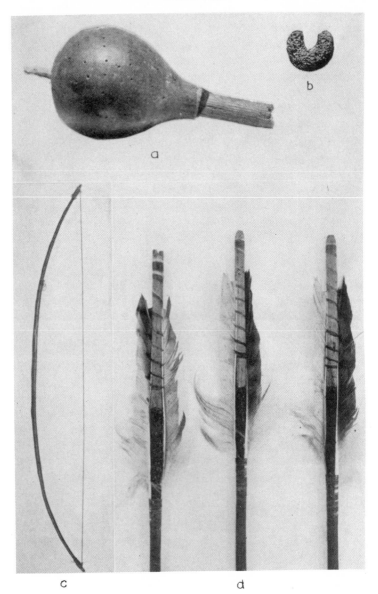

GOURD RATTLE, FISHING FLOAT, AND HUNTING BOW AND ARROWS

curving abruptly near the ends, and being always kept strung, they retained the curvature they were given. A hunting bow which I obtained (Pl. XII, *c*)[32] was fifty inches long; had a depth from string to belly of six inches, and measured one and a half by half an inch at the grip. A similarly shaped boy's bow seen, made of mesquite, was four feet three inches long, six inches deep, with a grip one inch by three-quarters. These were normal lengths for shorter bows. They were cut tapering uniformly toward each end: the width and thickness at the middle were measured only by the feel of the grip in the hand. They were given the desired curvature by burying the still green bow in hot ashes and bending it over the knee. The tips were squared across and provided with a notch on each side. Bows were painted black and red except for the grip which was ordinarily left unpainted. The strings were made of soaked sinew rolled on the thigh. Bows were not kept in cases when out of use, but hung horizontally inside the house on two pegs driven into the wall.

Sinew-backed bows had sinew laid on the back, where it was held in place by sinew bindings every few inches, but not glued. This was probably a bundle of sinew cords or a single large cord, not a layer lying flat; yet such bows were called "sinew-plastered" (gucĭma'mhotcŭ'k). The sinew was brought to the very tips but not over them. These bows differed from self bows only in their flatter cross-section.

When shooting, the bow was held nearly vertically, the hand gripping it exactly at the middle. The arrow passed on its left side, steadied by the left forefinger. I was told that only the primary release was used, that is, the nock was gripped between thumb and forefinger. This may well have been the intention but in demonstration by two old men, their second and third finger tips pulled on the string (Pl. XI). It is my notion, borne out by this case, that the so-called primary, secondary, and tertiary releases are everywhere simply variations of one theme, namely, the secondary.[33]

Arrows were perhaps invariably made of arrowweed (*Pluchea*).

[32] Washington State Museum, No. 2–11919.

[33] Cf. Kroeber, *Arrow Release*.

Reed arrows are ascribed to the Yavapai by Kutox: "we dare not touch them," presumably because one would be defiled by anything pertaining to the enemy. On the other hand, Last Star said that reed arrows were used, but rarely. The standard length of wooden arrows was that of the arm, from the fingertips to the armpit; their diameter was that of the peeled weed, a scant three-eighths of an inch. They were run through ashes to soften the bark so that it could be peeled off and scraped smooth with a fragment of stone. To straighten them, the dried sticks were warmed over a fire (not in the ashes) and bent with the aid of the teeth, sighting along the shaft for alignment. The butt end of the stick was used for the forward end of the arrow. Arrows made from the arrowreed were straightened on a heated stone (any odd stone, not a prepared grooved straightener). War and hunting arrows did not differ in length, but in their heads and feathering. War arrows were infrequently provided with stone heads: a wooden model of a head made for me was about an inch and a quarter long, triangular but with convex edges, straight base, and notched in the edges near the base. These were set into the split end of the shaft, held in place with sinew and the gum which exudes from the stems of arrowweed. Other arrows lacked stone points, the end being merely sharpened and hardened in some fashion unknown to informants.

Any stiff feathers were used on arrows: hawk, buzzard, crow, and sometimes eagle. Of the last they say that the feathers were too dangerous to touch unless they had first been purified by a shaman. Shorter wing feathers were alone used. These were carefully split; the quill scraped to a uniform width and thickness so that it would lie close to the shaft. The vanes must not face in the same direction, hence the halves were not used on the same arrow, but corresponding halves from different feathers. The vanes were laid parallel to the axis of the shaft, bound with sinew (pitch not used). War arrows had three vanes, fastened only at their extremities; hunting arrows bore two, but fastened at the middle as well (Pl. XII, *d*).[34] The vanes were placed just short of the nock so as to provide a meager grip. Their outer edges

[34] Washington State Museum, No. 2-11920E., C, D.

were trimmed parallel to the shaft, and were not cut serrate. The shaft was ordinarily painted red for half its length from the nock end, but some drew zigzag lines on it with their finger tips dipped in paint.

Quivers were of deerhide or a fox skin with its tail pendent; in fact, any skin, such as mountain lion, might be used. In this some twenty arrows were carried. It was tied to the belt in back with the mouth at the left floating ribs. In contrast, my informant pointed out, the Yuma slung it low on the left thigh, the Yavapai carried it on the back pointing over the left shoulder. ("They [the latter] were always creeping along.")

A bowguard was worn on the wrist of the bow-hand. Nothing could be ascertained beyond that it was of deerhide, laced with thongs. When they dressed for a dance, they wore this as an ornament (as the Navaho still do); a broad band with fringes hanging, by which girl partners would hold.

Poison was always applied to war arrows, it was said, but the "poison" (matápu'i) was jackrabbit blood and nothing more! "The jackrabbit is closely related to the cottontail. The latter was bitten by the rattlesnake at the creation, hence the jackrabbit contains the poison."[35] Hunting arrows were not poisoned.

Clubs were made of mesquite and ironwood, and were for use only in warfare. The conventional form had a cylindrical head with a long straight handle, sizable for gripping, in one piece; the whole about eighteen inches long. A specimen, made under the direction of old Kutox by his grandson, has an elongated knob head which only approximates this shape (Pl. XIII, e). It is also provided with a wrist loop tied in a groove encircling the tip.[36] Another, made by Charlie Redbird, has the same shape. This is generically the "potato-masher" type of the Pima and Mohave[37] but without the sharp contours. But the Maricopa, seizing the enemy by the hair, always used it with a downward smashing stroke at the temple, not punching upward as the Mohave habit. A straight club of the same length was also carried to be used

[35] See p. 348. [36] Washington State Museum, No. 2–11916.
[37] Russell, *Pima Indians*, p. 96; Kroeber, *Handbook*, p. 751.

should the mallet be lost to the enemy. Only the bravest and most agile warriors carried clubs alone. They were provided with small shields for parrying. According to the Halchidhoma Kutox, his people did not use the long pole-like clubs of other lower Colorado Yumans, at least not normally.

The shield in use was a small circular affair of skin, sixteen to eighteen inches in diameter; originally of deerskin but for a long time made of cowhide. This size provided protection only for the heart, they held. The hide was laid flat on the ground so that a disk could be cut from it, using a tray basket to mark out the circle. This was buried in ashes until soft, placed on a smooth spot, trod on to work out the wrinkles, and scraped clean. A specimen made for me has two disks laced together around the periphery with a thong.[38] Two short thongs were knotted through near the center to hold them together. Two others were provided to hold a hand grip at the center: a piece of wood covered with hide (Pl. XIII, *b*, *c*). A thong loop was fastened at two points near one edge so that the shield could be slung around the neck, lying under the left arm, or in retreat on the back. No feathers were tied to the shield.

The face of the shield bore painted decoration. Kutox described a common design as quartering the face by a cross, each arm of which consisted of a black, a white, and a red stripe. Within each quarter was a circle, each composed of three circles of the same colors placed concentrically. His grandson made the shield figured under his direction. While intended to have this design, it differs in that the cross is solid black, the concentric circles, one of red within a white; the thong lacing around the edge is painted red. Another design known to him was made by covering the palm with black or red paint, running the heel of the hand across the shield and putting the finger tips down. Four of these units covered the face of the shield. Particular designs bore no names.

Both the construction of the shield and the manner of its decoration was identical with that of the Pima.[39]

[38] Washington State Museum, No. 2–11917.

[39] Russell, *Pima Indians*, p, 120.

PLATE XIII

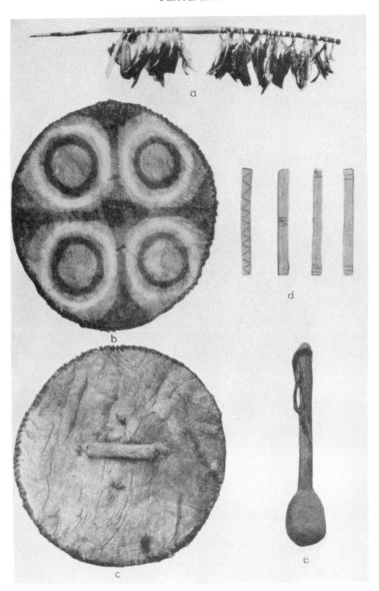

WEAPONS AND STICK DICE
(*a*, Feathered pike; *b*, *c*, shield; *d*, men's stick dice; *e*, club)

A short stabbing pike was sometimes used. This was simply a pointed wooden shaft, four or five feet long. A specimen was made for me[40] from the flower stalk of a narrow-leafed yucca (? bear grass; mahwĭ'tàma'cĭc, "bear eats"). It is painted red, with a feather pendant from the butt, and has the tip fashioned somewhat like a spear head. Charlie Redbird, who made it, said that these sometimes bore stone heads, but I am doubtful.

The native names of these weapons and their parts were as follows: bow, uti'c; bowstring, gwĭcĭma'c, "sinew," or descriptively gwĭcĭma'c uti'c muθau'wĭc, "sinew stretched on a bow"; arrow, ipa"; reed arrow, ipa"axta'c; wooden arrow, ipa"i'i; arrowhead, cĭu'ly or tcĭu'l; arrow nock, xucĭl_yàki'k or ipaucĭl_yàki'k; bowguard, hical_yăŏ'p; quiver, n_yĭgobĕ'tà or descriptively hĭl_yàpo'-và, "something in which to put things"; warclub, kĕlyahwai'; shield, kwacω'và or kŭco'và; pike, xucai'ĭc.

A series of negative points should be recorded. Arrows lacked an enlarged nock, cross-sticks or corncobs mounted on the point, grooves on the shaft, and were normally not made of reed. The grooved arrow-straightener and the arrow-wrench were unknown. The hook-like club of the Diegueño was unknown,[41] and my informant denied the existence of knobby protuberances on clubs ascribed to the Maricopa by Mr. E. W. Gifford's Southeastern Yavapai informant. (Nor did the Pima and Papago have them.) The stone axe was not their weapon, nor the club with a stone ball head incased in hide. Armor was unknown; neither the tunic nor stick armor, the mescal armor of the Yavapai, nor the curtain shield of the Havasupai.

[40] Peabody Museum, Yale University, No. 19112.

[41] Spier, *Southern Diegu,eño Customs*, p. 354.

CHAPTER VI

TIME RECKONING, DIRECTIONS, COLORS, AND NUMBERS

ANNALS

The Maricopa community was in possession of calendar sticks identical with those discovered by Russell among the Pima. Lumholtz discovered one, "the only one existing in the tribe," among the Papago near Tucson.[1] The Maricopa examples, bearing a series of notches like the other sticks, were no more than mnemonic devices: each notch represented the passage of a year, the owner being expected to remember the events of that year. A few additional scratches and dots interpolated between some of the year-marks helped indicate certain significant occurrences, but were so simple and non-pictorial as to give no clue to anyone else what the events may have been.

The years have been counted in this fashion "since the stars fell." Before that date (November 13, 1833) nothing of the sort was known. My informant believed the device invented by an old man of the Maricopa community. "At the meeting house an old man told the young people what happened each year. That is how it began. He decided he wanted the young people to remember." Nevertheless, there can be no doubt of their origin in common with the Pima records, identical in form and likewise beginning with the year of the meteoric shower. There is no certainty that even the Pima records are older than 1833. To be sure, Russell, after mentioning the five Pima sticks he located, and stating that the two explained to him began with 1833, writes: "There are traditions of older sticks that have been lost or buried with their keepers." This may mean that traditionally the records date from earlier times, but I would interpret it as no more than the statement I record below from the Maricopa, that sticks

---

[1] Russell, *Pima Indians*, pp. 34 f.; Lumholtz, *New Trails in Mexico*, p. 73.

PLATE XIV

TOOLS AND SANDALS

(*a, b*, Wooden ladles; *c*, travelling mortar; *d*, mush stirrer; *e*, sandals)

other than those seen, not earlier records, had been destroyed.
If there existed record sticks older than this date, it seems surprising that all the Maricopa and Pima examples known should
date uniformly from this particular event. My conclusion is that
all the sticks of both peoples were derived from a single proto-
type made after 1833. It may well be that the device merely
represents in material form an older custom of reciting annals at
village meetings. The solitary Papago example apparently began
with 1842.

> The time the stars fell is called xŏm⁴ce′kwàsïly⁴, "stars fall." They said the
> stars rained all over the sky. Then no more stars could be seen for a while that
> night; then they reappeared. They never gave a reason for this. This was the
> only time it happened; fourteen years before I [Kutox] was born [the correct date:
> he was born in 1847 or 8].[2]

Formerly several old people had these notched records, but
they were burned when they died. One alone remains. There
were no comparable records marked on skin nor knotted cords.

The solitary example remaining was in the hands of Mai′nyă′n
an elderly man, whose father was Kaveltcadom and mother Kohuana. But the device is not assignable to either of these tribes:
it was solely a product of the mixed Maricopa community. He
began to keep the record in 1873–74, having learned the earlier
annals from an old man of the other mixed Maricopa community
at Lehi, near Mesa. His recollection of events was acknowledged
to be good by Kutox, "but sometimes he makes mistakes and we
have to correct him." He is training his sons to continue it, "but
they don't pay attention." The stick itself is a store product,
which he has had for some years and uses as a staff. (It is four
feet long and an inch in diameter.) The notches, which are
spaced about one-half inch apart, are little square pits, made
with the knife-point, with every tenth year marked by a longer
scratch through it. It begins with 1833. He makes each mark at
the end of the year, i.e., in February. When I first broached the
matter of inspecting his stick on February 7, 1930, he said he had

---

[2] All the old men know their ages exactly; a most astonishing fact for an
illiterate people. The reason is obvious: they know the year of their birth as recorded on these sticks.

not yet added the mark for the year just passed; when I saw it on February 10, it included the 1929–30 mark.

The annals as he recited them follow. I was able to get from him no more than the events of the specially marked years.[3]

	1838	The first Kohuana group came here [to the Gila].
	1848	The Maricopa went to Yuma to fight.
	1852	An old man [Bismarck] was born this year.
	1857–58	The Yuma came to Sacate to fight. [This agrees with the date from Yuma, Mohave, and documentary sources.]
	1859–60	The informant [Maiⁱnyǎ′n] was born.
	1862–63	The first white man to have a store at Casa Blanca [Sweetwater] was captured by Texans. Soldiers came and fought near Tucson. [The reference is to Civil War episodes.]
	1863–64	Made a peace treaty with the Yavapai.
	1864–65	The Yavapai came down and stole horses; warfare started again.
	1865–66	Some men here [including Kutox] were taken to Fort McDowell as scouts.
	1869–70	The Maricopa left the Salt River opposite Phoenix and came here [in the Gila-Salt confluence].

[3] His wife objected. After placating her, I persuaded him to let me photograph and sketch the stick, and wheedled the meanings of the specially marked years. But no persuasion would make him go counter to his wife's wishes and recount the whole systematically.

1871–72 The Pima fought among themselves.

1873–74; 1874–75 The Yavapai were all captured. This year they killed all the Yavapai in the cave.[4]

1875–76 The Yavapai were concentrated at Fort McDowell.

1876–77 Halchidhoma at Sacate (?) lost a race to the Pima. [Russell, (*op. cit.*, p. 56) cites this "in the spring of 1877" as the first race between Pima and Gila Maricopa.]

1877–78 "About" fifty-two Maricopa and Pima went to the Mohave. Eclipse of the sun.[5]

1878–79 Measles killed many children.

1879–80 (The special mark a mistake?)

1882–83 Raced with the kicking-ball against the Pima.

1883–84 Measles again.

1887–88 Earthquake.[6] Established the boundary of the present reservation.

[4] Russell gives the date of the slaughter in the cave as December 28, 1872 (*Pima Indians*, p. 54).

[5] Solar eclipse of July 29, 1878, visible as a marked partial eclipse in southern Arizona (Abbe, *Solar Eclipse of July, 1878*, p. 61).

[6] This is the earthquake of May 3, 1887 (Heck, *Earthquake History of the United States*, p. 51); this was "the only earthquake in southern Arizona in historic times, according to old timers in the district" (Hawley, *Prehistoric Pottery*, p. 549).

1888–89   Another race with the Pima.

1889–90; 1890–91   Kicking-races with the Pima, won by the Maricopa each year.

1891–92   (No data.)

1893–94   Built the church here [near Laveen].

1896–97   Established the day-school here.

1899–1900   Snowed here for the first time that the informant knows; it lay four inches deep.

1918   Influenza epidemic that winter: many died.

1921–22   A man here murdered his wife.

1922–23   Made the big irrigation canal on the reservation boundary.

CALENDAR

The Maricopa year began in late January or early February with the budding of the trees. In 1930 the owner of the calendar stick, as noted above, marked its beginning sometime between February 7th and 10th.

The year begins when the yellow blossoms appear on the cottonwoods (late January). The star xaráϑoʹ appears at this time [information from Last Star]. The year starts in the spring when the trees bud leaves (about the second or third week of February) [Kutox].

Four seasons of the year (mat'a'mk) were recognized: bink, spring; nᵧakàpi'l, summer; iyo'rck, autumn; xatcw'Ràk, winter.

The days were known to vary in length, but the solstices were not watched for, nor were they even named.

Both informants interrogated (Last Star and Kutox) stated that twelve months were counted but that there were only six names, which were repeated. The calendar month (halya', month, moon) seems to have been the lunar month. Its exact duration was unknown, apparently a matter of no concern, and I could not elicit whether it included the dark phase of the moon. Kutox stated that the moon appears twelve times a year.

The calendar was associated, not only with the seasonal appearance of plants, but with the sibs, totems, and personal names. The names of the months were identical with those of sibs; the totemic plants were those gathered or planted during the month bearing the associated sib name; and the month name was said to "mean" corn and the like. Sib, month, and plant life formed a definite complex of associated ideas. Why sibs and months should bear the same names was a mystery to all informants. The association of months and plants was explained as ordained by the culture hero.

When Kukamat, the creator, died, people tried planting their seeds, but they did not know the right time. So they asked him to return. He said, "I do not know if you are strong enough to hear me." They all crowded into their one big house. When he came he spoke like thunder and they all fell asleep. All except Coyote, who tried to waken them. He told Coyote the proper time to plant and named the months so that he should know. Coyote told this to the people.

The usual difficulty was encountered in attempting to get the month names and their order: "Don't remember; very long since anyone used the names." The two informants agreed on the time the year began, the identity with sib names of at least some of the month names, and the plant-associations. The last point of agreement is important because it offers the possibility of arranging the names to agree with the seasonal round and their nearest Gregorian equivalents as follows:

February and August.........xavàtca'c
March and September........xamitu'tc (doubtfully)
April and October............xipa'
May and November..........lₓeω'c
June and December..........kŭmàϑi'
July and January............mavĭs or xamitu'tc

The actual month order given by the informants was as follows:

Kutox: xavàtca'c, xamitu'tc, macxipa's, xipa', kŭmȧϑi' (fifth or sixth month), another forgotten.

Last Star (1931): mavĭ's, kŭmȧϑi', xamitu'tc, xipa', lyeω'c, xavàtca'c.

Last Star (1930): macxipa's, lyeω'c, xamitu'tc, xavàtca'c, kŭmȧϑi', mavĭ's.

It is doubtful that Kutox's macxipa's and xipa' are actually different months. Last Star found great difficulty in giving the month order in 1930. On October 7, 1931 he stated that the new moon of this date marked the beginning of the month xipa'. This would make his first month of the 1931 list (mavĭ's) January–July. His 1930 list, said to begin in February, would also indicate that mavĭ's was January–July. Kutox and Last Star (1930) agree that kŭmȧϑi' came toward the close of the count. They also agree on having xamitu'tc followed by xipa', and Last Star is consistent by having lyeω'c follow this.

Further information is available from their descriptions of the months. Last Star described them indirectly as follows:

lyeω'c people praise that month, saying it was good for every living creature; it warms them and brings green leaves on the trees.

xamitu'tc people praise that month, saying the trees have come to life again, stand up strong, ready to bear mesquite beans to feed everybody.

xavàtca'c month is warm enough for plants to grow. They plant corn this month: because they are starving, they are glad to put in the seeds. It takes but four days for them to come up, hence they (xavàtca'c people) would praise the plants.

kŭmȧϑi' is warm enough for [giant?] cactus to ripen. It is known for this.

mavĭ's is the month they can do nothing. They cannot plant: in July it is too hot and the insects eat the plants, while in December (called the "freezing month") it freezes.

macxipa's is a good planting month again.

Kutox described the months as follows:

xamitu'tc cimu'l [sib: *sic*] "means" mesquite. They gather mesquite in this month, by the end of which the beans are gone. [Discussion revealed he meant July.]

xavàtca'c "means" corn. This the month they plant it [February and also August, when it was planted a second time].

xipa' "means" cholla cactus: the month these ripen is rainy [March or early April; September is rainy as well].

For kŭmȧϑi' and macxipa's, he could assign neither meaning nor time.

These ascriptions allow the identification of xavàtca'c as the first month, when corn was planted. This was done in early February and early August. Cholla cactus and rain (both totems of xipa' sib) fix xipa' as March or April and September or October. Kŭmȧϑi' is almost certainly June when giant cactus fruit were gathered; both ocatilla (i'ikŭmȧϑi'; i'i, wood) and giant cactus were totems of kŭmȧϑi'. Lyeω'c must be a period in the spring. There is difficulty with xamitu'tc: Kutox's definite statement that mesquite was then gathered fits July –August well enough, but placing it early in his list agrees rather with Last Star's description of what seems to be a spring month and with Last Star's order. Again as July–August or December–January, it conflicts with mavĭ's. Macxipa's is wholly uncertain, unless as a planting month it was synonymous with xavàtca'c.

There is just the possibility that macχipa's and mavï's are from the calendric system of some other Yuman tribe confused in this mixed community with Maricopa nomenclature.

Shorter intervals were indicated by counting nights, not days as we would, or by the moon's phase. The time for a dance, e.g., was fixed by saying, "You sleep four (or whatever) nights and on the fourth day come." Or they would say, "We will have our dance when it is full moon—or when the moon just appears." Neither knotted cords nor notched sticks were used for the purpose.

The intervals of the night were also indicated. The night was supposed to be divided into four parts, significant for dream experiences. The first and last quarter were productive of evil dreams; the second and possibly the third were the favorable quarters. These parts were named n$_y$axa'vŏk, "went down," evening; tinyă'mko'ʀŭm, "night (black)old," middle of the night; χacipa'nĭk, "nearing," before dawn; kwâliyo'ŭg, dawn.

CONSTELLATIONS AND NATURAL PHENOMENA

Maricopa star lore was inconsiderable. The major constellations, known also to other Yumans, were recognized, but equally obvious ones, such as Cassiopeia and Gemini, had no names. A few trivial tales were associated with the star clusters, but the esoteric values attached to them in southern California were unknown here.

For four, possibly five, of the six stars mentioned below, the significant position was dawn rising, not as is our customary mode of reference, evening ascension. Four of them were observed in autumn or winter.

The general cosmogonic notion was that there was a duplicate of this world above the sky. This was not the land of the dead, which lay in the west. It functioned in the myths and provided an explanation for the movement of the sun, but otherwise had no particular bearing on affairs of our world.

It is said that far above the sky is a place exactly like this world. There are people there doing the same things as here, and all the stars we see here are duplicated there. Our earth and sky are moving, so that from time to time there is an opening at the horizon. When the sun sets it goes through this gap. Then it rises in the world above and moves eastward to set. Then, coming through the gap once more, it rises again for us in the east.

The phases of the moon were named as follows: new moon, hapa′m; first quarter, tàωʀĭg; half moon, tĭnyakàðĭ′g (tĭnyă′m, dark; kàðĭg, come here); full moon, ĭnyămuyo′vĭg, lit. "[the moon] looks at the sun"; a somewhat uncertain name for the last quarter, puĭnyupai′, "disappearing"; the dark phase, tinyă′m, lit. "dark." Kutox, the informant, uniformly referred to these phases not by the appearance of the moon, but as it was opposed to or near the sun.

Two fragments of tales were related about the moon. Coyote wanted to marry the moon, a woman, but she refused. He went close to the moon, crying as hard as he could, opening his mouth wide. (This had no connection with an eclipse.) Another story has to do with Coyote stealing something. He tried to jump over the moon, and there he is.

The appearance of the constellations in the heavens was integrated in part with the calendar. "The stars (xomace′) change in the different seasons, so people will know when plants are ripe, especially the morning star." The significance of the last part of this statement is obscure, unless it implies that they recognized the variations in the time of rising of the planets that are the morning star. "They went for giant cactus fruit in the summer [mid-June] when the Pleiades (xĭtca′) appear on the eastern horizon [in the evening]." There was no tale about the Pleiades. When the constellation tcisalĭ′c or cipa′isaʀi′s (Cipa's, the culture hero's, hand or fingers; ical, "hand")[7] barely appears above the eastern horizon at early dawn, "they say the crops will first be frozen [December]." When it is well up at early dawn, it is freezing weather. This may be the cluster about Arcturus or the Corona.

The stars of Orion were collectively amŏ′s, "mountain sheep," which "comes up in the evening in early fall." The three stars of the Belt were recognized: the highest was a deer, the middle one a mountain sheep, the lowest an antelope. The associated tale was of a hunter who picked as his favorite food the mountain

[7] The Creation Tale tells how his finger marks were made in the sky.

sheep, and shot it. Three stars to the east, the apexes of a tri-
angle, were the head of his arrow; three to the west in a line (the
Sword?) were the feathers of its shaft. The hunter wants to get
around to the other side of the sheep, so he follows parallel to its
movement across the sky. He was called amokàtàve'Rà, "mountain sheep pursuer" and was identified with a star low on the
southern horizon, possibly Sirius. "When he appears in the evening [late March] it is too late to plant crops" [Kutox]. Last Star
referred to it by morning ascension: it appears well up just before sunrise in late August, almost due east, and a little south of
Orion's Belt. This is confirmation that the star is Sirius. Again
it was said that it served as a sign that it was too late to plant.
Later when the star was high in the sky before dawn, they referred to it by amokàtàve'Rà àxaxavikie''và, "mountain sheep
pursuer has crossed the water."

The Milky Way was called tcilgwiya'nᵧunyĕ'. An antelope and
a deer had a race along the Milky Way. The deer tracks are represented by spaced stars; those of the antelope are continuous
Two stars lie near it on the west: that to the north represented a
Yavapai wearing a cap (peaked forward from his forehead: the
stars form a V about a larger star); the southerly one was a Pima
with a banda about his head (a circle of faint stars about one
brighter). The latter star was called cakwĭlyu'k. "When these
two appear [on the eastern horizon at dawn?] it is the coldest
time of year [January]". These may be Vega and Antares. The
name of the latter suggests the Southern Diegueño cĭlu'k, a star
which rises in the morning in December.[8]

A cluster called axma "quail," lies close to the Milky Way (?).
It looks like a quail: a ring of faint stars forming the body, three
larger ones the head, surmounted by a single tiny star, the plume.

A star called xaRàðo' nᵧixa'a', "cold's cottonwood," appears
in the east before dawn in late January, "when the yellow blossoms appear on the cottonwoods," according to Last Star. It lies
at the lower edge of the Milky Way. This is clearly Altair.
XaRàðo', "cold," was the name of a hero in a tale: the star was
supposed to look like a cottonwood. They said, "XaRàðo''s cot-

[8] Spier, *Southern Diegueño Customs*, p. 357; cf. *Havasupai Ethnography*, p. 171.

tonwood is coming up; we are going to have buds now." Kutox also referred to it as xaʀáϑoʹ, "cold," and implied that it made its appearance in cold weather. The star was a Yavapai: "that is why the Yavapai can stand cold better than anyone else." Yet he stated that it made its appearance in the morning in autumn: he must have meant evening, either he or I being in error.

The North Star was known to my informants only by the Spanish name *capitan*, used locally to mean "chief." They knew it was immobile.

Ursa Major was known as xŏtáluweʹ yĭtavĭʹtc, "Coyote's net"; a group of seven stars.

The sky looks like a sea. Some people were fishing by the sea. Coyote had a net of his own, which he held by one end. Fishes were leaping to the east of the net, which moves counterclockwise [around the North Star. The constellation must be thought of as near the zenith.] He heard them splashing to the west of the net, and, being afraid of missing them, he turned around. That formed the bend in the line of stars [the handle of the Dipper].

A constellation maniʹc, "scorpion," was "directly overhead." It looks like a scorpion with its tail to the west. It was described as an arc of little stars facing the east, terminating at each end in two stars: a group of six stars lies west of the center of the arc; still farther west are three dim stars, and beyond, one alone.[9]

My informants did not know of any constellation called "buzzard," the Luiseño-Diegueño name for Altair. Nor did they recognize Cassiopeia or the Gemini from description.

The evening star was called "the star that travels through the sun," xomáceʹ ĭnyăʹmkwaʹm. There was no associated tale.

The morning star (xomáceʹ kovátaiʹá, "big star") was the old woman of the Flute Lure tale who took her station in the sky.

Then the old woman said she was going to change herself into the bright morning star. "Since I am an old woman, when an old person is dying, they will say he will be dead when the first morning star appears." (When an old person is dying, he always says, "I am not going to die until the morning star appears.")

People who dreamed of this star became brave, killed enemies.

The hero of the same tale, this woman's grandson, Kwiyaʹ-

---

[9] A statement recorded in Culin (*Games*, p. 202) identifies Orion with Mountain Sheep, Pleiades with Gopher, and notes the Scorpion as described here. The nformation seems, however, to be Pima as well as Maricopa in source.

homaᴿᵃ, became a comet (xŏmceaᴿŏsŏ′p).[10] Its appearance betokened the death of a prominent person or a general disaster. A variant of this segment of the tale, given in this connection, was as follows:

> An old woman started from the north with her grandson. When they had gone halfway, they said, "We have no home to go to. It would not be right for us to go to live with somebody else." As they stood thinking what to do, the little boy said, "I shall be a comet. People shall never see me except at the time a well-known person is going to die." He also said, "If they should happen to see a streak across the northern sky, people will know there is going to be sickness all over the world." As he said this, he changed himself into a comet. We see this once in a while.

Eclipses were called ĭnyacápu′i, "the sun dies," and xălăcápu′i, "the moon dies." No reason was assigned for the phenomena and there were no observances when they occurred. "We don't do anything [for the lunar eclipse], because they say it is the white man who uses his own trick on the moon." One eclipse of the sun was recalled, dating to possibly ninety years ago:[11]

> An old man told Kutox that when he [the old man] was a baby his mother was gathering mesquite beans at midday, when the sun was totally eclipsed. It was dark everywhere; the birds began to chirp and one could see the stars. The sun soon came back. They did nothing about it.

An earthquake (matᵃhĕ′nk, "earth shakes") was not considered significant. The reason assigned for quakes was that when the twin culture heroes died after the creation, they went back to lie under the earth; now when they are tired, they yawn and stretch, causing the earth to shake.

> Kutox remembered an earthquake when he was twelve years old (about 1859–60) and another fourteen years after they moved to Laveen from Sacate (about 1884). The annals above mention an earthquake in 1887–88.[12]

Thunder and lightning were two anthropomorphic beings in the sky. They had no names (the natural phenomena were re-

[10] Definitely not a meteor.

[11] Possibly the solar eclipse of November 30, 1834, but the season as indicated by gathering mesquite is wrong (Oppolzer, *Canon der Finsternisse*).

[12] The 1884 and 1887 earthquakes are probably the same, i.e., that of May 3, 1887, unless the earlier was the slight quake of July 6, 1886 (Heck, *Earthquake History*, pp. 51, 54).

spectively xuk'ŏs and xuʀŏ'vᵃ). People say the thunder strikes, not the lightning. They cry out to children, "Come into the house! The thunder will split you in two." Arrowheads (presumably those found in ruins) were dangerous for one to carry about; the thunder would be sure to strike him. They did not go close to a lightning-struck tree nor burn its wood: it would make them sick. Thunder was not associated with war by the Maricopa.

Men who dream of it say thunder and lightning have the form of human beings. One of them wears red clothing; the other is naked except for a skin around his loins. The latter carried a bow and arrow in his hands all the time. He has long bushy hair hanging over his shoulders. The man with red clothing does nothing but stand with arms folded: in talking to the other, he stretches his arms out, which makes the lightning. The one with the bow shoots at the same time: that is thunder.

What clouds are made of was not known, but "they come in the form of human beings";[13] a fundamental belief in the Pueblos. The Maricopa held that the Yavapai told the clouds to go to some spot in the Gila valley, so that it would cease raining where they lived.

The appearance of a rainbow (kwȧlice'rc) indicated the end of rain. A halo or corona seen around the moon (xal_yȧ'c kȧʀȧu'kȧm, "moon's ring") was not regarded as significant.

The whirlwind was a ghost, that is, one of the several souls each person had.

Little bees seen making holes in the ground was regarded as a sign of approaching spring.

DIRECTIONS, COLORS, AND NUMBERS

Six directions were named: the four cardinal points, zenith, and nadir.

ĭnya'cȧpa'k or ĭnya'djȧpa'k, "sun's rising place," or ĭnya', "sun," east
matxa'vĭg, matxa'k, north
kave', gĭve' or ĭnyaxa'pk, "sun went that way," west
xasa.i'l, south (lit. "salty water")
ȧmai', up (lit. "sky")
ȧma't, down (lit. "earth")

The term ĭn_yuxa'vȧ or ĭn_yuxa'p was volunteered for northwest, but this is palpably the term for west.

[13] The tale "Cloud and Wind" was told to exemplify this belief.

The Maricopa have transposed the normal Yuman word for south to west, a fact to which Dr. Kroeber has called my attention. For south they have substituted xasa.i'l, meaning salty water, the ocean; a word with identical meaning in all Yuman dialects known to me. There is cogency in this substitution, since the ocean in Maricopa mythology was set in the south and the Gulf of California lies substantially in that direction. If, as seems probable, kave' has come secondarily to mean "downriver" to the tribes residing on the lower Colorado, the Maricopa shift becomes intelligible: "downriver," i.e., down the Gila, is westward for them. And it may also argue their original location on the Colorado.

The word north is known to be that for wind, or contains the same stem, in several Yuman tongues, as Dr. Kroeber has also remarked (wind in Mohave is ma'thāk, and a possible case is Havasupai, ma'twi-, "wind"). Why this should be is anything but clear, because the prevailing winds of Arizona are southwesterly. But, although "wind" in Maricopa is matxa'c, my informants repudiated any connection with the word for north.

TABLE III

Tribes	North	West	East	South
Maricopa.....	matxa'vĭg	kave'	ĭnya'càpa'k	xasa.i'l
Mohave......	ma'thāk	....	-'inya	ka'veik
Yuma........	metva-	....	....	kavē-
Havasupai....	màta'vĭgà	[ĭ]nyato'povĭ (sun's setting place)	[ĭ]nya'djà'a'lovĕ (sun's rising place)	kàwe'vĭgà
Walapai	mat'a-'vᵉkᵃ	inya-to'poˋ (sun sinks)	inyatc-al'loˋ	kuwê'vek
Southeastern Yavapai	matava	inyadopo (where sun sets)	inyatcaauw (where sun rises)	weve
Northern Diegueño*.....	xitoʟ	awik	enyak	kawak

* Kroeber, *Phonetic Elements of Mohave*, pp. 62, 64, 82; *Handbook*, p. 800; Walapai Ms; Forde, *Yuma Ethnography*, p. 102; Spier, *Havasupai Ethnography*, pp. 169, 265; Gifford, *Southeastern Yavapai*, p. 247; Waterman, *Religious Practices of the Diegueño*, p. 333.

Directional sequence and color-direction association occurred here as elsewhere in the Southwest, but was slight. Nor was this symbolical patterning stressed in any degree like the constant repetition of their pattern number, four. The order of mention of the cardinal points was always east, north, south, and west, it was said, that is, not in a circuit. But when requested for the names of directions, Kutox had volunteered east, north, west and south. Later he corrected this, saying he had been careless: surely evidence that the sequence had definite form. He knew little of color-directional association, beyond reminding me that in the tale "Flute Lure" everything to the west was described as yellow, to the east as red (although he had actually omitted this entirely while narrating the tale). Last Star declared that he knew of no association in story or usage beyond that of the Killdeer dance. It is likely that this was not the whole of their associational habit. It is apparent that east and west were more highly significant for the Maricopa and Halchidhoma. This was the orientation of houses, activities connected with the purification of warriors, cremation, mourning rites, and concepts of the land of the dead, for example. North and south were relatively indifferent. At best the directional association seems but little developed or stressed, which stands in marked contrast to the exuberant symbolism of this order among Pueblos and Navaho, or even Pima and Papago.

A request for color names yielded the following:

nyi′lyĭg,   black   xama′ly^a,   white
^ahwĕ′tàm, red   k'wĕ′sàm,   yellow
xavàcu′,   blue, green (as the sky, grass, fresh leaves: the familiar blue-green
                confusion)
xacami′,   green (as slime in water, anything mouldy green)
ĭnyω′Rĭg,   variegated (as a pinto horse)

Brown, gray, and the like were not known as colors. Deer, e.g., were described as like the ground, dirt-colored (^ama′tĭg). White, red, and black were said by Kutox to be the principal colors, "because they were our paints" (as paints called respectively mat^amàca′và, ^agwe′R^a, and kwĭnyil,^a).

Numeration in Maricopa-Halchidhoma was as follows:

1	cĕ′ndĭg	11	caxŭ′kàmai′gcĕ′ndĭg
2	xavi′k	12	caxŭkàmai′gxavi′k
3	xamo′k	(13–19 were formed similarly)	
4	tcumpŏ′pk	20	caxŭ′kàxavi′k
5	saRa′pk	23	caxu′kàxavi′k maigxamo′k
6	xam^axu′k	30	caxu′kàxamo′k
7	paxkie′g	(40–90 were formed similarly)	
8	supxu′k	100	cĕndcĕndĭg
9	nyĭmxamŏ′k	200	cĕnxavi′k
10	càxŭ′k		

One to ten are independent stems, save six and nine which appear to contain that for three. The terminal syllables of six, eight, and ten are alike. Numbers of a higher order are transparent compounds. Since àmai′ means "high," "on top," it may be that eleven, e.g., can be etymologized as "one on top of ten." Twenty was etymologized as "two tens." Mrs. Redbird thought the element cĕn of the hundreds was of Spanish derivation, which is likely.

The only fraction said to be named was one half, kŭcluve′và ("middle" was tŏnyi′).

CHAPTER VII

SOCIAL RELATIONS

CHIEFTAINSHIP AND MEETINGS

National solidarity was strong among the Maricopa. This is the same sentiment recorded for other Yuman tribes of western Arizona and which sets them off so markedly from Californian peoples. The Maricopa constantly referred to themselves as a single homogeneous people, all participating equally in their group life and all united against their enemies. This despite the fact that their settlements were sprawling agglomerations of households spread over a considerable area.

The solidarity expressed itself in at least three ways. There was but one chief for the whole tribe so far as is known. Men of prominence might be found in the several villages but they had no formal status as chiefs. Again, there were no internecine feuds. In all the long discussions with informants, there was never so much as a hint of conflict between families or villages. And further, in warfare they presented a united front against their enemies, whether in attack or defense. Minor raids took place, to be sure, but what stands out in their minds are the massed battles in which a large proportion of their able-bodied men took part. This attitude of the Maricopa seems to have been duplicated among the tribes now resident with the Maricopa when in their original homes on the Colorado, although here our data are so slight as to be inconclusive. But once the remnants of these tribes had been incorporated in the Maricopa community, they felt themselves completely identified with their Maricopa hosts as forming one coherent whole.

Both Maricopa and Halchidhoma had chiefs whose position was hereditary and functions vague. It proved difficult to get adequate information about them. Dreamers (shamans and others) were mentioned frequently and voluntarily; specific questioning had to be directed to chieftainship with but unsatisfactory results. It would seem that others were at least equally prominent socially: shamans, song and dance leaders, the directors of funerals and mourning ceremonies, custodians of scalps, war leaders, orators, etc. All or most of them had the prestige that derived from dreaming the powers that entitled them to their positions. In a society that put a premium on dream-sanctions, it is intelligible why the chief, whose functions were of little moment, should receive slight attention.

There seems to have been but one chief at a time in each of the tribes. The difficulty is that our information relates to the period of joint community of Maricopa, Halchidhoma, Kohuana, and Halyikwamai. The groups were then impoverished in numbers and lived in mixed and scattered settlements interdigitated with Pima. There is also a question how far the chief's prestige or the office itself was due to recognition by Mexican authorities.

At the Sacate settlement when Kutox was a boy, about 1855, the Pima, Halchidhoma, and Kohuana had each their own chief. Sumĭlya'm, "down-feathers travelling," was the Kohuana chief. He was entering old age at the time, and while he might have been chief when they came from the Colorado (1838–39), Kutox was uncertain.[1] At about the same time Malai', a man of like age, was chief of the Halchidhoma, then a group of perhaps twenty families. He may have been appointed by the Mexicans when they were in Mexico twenty years before. Kutox did not know whether, in an earlier period, there had been more than one Maricopa or Halchidhoma chief at a time. It seems unlikely: since he could remember the ancestry of chiefs of his day, he should have known of plural chiefs in earlier times. Last Star declared emphatically that the Maricopa had but one chief at a time.

The Maricopa tribal chief was in reality the chief of the strongest village. Other villages lacked chiefs: "they came to that place when they wanted to find out anything." Practically he was chosen by the people of his village: they simply came to him for advice and to have him address them, until he came to be recognized as chief. In native theory, however, he dreamed his position. Last Star was not certain what spirit was the subject

[1] Papago-foot, mentioned by Kroeber (*Handbook*, p. 801) on Mohave authority as Kohuana chief about 1883, was, according to Kutox, not a chief but a respected old man. Last Star thought he may have been given a trial as chief, but could not have held the position for any great time.

of a chief's dreams, but presumed it must have been the mocking bird, because anyone who desired to become an orator dreamed of this bird.

His successor was his son or other close relative in the patrilineal line. The rule was not absolute but dependent on the competence or willingness of the logical successor. Normally the inheritor was a son (not of necessity the eldest son) because it was assumed that "the son had been instructed by his father, but they would pass over an incompetent son for a close relative on the father's side." The successor's competence was taken as a sign that he, in his turn, had had the requisite dreams. In default of a qualified son, the dead chief's brother or brother's son was chosen. The transmission was through the chief's sister only if she had sons while his brother had none. No woman could inherit the position. In the case cited below, the succession was to a filial grandson because the daughter could not hold office.

The first Maricopa chief who could be recalled by Kutox was killed by the Mohave at Sacate. "He had wanted his sister's sons [*sic*] to be chief in his place, but they [the sons or the people?] refused." Then the people chose his eldest son, but he too refused; the chieftaincy going to his second son Xan_yigwacxa'mᵃ, "frog beater." The latter was killed in battle in Yuma territory before Kutox was born (1847). He had a sister who had no son but a daughter. The son of this daughter was chosen chief. This man was Charlie Redbird's father. Charlie would now be chief if they had one. Last Star knew nothing of earlier chiefs, but thought the transmission was from an unnamed chief[2] through his daughter to Charlie Redbird's father. He is probably correct, but in either case the principle is the same; that transmission was always through the paternal lineage though not of necessity through males. It is obvious that the chieftaincy did not remain in a single sib.[3]

[2] Here occurred an instance of the emphatic refusal to name the dead, perhaps because Last Star was talking of his wife's ancestors (his wife being Charlie Redbird's sister) in the presence of Charlie's wife.

[3] The Mohave cited to Kroeber (*Handbook*, p. 801) the name of the Maricopa chief at the time of the Kohuana adhesion (1838) as Aha-kurrauva, and about

The first Maricopa chief mentioned was a great warrior against the Yavapai. When the Mohave came to Sacate he fled his house with his wife. Immediately he remembered he had left his feather bonnet inside. He said, "Even if I am killed, I must have it to wear." He went back, while his wife waited. By the time he rejoined her, the Mohave overtook them and killed both.

There is a suggestion in the single chiefly lineage known to the Halchidhoma informant Kutox that a man might rise to that dignity by his own efforts. Malai' was remembered as the Halchidhoma chief, who died at the age of seventy when Kutox was young (about 1855–60). His place was taken by his eldest son, Xatisa'là, "doghand," who died recently. Who was chief before Malai' was not known, but it was certainly not his Walapai or part Walapai father. This is corroborated by the fact that Kutox's paternal grandfather, Malai''s older half-brother, was not a chief. The son of Xatisa'là was never chief and was said never to have had pretensions. He was known as the dreamer of the Deer song. It is quite likely that his opportunity for succession came after the break-down of tribal society.

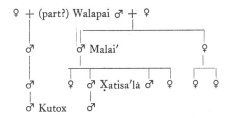

A Maricopa or Halchidhoma chief was called hutcàci'pĭc, "adviser," or pipavàtai', "big man," "because we think he is above everybody in the village. Everybody listens and obeys him." There were other designations for chiefs: gàmu'lvĭnc, "one who has the name [of honor]"; gwĭn$_y$ai'vĭc, "one who tells things"; hamu'lĭg, "well-known"; kina'pk, "praised"; but the last two terms at least were also applied to others, for instance, to those who had killed enemies.

1883 as Ahwanchevari (wantcàvaʀi' according to the Maricopa; named as Juan Chevereah in the *Report of the Commissioner of Indian Affairs for 1858*, p. 207). He also had power to cure (p. 287).

Xanavʀé was given as "king," meaning "anyone who was head over people."
This was not the name for the tribal chief, but for the leaders of Mexicans or
Americans. It is Spanish *general*, here pronounced henerala. (Dr. Beals suggests
that the terminal syllable may be from Spanish *rey*.) The Havasupai epithet for
the head chief, hanata'và, "superlatively good," was not recognized by informants.[4] Havasupai kahà't, "chief," Mohave kohota, "dance director," and Yuma
kwoxot, "chief," "dance leader,"[5] was here kwaxω''t or kwaxo'tĭnc, "good man''
(that is, good natured, kindly), not the name of an official. A dance leader was
here called nᵧima'càisk.

The functions of a chief seem to have been slight: his authority more admonitory than coercive. He rose early in the morning
and called the villagers. Talking to the men first, he admonished
them to go out to hunt, to feed their wives and children. He told
the women to hasten to prepare meal so the men could start. (A
woman who failed to have breakfast ready by sunrise was
scorned.) He looked after the meeting house and called men to
the meetings.

There appear to have been no speakers (repeaters) for the
chiefs or others.

Councillors were mentioned as chosen by the chief, two or
three men. Whether they had special functions or authority is
unknown to me. They were called matàsĭ'nyŭk, "those who
agree"; more recently matàwi'kĭk, "helpers."

There were evening meetings which any man might attend as
he chose, even young boys, but not women. They took place in a
special large house erected in the middle of the sprawling settlement. These were by no means legislative assemblies: decisions
were not binding. The opportunity was rather one for the expression of opinion at a convivial gathering. Nevertheless, the
proceedings were quite stereotyped.

It was customary for the chief to get the meeting house ready.
In mid-afternoon he started a big fire, which was kept up so that
by evening it was intensely hot inside. He would clear it of dé-

[4] Kroeber's derivation of the Mohave word for chief, hanidhala, from Spanish
general (Yuma, hon-ah-thal) may be correct but looks to me like folk-etymology
on the part of the Mohave (Kroeber, *Handbook*, p. 745; Trippel, p. 568). The
Cocopa, like the Maricopa and Havasupai, called the headman "good man" (information from Dr. R. H. Lowie).

[5] Forde, *Yuma Ethnography*, p. 137.

bris thrown inside by children, for they were not forbidden to play there. The fire was kept blazing during the meeting with the door closed, so that they would sweat. A pile of wood was stacked within the doorway on the south side for the convenience of the fire tender (autuʀa'k), an old man who alone had the duty of feeding the fire.

As evening came on, the chief would stand in the open to call the men to the meeting: "they might have something to discuss." He advised them to bring enough tobacco, so that the unprovided would not lack it. Meetings always began by smoking privately, not passing their lighted cigarettes around. Two or three were selected to do all the talking (whether orators who had dreamed or others is not clear). In the early evening they discussed "things like crops." Toward the middle of the night arrangements would be made for hunting. Warfare was discussed. (Young men were not supposed to go off on unauthorized raids, but if they did, they were nevertheless praised.) Talking would continue until the appearance of the morning star, which was taken as the signal to break up. They did not think it proper to leave early in the night: if topics were exhausted they sang until this star rose. No one was allowed to sleep, because the older men were delivering admonitions and advice to their juniors; telling them not to gamble, to treat their wives well, not to beg even though starving, not to be lazy, and the like. Anyone who slept was sent out. There were no guards at the door.

Such formal division of the night was a characteristic Maricopa pattern. Not only did it appear in the framework of dreamed experiences with spirits, but their actual sleeping habits were made to conform. Children were kept awake during the first part of the night and roused early before dawn to avoid dreaming during these ill-starred quarters of the night. Shamans, at least when working over a dying patient, abruptly changed their songs with the passage of the night's divisions. The night was supposed to be divided into quarters, but none of the experiences and practices cited to me conformed literally to this fourfold pattern. Here the meeting is described as of three parts: indifferent evening, deep night with its more serious problems, and pre-dawn. It may be that the conduct of the meeting followed the four-fold pattern, but it is far more likely that it existed only in native ideology.

The meeting house was in effect a men's club house and sweat house like those of California and the Pueblos, and, unlike the central Californian forms, not a dance house. The distinction is that it was not normally a men's dormitory: only in stormy weather, when an enemy attack was predicted, everyone in the village slept in it for safety.

WARFARE

FREQUENCY AND ORGANIZATION

Warfare occupied an unusually large place in the minds of the Maricopa for a people who by temperament were essentially mild-tempered and sedentary. They maintain that it was forced on them by raids of Yuma and Yavapai which had to be met or anticipated. While this seems much like the usual disavowal of aggression that can be heard from any of our western Indians, in this case I believe it to be true. No great premium attached to the man with a war record: the war leader was held in high regard, but the ordinary man who took a scalp or captive was not socially exceptional. Maricopa weighted dream experiences far beyond exploits of war. Nevertheless they talked a good deal of war, took pleasure in planning it, and brought up their sons to look forward to it.

The Halchidhoma situation was much the same, with this difference; that while they were still on the Colorado, they were caught between Yuma and Mohave, who hammered away at them with repeated attacks. While they were by no means supine and did counterattack, they had everything to lose by aggression. In the end, they lost their foothold on the river and fled into Mexico.

Both tribes shared unremitting warfare with Yuma, Mohave, Yavapai, and Western Apache. At least after their joint settlement on the middle Gila, this meant especially the Yuma and Yavapai, the nearer of the four. The Yuma were joined by Mohave and Yavapai, the Yavapai by Apache, for descent on the

Maricopa villages. Reciprocally, their allies were Cocopa, Kohuana, and perhaps Pima against the Yuma; the Pima against the Yavapai. Word having been dispatched to the Cocopa and the Kohuana, these people stole around through the desert to the east to join in the attack on the Yuma.

Every few years there was a raid or pitched battle important enough to rest in their memories. Culling through the Pima annals recorded by Russell,[6] I find mention of a Yuma raid against the Maricopa in 1833; of the Maricopa against Yuma in 1841; then three Yuma descents on the Maricopa between 1842 and 1845, followed at longer intervals by others in 1850 and 1857. My own information agrees only in that there were conflicts with the Yuma every few years. Kutox emphasized two expeditions apiece as worthy of recollection, yet he mentioned others indirectly. He placed a foray of Maricopa against Yuma as possibly in 1838, the return engagement some time after; again against the Yuma in 1848 or 1849, and the last descent of the Yuma on the Maricopa in 1856. (Documentary evidence makes this 1857 with certainty.) Peace followed in 1862 or 1863. The date 1848–49 is checked twice in the narratives given below. Kutox remembered the battle of 1857 as a boy of nine. Kutox' date 1838 may correspond to the Pima 1841, 1848 or 1849 undoubtedly to their 1850, and they agree on 1856 or 1857. Bartlett mentioned an engagement "a year before" 1852: this is probably Kutox' 1848 or 1849 and Pima 1850.[7] Kutox also mentioned a Maricopa party going to Yuma before he was born (1847); this may be that of 1838. A Mohave raid on Halchidhoma at Gila Bend seems to have been about 1835.

The Pima annals are filled with references to Yavapai and Apache attacks on the Pima as constantly occurring and mention reciprocal engagements. There can be no question that the Maricopa community as frequently suffered the same and went into the mountains to hunt down these enemies. These were different affairs from the pitched battles with the Yuma: a few Yavapai-Apache marauders picking off stragglers about the villages, or

---

[6] *Pima Indians*, pp. 38, 40–42, 44, 46. Some detail is given.

[7] Bartlett, *Personal Narrative*, II, 221.

the wiping out of isolated enemy families discovered in the mountain caves.

Two quite different modes of warfare were adopted. Against the Yuma and Mohave, the Maricopa followed the Colorado River custom of formally arranging pitched battles. These were preceded by challengers who first pranced up and down shouting insults at their opponents, until they clashed in single combat, followed by a general mêlée in which foemen stood against each other until they were clubbed down. Against the Yavapai, tactics were wholly different. While they still went *en masse*, it was rather in the nature of a foray, a quick blow and a speedy return, resting largely on their ability as bowmen.

Winter was thought the best time to go to war, especially on nights that were stormy. The enemy would think it too cold to leave their houses and would feel safe indoors. This was also the time that the Maricopa expected raids. On stormy nights, cold and windy, when enemies were thought to be about, everyone in the community gathered for security to sleep in the meeting house. It was on such nights that sentries (matŏ'au'm, "standing by himself") were posted. They went around the settlement at a distance, but built no deceptive fires as Russell records for the Pima.[8] Stockades were unknown to informants, although they are reputed to have existed in this area.

A shaman was called on at such gatherings to use his clairvoyant power to find if the enemy were approaching (see p. 292). He invoked the attendance of the spirits of the mountains by sucking up four piles of dirt. The mountains were thought to enter one by one and divulge the whereabouts and intentions of the enemy through the shaman's interpreter.[9]

However strongly they may have felt that winter was the proper time for warfare, the intoxication of the sahuaro drink roused them to frenzy for war at the time of the sahuaro celebration (June). "When they drank this they thought of war." The song peculiar to the celebration tells of "red water," i.e., blood, its appearance and "how it is made": that the enemy has come

---

[8] *Pima Indians*, p. 201.

[9] Mountains as champions of the several tribes are described on p. 253.

to join in drinking: they had joined in battle, now they would be together drinking. Intoxication and incitement, with their proximity to the mountains while gathering the fruit, led them to set out at once against the Yavapai.

Further, Russell's Pima annals indicate conflicts rather generally distributed through the year with the greater number in spring and summer. Thus, the Yuma came against the Maricopa in October, 1833, the autumn of 1842, and in the summer of 1843 and 1857. My own information is that the Mohave raided Gila Bend in midwinter (1835?). While this tells nothing of the time their own parties set out, it at least indicates when Yuma and Mohave might be expected. Pima and Maricopa were in much the same situation respecting raids of the Yavapai and Apache and their own retaliating attacks. The Pima annals yield the following where the season is identifiable. The Apache-Yavapai came down in spring five times, in summer the same, in the autumn once, in winter twice. Pima attacks on them, either alone or with Maricopa or Papago allies, were in spring once, summer twice, and winter twice. Bartlett saw a Maricopa party set out in July, 1852.

Dress for battle was no more than everyday wear: breechclout and sandals. Older men coiled the long braids that hung on back and breast around the head, confining them with a headband. They sometimes let them hang full length until the enemy was neared, then bound them about the crown with one braid, or, like younger men, tied the ends of the braids together as they hung down the back. I am not certain that war paint differed from that on gala occasions. This included a mask-like black stripe across the eyes and horizontal lines in white across the long back hair. Similarly, the feather headdress may have been only the everyday one: a bit of eagle down or an eagle feather pendent by a short cord from the back hair. A feather bonnet, a cap with eagle feathers projecting sidewise and vertically, was worn by some to indicate their bravery, but this also was gala dress.[10]

A war party was observed by Bartlett in July, 1852. "Such as had their own cotton blankets, placed them around their bodies in folds, and over this wound

[10] See pp. 100, 157.

their lariats as tight as possible; for the double purpose, I suppose, of bracing their bodies, and of protecting their vital parts from arrows. Those who possessed neither [trade] shirts nor blankets, remained as nature made them, with the addition of a little paint. On their head dresses, they had all bestowed more attention than on their bodies. Some had them plastered with clay, so as to resemble huge turbans. Others had decorated the great club of hair which hung down their backs with bits of scarlet cloth, but more of them with the richly-figured sashes or belts of their own manufacture. Some again wore their hair in braids tastefully wound around their heads, intermingled with pieces of scarlet cloth; while a few, less particular as to their appearance, wore it clubbed up in a huge mass."[11]

War parties comprised relatively large bodies of men, at least against the Yuma, although fewer may have participated against the Yavapai. Kutox persistently mentioned two hundred as the number in a party: while this need not be taken literally, it does indicate the order of their numbers. This is in striking contrast to the handful of raiders which the mountain tribes of Arizona mustered at any one time, and indicates clearly that warfare was a national affair of the sort carried on by the lower Colorado tribes. The contrast with the mountain tribes is not one of relative populations because the Maricopa were not very numerous in the second quarter of the last century, the period to which our data relate.

The organization of the parties was simple. There was a battle leader, one or two individuals who bore feathered pikes (the "battle standards" of the Yuma), several champions, and shamans who used their clairvoyant abilities to seek out the enemy and who tended the wounded. All these men had their functions by reason of special powers they had dreamed. Not one of them was more than a leader: they were not officers to issue orders. It seems reasonably clear that the tribal chief was not ordinarily war leader. Yet one at least among those is known to tradition as a warrior (p. 157).

There was but one battle leader at a time among the Maricopa. He was the only man who had the requisite dreams of war, and when he died, another dreamed in his stead. The dreams dwelt on surmounting dangers and killing the enemy. In his dreams he saw clouds of little flies (called kumanyihwi') fighting in the air,

[11] *Personal Narrative*, II, 216.

and by their actions he learned how to make successful issue of the battle. He dreamed only that he would be successful. His personal preparation was like that of all shamans: a series of dreams in which the spirits initiated him in the mysteries of his art until they were satisfied that he was fully prepared. There is a cactus more thorny than cholla, called ᵃxu'l. He dreamed he saw these fighting in the form of humans. When they saw he was fitted for his position, these spirits took him into a large cave, the hollow interior of a mountain located in the enemy country. As he entered he saw a club, a shield, and a pike hanging on the wall. Each time he was taken there, they gave him the opportunity to learn the use of one of these until he was proficient with all. Then he was ready to lead in battle. His song first described the morning star (xomáce′ kovátai′ᵃ, "big star"), which in some undefined way is connected with war. Just what was his function in battle was not ascertained. The last of such leaders among the Maricopa was named ḳa′ḳaiðo′.

The bearer of the feathered pike was a functionary known alike to Maricopa and Halchidhoma, and was represented among other lower Colorado tribes. He assumed no-flight obligations which placed him in the forefront of battle and in that sense was a war leader. But while Forde describes the pike of the Yuma as a battle standard sometimes planted in the ground and about which the forces rallied,[12] my informants explicitly and repeatedly denied this function among the Gila River tribes. The pike was carried by a man selected as the best warrior; quite infrequently two men had them. He used it as his weapon, supplemented by a club, and carried no shield. He was not the war captain, nor a dreamer. Carrying it entailed what was practically a no-flight obligation: the bearer must go always forward, never retreat. He was credited with fearlessness: even though his companions retreated, he rushed forward into the enemy's midst, to seize them by the hair and club them to death. Black paint covered his body and was drawn in a band across his eyes. His bangs were daubed red. At his death the pike was destroyed

[12] Forde, *Yuma Ethnography*, pp. 167, 265.

with the remainder of his personal belongings. Whether his position was transmitted was not disclosed.

This pike was a mesquite shaft, pointed at one or both ends, encircled at intervals by bands of red and black paint, and bearing pendent feathers. Kutox gave contradictory evidence regarding details: he stated that it was in length the height of its bearer, again that it was four to five feet long; that it was pointed at one end, again at both. A specimen which he had made for me (Pl. XIII, a)[13] is pointed at one end only and is forty-three inches in length. Another specimen made by Charlie Redbird is pointed at one end alone. The feathers were the largest plumes of buzzard and eagle, each bound individually to the shaft, leaving a space free for a hand grip at the middle. Halchidhoma and Maricopa made such pikes identically and alike called them hukwili'c.

Armament consisted of bows, short wooden clubs, and circular shields. Rarely a man might arm himself with a wooden pike. A warrior carried either bow, or club and shield; never both. Clubmen and bowmen went into battle as separate divisions; the clubmen always grouped to march in front, the bowmen following.[14] Each of these companies was said to have had its leader, presumably a spontaneous leader, since the absence of any special designation for them argues against formality of their status.

WAR DANCE AND SPEECHES

The night before setting out for war there was always a war dance (hupi'l‚ĭg). Everyone participated: women, old and young, as well as the warriors who would comprise the party. Songs of all kinds were sung, "because they might lose some of their men and this would be the last time they would ever hear these songs." These followed one another through the night. Toward morning, when the dances were over, everybody left. Meanwhile some women had prepared provisions for the war party. This consisted principally of ground parched wheat.

[13] Washington State Museum, No. 2–11918.

[14] This division aligns with Pima and Havasupai habit. But at least clubmen were not paired with bowmen in the manner of the Havasupai (Spier, *Havasupai Ethnography*, p. 250; Russell, *Pima Indians*, pp. 120, 202).

The songs may not have been peculiar to this occasion. Informants mentioned vuspo", "deserted," ce, "buzzard," and vitaʀi'c, "mountain killdeer," which were sung at other times as well. The Maricopa had pipa', "people," for both war and scalp dances; the Halchidhoma, hwĭcĭvau', "enemy standing." Ivȧðo' was named as peculiarly appropriate: the song of a stinging insect living by the rivers. But these three may also have been used at other times.

Pipa' told how the enemy fled for refuge and how they were found and brought as captives. It told ironically how, instead of being badly treated, they were well cared for; how a captive's father shed tears, not in sorrow, but for joy. Hwĭcĭvau', "standing up an enemy," told how a father acted when one of his family was taken prisoner or killed.

The dance forms varied with the songs. For Buzzard, there were two opposing rows of men and women alternately, who moved backward and forward together. Anyone, young or old, took part. In the middle of one row was the singer flanked by a man on each side, all three provided with rattles. Killdeer had also a definite dance form, or more than one, but it does not seem that the description fits the war dance performance (p. 231). Deserted and Ivȧðo' were songs without dancing: for the first, men and women remained seated, beating time with sticks on baskets; for Ivȧðo', they simply sat in rings.

It was assumed that before the war party set out, the shaman who was to accompany them had dreamed of their success. As they neared the enemy he exercised his clairvoyant power in the manner described below (p. 176) to reveal the location of the enemy. This was less necessary in the case of the Yuma, who lived in the open valley, than the Yavapai, who lay scattered among the mountains.

Four set speeches were always delivered to the out-bound warriors by one who had dreamed of the mocking bird. These were known as xwĭmtcȧkwe'ʀᵃ, "enemy speech." In content, if not in form, they were highly formalized. The first speech, delivered the night before they set out, encouraged them to go. It told that they would go together and help one another. The next night, when they had stopped to rest, the orator would tell how everyone wished them good fortune. The subject of the third night's speech was how anxious they were to see the enemy and how they would fare. On the fourth night he would exhort them to be indifferent; to throw themselves on the enemy or all return together. "We have come to fight the enemy and whatever becomes of us will be all right. If we are killed, we die with honor, but we may succeed in taking a scalp." Four speeches must represent an ideal form: how it was adjusted to the days actually necessary to move to the attack, I do not know. It took twice that time to reach the Yuma; the Yavapai were met within a day or two. But it does indicate how formal was the whole war procedure.[15]

Orators used in all speeches the abrupt, staccato, forced delivery described for Mohave and Yuma.[16] There is now no living orator. Last Star described the manner of speaking as follows:

When an orator called to the people in the morning, telling them to go for their day's food, his first three or four utterances were said slowly and quietly, then the rest was spoken forcibly, abruptly, and loudly.

PITCHED BATTLES AND RAIDS

So far as present information goes two quite different methods of warfare were used against Yuma-Mohave and Yavapai-Apache. At least the circumstantial detail given in what follows strongly indicates this. What it means in effect is that the Maricopa adapted themselves to the methods with which they had to contend: the highly formal pitched battle arranged by the lower Colorado tribes in contrast to the foray into the mountains against Yavapai and Apache. This does not mean that the element of surprise attack was lacking in the former nor that the latter lacked artificialities.

The pitched battle against the lower river tribes was attended by large forces on either side, who, if not succeeding in attempted surprise, gave notice of their intention, arranging for open hand-to-hand combat. Thus, the Pima annals record that

[15] The Pima shared this delivery of four formal speeches on as many nights on the warpath but it does not seem that the content was the same (Russell, *Pima Indians*, p. 202).

[16] Forde, *Yuma Ethnography*, p. 209.

the Yuma sent a messenger to the approaching Maricopa asking them to fight only with clubs, to which the latter agreed. He conducted them across the Colorado to where the Yuma waited.[17] As the contenders drew near, marching as compact groups, they halted, scratched a line on the ground, and stood along it facing each other.[18] Champions now sprang forward on each side to hurl insulting challenges at their opponents, until they had worked to the pitch of clashing in single combat. As soon as it appeared one of the champions was about to be bested, the whole body rushed forward in the wake of the victor. They met breast to breast in the mêlée, whacking away until their opponents were annihilated or broke and ran.[19] As soon as the battle was joined, there was no skirmishing, no flights of arrows; it was simple beating down of the foe with staves or short clubs. Mohave, Yuma, and Maricopa accounts all agree that of the several hundred engaged on each side not more than a handful of the vanquished, a half-dozen or a score, were left after the battle. It does not seem possible, that, as tradition relates, this type of warfare could have gone on from time immemorial. All of the nations alike would sooner or later have been reduced in numbers or wholly exterminated. That this actually happened in the case of the Halchidhoma, Kohuana, and Halyikwamai must mean that they always met overwhelming odds.

The challengers, who may not have been the actual champions, had their ability by reason of having dreamed of the mocking bird, that is, they were speechmakers. They marched along the long line drawn before their party, shouting insults at their opponents, whirling their bows in the air or dragging them with one end bouncing on the ground to make them dance up and down. Their performance duplicated their dream experience. The line represented a mountain, the long Sierra Estrella. They, like the mocking bird spirit of their dreams who led them the

[17] Russell, *Pima Indians*, p. 40.

[18] This is reminiscent of the Hopi in 1540, who stood on such a line to face Coronado's soldiers (Winship, *The Coronado Expedition*, p. 488).

[19] The whole affair is reflected in the pseudo-historic tale of the Dog Champion (p. 396).

length of the sierra, went shouting the whole distance without taking a breath.[20] Other dreamers too assumed this part, like the man who dreamed of his dog as a champion.[21] The verbal interchange at the time the Yuma and Mohave descended on the Maricopa in 1857 is characteristic.

The Yuma boasted they had been to the Cocopa three days before and killed everyone there.[22] They said they had come to stay a few weeks and marry [to trifle with?] some girls. The Halchidhoma champion replied, "When a girl wants to marry, she goes somewhere to stay a few weeks. So I think you came because we are handsome men. We will keep you three or four weeks, and if we do not like you, we will turn you away." Each side was implying that their opponents were women. When the Maricopa champion marched up and down, he said he had always been successful in battle; he would annihilate the whole Yuma tribe even though he die in the attempt. He was actually killed in the fight.

While the line that was drawn may have been a mark beyond which the enemy were dared to come, it was thought of as a mountain magically raised to give protection. The same device was used to impede runners in intertribal races (p. 335). When the Halchidhoma and Maricopa were surrounded by the Yuma in the latter's territory, they drew a circle around themselves.

How far the combat was a formal game is evidenced by their attitude toward the surviving enemy. When a single foe remained ("a very fierce fighter") they did not think it fair for all to attack together. They surrounded him; then one would go forward alone. When the enemy shot, the attacker parried the arrow with his shield, or, watching carefully, jumped aside. As this man marched deliberately forward, he began to count slowly, meaning that he would kill the enemy before he had counted four. "He always killed the enemy before he reached the fourth count."

A man who attacked a single foeman like this was one who had dreamed of it. He dreamed that as he approached some fierce animals (bears or mountain lions), they suddenly became quiet, so that he could reach them. So it would be with the enemy. If, on the contrary, he had dreamed the animals chased him, he would fail in this single combat. As usual, the Maricopa thought

[20] See p. 247.   [21] P. 396.

[22] Cf. Kroeber, *Handbook*, pp. 745, 751.

that success or failure must have been prefigured in a dream: "he did not tell his dream before he began, but might tell it much later when describing his battles."

The tactics of the Maricopa differed somewhat from their river foes. They made some use of cavalry, but wholly ineffectually. Their mounted men were elderly individuals and boys who went behind the footmen to encourage them and to charge. But the narratives relate how they sat their horses waiting for the outcome and charged through the mass, comprised of friend and foe together, depending on the weight of their steeds rather than any finesse of their arms. They too went down under the flailing clubs or were dragged from their seats to be butchered.

It is also astonishing that the Maricopa were backward in adopting the long staves which gave their Yuma opponents so much advantage. Beyond providing themselves at the last moment with poles, as the narratives relate, they depended wholly on their short clubs. This is intelligible if it meant learning definite procedure in fencing and parrying with these pole-length clubs, like the quarter-staff play of English yeomen, but there is no hint of such stereotyped handling of the weapons from Yuma sources.[23] My account also states that Yuma women and lads similarly armed gave support to their men, but it is noteworthy that nothing of the sort is said about the Maricopa when the Yuma and Mohave attacked them. What may have been a counter attempt of the Yuma to adopt Maricopa methods is implied in my Halchidhoma informant's statement that when the Yuma came in 1857, they did not use staves but their bows (and short clubs?) alone.

Not all conflicts with the Yuma were pitched battles. Occasionally a small body of raiders would visit the Yuma villages to do what damage they could (see p. 46).

Elementary strategy was sometimes employed. The warriors might be divided into three or four groups to approach the enemy village from as many directions. Then, when the enemy came out to attack the first party discovered, the others would rush the village.

[23] Cf. Forde, *Yuma Ethnography*, p. 170.

Once when the Maricopa went to attack a Yuma village situated opposite the present town of Yuma, they were discovered while still on the east bank. They arranged for a few men to go forward openly toward the village. The Yuma crossed the river and pursued this small body. When they had been drawn some distance from the village, the main body of Maricopa, who had remained hidden in the brush, then rushed to attack the pursuers from the rear. The women in the village shouted warnings to their men. When the Yuma heard this, they turned back to meet the second body. But the Yuma were surrounded and nearly annihilated. Those who escaped discarded their bows and plunged into the Colorado despite its high banks. The Maricopa did not attack the village on the farther bank.

It was held that such strategies must have been dreamed by the leader. "If he was successful, he must have dreamed it."

From the time of the creation, people quarreled.[24] So the Mohave took the Yuma on their side to help in their fights as children do. Our people [Halchidhoma] did the same: they took the Walapai and Mission Indians [Cahuilla] on their side. When the creator died, people scattered, but they still had those enmities. That was how the Yuma and Maricopa came to fight.

The Maricopa started to war with the Yuma [possibly in 1838]. They reached the Colorado late in the afternoon. Two or three Yuma, who were fishing at a little stream, saw the Maricopa approaching. These men told them to stop and go home, else they would be annihilated. Even the bravest warriors declared that they should return, since the Yuma already knew of their coming. Some of our people urged the older men to fight. They took willow limbs and beat them to force them to do it. They had not yet decided whether to go on, when two Yuma came up carrying a Maricopa scalp. They bore it on a long pole, dancing up and down on the bank. Then one elderly Maricopa declared the scalp was that of his brother. He said that even though he went alone, he was going to fight the Yuma. So all declared they would fight on account of the scalp. These were the best warriors we ever had. All said they would fight because if they retreated it would be to their shame.

They started westward across the Colorado. The Yuma had long poles for clubs, a little above their heads in length. Every man, woman, and child had such a staff. Before the Maricopa crossed, they saw the Yuma carrying torches; going off to collect their forces. This continued all night. Toward morning the Maricopa knew the Yuma had all collected opposite. They knew they would be killed, but determined nevertheless to fight them. Better to kill an enemy and be killed in turn than to return without fighting.

Where they crossed the river were some Yavapai armed with bows on the bank in front of the Yuma. A great many of our best men were shot as they were crossing.

[24] These narratives were given by Kutox, the Halchidhoma informant. Another is recorded on p. 245. For Mohave and Yuma accounts of the affair of 1857, see Kroeber, *Handbook*, p. 753; Gifford, *Yuma Dreams*, p. 63; Ives, *Report upon the Colorado River of the West*, p. 45; *Report of the Commissioner of Indian Affairs for 1857*, p. 300; see also Cremony, *Life among the Apaches*, p. 148; Russell, *Pima Indians*, p. 46 *et supra*.

They marched to close with the enemy. Some had hip-length clubs but these were not long enough. Before they were close enough to use them, the Yuma beat them down with their long staves. Our men, striking at legs and hips, brought some of them down. But as the Yuma had much longer clubs, they knocked down a good many of our men with one blow. The Yuma had all put mud over their faces and bodies, down which they had scratched lines with their fingers, so that they should recognize their men in the fight. Both sides came up in several ranks, until they stood so thick one could hardly get through. As those in the front rank were knocked down, the men behind would step into their places.

Our men had a few horsemen with them, perhaps twenty or fewer. These rode once through the mob of Yuma and once back again. They charged through twice and no more. No one knew what became of our horsemen; perhaps the Yuma pulled them down and killed them.

This left our clubmen standing in a group, surrounded by Yuma, men, women, and children. The battle began about nine or ten in the morning and lasted until late in the afternoon. By that time all our people had been killed except two or three of the two hundred or more who went there. These few crawled back under their own men's legs as they fought the Yuma. That is how they were saved. (It is shameful to tell this, for these were the very ones who coaxed the others to give fight.)

Soon after that the Yuma came to our village near Sacate to fight. They had about the same number of men as we had at this village, and about one hundred Mohave came to help them. Our bravest warriors had been killed but we had some left, so the Yuma decided to come here to exterminate the whole tribe. The enemy and our people lined up a short distance apart. A Yuma walked up and down in front of their line, saying that he had come to live with the Maricopa, to be friends; that he had brought his men to take care of [rape] all the widows [they would create]. Then our man said that he had thought of going to the Yuma villages to take care of all the widows there, but thought he had better wait for some childish people to come to play with him. He might play a day or two, then he would start for the Colorado.

After the talk was ended, both sides shot at each other. Then the Maricopa sent word to the Halchidhoma, who lived [to the east] near Sacate, and to the Pima. Shortly after the fighting began, the Mohave deserted. When the Yuma saw the Halchidhoma and Pima horsemen arriving by hundreds, they felt afraid and fled. The Maricopa drove the Yuma toward the Gila, but killed nearly all before they had gone far. Only a few men escaped: some count five, some six.

The second trip of our people against the Yuma was much like the first. I was one year old at the time [1847 or 1848]. They crossed the Colorado, went north and then west, before circling back to the river. This was in the early morning before dawn. They were fairly certain that no one had seen them cross the river. Their idea was to return toward the bank, and if they found no one, to recross the river and return home. But the Yuma, who had discovered their tracks, gathered in a great crowd near the bank to cut them off. When they found themselves discovered, some went off to cut long poles for clubs. The Yuma again had long staves with which they easily beat down our men. Our men dropped so rapidly this time that the Yuma were sure all would be slain by noon. By that time there were but twenty or fewer of the Maricopa, but they kept up the fight until late afternoon, although completely surrounded by Yuma. Only a single Maricopa escaped this time; one who had cowardly fled to the other bank. He crossed the Colorado while the others fought, and hid in the bushes where he heard all that was said.

The second time the Yuma came here I was about nine years old [1857]. I can remember it pretty well. There were about three hundred Yuma with a few Yavapai and Mohave. We heard them coming early in the morning. All our women and children fled to viva'vĭs [Pima Butte near Sacate]. This time the Yuma and Mohave did not push on, but stopped at the first house of the village. Some were sent into the houses to collect all the food stored in them. Then they prepared something to eat, since they had come without eating. They remained there all morning.

Our men then tried to scare them away. But instead of retreating the Yuma advanced. The Maricopa of this village sent for the Halchidhoma and Pima again. Then the two parties clashed. But when the Yuma saw the horsemen arriving one by one, lines of them converging on the battle, they thought they were lost. At noon they fled. This time, instead of forcing the Yuma down to the river, the allies drove them south [southwest?] to the mountains [probably the Sierra Estrella]. The slain lay in piles, struck down as they fled. Only a few were left. These went on southward until they almost reached the foot of the mountain. The Maricopa left it to a few clubmen to finish these Yuma, but when they saw they might escape, the horsemen ran them down, so that those with clubs could beat them to death. Not one escaped this time.

Six years after this they made peace. I was then sixteen years old.

At the two attacks on the Yuma, there were only Maricopa and Halchidhoma. The Pima claim that some of them took part, but it was not so.

On another occasion before Kutox was born they attacked the Yuma. They were coming back without an engagement when they met the Yuma halfway between the Colorado and Gila Bend. The Yuma had circled around them to approach from the east. With the Maricopa were two Mexicans, one named pau̯ᵃlĭn. The Maricopa could swim the Colorado, which was in flood, but the Mexicans could not. They were put on a raft formed of two logs with tules laid across, together with clothing, provisions, and drinking water, which the Mexicans paddled. But when they had almost crossed, the raft struck a snag, turned over, and one was drowned. The other was left for dead after the battle. Late in the day, he rose and attempted to follow the Maricopa tracks home. He got lost in the desert. Nine months later he wandered into the Maricopa village. Shoes and clothing were worn out: he was footsore. With bits of wood and strips of his clothing he had made makeshift sandals.

An account of an attack by Mohave was told as an example of the anecdotes told by the Maricopa to demonstrate the ludicrous behavior of the Halchidhoma, although the narrator (Kutox) was himself an Halchidhoma. The incident relates to a party of Halchidhoma who in the midwinter following their return to the Gila from Mexico, that is, about 1835, were visiting at Gila Bend.

The Halchidhoma men were assembled in the meeting house where they had been singing all night. When nearly dawn, the Mohave arrived in great numbers. A woman grinding outside repeatedly warned them. They did not heed; only told her to save herself. As people fled by the house, they put their heads inside and told the inmates to get their bows. But the old men only sang the louder with each warning until they could be heard at a great distance.

The singing brought the Mohave crowding around the house. They did not enter but broke holes in the walls to shoot through and crowded about the doorway to shoot in. Finally those inside—there were about one hundred—said, "It is not right for us to be burned in the house. Let us go out to fight like men." They called to the Mohave to clear away from the entrance. They painted their hair red and drew a black band across the eyes. They came out three abreast, moved forward a little so that three more could follow, and so on. They fought for a while but were all killed.

The Mohave cut off the heads of every one and carried them to the village, where they camped. They scalped the heads. They built a big fire in a hole, and when it had burned to coals, placed the heads around the fire, as one bakes pumpkins, as an insult. They warmed them on each side, raked away the coals, and baked the heads on the ground like pumpkins.

Raids against the Yavapai and their Apache neighbors may have been undertaken by large bodies of men but it is quite unlikely that they mustered for this purpose anything like the number who set out against the Yuma. Still the indications are that their number was frequently considerable, certainly more than the Yavapai were accustomed to send against them. The reason is obvious enough: a handful of Yavapai marauders were sufficient to pick off the more or less concentrated and settled Maricopa, where a far larger number was required for any effective campaign against these scattered, migratory mountain dwellers. Punitive expeditions into the mountains must have been far more infrequent than Yavapai attacks.

In this type of warfare the methods resembled those of the Yavapai themselves; a secret concentration near the enemy, a surprise attack, and an immediate return. The impression is that bows were used far more than in battles with the river Yumans. Battle formation was described as a line of bowmen, who were nevertheless close to the enemy for the reason that the arrows neither carried far nor were especially effective. Dependence was still on the short club. It seems probable that there was again something of a division of function, bowmen separate from clubmen; at least it was said several clubmen would proceed together. Half the party was said to have been mounted in these engagements.

Bartlett saw a party set out against the enemy north of the Salt River in July 1852. "Their arms were solely the bow and arrow: most of them had a skin quiver hung across their backs; though a few carried their arrows in their girdles." And in speaking of Pima-Maricopa armament in general, he wrote, "The only weapon used by these tribes is the bow and arrow. The short club of the Yumas and the long lance of the Apaches I never saw among them. The constant use of this weapon has rendered them excellent marksmen. Even the boys are very expert in the use of it."[25]

Moving northward toward the mountains, they would start out slowly and camp hidden in the thickets of the Salt River bottom. During the night the journey was resumed, bringing them near the enemy toward dawn. There they would rest all day. Late in the afternoon they moved to the actual attack. Only a little ground parched wheat was carried for provisions. Rabbits might be killed on the way; these were roasted if it was safe.

A clairvoyant was always included in the party; one who had dreamed of Buzzard or Coyote. While they were resting in the mountains, an older man would ask him to locate the enemy. Everyone must be quiet: the horsemen would lead their horses aside. The clairvoyant, standing beside a fire in the center of the circle of seated men, proceeded to smoke four cigarettes. By the time he had finished smoking the first, he thought he was lifted off the ground a little. With the second and third, he was still higher, and when the fourth was finished, he dropped as though dead. After a few minutes he sat up. The man who had requested his aid now lit a cigarette to give him. The clairvoyant would then tell how Buzzard had taken him to the highest mountain to reveal the location and numbers of the enemy; had told him from which direction to approach, how easily he would find and kill them. The warriors then set off, led by this man.

When they reached the enemy, all rushed forward to see who would kill the first enemy. If the enemy were surprised asleep, everyone in the camp was killed, three or four families. They did not look on a slain enemy's face any more than was necessary. As soon as they knew he was dead, they faced toward home, with their backs turned to the corpse and to the mountains, which were also conceived as enemies.[26] Apparently they were quite

[25] *Personal Narrative*, II, 217, 237.   [26] See p. 253.

satisfied with the killing and scalping of a single enemy. They preferred, if possible, to scalp their victim alive: together they rushed the man selected, sat on him, and cut away the scalp. It was sometimes taken from the dead, but "they do not call that a brave deed." Immediately it was thrown into the air and allowed to fall to earth. (It was not kicked in Yuma fashion and the singing and dancing which Cocopa and Yuma indulge in at this point were absent.)

As soon as they were ready to return one of the younger lads was dispatched with the news, whereupon everyone gathered at the meeting house to await them. Some of the old people might join in expressing their happiness by such songs as Ivàðo' and Mountain Killdeer.

Only a man who had dreamed of it could scalp, hence the taking of a single scalp was sufficient to establish the fulfillment of his dream. His dreams were of winning battles against fearful animals. If he had not the requisite dream, no man, no matter how brave, would take a scalp. There was a saying that if he had not dreamed but forced himself to take a scalp, the dead enemy would grin, so that he would flee in fear. Scalps were exceptionally dangerous: they caused paralysis unless those that took them or handled them underwent the purification described below.

The scalps taken were those with long fine hair: not all the slain were scalped. They took the whole skin of the upper half of the head cut away just below [sic] the eyes and above the ears. (The scalp was hie'ðau'g, "hair taken.") Sometimes the ears were taken separately, but not the whole head nor other parts of the body.

Dead foemen were eaten by the Yavapai, according to Kutox; a practice quite willingly corroborated by Mr. E. W. Gifford's Southeastern Yavapai informant[27] and recorded by Dr. Kroeber for the more northerly Yavapai. The Maricopa and Halchidhoma never did (nor, according to Kutox's knowledge, the Yuma and Mohave), not so much because of repugnance as because

[27] Who, however, accused the Maricopa of the practice (Gifford, *Southeastern Yavapai*, p. 186).

they feared it would cripple the eater. The enemy were believed "diseased": scalps, captives, and those who had taken or slain an enemy, all had to undergo a lengthy purification.

Two accounts of the practice which may refer to the same case were obtained from Kutox. Once before he was born some Halchidhoma from the Maricopa Wells district were on their way to the Kaveltcadom at Gila Bend. (This places the incident between 1835 and 1845.) Just west of the Sierra Estrella they were surrounded by Yavapai and Apache, who killed all twenty, carrying off a woman and her child. They took them northward to the mountains, where they cooked and ate the child. Kutox has seen the place. All their allies were invited to this. In the early evening they made the woman and the little girl dance. They then dug a long pit in which they burned logs until reduced to coals, on which they roasted a deer. They dragged the screaming girl away from her mother, and held her down on the coals until she died. Then each ate a piece of deer flesh and that of the girl. The woman later escaped and returned home.

Four women went to gather mesquite. One, who was somewhat apart from the others, had a girl of seven with her. The Yavapai caught these two and hurried them off to the mountains. They called all men and women together and danced beside a big fire. When the fire had burned down, they threw the little girl on the ashes and roasted her alive. The woman lived with the Yavapai for some time before she had an opportunity to run away. She said they had forcibly made her eat part of the girl's flesh.

Shamans also accompanied war parties to heal the wounded. These were not general practitioners, but those who had the proper dreams for wounds (p. 287).

Those who were killed in enemy territory were cremated on the spot if possible. The pyre was quietly built at night and as soon as well ablaze they left the spot. No attempt was made to carry the ashes home.

On one occasion the Maricopa went to fight west of or below Fort McDowell. The war leader chose a number of men to accompany him. A scout sent forward was seen by the enemy. Almost caught, he abandoned his horse and fled to warn the approaching Maricopa. These returned south of the Salt River, where they camped. In the evening the leader spoke, expressing his disappointment that his plan had miscarried, but saying they would try again. He argued that since the Yavapai had taken the horse, they would feast on it through the night. Perhaps they could be attacked when they finally fell asleep. At midnight the Maricopa again moved close to the Yavapai encampment and sent a spy ahead. He found that the Yavapai had feasted on the horse and, near morning, reported them asleep. The Maricopa then attacked and killed all the enemy. Since this event the locality has been known as xukávĭ'k tatápoi'ic, "the returning and killing."

Kutox's account of his own experience about 1865 also illustrates the character of this fighting with the mountain tribes.

A hundred Pima and as many Maricopa were given guns by the soldiers and sent travelling over the mountains, but killed never an enemy. The Yavapai had come down and killed some whites and their mules, taken the harness and burned the wagons. The Pima-Maricopa went to Fort McDowell, where they stayed a year looking for Yavapai. They came over to Sacate near the Maricopa villages where they heard Yavapai were stealing horses.

They pursued the Yavapai. There were three of them, armed one with a gun, another a bow, the third a sword. Some followed their tracks directly northward toward the mountains. Others, a large number including the boy Kutox, circled to get ahead of them.

The three Yavapai walked along side by side. When someone rushed at them, they turned to face him and the one with the gun made as though to shoot. Those following came up with them first, but no one dared go close. They continued following. Toward morning the three came to where Kutox's party was. Kutox started toward them to see if he could not beat one down. The man with the gun was facing those following, so he thought he would chance it. But as he drew near, the bowman turned on him; so he retreated. The one with the sword disappeared; perhaps crawled under a bush. The man with the gun walked backward, holding off his pursuers, so they kept trying for the bowman. Kutox tried again. Just as he got close, someone at a distance shot the Yavapai. He tried to rise, but Kutox dismounted and hit him on the head with a stone, killing him. (Because of this Kutox would have had to undergo purification when he returned, so he gave the credit to the one who had shot the Y. vapai, "rather than starve", he said.[28]) This was at early dawn.

They knew two had escaped, so they scattered to search. Kutox felt very sleepy. He came close to a giant cactus, which he mistook for an enemy. He was afraid, so he dismounted and ran away. This has always been told as a joke on him.

PURIFICATION

The theme that physical contact with the enemy was defiling threads through all the proceedings that follow on the return of the war party. The enemy, his scalp, his women and children who were made captives were all extremely dangerous. They were "diseased"; they brought sickness to such as touched them; they had potentialities for harm of a magical order. Once struck down, the very sight of the enemy must be hurriedly avoided. Even the mountains of his land, spiritually his in a literal sense, must no longer be looked on. This was clearly not for fear of the dead as such, for they had no comparable strong concern for their own dead, but because the enemy had maleficent powers on his side. All persons and things that had had intimate contact with him must undergo a stringent rite of purification (mata-

[28] Gifford recorded the same yielding of credit among the Cocopa. The one who took the credit had to undergo purification (Cocopa Ms).

Rằě′k): those who had slain an enemy, those who had taken scalps or captives, and the captives, the scalps, and their permanent keeper. The sentiment was not foreign in other fields of Maricopa thought. Eagle feathers were not casually gathered: they had to be purified by a shaman before they could be used. One had to tread softly, speak circumspectly, move slowly, where mountain sheep were concerned.

It is not wholly clear that such sentiments held with respect to all enemies. All references to the necessity for purification I gathered were to the Yavapai and Apache: not once during the more numerous references to the Yuma and Mohave was it mentioned. Unfortunately I neglected to direct questions to the point.

When the war party was ready to return from the mountains, one of the younger boys was sent ahead to carry news that they had killed the enemy. Some of the men at home then hastily built huts in preparation for their coming. These were close to the Gila at some distance from the village. They were like those built for the girls' puberty rites, with their openings always to the east. It was also essential that they stand in a row, but the direction of the row was immaterial. One hut was built for each man who had killed an enemy, taken his scalp, or made a captive.

Such men did not return with the main group of warriors, but followed. They walked slowly in single file and preserved an absolute silence. Sometimes the warriors ahead would try to scare them, to shake them from this course, but the killers always marched on slowly. Even when the whole group stopped for the night, these men camped at a distance.

Before they started home, these men twisted their hair into a knot behind, and thrust into it some sharpened twigs of ivusĭ, a medicinal plant, as hairpins. Another such stick for a scratcher was stuck into the side hair. If they used their fingers, their hands would get sore. This scratcher was about six inches in length: to the butt a bundle of feathers (for wiping the face) was attached by a short willow bark cord. These men must not spit on the ground but into the middle of a bush, because the spirit of the enemy was following and would breathe it up, causing them to fall sick. All the way home they were given very little to eat and drink.

When they reached the Salt River they drank all they could. Then an older man raised each one up and ran a well scraped arrowweed down his throat to make him vomit. They then stooped again and rinsed their mouths without drinking. They approached the river still in single file and preserved this order in whatever they did. When the first finished drinking, the second stood on the same spot, and so on.

From this point their sixteen days of purification began. At the Salt River each one bathed. When they arrived at home, they entered the huts prepared for them in the order they had been marching. There they remained fasting for the sixteen days, being given only a little soup of mesquite bean flour, and that only at dawn as the sun barely showed above the horizon.

The program of the sixteen-day period was divided into sets of four days. Beginning with the Salt River crossing, they bathed every morning of the sixteen before dawn. At night, for the second four days, each man daubed his head with a mixture of mud and boiled mesquite bark; for the third set of four, with mud alone; for the fourth set like the first, this was omitted and only the customary morning bath was required.

During this time, a man who had scalped hardly let the scalp out of his hand. Every time he bathed he carried it into the water: when he slept he laid it on his chest. At the end of the whole period he gave it into the keeping of an old man, a former warrior, who as the custodian of all scalps, placed it with others in a large jar stored in the meeting house.

Every evening of the sixteen, old warriors went to the huts to talk to the men undergoing purification. They continued their harangues until midnight. They told them to be kind and agreeable to everyone, not to steal nor beg, not to be lazy.

The hut was left at the end of the sixteenth night. The occupant rose early on the following morning and returned to his dwelling. He did not enter it until just as the sun appeared. He walked in straightway and seated himself at the back, facing the west, with his back to the family. He slept in the dwelling and ate when the family did, but during all his waking hours for the next four days he maintained this position. From time to time other men would visit to see if they could make him laugh at their remarks. Each of these days he also bathed before dawn. This terminated the purification. "By the end of these twenty days, he was so thin as to be scarcely recognizable." The whole performance had to be gone through should he again kill an enemy.

Not many captives seem to have been taken. This was certainly not an objective of their warfare. Small boys were made captive, less commonly girls and women, but larger lads were killed because, being able to escape, they might lead the enemy against their captors. Women were seldom taken for the same reason. When they were captured, they were always hurried off to sell in Mexico. Children were usually kept until they too were old enough to sell.

Captives were thought to carry sickness which would fall on the captor unless he got rid of them or they were purified. A child was immediately handed over to an older man to rear. Women and girls were given into the custody of old men, who, since they had not much longer to live, might chance the danger of keeping them. As with the Mohave, who had the identical reason,[29] it seems fairly certain that captive women were not violated.

Purification for the captive was much like that of the captor. The child was given very little food and made to bathe and put mud over his hair for the twenty days. It was kept away from the family for this period; made to sleep in a separate part of the dwelling, and they dared not eat from the same bowl with it.

Children were sometimes kept for life, reared by the men they had been given to as members of their families. The owner's daughter might interpose on behalf of a little girl of whom she grew fond. Boys were brought up with the thought that ultimately they would serve as guides and fight against their own

[29] Kroeber, *Handbook*, p. 752.

people. Some people would pity them; those who reared them were kind; others outside the family might abuse them. But abuse ceased and their foreign origin was forgotten after these boys and girls had married Maricopa. Several Maricopa now living are known to have Yavapai blood, possibly all derived from a single captive ancestress.

A grown girl was captured from the Apache [Yavapai?]. Her owners treated her exactly as their own daughter. She rode with us against the Apache, showing the way. When she first arrived she was unintelligible, but by the time she was grown she could speak Maricopa and Pima.

Captives were collectively known as n$_y$ixu′alyacϑu′m, "———— taken be mistreated" (n$_y$ixu′, meaningless ?; alyac, "to mistreat," as by throwing dirt; ϑu′m, "to take"); a single captive, n$_y$ixu′-alyaϑau′. A captive who had been kept for a long time was called n$_y$ixu′alyikω′ʀĭc, "old captive" (from n$_y$ikω′ʀᵃ, "old," "ancient").[30]

[30] It seems probable that the last is the original of the term for captives used in the Spanish documents, *nixoras* (*niforas*). By its context the word seems to have been derived from the Yuman tongues. Font (1775) wrote: "They [the Yuma] usually . . . . try to capture a few children in order to take them out to sell in the lands of the Spaniards. These captives are called Nixoras by us in Sonora, no matter where they come from." But while here the word appears Sonoran, hence presumably Piman, he corrects this impression later (see below). Anza, for his part, wrote as though the Nixoras constituted a separate tribe: thus, in enumerating the personnel of the expedition of 1775, he listed "five interpreters of the Pima, Yuma, Cajuenchi, and Nifora languages," and in a letter of December, 1775, "This tribe [Cocomaricopa?], together with the preceding tribes and the Halchedunes, Niforas, Cahuenches, and others." But Font specifically corrects this: "I asked him [Anza] to tell me how he understood the entry which he knew he had made in his diary, that is to say, 'five interpreters for five tribes,' for I did not find more than three, and four at the most, counting as a servant of his an interpreter of the Pima tribe. . . . . The fact is that in order to heap up the salaries he had listed one as an interpreter of the Nixora tribe, though there is no such tribe; for in the Pimería they call Nixoras the Indians whom the tribes of the interior in their wars capture amongst themselves, and whom afterwards the Yumas and Pápagos bring to El Altar and other places to sell as captives or slaves, no matter what tribe they may belong to." As a matter of fact, Anza nowhere else wrote of the Nixoras as a tribe. Garcés several times used the name as a tribal designation, but with vagueness; he finally assigned "Niforas or Cuilsnivors or Naxi" to those Yavapai (or better upland Yumans) living northeast of the Halchidhoma. But there is no conviction to be derived from his usage that this was actually a tribal name (Bolton, *Anza's California Expeditions*, II, 382; III, 2; IV, 102, 513; V, 305).

The scalp dance, which followed the sixteen days of purification, comprised a dance by day, followed by singing throughout the night. Old men and women alone took part, even the men who had taken scalps being excluded with other young people. The old women alone danced, but they as well as the men took part in the night performance.

The scalp was mounted on a tall pole by an old man, its permanent keeper. The performance derived its named from this, "enemy standing" (hwĭcĭvau'). Had an enemy been slain while raiding the village his corpse was mounted on another post beside it, facing the east, tied upright as high as could be managed.[31] There it would stay until it rotted away. The scalp had been previously prepared. It was fastened to a deerskin-faced hoop and the hair redressed in Maricopa style, with a feather on top and white lines drawn across the long braids. Every morning for sixteen days the scalper had washed it while he bathed, in order that by this purification it might become one of themselves, no longer an enemy. This accounts for the redressing in Maricopa style.

A ring of participants was formed around the pole with the singer and his helpers beside it. The old women wore their finery, painting their faces always with a black mask-like stripe across the eyes like warriors painted for battle. The circle of women moved counterclockwise facing the scalp, clasping one another's hands. Some would point at the scalp; others throw dirt at it. They yelled and howled in mockery, pretending their own scalps had been taken. The old men outside their circle joined in the cries. Captive children were also made to take part, being stripped naked and forced by the women to run about in the circle. A child too small to run well had its arms squeezed till it screamed and was forced to run until it could barely stagger. The dance continued all day.

[31] The Pima annals mention the Maricopa tying an Apache corpse to a post (apparently distant from their village) where it was allowed to remain. On another occasion the Pima strangled an Apache captive and left her body tied to a post (Russell, *Pima Indians*, pp. 49, 50, 203). Browne in 1864 saw a "crucified" Apache near Maricopa Wells (*Adventures in the Apache Country*, p. 104).

Singing alone comprised the night performance within the meeting house, where the scalp had been set on a short post just within the doorway. (The Maricopa never danced in this house.) The old women joined the men in singing on this occasion, although normally they never attended formal gatherings in the meeting house. The singers used rattles or beat and scraped on overturned baskets by way of accompaniment as the songs dictated. The singing continued throughout the night.

There seem to have been no songs peculiar to the scalp dance with the possible exception of hwĭcĭvau', "enemy standing," and tuxa'ʀᵃ, "pasted, sealed." The former bore a name identical with that of the whole performance; the latter was said never to have been sung for mere amusement. But these songs, like pipa' (people), kapĕ't (turtle), and cĭmáꝰulᵧᵃ (red ants) were sung at both preparatory and victory dances. Hwĭcĭvau' was said to be Halchidhoma, kapĕ't Kohuana, and the three others Maricopa. All were sung at the joint performances of the mixed community. Tuxa'ʀᵃ and hwĭcĭvau' had rattle accompaniments. The singer of the last-named dreamed of the enemy teaching him the song. The song related how the enemy treated prisoners and how appalling the enemy thought it that one of them lost his scalp. It also told of insects fighting among themselves.

The scalp now went into the permanent keeping of its elderly custodian, who placed it with others collected in the past in a special receptacle in the meeting house. Each morning before dawn for four days he bathed, washed the scalp, and replaced it. The receptacle (called 'ie'rhĭlᵧátca'vĭs, "hair container") was especially made for the purpose: a large undecorated pot, nearly globular, with a small mouth and no neck, covered with a clay plate. For these four days he slept alone in the meeting house, lying on the south side with the pot to the east near his head. No one else dared sleep there for fear of the scalps. The keeper would hear the scalps talking together in the pot; would hear them go outside to play, open the door, and re-enter the pot. He would sometimes announce, "Something is going to happen to our people, because I heard the scalps laughing and having a good time"; laughing because a Maricopa was going to be killed or die at home.

But if an enemy was doomed, he would hear the scalps weeping. Why he slept with them is not clear: "they put the pot at the old man's head because if it was elsewhere, the scalps might act as enemies and make him sick." The jar containing these trophies remained permanently in this spot, although he no longer slept with it.

The scalp dance might be repeated at any time, presumably as much for entertainment as for any other reason, taking exactly the same form. At their request the old man would bring out the scalps, wash and dress the hair; and again bathe and sleep with them for four days. They never asked directly but said, "Dress up our visitors and let them visit us."

Scalps were never used to bring rain nor to cure the sickness they caused, as by the Pima,[32] nor were they carried to war in Yuma fashion.

THE SIB SYSTEM

The Maricopa and the allied Halchidhoma, Kohuana, and Halyikwamai shared a single system of sibs (clans) of the type established for other lower Colorado Yumans by Kroeber.[33] These were patrilinear, definitely named groups, strictly exogamous, and "totemic." They not only bore names the same as or analogous to those on the lower Colorado, but these tribes shared the peculiar habit of naming women of the sib for the totems in an indirect fashion. Further, the sib system was definitely integrated with the calendar of months and hence with the economic round. There was no suggestion of localization of the sibs.

On the other hand, the system had no relation whatever to their religious life. Yet this would have been quite possible. The basis of Maricopa religion was dream experience with spirit birds and animals. The spirit dreamed of might well have been one of the totems of the dreamer, yet such was not the case. There is not a single instance of this, and it was quite remote from their minds that one should dream of his totem.

[32] Parsons, *Notes on the Pima*, p. 461.

[33] *Handbook*, p. 741.

There were differences between these sibs and those on the Colorado, or at least those of the Mohave as Kroeber describes them. Mohave sibs are said to be nameless; all the women of a sib were called by a single name, which had totemic reference; and the totemic name was not the everyday word for the totem. Thus, all Mohave women of a particular sib were called hipa. This name was said to "mean" coyote although in normal Mohave speech the coyote was hukθara. According to Mohave myth, certain men originally named Coyote were instructed by the culture hero to call their female descendants through males by the term hipa "corresponding" to their name Coyote. Similarly myth provided each one of the women's names with its associated "totem."[34]

In the Maricopa community there were phonetic equivalents of the Mohave women's names which served explicitly as names of the sibs. This is unlike the Mohave situation. The sib name was regarded as only potentially the name of all the women of the sib; many of them were called by the name of the sib, but only after marriage. The sib names might thus replace their personal names but this was by no means automatic and universal. They were rather used as convenient alternatives for the personal names. The feature of the Maricopa-Halchidhoma naming practice which contrasts most strongly with the Mohave as Kroeber describes it, is that most of the women had individual personal names, many of which had totemic import. Usually the names referred indirectly to the totems, but they were sometimes the everyday names of the totems. Some men, in addition, had names of the same sort.

To take the parallel instance, the Maricopa[35] sib χipa', one of whose totems was coyote (χatàluwe'), included forty-three women and girls. Eighteen of them bore names referring to the totems of this sib, while thirteen had names devoid of such reference. (Of the remaining twelve, some had no native names, for others it could not be recalled by my informant.) Four of the eighteen were called sim-

[34] Ibid.; Preliminary Sketch of the Mohave, p. 278.

[35] Strictly speaking, this refers collectively to the χipa sibs of Maricopa, Halchidhoma, and persons of Pima descent in the Maricopa-speaking community. It proved impossible to separate the names according to tribe in any satisfactory way (see p. 198).

ply x̱ipa'. The names of two women will illustrate the indirect reference of the remainder; one is named "invisible," referring to the clouds; another, "winding," referring to the wild gourd vines; both clouds and wild gourd being among the x̱ipa' totems. Thirty-one men belong to this sib, but only one has a totemic name.

The sib name thus serves as an auxiliary designation for all the women of a sib. Some women have no other personal name. More specifically it is a common term of address used by a man's relatives for his wife. For example, Mrs. Redbird of kwĭtk_yĭ'l_y^a sib has the personal name nĭk_yĭnk_yĭ'k, "iridescent green" (referring to the totem lizard), but is called kwĭtk_yĭ'l_y^a by her husband's sister. This has its counterpart in the bestowal of a nickname on a husband by his mother-in-law or someone of his wife's family.[36]

The feeling is marked among these people that all the Yumans have one sib system. That particular sibs of their own are not present in other tribes is a matter of no moment: that, they would say, is due to the fact that what we are here calling sibs are to them single lines of descent, and it is but natural that some lineages are not found in other tribes. What impresses them is that everywhere on the Colorado there are patrilineal lineages, within which the women alone are designated as pertaining to the lineage, and which function exogamously. They are conscious of a system; that details differ is immaterial.

The feeling for the system is very strong. They equate the patrilineal sibs of the Pima, or rather their moieties, with their own sibs, although the basis of Pima organization is different. All the local families derived from Pima paternal ancestors are reckoned in the sibs x̱ipa' and l_yew'c. They object violently even today to allowing their daughters to marry men of sibless tribes; the children would have no sib affiliation. Naturally, it is quite permissible for men to do so. There are several cases in the present generation of women who have married Indians from California. No attempt was made to assign these men to particular sibs, hence

[36] The Yuma situation also differed from that of the Mohave. Yuma sibs had definite names; these served as women's names, but the women also had personal names which referred indirectly to the totems. The Yuma differed from the Maricopa-Halchidhoma in that the sib name regularly substituted for the personal name in later life (Forde, *Yuma Ethnography*, pp. 142–47, 149).

their children are not placeable. The bastard origin of one woman can never be forgotten, since she belongs to no sib, her Indian father being unknown. I do not know how the matter came to be resolved in the case of several individuals known to be descendants of white men, but they have sib affiliation. On the other hand, all the known members of the Halchidhoma sib kwĭtk$_y$ĭl$_y$^{a} are derived from a remote Walapai ancestor. They do not know how he came to be called kwĭtk$_y$ĭ′l$_y$^{a}, but presume that the Walapai must have sibs, which is not the case.[37] They would be distinctly nonplussed if their women married men of a matrilineally organized tribe, such as the Apache or Southeastern Yavapai, but no such marriages have occurred, since these were mortal enemies. There is a recent instance, however; a marriage of a Maricopa girl to a Hopi man, now resident in nearby Phoenix. The girl's family, with whom I discussed the case, looked upon the placing of their two infants as an unsolvable problem.

Lists of sibs (cimu′l) of the several local tribes were obtained from several individuals. They were not always in agreement as to the tribal origin of particular sibs: the most probable ascription appears in the following list (Table IV). There may have been other sibs among the Halchidhoma, Kohuana, and Halyikwamai before they joined the Maricopa. But it is improbable: since the migration occurred only in the generation preceding that of my older informants, other sibs would have been remembered.

Some of the ascriptions are certain: Halchidhoma, kwĭtk$_y$ĭ′l$_y$à; Kohuana, cĭnyikwĭ′s and xĭlyi′; Halyikwamai, tŏxpa′s; Yuma, cŭkàpa′s; Halchidhoma and Kohuana, cĭkàma′; Kohuana and Halyikwamai, sala′l. It was thought probable that Halchidhoma kwŭc^{a}ku′ and l$_y$àmu′c were derived from the Kohuana. There is some doubt that the Halchidhoma originally had the sibs they share with the Maricopa, but the probability is high. Maricopa mavĭ′s is extinct or may never have existed as a sib. (It is one of the month names.) My informants had never heard of anyone locally with this sib affiliation, but one man knew it as a Yuma sib. Yuma cŭkàpa′s and Pima l$_y$ew′c and xipa′, given in this list, refer to individuals of immediate Yuma and Pima descent.

Some of the Maricopa and Halchidhoma sib names were the same as the six month names. This, incidentally, makes it more certain that both peoples had the same sibs, as they seem to have

[37] There is a Mohave sib kutkilya with which he may have been affiliated (Kroeber, Handbook, p. 742).

had the same calendar. These months are xavàtca'c, xamitu'tc, and kŭmàϑi'. Other month names were doubtfully the same as sibs: Last Star added lyeω'c and mavĭ's as month names, Kutox added xipa'. Both gave macxipa's as the name of a month, but Last Star maintained that this corresponded to the sib name

TABLE IV

Sibs

Maricopa*	Halchidhoma	Kohuana	Halyikwamai	Pima	Yuma
lyeω'c........	lyeω'c	....	....	lyeω'c	....
xipa'........	xipa'	....	....	xipa'	....
xavàtca'c....	xavàtca'c	....	....	....	....
xamitu'tc....	xamitu'tc	....	....	....	....
kŭmàϑi'.....	kŭmàϑi'	....	....	....	....
pakĭ't.......	pakĭ't	....	....	....	....
	cĭkàma'	cĭkàma'	....	....	....
	kwŭcᴬku'	kwŭcᴬku'	....	....	....
	lyàmu'c	lyàmu'c	....	....	....
		cĭnyikwĭ's	....	....	....
		sala'l	sala'l	....	....
mavĭ's (?)...	....	....	....	....	mavĭ's
	kwĭtkyĭ'lyᴬ	....	....	....	....
		xĭlyi'	....	....	....
				tŏxpa's	....
					cŭkàpa's

* Kroeber (*Handbook*, p. 742) gives a list of sibs purporting to be Maricopa, but it is palpable that these refer to the several Maricopa-speaking tribes now forming the joint community. Kwaku is evidently Halchidhoma and Kohuana kwŭcᴬku'. Ksila, sand, does not occur in any of my lists. The following sibs among the "Maricopa from the Cocopa," which Kroeber interprets to mean the Kohuana, do not occur in my list of local Kohuana sibs: halpot, a bush; kwutkil, any yellow animal; mave, rattlesnake; kwinis, deer; hutpas, sedge (see also Gifford, *Clans and Moieties*, pp. 158 f.). Of these, only one (kwutkil) is known locally. It may be that these Kohuana sibs exist among remnants of this tribe elsewhere.

xipa'. The significant point is that both felt that the sib system was in direct relation to the calendar round. The plants that are cultivated, or which ripen in a certain month, are the totems of the sib having that month name. Thus, corn is planted in the two months named xavàtca'c (February and August); xamitu'tc is the month for gathering mesquite; cholla cactus ripens in xipa' and the giant cactus in kŭmàϑi'; xipa' months (April and September) are also the months of rain. Corn, mesquite, cholla, suhuaro, and rain are all totems of the correspondingly named sibs.

Curiously enough the general creation myth, which tended to account for all items of culture, did not directly refer to the establishment of the sibs. It told how the culture hero instructed the people when to plant and when to gather fruits, and how he named the months that they might know the proper time, but my aged informant could only infer that the sibs and their totems were fixed at this time.

The totemic references of the sibs are as follows:

lyeω'c	buzzard, fire, beetle,[38] sun
xipa'	coyote, fox, eagle, rain, clouds, opuntia cactus, cholla cactus, moon, wild gourd
xavȧtca'c	corn, beetle,[38] wildcat, frog
xamitu'tc	bean mesquite, road runner, lizard[39]
kŭmȧði'	ocatilla cactus, giant cactus
pakĭ't	buzzard
cĭkȧma'	giant cactus
kwŭcᵃku'	dove[40]
lyȧmu'c	(unknown)
cĭnyikwĭ's	(unknown)
sala'l	bean mesquite
mavĭ's	rattlesnake
kwĭtkyĭ'lyᴬ	eagle, lizard[41]
xĭlyi'	(unknown)
tŏxpa's	(unknown)
cŭkȧpa's	red ants, deer

It proved impossible to discover which totems pertained to the similarly named sibs of the several tribes; those of xipa', e.g., to Maricopa or Halchidhoma. The informants' view was that every sib of the same name would necessarily have the same totems.

The idea prevails that these were not all the totems of the sibs; rather that they were more numerous. Even with the relatively small number given for lyeω'c or xipa', for example, no single informant named them all at one time. It is really doubtful, however, that there are many more than are cited here.

The "totemic" relationship is only slightly developed. It is

[38] A red or yellow beetle.

[39] A rare lizard having a green back.

[40] Not the whitewing.

[41] A lizard living near the water, having a curved tail bearing black marks and an iridescent green breast.

felt that there is an association between the totem and the tote-
mite, but the character of the relationship is not defined. Its
chief expression is in the naming-habit. Perhaps the quality of
the association is best expressed in the manner in which it was
translated: lyew'c "means" buzzard; it "refers" to fire; it "takes
its name after" the sun; mavĭ's "prefers" the rattlesnake;
xavàtca'c and lyew'c "have the same insect." For the rest, the
totemites praised their totem or boasted of it; they looked on it
as peculiarly theirs. People in general called the totem by the sib
name on more solemn occasions, though not in everyday parlance. There were no taboos of any sort surrounding the totems;
they did not hold them in any degree of veneration or awe, nor
did they address prayers especially to them. All in all, the emotional quality of the association was very slight.

The following statements define the attitude:

People of lyew'c sib say the sun makes the plants grow: they
would praise it. They call the sun lyew'c, and say "Look down on
us and make us feel happy. Come out and shine brightly on us;
shine on our plants." People of other sibs would also call it
lyew'c and pray to it the same way. Those of this sib would
praise the month lyew'c, saying it was good for all living things,
making them warm, and bringing green leaves on the trees.

Xipa' people regarded the rain prayerfully, saying, if it was
cloudy, "Rain on the people so they may have plenty to eat."
Other sibs would say, "xipa', look down on us and give us plenty
of water." When one is eating opuntia fruit, he says "xipa', turn
your back," meaning the spines should turn away so the eater
will not be pricked.

In xavàtca'c month it is warm enough for plants to grow.
Corn is then planted; because they are starving, they are glad to
put in the seeds. It takes but four days for the corn to come up.
Hence, they, the xavàtca'c people, praise the plants. Xavàtca'c
praised the corn as the prettiest thing that ever grew in the fields.
If one was about to plant, the field being ready, he would get a
man or woman of xavàtca'c, who would say, "Put me down in
your field; bury me. I will be glad to come up," meaning he was

the corn himself. But these xavàtca′c people would eat corn too: they would only praise it.

Those of xamitu′tc praise that month, saying the trees had again come to life, were standing up stoutly, ready to bring mesquite beans to feed everyone.

Pakĭ′t would boast, speak well of the buzzard. (One of them said, "Our white friends have dreamed of the buzzards; that is why they make airplanes.") At harvest time when it is cloudy, and buzzards always fly about when it is overcast, pakĭ′t people say, "cimu′l (sib), drive all the clouds away, so rain will not destroy our crops."

Kwĭtk₍y₎ĭ′l₍y₎ᴬ sib looked on the eagle and lizards as its friends, and as friends, would not kill them. Kutox (of this sib) said, "When I see the little lizard, I praise it and boast of it as something big. I pray to the eagle when I go to bed, 'You are way above the sky and can look down on me and protect me. When I am asleep and there is any harm near, wake me.' To the lizard, I say, 'You are creeping on the ground just like the poisonous snakes: try to keep the poisonous creatures away from me.' "

Although several sibs had the same totems, there was no tendency to group them on this basis in phratries. That is, they recognized that two sibs had identical sentiments for a particular totem and that their relationship was therefore different from that with other sibs, yet there was no temptation to consolidate such pairs. Several statements describe this position. The Maricopa sibs xavàtca′c and l₍y₎ew′c "have the same insect" (a red or yellow beetle), so they are "almost alike," yet they could freely intermarry. Pakĭ′t and l₍y₎ew′c both refer to the buzzard, but they do not consider themselves related. Pakĭ′t people call it pakĭ′t, while l₍y₎ew′c call it by their sib name. Contradictory to this, the single Halyikwamai family of sala′l sib have mesquite for a totem; so has Maricopa xamitu′tc, hence "these would consider themselves as belonging to one group."

It is significant that although the Maricopa community knows the Pima quite well, my informant had no inkling of Pima social structure. The Pima have five patrilineal sibs bearing meaningless names, three of them grouped in one moiety, two in the other. The moieties are called Vulture (buzzard), Red People, or Red Cow-Killer, and Coyote, White People, or White Cow-Killer.[42] My informants did not know why those of Pima ancestry were classed invariably as either xipa' or l$_y$ew'c. They knew only that the part Pima of xipa' sib say that their sib refers to the coyote. The reason is, however, transparent: since Maricopa-Halchidhoma xipa' refers to the coyote, l$_y$ew'c to the buzzard, the Pima married into the Maricopa community have been equated by their moiety affiliation with the local sib system.[43] (This raises the question, incidentally, whether the essential Pima unit is not the moiety rather than the sib.)

The relative numerical strength of the sibs, as checked from an allotment list of 1915, is as follows: xipa', 83; l$_y$ew'c, 55; cĭkàma', 21; xavàtca'c, 16; sala'l, 14; cĭnyikwĭ's, 12; kwĭtk$_y$ĭ'l$_y$ᵃ, 12; xamitu'tc, 9; cŭkàpa's, 9; pakĭ't, 5; kwŭcᵃku', 1; l$_y$àmu'c, 1; tŏxpa's, 1; xĭlyi', 1 (total 240). Kŭmàði' and mavĭ's are extinct; the latter, at least, may never have existed. Since tŏxpa's and xĭlyi' are repesented only by women, they too are about to be extinguished. My informant Last Star believes that xipa' and l$_y$ew'c were the largest sibs in earlier times as they are today.

While all the members of a sib were regarded as in some sense related, it was recognized that there were several distinct lines of descent within it, between which blood relationship could not be established, or at least was not definitely known. Hence people of one's own sib, not relatives, were not called by kinship terms. The terms in use were "friend," kiyi' (used between men) and ciyi' (when one or both persons were women). So also a man might marry in his mother's sib anyone not related to her by blood. On the other hand, marriage to a non-relative of one's own sib was prohibited.

There seems to have been no preferred marriages between par-

---

[42] Russell, *Pima Indians*, p. 197; Parsons, *Notes on the Pima*, p. 455; Lloyd, pp. 147, 163; Gifford, *Clans and Moieties*, p. 174.

[43] It is interesting to note that my informant remarked that "the Pima say tcĭk$_y$ä'và (man's cross-cousin) for cimu'l (sib)." Parsons found that the Pima referred to the moiety by the term that is used for cross-cousins (*op. cit.*, p. 456).

ticular sibs. To be sure, I understood Last Star to say that lyeω'c, xipa', and xavàtca'c preferred to marry, but he may have meant no more than that they did intermarry most frequently. Since they are the largest sibs, chance would inevitably make this the fact. A record of sixty-two marriages covering the present and past generations is appended. There does not appear to be

TABLE V

DISTRIBUTION OF MARRIAGES ACCORDING TO SIB

	lyeω'c	xipa'	Pima xipa'	xamitu'tc	xavàtca'c	cïnyikwï's	pakï't	kwïtkyï'lyᵃ	cïkàma'	kwŭcᵃku'	lyàmu'c	sala'l	xïlyï'	tŏxpa's	cŭkàpa's	Unassigned
lyeω'c.........																
xipa'.........	7	3														
Pima xipa'*....	1	2														
xamitu'tc.....	1															
xavàtca'c......	6	1														
cïnyikwï's.....	1	2		1												
pakï't.........	1	1			1											
kwïtkyï'lyᵃ.....	1	4		1	2											
cïkàma'.......	2		1	1		1										
kwŭcᵃku'......									1							
lyàmu'c.........		1														
sala'l........	1	2	1		1				1							
xïlyï'.........		1			1											
tŏxpa's........														1		
cŭkàpa's......	1	1														
Unassigned....	4	2						1						1		

* These are xipa' individuals of Pima descent.

any clear-cut marriage preference. The distribution seems random: the number of cases is too small to make it worth while to calculate the probabilities.

The sibs were strictly exogamous in theory, but it will be observed that they were not so in practice. The breach occurs in the largest sib, xipa': three were marriages among xipa' of the local community and two with individuals who were either Pima or of Pima descent. Of the first category, two marriages occurred some time ago, and in one case husband and wife were close blood relatives. In the other two marriages within the local xipa′ group, the couples were not related. One of these cases is interesting: a Maricopa xipa′ woman married first a Pima classed as xipa′ and later a Maricopa xipa′. Breach of the exogamic rule is implied in aboriginal times, for a stereotyped reaction was described which I doubt ever occurred with the modern marriages.

A man could not marry any known blood relative of either parent, nor any woman of his own sib. Hence he could marry an unrelated member of his mother's sib. If two related individuals did marry "without their parent's consent," they were regarded as dead. All their relatives would gather at the girl's home and mourn all day. They would set fire to the house, and break up and destroy all their belongings, just as though the girl had died. The man's parents did the same thing. The old people then told the couple they must never part, never remarry. It was held that children born to them would be weaklings.

In recent times the reaction was not so drastic. Sixteen years ago, B. J., a shaman now dead, married a girl of his own sib, xipa′, who was in addition a close relative. His mother and this girl called each other by first-cousin terms; the exact relationship is unknown. The wife called him ĕnω′, older sister's or cousin's child. He was an orphan who lived with her parents. People tried to prevent their marriage; they thought it revolting.

In another instance, a man married his paternal grandfather's sister's daughter (hence of another sib). I was told that in the old days this could not have happened. After nearly ten years, the aged grandfather is still unwilling to forgive, although he lives with the couple.

NAMES

Babies were given non-significant names, nicknames, by their mothers. It was not until they were several years old that real names were chosen, and these are given casually by anyone, without formality.[44] Boys' names were chosen indiscriminately, but girls were commonly named with reference to their sibs. Thus, xamitu′tc sib had for its principal totem the bean mesquite, hence the girls of this sib were commonly named for parts of the mesquite, and sometimes the boys. One little girl of this sib, e.g., was named by her maternal grandmother's sister,

[44] The Pima naming ceremony with godparents was unknown here (Russell, *Pima Indians*, p. 188).

wanyuwa′n, "hanging in bunches," having reference to the clusters of mesquite beans on the trees. Somewhat less commonly children were nicknamed for physical peculiarities or habits, and still other names were of random origin and meaningless, or at least the reason for their use was not obvious to others nor generally known.

A small boy, W——, received his name from an old man, who said he dreamed he was in the desert where he saw a group of men seated in a circle. There was a little boy coming alone in the desert. They selected a name for him. They turned around and called him munyoi′xȧxdăt, "tarantula's backbone." The old man was anxious to see who the little boy was: when the boy drew near, he saw it was W——.

Such names of girls persisted through life. Sometimes they came to be known only by the names of their sibs, since it was the custom for the husband's relatives to call the wife in this fashion. Men, however, usually acquired a new name at marriage, the childhood name either being dropped or falling into secondary use. The man's new name was a nickname, said to be applied to him by his mother-in-law, but perhaps more commonly given by his friends who then declared his wife's mother had so styled him. This nickname was a derisive reference to his appearance, likened him to any ugly animal, or to his habits. For instance, one man was called *Prescott*—matkȧvĭ′chwatcĭpŏ′mihwu′, "the Prescott train's smokestack-nose." Doubtlessly such names frequently had gross sexual reference, but I was not told so.

The names of the dead and of the living were equally tabu and emphatically so. Kinship terms were used for reference, or some indirect description. Kinsmen were never addressed by name; it was thought horrible even to call a brother by his name. Even my interpreter, an emancipated woman, invariably avoided using names and, on that account, was sometimes unintelligible. Yet, while they were very uneasy at hearing their names mentioned, they had no hesitation whatever in naming themselves. There is no analogue to the Pima rule that boys and girls must not utter their own names.[45] The tabu was hardly slighter for the living than the dead, where it was intense. Yet they did not

[45] *Ibid.*

think of renaming objects for which the dead had been named, nor of using circumlocutions. This tabu, coupled with the freedom with which new names were coined, brought it about that there was no inheritance of particular names.

Maricopa names had thus a contradictory character. They were significant in that many of them had totemic reference and in that they were not lightly used, but they were not emotionally significant. The tabu was on the whole not emotionally rooted; it was rather a matter of etiquette, of good form. Their non-significant character is borne out by their nickname nature, the fluidity of composition, the casual way in which they were bestowed, and the readiness to change. Even the names having totemic reference are one with the avowed nicknames in that they are mere designations, just as dogs were named for convenience of reference.

The names of all persons in the Maricopa community which follow are based on an allotment list dating from about 1915. These were obtained with difficulty from my interpreter, who invariably interrupted the procedure when a third person approached. It was striking that she knew the sib affiliation and the complicated tribal lineages even in cases where she could not recall the person's name. All the persons listed are Maricopa-speaking members of the single community despite their diversity of tribal ancestry. Probably every one of them is of mixed tribal blood, so that only in those few cases where this is not known to be the fact, could we describe them as specifically Maricopa, Halchidhoma, Kohuana, or Halyikwamai. The tribal designations in the following list do not mean that the individual is reckoned an Halchidhoma, e.g., but that the patrilineal descent is from the Halchidhoma sib of that name rather than from the equivalent sib of one of the other tribes.

The names are grouped by sib and sex, so that all names of sib reference appear first (marked by an asterisk), then those referring to personal appearance and habits, other names with meaning, and those for which my interpreter knew neither meaning nor the reason for the bestowal of the name. In all cases where meaning is recorded, a satisfactory etymology was obtained. In no case did an etymology seem forced or a folk-etymology attempted. All names are in the Maricopa language.

Certain features appear clearly from this list. Not all the "totems" of a sib are referred to: for example, lyeω'c names refer to buzzard, fire, and sun, but not to the beetle. A surprisingly large proportion of women's names have sib reference, fifty-eight in a total of eighty-eight. The proportion is uniform in all the sibs. Actually the habit of bestowing sib-names is not randomly distributed, but prevails rather in certain families. If these are excluded, the proportion of sib-names drops appreciably. So far as I know this fact has no sociological significance, but seems solely a matter of preference for this type of name.

For instance, in kwĭtkyĭ'lyᴀ sib, numbers 166 and 168 are brothers; 166 is the father of 170, whose children are 169, 165, 164 (sons), and 159, 160 (daughters); a third daughter having no native name. The son of 168 is 167, and 171 the son of 169. Of these, the brothers and sisters 159, 165, 160, and 164 have names all referring to the lizard. Again, in xamitu'tc sib, the sons of 123 are 124, 125, and W—— (referred to above), the daughters 119, 120, and 121. Names 119 and 120 refer to the mesquite beans; 121 to the roadrunner.

The list is presumably deficient in at least one way: there are no names which refer grossly to sexual matters, which might have been expected, since this is general among the Yuman tribes. I can only believe that my interpreter deliberately avoided mentioning these, just as she avoided coarseness at all other times. It may be that the untranslated names and those of people whom she declared had no native names, are of this character.

TABLE VI

List of Names

sib: lyeω'c

Women

*1	saxavàcu'ĭc........	bluish forehead	The sun's rays, as it rises, are blue.	Maricopa
*2	xaʀàǎ'sk..........	sun rays		Halchidhoma
*3	hàʀa'............	blaze	Refers to fire.	Maricopa
*4	nyikama'.........	untouchable	Refers to fire.	Maricopa
*5	nyika'm..........	——	Refers to fire.	Maricopa
*6	oi'ĭv............	moving to and fro	Refers to the blaze of a fire.	Maricopa

TABLE VI—*Continued*

*7	lʸeω'ciyĕʀȧ.......	[buzzard?] flies		Maricopa
*8	lʸeω'canĕ'x.......	dignified [buzzard]		Maricopa
*9	matcănyau'.......	pretending to hide	Refers to the buzzard soaring on high.	Maricopa
*10	lʸeω'c............			Maricopa
*11	lʸeωcȧxa'n........	good (true, real)		Maricopa
*12	lʸeω'c............	———		Maricopa
*13	lʸeω'cʻite'vȧ......	unfastening ———		Maricopa
14	kȧlȧa'lk..........	slender	She is slender.	Maricopa
15	vikwatŏ's........	stone-bumping [head]	Named after one of her Yavapai ancestors, a captive girl who was thrown on a stone because she resisted.	Maricopa
16	tȧmȧckwi'n......	twisted		Maricopa
17	sĭnyŭ'x..........	ashamed		Maricopa
18	matkuȧ'lʸᵃ......	appearing		Maricopa
19	xamĭkŭmacȧʀai'...	——— angry		Maricopa
20	tȧtcu'vȧ.........	———		Maricopa
21	xutca'c..........	———		Maricopa
22	kwȧxa'ʀȧ........	———		Maricopa
		Men		
*23	yĭmĭnyai'........	[sun]light path		Maricopa
*24	ĭnyȧ'sumĭ".......	sun's down [feathers]		Maricopa
*25	hiye'ʀȧkwĭcȧmpŏ'p.	four things flying	Refers to the buzzard as huge.	Maricopa
26	tcĭmȧϑu'lha'vȧ....	red ant going in		Maricopa
27	tcĭmȧϑu'lʸhiϑo'....	red ant's eye		Maricopa
28	kwȧxaŏʀutu'ʀȧ....	starving at hoop and pole game	He was thin and delicate. He walked as though falling from hunger. In the spring, at the time they play this game, people are starving and can not run.	Maricopa
29	tacȧvu'i..........	shriveled	He was underdeveloped.	Maricopa
30	⎰ maxaikwĭlʸȧŏ'k....	old man-lad	Boyhood name.	Maricopa
	⎱ pantalo'n........	(Spanish)	Every time he went off, he came home with no (new?) pants.	

TABLE VI—*Continued*

31	tinyamkwaiya′m...	moving the night		Maricopa
32	tcumĭcl_yămĕ′m....	[a foreign] tribe mourning	Refers to the enemy's mourning.	Maricopa
33	xatĭlăwe′ᵃpŭm.....	burnt coyote		Maricopa
34	ma.u′l_yᵃ.........	antelope	He took part in races; his wife's mother called him thus.	Maricopa
35	xanyamĭca′vȧ.....	kingfisher (?)		Maricopa
36	tcȧωRȧhimisi′l_yᵃ....	chickenhawk's thigh		Maricopa
37	uvuti′c..........	tobacco-bow		Maricopa
38	ᵃxaniwa′.........	real (good) heart		Maricopa
39	cuwe′m..........	shifting		Maricopa
40	cutĭ′k...........	barely touch		Maricopa
41	ĭcȧoRiya′.........	chickenhawk's mouth		Maricopa
42	cota′n...........	gathering in bunches		Maricopa
43	pĕn_yȧva′.........	beaver's house		Maricopa

SIB: xipa′

Women

*44	su.u′rtk.........	mixed	Refers to the interlaced branches of cholla (?) cactus.	Halchidhoma
*45	xloi′ⁱ............	something gone (?)	Refers to the calyx of the cholla from which the fruit has been plucked.	Maricopa
*46	ȧmŭsu′l_yᵃ........	sour	Refers to the sour fruit of the cholla.	Maricopa
*47,48	vȧcȧwo′.......	[spines] sticking out	Refers to the cholla.	Maricopa
*49	packua′l_yᵃ........	[moon] appears and shows plainly	Refers to the moon.	Maricopa
*50	hĭl′ĭnyo′m........	invisible [clouds]	Refers to clouds.	Halchidhoma
*51	ᵃnŏ′mp	[clouds] pressing down (lowering)	Refers to clouds.	Halchidhoma
*52	tcĭnă′ldj.........	hanging [clouds]	Refers to clouds.	Maricopa
*53	xacmȧu′ltc.......	smoke bank	Refers to clouds as they lower over the mountains.	Maricopa
*54	kolȧĕ′m..........	distant	Refers to distant thunder.	Maricopa
*54a	n_yimackwĭ′n.......	winding	Refers to the wild gourd vine winding over tree branches.	Maricopa
*55	xipa′............	———		Halchidhoma

TABLE VI—*Continued*

*56,57,58	xipa'.......	———		Pima
*59	xipacârĭ'k........	——— holding	May refer to an edible caterpillar, which was caught and held in a peculiar fashion.	Maricopa
*60	xipa'nĕx.........	——— dignified		Maricopa
61	mĭcxaimu'lᴬ......	becoming a girl		Maricopa
62	xĭlyᴬtĕ'và.........	sprouted		Halchidhoma
63	nyivàca'lyᴬ.......	sprinkling		Maricopa
64	siva'mᴬ..........	[sun] slips below [horizon]		Maricopa
65	hĭlyiu'c..........	keeping something in sight		Maricopa
66	tcaiⁱya'..........	———		Halchidhoma
67	cici'm..........	———		Halchidhoma
68	mai'kàti'c........	———		Maricopa
69	kwĭcilyu'c........	———		Maricopa
70	tacpŏ't..........	———		Maricopa
71	xame'kĭnyàme'và..	———		Maricopa
72	satckàsa'tc.......	———		Kohuana
73	ulyàu'l..........	———		Maricopa

Men

*74	xa'lyààlyàϑi'k.....	appearing in the moon	Refers to Coyote who appears in the moon.	Maricopa
75	tcakwa't.........	yucca (or whip)	He has little hair, which is also curly. (Yucca is used by the Pima for washing the hair. Its leaves are fringed with curling fibers.)	Maricopa
76	hiye'ʀàmatxa'.....	flying wind	He walks rapidly; always quick at his tasks.	Maricopa
77	tcipai'iϑo'........	gnat's eyes	His eyes were very small.	Maricopa
78	xa'aʀàkŏ'k.......	tail straight down	He always wore his long hair only down the back.	Maricopa
79	unyĭcĭma'........	dreaming of a road	He never stayed home: his mother-in-law said the reason must be that he dreamed of all the roads.	Maricopa

TABLE VI—*Continued*

80	nĭmauȧca'k.......	paternal grand-mother's bones	Implies that the enemies' grandmothers' bones lay about, so many were killed.	Maricopa
81	nĭxnĭxkwĭʀau'.....	humming bird—good runner		Maricopa
82	ima'tkwĭsȧmhai'...	rubbing his body		Maricopa
83	halyȧau'ᵃapa's.....	hidden rabbit		Maricopa
84	mȧxainᵧunᵧĭ'......	boy's road		Maricopa
85	tcȧo'ʀȧkwĭsa'ʀȧ....	left-handed hawk		Maricopa
86	matkui's.........	stretching (when tired)		Maricopa
87	ᵃvitcuhu'i........	pouring pebbles		Maricopa
88	taʀi'cvaxa.......	killdeer guts		Maricopa
89	mahwĭtȧpa'vȧ.....	roasting bear		Maricopa
90	kilᵧᵃahwai'.......	club		Maricopa
91	ḳwaʀȧo'..........	knife		Maricopa
92	ĕnyo'ʀᵃ..........	variegated		Halchidhoma
93	maiᶫnyă'n........	managing		Kaveltcadom
94	tinyă'mkwĭlyŏ'x...	patting the night gently		Maricopa
95	ce'ĭkwĭcȧkwŏḳ'....	buzzard-husking [corn]		Halchidhoma
96	cuma'kȧxwi'vȧ....	dream-odor		Halchidhoma
97	ðŭnyȧmicȧðau'....	mad-taken		Maricopa
98	xamkĭmxai'.......	bird-boy		Halchidhoma
99	maxai'kwȧkĕ'tc....	shooting boy		Maricopa
100	xai'ĕmᵃgwĕnĕ'x....	move—dignified		Maricopa
101	unyĭkwaðu'lᵧᵃ.....	hidden road		Maricopa
102	'unyi's...........	———		Maricopa
103	mŭski'ʀȧ.........	———		Maricopa
104	iʀĭ'k.............	———		Pima

sib: xavȧtca'c

Women

*105	xavȧtca'cᵃpŏ'k.....	——— popping	Refers to the popping sound of corn being parched.	Maricopa
*106	xavȧtca'ckuwa'lᵧᵃ..	——— appearing	Refers to corn.	Maricopa
*107	ᵃxuᵘt.............	pretty...........	Describes the appearance of the corn.	Halchidhoma
*108	tŭksa'vȧ.........	slow	Corn comes up slowly.	Halchidhoma
109	xavȧtca'c........	———		Maricopa
110	ta'vĭcmĭsŏ'm......	light (weight) flower		Maricopa

TABLE VI—*Continued*

Men

111	ma.i'lyᵃ..........	worm	He was afraid of worms when a little boy.	Maricopa
	matᵃkwĭ'cŏksŭ'm...	light (weight) shadow		
112	tcȧoʀokwĭ's.......	yellow hawk		Halchidhoma
113	ĭnya'tcĭpakwa.u'l..	holding the sunrise		Halchidhoma
114	matᵃxa'..........	wind		Halchidhoma
115	muxoi'ⁱ..........	steam		Halchidhoma
116	cakwĭ'..........	branching (as a tree)		Halchidhoma
117	kŭmᵃcĕ's..........	———		Halchidhoma

SIB: xamitu'tc

Women

*118	tavĭcunȧ'u'n.......	flowers short lived	Refers to the mesquite blossoms.	Maricopa
*119	wanyuwa'n........	hanging in bunches	Refers to the green mesquite beans which hang in bunches.	Maricopa
*120	hĭlnyȧtȧma'g......	leaving it lying	Refers to the poorer mesquite beans which are left on the ground.	Maricopa
*121	yux..............	crawling	Describes the road-runner as it runs with its head down.	Maricopa

Men

122	avĕxaka'm........	snake going through [water]		Maricopa
123	matȧkwĭsnunyĕ'...	yellow road		Maricopa
124	sumĕmiyĭ'm.......	walking over down (feathers)		Maricopa
125	tcie'ʀȧma'm.......	waking birds		Maricopa

SIB: pakĭ't

Women

*126	pakĭtsi'x..........	——— snuffle	Refers to the buzzard which sniffs (detects) dead animals first.	Maricopa
*127,128	pakĭ't........	———		Maricopa

TABLE VI—*Continued*

Man

129	ᵃmatàlïvŏ'x........	big hole in the ground		Maricopa

SIB: cĭkàma'

Women

*130	ïlyàϑau'.........	appearing	Refers to giant cactus fruit.	Kohuana
*131	ïlyàva'c..........	they are appearing	Refers to giant cactus fruit.	Halchidhoma
*132	{cĭkàma'..........	——		Kohuana
	{kwĭca'a'ʀà.......	slender	She was slender when a child.	
*133,134	cĭkàma'.......	——		Halchidhoma

Men

135	moϑïlxacu'i.......	bread without salt		Kohuana
136	tălyă'n..........	(Spanish *Italiano*)	Looks like an Italian.	Kohuana
137	xanàpa'tc.........	real (good)—lying down		Kohuana

SIB: kwŭcᵃku'

Man

138	vanŏ't...........	(a plant)		Halchidhoma

SIB: lyàmu'c

Man

139	hatàluwĕ'cupa'....	coyote scratches [himself]		Halchidhoma

SIB: cĭnyikwï's

Women

140	kwĭsmĭnyo'ʀà......	painted yellow		Kohuana
141	tcuma'k..........	——		Kohuana

Men

142	kwiϑuyito"........	watermelon belly	When he was a baby, they tapped on his protruding abdomen as on a ripe melon.	Maricopa†

† The men, Nos. 142, 143, and 144, are members of a single family, said to be "Maricopa and part Yuma." The sib cĭnyikwï's is not Maricopa, but sinʸkwa'tʟ is given by Harrington and Gifford as a Yuma sib, hence we may infer that the lineage is really Yuma (Harrington, *Yuma Account of Origins*, p. 345; Gifford, *Clans and Moieties*, p. 158). According to Forde (*Yuma Ethnography*, p. 143), this may rather be a Diegueño sib.

TABLE VI—*Continued*

143	kwĭtcagŏnti'n......	canteen head	His occiput is flat like a canteen.	Maricopa
144	xako'ḵutcu'c......	carrying his daughter's child		Maricopa
145	xŏmȧce'kupa'ʀȧ....	last star	He was an only child: when one sees the last star, it is the only one.	Kohuana

SIB: sala'l

Women

*146	tavȧcuse'vȧ.......	drinking flower	Refers to the mesquite, when it first blossoms.	Halyikwamai
*147	tcĕcxama'ly ᴬ.......	stored—white	Refers to the mesquite: if the green beans are stored, they turn white.	Halyikwamai
*148	ḵuḵu't...........	mesquite bean bearers	The word means a group of women bearing loads of mesquite beans.	Halyikwamai
*149	nyĭmiyu'vȧ........	shows plainly	Refers to the appearance of ripe mesquite beans.	Halyikwamai
*150	ta'vȧcĭlyaᵭi'k.......	flowers appearing	Refers to mesquite.	Halyikwamai
*151	nyikȧwu'mkăᵭau'..	starts picking from the beginning	Refers to mesquite beans.	Halyikwamai

Men

152	sumĭ'kwĭckĭt......	cutting (downy) feathers		Halyikwamai
153	matȧpŭ'cᴬ........	mud filled (packed)		Halyikwamai
154	unyĭ'ḵwaxavĭ'k....	two roads		Halyikwamai
155	xȧlyȧsmo'kutcuaŏ'k	kicking a fly		Halyikwamai
156	hĭlyȧmi'c........	———		Halyikwamai

SIB: tŏxpa's

Woman

| *157 | tŏxpa's.......... | ——— | | Halyikwamai |

SIB: xĭlyi'

Woman

| 158 | xĭlyȧko'vȧ........ | no more | Refers to enemies exterminated at the Kohuana village. (xlĭ'kwĭp is the Kohuana form of this name.) | Kohuana |

TABLE VI—*Continued*

SIB: kwĭtk$_y$ĭ'l$_y$$^{\dot{a}}$

Women

*159	nĭk$_y$ĭnk$_y$ĭ'k........	iridescent green	Refers to a lizard, whose breast is iridescent green.	Halchidhoma
*160	ta'vĭcuʀȧu'k.......	flower-curl	Refers to the lizard's curved tail.	Halchidhoma
*161	kwaiŏliyŏ'l........	———	(Refers in an obscure way to the sib.)	Halchidhoma
162	matmȧso'$^{\dot{a}}$........	eating herself	She was a cranky child.	Halchidhoma
163	matȧstu'm........	gathering dirt		Halchidhoma

Men

*164	'uvȧau'nyuti'c.....	rain—bow (not rainbow)	Describes the lizard's tail, which is thought to resemble a bow, hence also a rainbow, and hence the rain.	Halchidhoma
*165	mankwȧʀau'......	sudden runner	Refers to the sudden running of the lizard.	Halchidhoma
166	uwȧ'n$_y$$^{\dot{a}}$...........	carries all the weight	Childhood name. He was a stout child, whom they would bounce up and down.	Halchidhoma
	kutŏ'x̣............	women's dice (also playing cards)	His explanation is that his face is lozenge-shaped like the pip on a card. The common explanation is that this name was given by his mother-in-law because he spent all his time playing cards: she said he was full of the figures on the cards.	
167	tcuve'kȧmĭ'c.......	returning mourning	Named for the mourning ceremony.	Halchidhoma

TABLE VI—*Concluded*

168	tĭlĭke'.............	top-heavy	Childhood name: because as he walked he nodded his big head.	Halchidhoma
	tĭnyămkwăʀau'....	night [is] a good runner		
169	matăxa'kwĭnyuwĭ'c.	wind owner		Halchidhoma
170	sŭmĭ'kwĭctĕ'vă.....	tying downy feathers		Halchidhoma
171	tcie'ʀăkwŏtkwi'ʀă..	following a bird		Halchidhoma

sɪʙ: cŭkăpa's

Women

*172	tŏtkăva'k.........	coming back and forth	Refers to the movements of red ants. Kutox says it refers to the tracks of deer going to and fro.	Yuma
*173	mătnᵧiϑi'.........	coming toward each other	Refers to the red ants.	Yuma

Men

*174	cuϑŭ'lᵧᵃ..........	hiding	Refers to red ants, whose nests are difficult to find and destroy. Kutox says the one who named this man meant the deer hiding.	Yuma
175	tcieʀătŏp.........	bird-throw		Yuma

THE KINSHIP SYSTEM

The Maricopa kinship system closely resembles that of all other Yuman tribes in the stress laid on age distinctions among brothers and sisters and their descendants. It goes farther than most in the systematic way in which these distinctions are carried out in terminology. Add to this that brothers and sisters are called brother and sister only when full brothers or sisters, or when derived from the same mother, but not when they have only a father in common. The general impression is one of bewildering complexity, yet it is clear that they operate with a few simple principles.

The word "system" is quite legitimately employed for this body of kinship designations. It became quite clear that the Maricopa themselves think of it as a well-defined system. Thanks to my interpreter, Mrs. Redbird, it was possible to enquire systematically into the relationship of every person in the collateral lines derived from common greatgrandparents. She needed to know no more than the sex and relative ages of the siblings from whom the lines were traced to give without hesitation the terms used between any pair in the succeeding generations to no matter what degree of remoteness. She was frankly operating with a system. Every one of the usages obtained from her was checked and cross-checked, and in nearly every instance her first response was found to be correct. Not so her mother, an old-time Maricopa of nearly sixty, who, her daughter told me, could never tell what her relatives of even slight remoteness were called. Obviously, individual interest in the subject varied widely.

It is important to note that the kinship system bears no relation whatever to the sib system; kinship groupings do not follow sib lines.

The essential principle of the system is that the relative ages of brothers and sisters are given terminological expression, and the terms for their descendants hinge on this. These distinctions appear at every point, yet the curious thing is that age distinctions between siblings have no social existence. Neither I nor my interpreter, with whom I repeatedly discussed the matter, could find any feature of social life which might give rise to this. It may exist, but Mrs. Redbird's opinion was that the terminological distinctions existed only for their own sake.

Coupled with this basic principle is the fact that half-brothers and half-sisters are considered brother and sister, but only when children of the same mother.[46] The classification of parallel cous-

[46] By implication this may also be true of the Yuma and Mohave, but not of Cocopa, Kamia, and Northern Diegueño (Gifford, *Californian Kinship Terminologies*, p. 62; Kroeber, *California Kinship Systems*, p. 341). Terms given for paternal and maternal half-siblings among Yuma and Mohave are identical with those recorded here for the Maricopa. It may therefore be that these Colorado

ins follows from this, but only in part. True enough a father's brother's children and a woman's mother's sister's children are called brothers and sisters when the father and his brother or the mother and her sister are half-siblings by the same mother. But instead of calling these parallel cousins brother and sister as well when the parents are full brothers and sisters, they use special terms for them.

The reason for considering half-siblings as full siblings when derived from the same mother but not from the same father is inexplicable, especially in face of the marked patriliny prevailing otherwise in their social structure. Obviously, with different fathers these children may have belonged to different sibs, hence the blood-bond here overrides sib affiliation. Informants were wholly at a loss to find any correlated social function. It seems that it must be correlated in some way which I do not understand with the importance of the two mothers-in-law in determining the relation of their child's spouse to their own families, to the function of the mother-in-law in supplying a woman of her own family to the widower son-in-law, and to the attitude of considering women as essentially the carriers of patrilineal sib affiliations; but the clue to their interrelation is lacking. It might be thought to be based on a belief that a woman alone was concerned in conception, the man's part being secondary. But nothing of the sort developed in a long discussion of the relation of conception to dreams nor in the many other opportunities when it might have come out.

Sex, on the other hand, is not an important basis of classification. The speaker's sex does make a difference, to be sure, but rarely that of the kinsman addressed. It is partially ignored between brothers and sisters and with cousins of one's own generation. It is practically ignored in one's children's generation, and does not figure at all in the generation of grandchildren and greatgrandchildren.

River tribes reckon half-siblings as full siblings when the bond is through the mother, but we are not told so. Similarly it may be that this blood bond figures in the classification of parallel cousins, as it does in Maricopa, but these authorities are also silent on this point.

Mother's and father's kinsmen are distinguished among uncles, aunts, and grandparents. But the two lines are merged for all kin more remotely related: greatgrandparents, granduncles and -aunts, and their descendants. Correspondingly, distinctions are minimal among the descendants of one's son and daughter.

Within the immediate family, men and women employ the same term for mother but not for father. Correlatively a man has separate terms for his son and daughter, a woman a single word for her children. A father's father is differentiated from a mother's father and a father's mother from mother's mother; corresponding to this a son's children are distinguished from a daughter's children. Greatgrandparents and greatgrandchildren are brothers and sisters, but curiously it is the senior generation that is called younger brother and sister.[47] The father's siblings are distinguished from the mother's siblings. The father's brother and the mother's sister are distinguished as older or younger than the corresponding parent. The relative ages of father's sister and mother's brother have no terminological expression, but are taken into account in the terms for their children, the cross-cousins.

Brothers and sisters are classed as elder sibling, younger sister, and younger brother. Parallel and cross-cousins are called brothers and sisters under certain circumstances. When a father's brother and the father are half-brothers by the same mother, the father's brother's children are termed siblings. Similarly a mother's sister's children are siblings when the parents are half-sisters by the same mother, but the latter seem to hold for a woman speaker alone. Otherwise parallel cousins are called by special terms, differing for the two sides of the house. Cross-cousins of the opposite sex are brother and sister, those of the speaker's own sex are known by special terms, but the difference between father's and mother's kinsmen is ignored.

Although age distinctions are made among all siblings, these are partially ignored in the designation of their children. A man distinguishes his older and younger brother's children, a woman

47 This may rest on the same notion that has the first born of twins the younger, because a younger person, they say, alway goes first.

her older and younger sister's, but for children of siblings of the opposite sex the distinction is ignored. A man's younger brother's child and a woman's younger sister's child are called by the same term; otherwise separate terms are used for each nepotic category. This, of course, correlates with the age distinctions among father's brothers and mother's sisters, and their absence among father's sisters and mother's brothers. The children of parallel and cross-cousins, and of cousins of the speaker's generation in the collateral lines, are classed with the appropriate nephew-niece group, regardless of whether the cousins are called brothers and sisters or by special cousin terms. The grandchildren of cousins are classed with grandnephews and grandnieces.

The collateral lines are merged with the line of direct descent. The avuncular relatives of the speaker's parents are grouped by sex alone without regard to the side of the house they are on, as we say granduncle and grandaunt. But the children of these granduncles and grandaunts, that is the parents' first cousins, are classed with the father's brother (older or younger) and sister or the mother's sister (older or younger) and brother according as they are related through the father or mother. Their children in turn are classed with the parallel and cross-cousins and the two succeeding generations fall in the categories of nephew-niece and grandnephew-niece. Those of the collateral cousins of the speaker's generation who are equated with cross-cousins are called by cross-cousin terms, but those who are equated with parallel cousins are called siblings. This is true of the speaker's actual parallel cousins only in certain circumstances to be discussed below.

These statements regarding collateral relatives are based on specific inquiry concerning terms applied to each and every relative stemming from the speaker's greatgrandparents. A few collateral cousins in the speaker's generation and some of their children were inadvertently overlooked, but since these cases are random and the remainder of the cases conform to the general statements immediately above, I see no reason for assuming any nonconformity here.

The age distinctions among parallel and cross-cousins are made, not on the basis of the relative age of the cousin and the speaker, but on the relative age of the speaker's parents and their brothers and sisters. This correlates with the classification by the speaker of father's or mother's first cousins as older or younger parents' siblings according as the parents call them (i.e., their cousins) older or younger brother or sister. The children of these parents' first cousins (i.e., the cousins of the speaker's own generation in the collateral lines) are accordingly older or younger siblings of the speaker depending on the assumed relative ages of their parents with the speaker's parents. The general principle then is to equate all relatives in the collateral lines with those of the direct line, preserving the horizontal stratification of generations, and making the age distinctions in one's parent's generation and one's own according to the relative ages of the connecting relatives in the grandparents' generation. With these collateral cousins of one's own generation it does not matter whether the connecting relatives are full or half-siblings.

As an illustration: a man's father's father's sister is cǐn_yàkǐ's regardless of whether she is older or younger than the paternal grandfather. But this woman's son is nàvi' (older paternal uncle) or n_yiku's (younger paternal uncle) like a true father's brother, depending on whether she is older or younger than the paternal grandfather. And again this son's son, in the speaker's own generation, is ěndjě'n (older sibling) or àcu'tc (younger brother) according to the same relative ages.

As illustrated by the genealogy below: Kutox's father D could not have called F dǒkxǎmi'k (father's brother's child) because D's father and his brother were not full brothers. Instead he called him àcu'tc (father's younger brother's son) because A was older than B. Kutox called F and G n_yiku's (father's younger brother), "because their side was younger," and their sisters, E and H, nàbi' (father's sister). These brothers called Kutox yěck_yiwa' (a man's older brother's child) and their sisters used měràpi' (a woman's brother's child).

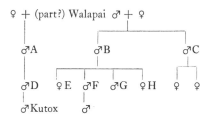

An alternative term, kiyi', "friend," is used by a man for certain of these collateral cousins of his own generation (but not for his first cousins). These are cousins whom he calls older and younger brother; the children of his parents' cousins who figure as father's brothers and mother's sisters. There is an exception, however; it is not used for the cousins derived from his father's mother's sister or his mother's father's brother. On its face this implies that the excepted lines of descent are more closely related to the direct line than the others, but the reason is obscure. The word is also used as a term of greeting to a non-relative, when the speakers are both men. The corresponding form is ciyi', used by two women, or when addressing an acquaintance of the opposite sex.[48] These are the terms used between members of the same sib when they are not blood relatives.

Relatives by marriage are grouped so that all women married to the men of one's own family are called by the same term (unyi', the wives of a brother, son, grandson, and of the parents' brothers, and with them the step-mother). This corresponds to the practice of all members of the family, but especially the women, calling these wives each by her sib name. The same stem appears in the single term applied by a woman to her husband's family (inkunyi',[49] his siblings, parents, grandparents and his children by another wife). Corresponding to this we might expect a man to use one term to designate members of his wife's family, including his step-children, but this does not occur. He groups some of his wife's relatives (her brother and grandparents) with some of the husbands of women of his own family (his sister's and granddaughter's husbands). A woman also calls her granddaughter's husband by this term (ucu'). A man's stepchild is kitca', a step-father the same (ᵃnᵧakĭ'tc); corresponding to unyi'c for step-mother and a woman's step-child, but without

[48] Kiyi' as an alternative for brother has an analog in Yuma, Kamia, and Cocopa. Where in Maricopa greatgrandparents and greatgrandchildren call each other siblings, in the tongues named these relatives call one another kiyi and siyi (Gifford, *Californian Kinship Terminologies*, pp. 62, 65, 67). Further, kiyi is used between males, siyi between male and female or between females, exactly as in Maricopa.

[49] This may be ĭ-nᵧa-k-unyi'; nᵧa-, the first person possessive prefix. This is borne out by Mohave: Maricopa unyi' and inkunyi' are covered by unyi-k in Mohave (Kroeber, *California Kinship Systems*, p. 342).

the extension of that word. (However, these words also mean a man's sibling's grandchild and grandparent's brother.) Reciprocal usage accounts for the same stem in son-in-law (ĭŋgwaxl$_y$áau′á) and wife's parent (ĭnxĭl$_y$áau′), but it is not clear why the wife's parents are not grouped with her other relatives. The sororate accounts for another exception: the words for wife's sister (ĭnyahwĭ′) and a woman's sister's husband (ĭnkwĭnyáhweya′) are similar.[50] The levirate is not reflected in any analogous way. It will be observed that the grouping of relatives by marriage does not follow sib lines. There are no terms in use between the parents of a couple, for a parents' sister's husband, nor for step-siblings. They are not related. While some of the cousins of the collateral lines in the speaker's generation are called brothers or sisters, their spouses are not called by brother- or sister-in-law terms. The wives among them are called by the names of their sibs.

One feature of some western systems is absent here, namely, the change of a term on the death of the connecting relative. However, after the death of a husband or wife, the terms for their relatives are dropped: they are no longer related.

Verbal reciprocity is only weakly developed. The following reciprocals occur:

nàvi′, father's older brother
nàpi′, father's sister
nàgwo′, maternal grandfather
nàkĭtc, grandparent's brother, step-father
cĭn$_y$ákĭ′s, grandparent's sister
ĭnxĭl$_y$áau′, wife's parent
ĭnkunyi′, husband's parent, husband's sibling, husband's grandparent, a woman's step-child
ĭnyahwĭ′, wife's sister
dŏkx̌ámi′k, a man's father's brother's child

vĕta′, a man's younger brother's child
mĕrápi′, a woman's brother's child
xaxgω′g, ŏx̌ko′, a man's daughter's child
kitca′, a man's sibling's grandchild, a man's step-child
ákĭ′s, a woman's sibling's grandchild
ĭŋgwaxl$_y$áau′à, son-in-law
unyi′, son's wife, brother's wife, grandson's wife, step-mother
ĭnkwĭnyáhweya′, woman's sister's husband

[50] They are probably more nearly alike than they are written; this was not checked. Together they are cognates of Mohave inyahuvik, wife's sister and woman's sister's husband (*ibid.*).

dŏkpȧsi'ṇk, a woman's father's brother's daughter
ĕstcuma'vȧ, mother's sister's child
tcĭkyȧ'vȧ, a man's male cross-cousin
ïlya', a woman's female cross-cousin

It is noteworthy that all the terms of the parental and grand-parental generation carry the possessive prefix, nȧ-, nyȧ-.

The Halchidhoma kinship system is identical with that of the Maricopa, except for slight phonetic differences, according to Kutox and Mrs. Redbird. As an example, the latter cited Halchidhoma mĭʀȧpiga' for Maricopa mĕʀȧpiya'. They may have meant, however, nothing more than that the terms and their use for close relatives are the same. Whether all the connotations are the same was not enquired into.

In the following list of Maricopa terms, the extensions into the collateral lines are not given, i.e., the classification of descendants of the grandparents' siblings. These are summarized above.

nȧpau'	father's father
nȧgwo'	mother's father
nȧmau'	father's mother
nȧkyiu'	mother's mother
nȧkĭ'tc, nyȧkĭ'tc, nyȧkica'	grandparent's brother, step-father
cĭnyȧkĭ's	grandparent's sister
nyĭko"	a man's father
ĕnȧ'ai'	a woman's father
'ntai	mother
nȧviya' (vocative), nȧvi' (non-vocative)	father's older brother
nyiku's, ĭnyiku's	father's younger brother
nȧbiya' (vocative), nabi' (non-vocative), nĕbi'k	father's sister
ĕnȧsi'c, nȧsi', nȧsiya'	mother's older sister
nyȧmuyi'c, nȧmuya'	mother's younger sister
nȧgwi'c, nȧgwiya'	mother's brother
xavi'kĭc	"two [of us]", sibling (probably non-vocative)
matxacȧvȧva'k	siblings (more than two; probably non-vocative)
ĕndjĕ'n	"straight," older sibling; father's older brother's child; a man's father's older sister's and mother's older brother's daughter; a woman's father's older sister's and mother's older brother's son; a woman's mother's older sister's child, when the mother and her sister had the

	same mother; greatgrandchild (all grand-children's children) (ĕndjĕ'n kuʀàŏk was recorded for elder brother in a myth; from kwuʀàŏ'k, "old man.")
ĕsdja'.....................	younger brother (but àcu'tc is regularly employed for parallel, cross, and collateral cousins)
àcu'tc....................	a woman's younger brother (seldom used); a man's or woman's father's younger brother's son; a woman's father's younger sister's and mother's younger sibling's son; greatgrandfather (all grandparents' fathers)
ĕnyŏka'..................	younger sister; father's younger brother's daughter; a man's father's younger sister's and mother's younger brother's daughter; a woman's mother's younger sister's daughter, where the mother and her sister had the same mother; greatgrandmother (all grandparents' mothers)
yŏvàk_yau' or matia'vàk_yaug..	half-sibling by the same father (When half-siblings have the same mother they call each other by the above brother and sister terms or tàvàa'l_yĭ'c, "tied together.")
dŏkχàmi'k................	a man's father's brother's child and a woman's father's brother's son when the father and his brother are full brothers
dŏkpàsi'n̥k...............	a woman's father's brother's daughter, when the father and his brother are full brothers (When they are half-brothers by the same mother, the father's brother's children are called by brother and sister terms.)
ĕstcuma'và...............	mother's sister's child (But this term was used by a woman only when her mother and her mother's sister were half-sisters by the same father, otherwise she used brother-sister terms for them.)
tcĭk_yă'và................	a man's father's sister's and mother's brother's son
ĭlya'.....................	a woman's father's sister's and mother's brother's daughter
kiyi'.....................	"friend" (used between male strangers); used alternatively for ĕndjĕ'n and àcu'tc (older and younger brother) in the following cases: a man's father's father's sibling's son's son, his father's mother's brother's son's son, his mother's father's sister's daughter's son, his mother's mother's sibling's daughter's son
ciyi'....................	"friend" (used between strangers where one or both are women, but the word is not used as a kinship term for collateral cousins)

xumai'....................	a man's son
vĭtci'....................	a man's daughter
sà'auwĭ'c.................	"issue," a woman's child (no specific terms for son and daughter)
yĕck̯yiwa'.................	a man's older brother's child; a man's parents' older sibling's son's child (It makes no difference with this and the following terms whether the father and his brother were full brothers.)
mĕRȧpiya' (vocative), mĕRȧpi', mĕRȧpi'k (non-vocative)...	a woman's brother's child; a woman's parents' sibling's son's child
vȧna' (vocative), vani'c (non-vocative)................	a man's sister's child; a man's parents' older sibling's daughter's child; since this also means a man's mother's younger sister's daughter's child and his father's younger brother's daughter's child, it probably means a man's parents' sibling's daughter's child
ĕn'ω', ĕnᵃω'.................	a woman's older sister's child; a woman's parents' older sibling's daughter's child
vĕta', ĕvĕta'................	a man's younger brother's child; a woman's younger sister's child; a man's parents' younger sibling's son's child; a woman's parents' younger sibling's daughter's child
auwȧ'....................	son's child
xaxgω'g, ŏxko'..............	daughter's child
kica'....................	a man's sibling's grandchild
ȧkĭ's....................	a woman's sibling's grandchild[51]
n̯yave'....................	wife
huða'vȧ..................	"partner," wife
akoi'....................	"old woman," wife when older
tavi'k, mataxavi'kĭk..........	co-wife (i.e., a woman speaking)[52]
n̯yikwĭRȧŏ'k................	husband[53]
kwuRȧŏ'k.................	"old man," husband when older
ĭnxĭl̯yȧau'.................	wife's parent
ĭngwaxl̯yȧau'ȧ..............	daughter's husband
ĭnkunyi', ĭnkun̯yiya'........	husband's parent, husband's brother, husband's sister, husband's grandparents, a woman's step-child

[51] The field-notes at one point give kica'and ȧkĭ's as vocative and non-vocative forms with this meaning, but I think rather that these are man's and woman's terms, corresponding to the forms for the grandparents' siblings.

[52] The word contains the stem xavi'k, "two."

[53] Although the word looks suspiciously like that for "old man," Mrs. Redbird said it does not mean this. She distinguished the following term, "old man," for a husband when older.

| unyi', unyi'c, un_yiya'........ | son's wife, brother's wife, grandson's wife, father's brother's wife, mother's brother's wife, step-mother |

unyi', unyi'c, un_yiya'........ son's wife, brother's wife, grandson's wife, father's brother's wife, mother's brother's wife, step-mother
kitca'..................... a man's step-child
ucu'..................... a man's sister's husband, his son's (and daughter's?) daughter's husband, wife's brother, wife's grandparents, a woman's daughter's (and son's?) daughter's husband
ĭnkwĭnyȧhweya'............. a woman's sister's husband
ĭnyahwĭ'.................. wife's sister

MARRIAGE AND FAMILY LIFE

The curious feature of Maricopa marriage is that its apparent informality belied a strictly formulated social configuration that resulted from it. Marriage ritual was lacking except for a purely formal test of housewifery. Despite the rigid control of their choice by the parents of the young couple, the mating seems casual enough. Nevertheless, the movement toward the union once initiated by the young people themselves, their relation to the two families becomes increasingly fixed in a rigid mould.

Marriage possibilities were limited by blood relationship and sib exogamy. A man could not marry any known blood relative of either parent regardless of sib affiliation, nor any woman of his own sib. Hence he could marry an unrelated member of his mother's sib. I was several times informed that he could not marry either parallel or cross-cousins (although his parents' several nieces were not members of his sib except by chance).

My aged informant denied that young men went courting: the most he would admit was that during night dances some would play their flutes at a distance to attract girls. Yet I received strong intimations elsewhere that young people made their own choice. There was at least no open courting, even through the intermediacy of a friend in the Pima manner.[54] While their elders might insist on industry and good temper as sufficient qualifications, young people were also interested in handsome mates. Good looks are not easily defined: I was told at least that one should have long thick hair and that girls as well should be broad in the hips. In a reference to beautiful women (axo'tk, "beauty,"

[54] Cf. Russell, *Pima Indians*, p. 183.

i.e., "good") it was explained that fleshy women were meant. Further, cradles for girls were made with the cross bars widely spaced so that the infants would grow to have large buttocks. They had a common saying that a handsome man will never marry a good-looking woman, while an ugly one would always get several wives. They had also the saying that a woman would give her good-looking daughter to a successful deer hunter. On the other hand I was told that one who was lucky at hunting and in games would not be lucky in love.

A girl might marry a few months or half a year after her puberty celebration, but some did not marry for several years.

Theoretically, at least, young men asked permission of their parents to marry. The parents selected the girl: even if their son did not care for her, he nevertheless obeyed them. "That is why some couples did not get along; because the parents did the selecting," Kutox observed.

The youth did not court the girl. Instead, he crept to her bed at night and lay beside it, but he refrained from touching her.[55] (This seems incredible but was convincingly affirmed by several informants.) Occasionally he would take a bosom friend along, point out where the girl lay, and send him off.

This gave rise to a saying: when a man reaches for something and his joints crack, he ejaculates, "No, I am not trying to get married"; because a lad's joints will crack, no matter how quiet he may be when he tries to crawl in beside the girl. It is reported that one man now living said he could never get married because this always happened to him. He said he exercised so his joints would not crack, but they always did.

If the girl woke, she sent her suitor away. She might go over to her parents and lie between them. Then the young man would tell one of them to get up, so that he could lie beside her.[56] Sometimes, if she did not wake, he remained until morning. Then, when her parents found he had been there, they persuaded her to marry him. Even if he came but once, they would force her to marry. It made no difference if she protested her dislike. Her

[55] They were not continent for four nights following marriage like the Yuma (Forde, *Yuma Ethnography*, p. 156).

[56] Again, this seems actually to have happened.

parents would remind her that death might take them and she would be alone in the world. "Children are supposed to obey; so she married him even if she did not like him." Yet she might finally refuse to go when the groom's mother came to fetch her.

When the youth told his parents that he had spent the night with the girl, his mother went for her. But before leaving, she sent word throughout the village that her son had been married. Then all the men and sometimes women gathered at his home to await the arrival of the girl. As soon as she arrived, she performed the stereotyped task of providing a meal for them.[57]

When a girl married, she was supposed to know all about cooking and grinding wheat. The latter was looked on as the most onerous task that could be set a young girl. The man's parents gave her a big basket of wheat to grind as soon as she arrived. Sometimes she would finish grinding the whole of it, but some could do no more than half. These would attempt to hide the unground grain in a hole beneath the end of the metate. Sometimes the girl would be so ashamed of her failure that she would run off home. Then others thought the parents mean to have given her so hard a task.

They also made her fetch a large vessel of water, perhaps from quite a distance. A girl friend might secretly help her; filling the pot after the bride had lifted it to her head. Sometimes she would leave the vessel on the river bank and run home.

Girls who could not perform these minimum accomplishments of any proper housewife, grinding quickly and well, and keeping an adequate supply of water on hand, were not wanted. Such a girl was permanently rejected by her intended husband's family. But when someone else wanted to marry her, they would bring up this defect in her character.

Nothing in the way of payment, not even gifts, was made to the girl's parents. But the man's parents made presents of such things as shawls to the girl before she married. A girl might be receiving gifts from one family when another selected her for

[57] There is no ceremonial washing of the couple as among the Navaho and Havasupai (cf. Spier, *Havasupai Ethnography*, p. 326).

their son to marry. Then the first family would say nothing whatever of their gifts: this was quite within her rights.

The young couple took up their residence in the home of the groom's parents. In fact some households became quite large when several sons brought home their wives. It was sometimes convenient for them to build a house of their own at once: they always did so following the birth of their second child. Their house might be located anywhere in the village, not of necessity beside the husband's former home. Since the farm lands, which were inherited, were located at a distance from the village and house sites were not heritable property, there was no compulsion in the forms of inheritance to do so.[58]

It was thought unnatural for a man to live with his wife's family, unless his help was really needed there. They believed he must be jealous that he kept his wife from his family or his erstwhile companions who still frequented his former home.

> It was a saying that a younger son or daughter would stay at home with their parents. Such a daughter would be joined by her husband. The older sons brought their wives home, but went off later to establish homes of their own. The older daughters marry elsewhere. Then the youngest at home inherited (Kutox). [This was obviously a matter of chance rather than any formalized junior inheritance.]

A new social configuration settled about the couple. From this time forward, the bride was regularly called by the name of her sib by the husband's family, especially its women members. Similarly, the groom was derisively nicknamed by his wife's relatives. They called him ugly like an animal or referred to some discreditable habit. The invention of the nickname was uniformly credited to his mother-in-law, although she may not have been its originator at all. A man was expected to treat his mother-in-law just like his wife. There was no mother-in-law taboo, nor one between father- and daughter-in-law. Brothers-in-law considered themselves close relatives and made it a point to help each other. Between brothers- and sisters-in-law a certain amount of licence was permissible: they might say anything to each other, even to obscenity, without offense.

[58] Cf. *ibid.*, p. 228.

The levirate was compulsory; the sororate common but not wholly obligatory. The levirate was compulsory, I was told, because the woman was a member of her husband's family and they did not want to give her up. It made no difference whether or not she had borne him children. If her deceased husband had no brother (there was no rule of junior or senior levirate), she must marry one of his relatives, sometimes her father-in-law. More commonly it was his father's brother's son or his brother's son (but not his sister's son); that is, someone of his family and sib. If the brother already had a family, she commonly married the parallel cousin. She might not like the brother and might marry outside the family, but this was regarded as disobedience of her obligation: she was willful like a child.

The sororate was customary rather than obligatory. When the wife died, her mother supplied in her place a sister of the dead woman (almost inevitably a younger sister) or some other relative of her own family. This might be her mother's sister's daughter, but not her mother's brother's daughter, nor any feminine relative of the father-in-law. In this case the second spouse was not of necessity of the same sib as the first, but it exactly parallels the case of the levirate where the substitute husband is by male linkage a member of the deceased husband's father's family, not his mother's. If the younger sister did not like the widower, she need not marry him. In earlier times a man did not marry his mother-in-law, but there is at present a case of this.

A few widows and widowers remarried only a few months after the death of their spouses, but it was usual to wait a year or two. Some never married again.

Plural marriages were not common. Some men had three or four wives. "Yet such a man would nevertheless go starving all day long!" each of his wives thinking the others had provided for him. He was not necessarily a handsome man; it happened rather because he had dreamed of the mocking-bird. He seemed handsome in his dream. He dreamed of the orange-winged blackbird and the mocking-bird(?), who are friends and always in pursuit of women. They have a big house so full of wives that they have to build another to hold them; blackbird's wives in one, mocking-bird's in the other. When he saw this in a dream he acquired two or three wives.[59]

When he married the first time, he brought his wife to his home. Later at a dance or a meeting, he might decide to speak to another. When the girl's parents discovered this, they might make her marry him. When he married a third time, they might think the third wife should stay at her own home, where he joined her. A man might keep all his wives in a single house, or they might remain with their parents. But he did not build a separate residence for each.

Plural marriages were sometimes with sisters, but not often. In response to specific questions concerning Navaho and Miwok types of marriage, I was told that a man sometimes married a woman and her adult daughter by another marriage, or a woman and her brother's daughter, but that neither was a regular form of marriage. There was no set preference for marrying wives related to each other, but there was some feeling that sisters would get along together better than non-relatives. Polyandry was unknown.

The following words describe the married state: matàtcu'ig, married; sinᵧàŏ'kàðau'g, having a wife; taxavï'g, having two wives (from xavi'k, two); sinᵧàŏ'kïcᵃða', plural wives (i.e. more than two).

Separation and divorce may have been fairly frequent. Incompatibility, infidelity, and barrenness were named as causes. They held that ordinarily a bride could get on with her husband's family if she remembered what she had been taught by her parents: to be industrious, to avoid quarrels and to be unselfish. If a man beat his wife, her parents would have nothing to say: she belonged to him. Even if he wanted to kill her, he could do as he pleased. This sounds much like Moslem despotism and theoretically it was, but actually, it seems, no man would have thought of unrestrained tyranny. The reaction to a wife's infidelity belies the theory.

If a man found his wife in adultery, he would say calmly

[59] See the tale, p. 405.

enough, "Perhaps she wants something to eat or wear that I can not give her," and let her go to her lover. He made no attempt to harm either of them. But he would never have anything to do with her thereafter.

X left his first wife, who took her infant son with her when she married a Kohuana. The Kohuana could not have been more fond of the boy had he been his own son. For instance, when the lad was returning from a visit to the Mohave, he injured his foot badly. His companions who came ahead reported that he might die of thirst in the desert. The Kohuana step-father immediately rode out to fetch him. X would have nothing to do with his ex-wife. He always drove the lad away with a stick and extended this unkindness to his son's children. People now ask why those children care for X, now that he is old, since he treated them so badly, but they reply simply that he is their relative and needs their help.

Women fought to retain the affections of unfaithful husbands. If a man was repeatedly remiss, his wife would give him up to her rival. If she left him for this reason, he might try to persuade her to return but she would refuse. She went to her relatives to live, because her husband was bringing a new wife to his home. However, if they had children, the wife would stay with her children. If nevertheless she decided to marry again, she told no one, not even the children, whom she abandoned there. Such abandonment is confirmed by an incident related below.

Ordinarily a barren wife was divorced. It was a common saying that a home was incomplete without children. Occasionally the wife might be kept if she was good-natured and industrious, and an additional wife might be taken. Both sexes were known to be impotent: they were called yĕsa'a'n.

Much the same attitude was displayed to a wife who bore girls. Girl babies were not wanted: they always said a girl was an enemy, because she might some day be married to an enemy and tell how to attack her own people. If the wife of a first marriage bore a girl first, her husband discarded her; but if she bore a boy, his people praised her.

While the Halchidhoma were still on the Colorado, a woman bore no children, so her husband sent her away. She married another man—it was his first marriage—and bore him a girl. His family made him put her away and take another wife. The woman said it was not right to raise a girl who had no father, implying it was no better than a bastard. It ought to be killed; so she threw the baby into the river.

Since aboriginal conditions are almost wholly a thing of the past, it is not easy to say what was the nature of family life. Relatives lived close together in a village. Two or three families lived together in a single house at times ("when they loved each other so they could not separate"), but such joint households were not common. Joint households were ordinarily comprised of patrilineal relatives.

They take more pride in that family. Of course, they do have respect for all their relatives, but more for those on the father's side.

A description was obtained from Hoot of the composition of the household in which she lived as a girl. She remembers a large house, her father's sister's home. Her aunt, uncle, and their two children slept on the south side; on the north side were her own parents, a younger brother, and herself. The southwest quarter was reserved for her father's mother's sister. Later this household broke up when her parents built a home of their own. There her parents slept on the south side; she herself was on the north side, but she never slept alone. At times the younger brother slept with her, but he, a little boy, would sometimes sleep between his parents. Then she would prevail on a girl friend to stay with her. Cooking utensils were stored on the south side near the door, so as to be handy for her mother when she arose. The rear of the house was left vacant for a visiting relative or friend.

When Last Star was a boy, in his house there were only his parents and his father's mother. He was an only child. His parents slept on the north side ("Parents always sleep on the north side"), his grandmother and himself opposite. The rear of the house was left for storage; food and water stood opposite beside the door. The fireplace was between the eastern pair of main posts.

All elders of a household assumed parental relation to the children, feeding, admonishing, and training them.[60] A boy's father or either grandfather made him his first bow, for example. Step-parents assumed the relation of parents to their step-chil-

[60] The special influence of the mother's brother, as among the Hopi, and that of the maternal grandfather, known among the Paiute, was wholly absent.

dren: nevertheless, they would never think of using parent-child terms for one another. They would be horrified by the reference to the dead. Adoption of children was frequent because of the wars. Even distant relatives would take them. When the child was adult, he would look on his foster-parents as he would on true parents. They have a saying: "never abuse a child, because the day will come when you too will be [as] a child." Yet occasionally orphans and step-children were mistreated. Despite this sentiment, there was a curious detachment toward children. No one would wholly blame a woman for deserting her children if her husband had given her sufficient cause.

An illustrative incident dates from about 1840. There was a Kohuana woman of the Kohuana village at Gila Crossing whose husband had died. She had two little children, a boy of six and a girl of two. She decided that she wanted to live with her relatives still on the Colorado. She thought the little children could never travel that far afoot. So she prepared provisions for herself, sent the children off to play, merely telling them to wait for her, and stole off to join the group that was going. When she failed to return, the boy led his little sister by the hand from house to house, inquiring for her. At night he would take her into the meeting house and build a fire to keep warm. In the morning they would go to someone's house to be fed. They had no relatives there. The boy said, "If I have no relatives here, I will call you all ciyi',[61] strangers." The two were inseparable. People took care of them. When they were grown, he said, "I have taken the trouble to bring up my sister; now someone should take the trouble to marry her." Both have long been dead.

A brother and sister had the highest respect for each other; they would not use obscene words in the other's presence, for example. Yet I received the impression that this had none of the stringency of Crow custom,[62] but was rather our own middle-class attitude.

Relationship seems to have imposed an obligation to be at least friendly and helpful if needed. Today, relatives gather to till each other's fields, expecting no more than to be fed by their host, or they tend each other's children.

Something of this sentiment is reflected in the following tale. In the early days an American beaver hunter living west of the Gila Bend Mountains was friendly with the Maricopa. He had bags of dried beaver skins there. Some

[61] The use of this form (ciyi' instead of kiyi') indicates that he must have been addressing the women.

[62] Lowie, *Social Life of the Crow*, p. 214.

Maricopa, visiting him, found him slain by the Yavapai. They thought they had best flee so that they would not be accused of his murder. One Maricopa, however, insisted on carrying off one of the bags, thinking it contained the much desired miner's shovels. The others crowded around him, ingratiatingly calling him "uncle" and by other kinship terms. When they opened the bag, they found that what had felt like shovel blades were only the stiff, flat tails of the beaver. So they thought it a joke on him and pushed him about.

They did not refer to father's and mother's kinsmen in the Mohave manner as on the right and left respectively,[63] but a simple reference to "on the man's side" (ipa'gȧwŭ'm) or "on the woman's side" (sĭn_yȧŏ'kȧwŭ'm) would be fully understood.

[63] Kroeber, *Handbook*, p. 749.

CHAPTER VIII

DANCES

Maricopa dances seem to have been purely social affairs. Ritual dancing was unknown, at least in anything like the form it took among the Pueblos. The dances appropriate to the several song series, while in some instances of fixed form, were so simple, so unorganized and with the pleasurable element uppermost, that they could be called no more than rudimentary attempts at ritual dancing. The sole dance having any elaboration was that in connection with the Mountain Killdeer song; the dance elements may have been taken over from the Papago-Pima Vikita complex.

Dances occurred at irregular intervals throughout the year. The big dances were held especially in winter (January–February), "when their wheat comes up nicely and they feel proud," and at harvest time (late August–September). These social dances were called xima′k (or hima′tc; hima′k, the dance step): "dances at other times would not really be called dances." This is significant, for the one general dance of the year held by the Havasupai (at harvest) was also alone called yima′gȧ. Similar celebrations of the Yuma were also yimut or nyima′ts.[1] Any dance leader was here called nᵧima′càisk, obviously based on this word. Such a leader held his position informally.

Other dances were coupled with the sahuaro drinking bout in the middle of June (p. 57), with the girls' puberty rite (p. 326), war and scalp celebrations (pp. 166, 184), and at the funeral and mourning rite held for a singer. From time to time when they were impoverished they exchanged visits with the Pima to gain foodstuffs by singing for their hosts. Still other dances for pure entertainment came at uncertain intervals to the accompaniment

[1] Spier, *Havasupai Ethnography*, p. 261; Gifford, *Yuma Dreams*, pp. 58, 62; Forde, *Yuma Ethnography*, p. 118.

of the song cycles, but with these it is clear that the song was by far the more significant element. Two dances of this type, more ambitious than most, are described below.

Dancing always took place in the open, never in the meeting house. The big dances, at least, were usually held when the moon was full. Gathering early in the evening, a few boys and girls would commence dancing; when it was dark, the dance got into full swing with many participating, and continued until the sun rose. There was little special dressing for dances: they washed their hair, men tied feathers in it and painted their faces, while women wore beads on neck and wrist. Invitations were freely extended to other tribes, beside those of the local mixed community, particularly the Pima. There was no formal manner of issuing invitations; no knotted string or notched stick sent, for example, to indicate the days before the dance would take place. An elderly man, a good speaker, was dispatched.

The dream songs were used at these big social dances; only one singer being chosen to sing his series throughout the entire cele-bration. He sat at the center of the dance circle, with others who were accustomed to sing with him. Dancers did not sing. The singer accompanied himself as his particular song required, with either a gourd rattle or a basket, which he either beat or scraped. A peculiar accompaniment, a combination of the two, scraping on one side of an upturned basket, pounding with his hand on the other, had a specific name, haxwe′ʀig.

The dance form was the round dance common in the Great Basin area. The dancers formed a circle about the singer, men and women alternately, their hands clasped (fingers not inter-twined). Partners were not paid, as among Havasupai, Navaho, etc. They circled counterclockwise, their step depending on the rhythm: if the singer beat slowly they shuffled along, if rapidly they hopped. The circle stood waiting after the song began until some selected man gave the order to start. The singer still beat time after his song ended, the dancers continuing to circle, while he picked up the next verse of his song. It was not customary to abandon the accompanying instrument (rattle or basket) on the dance ground, as the Havasupai their drum.

Shamans performed their feats at these celebrations.

In times of starvation they would go to other tribes to sing for them in order to receive gifts. The Pima also came in this fashion when they knew the Maricopa had plenty. Several days before the Maricopa set out they sent one of their number to the host village, provided with as many sticks as there were families intending to visit. A Pima man, acting for the hosts, collected an identical number to aid his memory. After the group arrived, these two told off each Maricopa family to the care of a Pima household. The latter would feed them in the evening and after the meal all gathered to dance. During the dance the Pima made gifts to their visitors: beads, baskets, bundles of mesquite beans or wheat, great jugs of sahuaro syrup, horses, and cattle. After their return the Maricopa would trade these among themselves until each had what he lacked.[2]

The Mountain Killdeer song had two disparate performances associated with it; one a display of power, the other a dance. In the display according to Kutox, the singer caused models of butterflies to flutter in time to his tune. A circular, roofless enclosure of willow poles was built, walled in with leafy branches. Across the top ran a series of parallel strings along which many yellow butterflies, cut out of mountain sheep skin, were tied. The singer sat at the center of the enclosure, which was about twenty feet in diameter and seven feet high. Others also sat within it to help him sing. As he sang, he beat on an inverted basket with one hand, scraping a stick (a foot long) on it with the other. "This made the butterflies look as though they were fluttering, as though they were dancing." This was simply a feat, not for curing.

The dance form coupled with the Mountain Killdeer song was used in the war dance (the performance preparatory to setting out to war), but also on other occasions. At the latter, Pima attended and a clown took part. Again the singer was seated. The dancers remained in hiding until he began to beat his basket: they then came forward in single file. Ten girls and ten young

[2] I was not told of the guest assuming the host's name, as recorded by Russell (*Pima Indians*, p. 171).

men took part, alternating in the line, with a man leading. Their bodies were painted white and red. Good-looking, long haired girls were chosen. Every dancer carried in each hand a four-foot stick, painted red and white, and along which were fastened alternately little wooden birds painted to resemble the mountain killdeer and butterflies made of deer skin or mountain sheep skin, with feathers between. The file of dancers stepped slowly and jerkily forward in a circular course, counterclockwise, around the singer. They stooped, thrusting their sticks forward alternately with each step, piston-rod fashion. The sticks were grasped by the middle. At the "chorus" they crossed them in front.

When the Pima attended, some of their women would hang on to the sides of the dancers, men or girls, and go with them to dance in the dance space. Relatives of those dancers who had Pima companions then made gifts to the latter: necklaces, beads, shawls, blankets, and the like.[3] Finally the Pima chief would tell the Pima participants to leave off and let the dancers perform.

A clown was described in connection with this dance by Kutox, as participating in any dance by Last Star. He was an active man, carried a long pointed stick in his hand as a spear, and had his face painted or wore a mask. When he wore face paint, one half of his face was red, the other black, "to appear comical," and a headdress woven of willow twigs as a disguise. The mask sometimes worn was of cotton cloth, bag-shaped, with a long nose of cloth, and a mouth painted on it, with fringes to represent whiskers. The essential part of any costume he might wear was a strong belt: a mescal fiber rope, or of cloth. He danced violently, principally by himself, used inverted speech (but not inverted actions), and in general, tried to behave ludicrously. If he joined the ring of dancers, he would not let women grasp his hand but would jerk away. Women would lay hold of his belt trying to dance with him, but he would whirl them around. His relatives would then make presents to these women. This clown was called ϑokwutai'ás, an unanalyzable word.

[3] Precisely as in the Pima "name song," the begging performance mentioned above.

Such masks (iϑŏmataŏ'm) were said by Last Star to have come into use only in his parents' day, that is, in the middle of the last century. He did not know where they derived the idea.

A combination of these two forms of the Mountain Killdeer dance was described by Last Star. He had heard it referred to as the greatest dance they had ever had. (It occurred before he was born.) "Once" the singer had made a large circular enclosure of arrowweeds stuck into the ground. It was provided with four openings, one at each of the cardinal points, and within each opening a pole was set up. From each pole hung an image of a butterfly made of leather: that on the east pole was painted white and black, on the west yellow, north blue, and south black. When the dancers entered, "their breathing and dust" made the butterflies flutter as though dancing. The singer sat on the western side within the enclosure, together with several men who sang with him; all scraping on a single basket. Behind them were some women who also sang with them. The audience entered by east, south, and west openings to sit about inside. The dancers were mostly young women and men. Each was provided with a stick bearing many pendent feathers: in their other hands they each held a skin image of a butterfly. They kept time with their sticks, moving their arms piston-rod fashion. When the "chorus" was sung, they held these objects high. The dancers entered by the northern opening, moving in a counterclockwise course in single file within the enclosure. There was no masked clown at this dance. This dance occurred at an occasion for jollification; not when news of slain enemies had been received.

The last time this dance was given, according to the same informant, the enclosure was presumably lacking. Each dancer held an image of the mountain killdeer in one hand with which to keep time; something else in the other. The image was made from the chocolate-colored root of a plant growing near the river, in shape resembling a sweet potato. A band scraped white resembled that about the neck of this bird. The image was mounted on a stick.[4]

---

[4] It is possible that the Mountain Killdeer performance and the masked clown are to be identified with the Vikita-Navitco dance complex of the Papago and

A spectacular dance called Moving the King Around (xan-àvʀe' gĭcpa'càm, "to move out the king") may have been coupled with the song Dragonfly (xanavàʀe'). The word xan-avàʀe' meant not only dragonfly, but the leader of the whites, as king or President. This looks like the confusion of a native term for the insect with a Maricopazation of Spanish *general*. The reference in this dance was to Montezuma, a figure of local myths, who was identified in some fashion unknown to me with the Sierra Estrella. The mountain was called "Man lying on his back" beside its esoteric name "Berdache Mountain," and a peak at the eastern end, "Two heads." These are recorded on modern maps as "Montezuma Sleeping" and "Montezuma's Head." The word mŏntĕsu'm, according to Mrs. Redbird, meant "unknown people"! The performance was based on the circumstance that "in the early morning the Sierra Estrella looks as though there was a great building there, a castle, or a row of cottonwood trees, or the like. It will stand this way for a time and suddenly disappear." This is simply due to the morning light sharply defining the pinnacles on its northeastern front for a time.

The man "who started it again [the song?] said he was going to make something like they see in that mountain." He painted a cloth to resemble the mountain. He danced with others, all "going around" several times; then he stretched the painted cloth to cover them all. Baskets were used to mark time; some beaten, others scraped. This dance took place in the open during the day. "They thought it the greatest performance ever held. He never tried it again."

The dance forms of the Maricopa appear in summary as two alone: a circular dance and one in which two opposed lines of dancers trotted backward and forward together. The circular form was used in the big social dances described above, the scalp dance, and with Mountain Killdeer singing. The direction of movement was counterclockwise in all three, as in all Maricopa

Pima (cf. J. A. Mason, *Papago Harvest Festival;* Davis, *Papago Ceremony;* Russell, *Pima Indians*, pp. 266, 328; Parsons, *Notes on Pima*, pp. 461 f.; Curtis, II, 12).

circuits. The form with opposed lines was recorded, so far as my scanty notes go, in the girls' puberty rites and with Buzzard singing. For other songs, the stereotyped procedure was simply sitting or standing about. The lack of variety in dance steps is noteworthy.

The rhythmic accompaniment for songs and dances was with gourd rattles or baskets which were scraped or beaten. Other instruments were unknown: the drum, the trench drum described for the Mohave, deerhoof and cocoon rattles, and the notched rasp. The Yuma and Pima were credited with the deerhoof rattle, the former in their mourning rites; the Pima clown used the cocoon rattle, and the Pima again the notched rasp in the cure of rheumatism and to bring rain.

The rattles (ᵃxna'lᵧ,ᵃtatci'n, "shaken gourd") were always made of gourds they cultivated. These were mounted on wooden handles which projected completely through them, with small pebbles inside. The rattle was pierced with many little holes "to get all the noise out." In examples for secular use, these were arranged in longitudinal and transverse rows (Pl. XII, a),[5] but shamans, according to Kutox, who alone described their use in curing, had the holes grouped in little circles. The reason for the difference was unknown to the informant. Arrangement of the holes to represent the constellations, as recorded for the Navaho, was unknown.

[5] Washington State Museum, No. 2–11921.

CHAPTER IX

RELIGIOUS BELIEFS AND PRACTICES

THE DREAM EXPERIENCE AND SPIRITS

At the heart of Maricopa culture was the dream experience. It was the one thing of which they constantly talked, the significant aspect of their life as they saw it. It is this more than any other single element that establishes the unity of their culture with that of the lower Colorado Yumans, and this holds equally for the other, originally Colorado peoples among them, Halchidhoma, Kohuana, and Halyikwamai, so far as one can now judge. At the same time, the Maricopa emphasis on experiences with particular spirits seems more like the generalized North American relation with guardian spirits than does the Mohave, with its myth framework in the phrasing of the dream.

Dream experience was at the bottom of all success in life, and as such their constant preoccupation. Learning was displaced by dreaming, and while it was recognized that an individual acquired skill by practice or imitated songs on hearing others, his activity or knowledge would be neither wholly successful nor significant unless he had dreamed. A single statement of Last Star's epitomizes their attitude: "Everyone who is prosperous or successful must have dreamed of something. It is not because he is a good worker that he is prosperous, but because he dreamed." All songs and song performances were revealed in dreams and their content was the dream experience; on the experience was based the conceiving of children, oratorical power, curing, bewitching, and shamanistic feats; clairvoyance and prowess in war, and the ability to lead in war or to serve as chief. In short, all special abilities were to be had by dreaming, and by dreaming alone.

Supernatural power came only in dreams and almost always involuntarily. Dream and spirit were called by a single word, càma'g. As Mrs. Redbird put it when asked for the word for spirit, "The only way to express 'spirit' is that it comes in dreams." The word gwïstama'tc, "one who has power," i.e., one who has dreamed, seems based on the same stem. The core of the concept seems to be that what we are here calling spirit and dream were shadowy doubles of the same thing, namely, the experience with spirits in dreams. Asked to explain how the spirits entered into dreams, Kutox gave a halting explanation. "Here is my shadow. Now the Owl somewhere sends his spirit to meet others. We call that hucamai'ïg. If I am asleep here, there is my shadow. If the spirits wanted to talk to me, they would take me out, that is, that part of me something like my shadow." The word hucamai'ïg was then rendered "shadows meeting each other," but it is palpably based on càma'g, "dream," not on matkwïca', "shadow" (of a man, animal, or object), "reflection" (as in water). At another time he said that "a dreamer's shadow (matkwïca') has the experience with the spirit birds, not his soul (wipai')." This is unsatisfactory: it is at once too vague and too much objectified. The difficulty seems to be that the Maricopa were not interested in sharply crystallizing the concept. So far as I can see it sums up in this fashion: what we are here calling a spirit has no existence or at least never manifests itself except in dreams: the dream is not as we would say a phantasy based on a particular physiological state, but is a state in which some spiritual quality of the dreamer goes out to meet the spirit: in other words, it is the dream experience which is at once the dream and the spirit.

The same concept and stem appeared in the words lucky, càma'sàxωtk (lit. "dream good"), and unlucky, càma'mŭk. These were explained as derived from the quality of one's dreams, which in turn depended on the time of night one dreamed. "To be lucky is to dream good. In the early evening one has bad dreams," and again "before dawn, when the spirit birds are fighting and eating each other, what with all their bloodstains, if one dreams of this he will get sick." Lucky dreams came in the middle of the night (see p. 248). On the other hand, some expressions for having power were based on another stem:

gwĭdĭcʋĭ'sk, "they have power"; gwĭsĭʋi'k, "one has power"; gwĭsiʋe', "shaman."

In native theory dreaming was almost wholly unpremeditated. Quite rarely a man visited certain caves in which the spirits were known to dwell in order to induce dreams of them. But there was no such thing as deliberately going out to seek a vision (as distinguished from a dream). In fact, the only vision in a waking state known to my informants (that of the war tale below) came as involuntarily as the usual power-bestowing dream.

Dreams, by reason of their involuntary character, might come to anyone, but the evidence is that relatively few had dreams bestowing songs or the ability to cure, or to foretell or bewitch. Men shamans numbered only five or six at a time and those who bewitched even fewer. There is some question whether women were ever shamans. Similarly, singers, who had their gift by dreaming and were men alone, were a handful, orators even fewer, and there was but one war leader and one chief. The impression was that those who had power never numbered more than a score in the whole community. This does not mean that the rank and file did not have dreams of the same stereotyped sort, since, for instance, falling ill was commonly attributed to dreaming of the dead or of certain plants, and children were born as the result of dreams, but their dreams did not result in power or song. There was a saying that a handsome individual never dreamed of spirits. That, explained Kutox, my informant, accounted for himself!

Professional segmentation among those having power was marked. These individuals were set off from one another by the possession of discrete powers from particular spirits. Thus, Coyote and Buzzard gave power to cure, Eagle power to sing, Mocking Bird to orate, Frog to bewitch. The differentiation was not a quantitative one in the sense of some having more power, of having dreamed of more spirits, although this may have been true of shamans who cured. Dreaming of various spirits very probably occurred, as suggested by the fact that a single individual did dream more than one song cycle. Against this particularism in professional activity is the fact that while Buzzard, for instance, gave the ability to cure wounds caused by the Yavapai, he also gave clairvoyant power to discover the enemy's whereabouts. Further, it is not certain that shamans who cured and those who bewitched were different individuals. An explicit statement affirms that they were, but to the contrary is the fact that shamans who failed of a cure were accused of witchcraft. Perhaps the test would be if the word for curing shaman (gwïsiθe') was also applied to the witch: I do not know. There was at least an overlapping of powers in that both shamans and song leaders dreamed songs, the shamans sometimes singing for entertainment like song leaders.

Ordinarily the dream first came in early childhood, but it could be had by an adult. At any rate, it is clear that it was not connected in any way with puberty. The spirit visitation recurred to the dreamer over a long period. Further properties of curing were revealed; he was trained as orator or warrior, or more of the song was given him. During this time he must reveal his dream to no one. Not until the spirits pronounced his preparation complete could he use the powers they granted; otherwise they were angered and withdrew their gifts. The following statements of informants will illustrated these points.

Any man, even a child, might be asleep. Some bird or animal likes his ways and takes him way up in his dream. A child would not speak of his dream until he was a man. He dreams repeatedly of the same bird. When the bird has shown him everything, he tells the lad to begin singing and curing. The lad would then be in his late twenties.

A man started dreaming when he was a child if the spirit liked him. When he began to get gray, he realized what he had been taught and then began to cure.

A man returning from hunting, tired, might lie down to dream that some bird comes to him and sings. When he gets home he may dream again that the bird comes and takes him to a mountain where there is singing and dancing. Men do not tell what happens on these occasions. Such a man always wants to sleep so as to dream again as quickly as possible. Even if they are off to war, when it is dangerous to sleep, such a man persists. Then they know he is dreaming of these things. They would ask him but he would not tell. He dreams he is taken off into the mountains and shown the enemy. One does not tell of his dreams until he is turning gray. Then he tells just a little, but he never tells what kind of bird it was.

Men would not tell plainly of what animal or other spirit they had dreamed. They did not name it in the song but would nickname it and hint at its behavior; then people would understand. Nothing was worn to show what it might be.

The incipient stages of dreaming in childhood, the setting from which the significant dream might mature are revealed by two anecdotes.

When W——was but a few years old, he was followed everywhere by his pack of pups. He said he could understand what dogs said. When one was barking in the distance, he said, "He is telling us to come: he knows where there is meat hidden." Or "He is telling us that he is being beaten. He says, 'My master is not kind to me.'" The old people said he must have been dreaming of dogs.

The important point here is that the elders were implying that this precocity could be turned to account in later life by assuming that the boy's course of dreaming had already begun. The other anecdote shows a course of dreaming well begun in a lad of about sixteen. The setting of the dream is modern, but its repetitive form is of the old type.

A boy kept repeating certain words to himself, "Children of Castovia."[1] He said he could not get them out of his mind. He always dreamed he was going along a wide straight road, with nothing but right hand turns; at each turn was a sign "Children of Castovia." He said he reached the place (directed by these sign posts): it was a big house, full of children, with this sign on the door.

Inheritance of power, so far as it occurred at all, also revolved about such incipient stages of dreaming in childhood, but the powers were not used until the heir was adult and until the death of the parent.

A father who had dreamed songs would tell his child as soon as he was old enough to understand, how he came to see these things and how to go about seeing them. Then when the child grew to be a man, he always took after his father, that is, always after the father died.

A case in point, cited below, is the attempt of a son to take over the Mountain Killdeer songs of his father by dreaming of this spirit after his father's death. A specific case of inheritance was that of xatisa'là, the Halchidhoma chief, who dreamed the songs Deserted (vŭspo') and Enemy Standing (hwĭcĭvau'). His son, who was not chief, was known as the dreamer of the Deer song. All that seems to be inherited in this case was the tendency to dream. I do not know of any connection between these songs.

[1] This was said to be meaningless by the narrator of the anecdote, but it is palpable he was repeating the slogan of a common patent-medicine advertisement tacked up at every fence-corner.

Inasmuch as it was said that "there was one war leader [at a time]; when he died another took his place at dreaming," the suggestion is that, in general, the normal course was for a successor to dream the specific powers. This was specifically the case with chieftainship: the dead chief's successor (normally his son) dreamed the necessary oratorical powers. From this point of view, filial inheritance is to be regarded as only a special case. Certainly filial inheritance was not stressed. My informants repeatedly referred to shamans and singer without remarking that their fathers had had these capacities before them.

Both the progressive change in the character of the songs as they were learned in dreams and their withdrawal by the spirits because they were sung before the revelation was completed are exemplified by the following account.

A man sang the Mountain Killdeer songs [when young]. He would sit in broad daylight working on the cotton he was going to weave and still hear the bird's songs. He could hear them just as though a person was sitting beside him singing. He sang that he was taken by this little bird during the night to the bird's home at vikwàme' [the Mohave sacred mountain], where he was taught the songs by the bird. Mountain Killdeer had sung these songs to him for more than a year. He called it vitaRi'c nᵧĭmsa'và, "white mountain killdeer." Then he went to Mountain Killdeer again, who now sang to him that his songs had turned black, meaning that he did not like this man because he had sung too early. The man told this, singing:

avinyaya'ka	mavinyaya'ka
he is going	
vĭtaRi'cvas	kwinyamusa'vic
mountain killdeer	twilight
amicova'Rà	matininyamviyak
song	dark going

He sang this song at gatherings.[2] He no longer mentioned "white" in his songs. He would tell how the bird had said that he, the young man, had had his songs taken back. The old people said he would die young: he did.

The son of this man said it was queer that he did not dream of this, get it, after his father died, because this usually happened to a child. Then he did dream of it twice. He dreamed he was taken to a butte near Tempe and then to another. When he woke late he told his grown daughters. He then dreamed again that the person [spirit] appeared to him and was angry because he had told too soon. The person said, "I will never take you again." To make him forget what he had

---

[2] The method of singing and the associated dance are described elsewhere (pp. 231-33, 266).

learned, the person then smeared ashes over the man's lips, and, turning his back on him, struck him on the mouth, taking away the song. He told his daughters it was taken away because he talked too much. He was a notorious chatterer.

While it was decidedly advantageous for one to begin dreaming while still a child, there was real danger in overdoing it, in dreaming too much. A boy or girl "who dreamed too much of any one thing" would suffer a change of sex. "They had, in fact, too much of this dreaming; that is why they changed their mode of life. The change was caused by some spirit." Transvestites were never shamans; although they had been given the power to cure and sing, they had been given too much. The other spirits might interfere, taking the boy and changing him into a woman. Sex changed at puberty, "about the time the voice changed."

On the other hand, the same informant ascribed the transformation to a dream of a specific type. It was believed the Sierra Estrella had a berdache living inside, hence the name of the mountain, ᵃvial_yxa", "berdache mountain." "Any man who dreams of this will become a berdache." Another mountain at Yuma, called by the same name, also had the power to transform men. "As one sees them in dreams, the two mountains are young girls." The Sierra Estrella invited the mountain at Yuma to play games. If the Yuma mountain, e.g., lost, then the Yuma lost a man; he became a berdache. ("But to us as we now look at it, we would never think it could do this.")

The signs of transformation came early in childhood; which corroborates the statements that all courses of dreaming began at that time.

When a boy begins to toddle, they would not think of letting him run around without bow and arrow, nor a little girl without a basket to use like her mother. But if the boy was going to become a berdache (ĭl_yȧxai': cf. cĭl_yȧxai'g, "girlish," mȧcȧxai, "girl"), he threw away his bow and took a basket or continually used a metate. Older people would comment, "He is going to turn out to be a berdache"; by his actions, they knew he would change sex.

If they did not wish to embarrass transvestites by calling them ĭl_yȧxai', the word yĕsa'a'n, "barren man or woman," was used.

Such transformations were rare. Kutox remembered but one berdache in his day and another in the previous generation, with not more than one transformed woman at a time. Berdaches behaved like women; gathering mesquite, etc. They always went about with women, not with men. They married men and had no children of their own. Men approved, "treated them like girls," but the women were uneasy of them. Women who passed for men (kwĭraxamĕ′, which cannot be etymologized) dressed like men and married women. There was no ceremony at the transformation as among the Mohave.

Since all success depended on dreaming, it must have been frequent in adult life. In fact, the evidence is that the interpretation of dreams was a relatively common topic for discussion among friends. For instance, a significant dream came to a man or woman before they had intercourse; by it they knew whether they would have children. A man might dream that he was gathering little birds or puppies, dream that he was fond of them; that was a sign that he would have children. A woman might equally have such a dream. The dream did not give power to conceive: it was merely a forecast. Only in this sense, said informants, could it be said that a man knew the woman would conceive before she did.[3] Or on telling a dream, someone would interpret it: "That is a sign that you are not going to have a child." This type of dreaming had no special designation.

Similarly a man who had dreamed of marching up to fierce animals, who suddenly became quiet, could in the same manner march up to and kill a foeman.

Beside spontaneous dreaming, there was the possibility of inducing dreams which would yield occult power by taking jimsonweed. While under its influence, a man dreamed that the birds sang to him and told what he should do. Some days later he began to sing, having gotten power to cure. Such a person would not live long, they believed. For other persons the reactions to the narcotic were interpreted differently: their actions while under its influence foretold their future. If a man "was interested in fishing," he might jump into the river fully-clad,

[3] Of the Yuma, Forde writes: "Actual conception is known to the man before it is to the woman. . . . . To him, it is believed, comes the power to create the child. Conception can only occur when the man has received this power of which he should normally dream beforehand. Without this sense of spiritual exaltation intercourse cannot be fruitful, and he is immediately aware if he has achieved impregnation. The woman, for her part, can also resist conception by merely refusing to desire a child" (*Yuma Ethnography*, p. 158; cf. p. 159). Perhaps; but I suggest that his informant meant no more than the Maricopa forecast.

and snatch up bits of wood and stones under the impression they were fish. If he was to be a great warrior, he seized a stick and brandished it, whacking away on a stump. It is not wholly clear that this typifying activity was thought different in nature from the induced dream. A statement suggests otherwise: "they dream how to become good hunters of a particular animal, as jackrabbits, cottontails, deer, or mountain sheep."

Jimsonweed (*Datura*, cmalgapi't, "deaf ear") was used by any man; usually younger men and boys. The inner portion of the root was chewed and swallowed, a decoction of the mashed leaves was drunk, or the latter rubbed on the body. The part of the plant from which the roots or leaves were taken was not prescribed. "They do not eat much: too much will kill them. It makes them crazy: they will not come close to a person, but sneak away." Beyond the fact that young people took the drug, inquiry failed to reveal any specific parallels to the toloache rite of southern California. Nor were thieves detected under its influence as at Zuñi.

A deliberate quest for dreams, like the vision-quest of northern and eastern Indians, was rare. My informant knew of only two places, two caves, to which one went to get in touch with the spirits. The first cave, on the western (?) side of the Painted Rock Mountains, was the home of a spirit named kukupu'Rá (hence the mountains were called his house, kukupu'Rniva). The nature of this spirit was unknown. One can barely creep through the entrance to this cave; far inside is a large room, and the cave extends indefinitely beyond. "Whenever a man wished to be rich or to become a shaman, or have crops prosper, be a good runner, or have many girls about him," he sat in this room facing the opening and holding his right hand out. He prayed for what he desired. Then he heard something coming from the rear of the cave: there was a great draught and the sound of a whirlwind. The spirit put something very cold in the man's hand. He clenched his fist tight and crept out. When he reached home, he avoided fats and salt, "fasting" for four days, and bathing each morning. "Then his wish came true." If the seeker fled from the cave in fear, he would become blind and perhaps insane.

A second cave, also difficult of access, was halfway up the eastern face of a little butte south of Tempe: called kumpa'n$_y$-ïkn$_y$iva', "Bat's house." "There must be a spirit there, the bat." Lying in the cave were stubs of reed cigarettes of varying length, some old, some new, each was plugged with a wad of cotton and contained a white powder which could be smoked.[4] Most men dared not touch these, but if a man smoked one, he would either die right there or dream of something to become a shaman. (An instance in which this was done by Papago Foot is cited below.) There was also thought to be a gourd rattle in the dirt of the cave floor. But no ordinary man could find it; only an especially favored shaman, one who dreamed of the spirit. He would replace it where he found it.

Visions (as distinguished from dreams) were not had by the Maricopa. The only instance of a vision experience was recounted in a war tale, which follows. Here the spirit birds act as they do in dreams, condescend to pity the visionary and give him ability to perform an otherwise impossible feat. But the vision does not take the stereotyped form of the dream experience.

This happened to a Maricopa who was born two months after the stars fell [1833] and who died just over a year ago. He went to fight the Yuma when he was fifteen years old (1848–49). He never said whether he had had any dreams of these birds before this experience.

He started with his father and his father's younger brother. All three rode horses. There were more than one hundred on foot and as many horsemen. When they crossed the Colorado, he was told they would let the footmen go ahead because they were armed with clubs. The whole Yuma tribe gathered clustered into a space of three acres. There were women and children fighting on the Yuma side. When there were only forty or fifty Maricopa left, surrounded by Yuma, the waiting horsemen decided to charge. They were armed, some with bows, some with clubs. The Yuma beat some down, dragged them off their horses and killed them. This man did not know how he ever got through the crowd without being hurt. Only a few horsemen were left, but they decided to charge back through the Yuma once more. He did not know what had happened to his father and uncle. He escaped and raced away through the thick willows. The paths were so narrow that people had to go single file. As he was going through, he heard two Yuma coming toward him on the path, so he hid himself in the bushes until they passed. Then he went on to the river. He did not return by the way they had crossed. He had a shirt of woven cotton, which he took off and tied on top of his head. He got on his horse and entered the water. Just as

---

[4] In this connection it must be noted that these were not Maricopa offerings. They made no offerings to spirits nor planted prayer plumes.

he reached the other side, his horse got away from him. He felt around for the tail, but managed to catch the halter rope. He felt sure that if he missed it he would drown. The lad kicked out until he felt the sand under foot; then he stood up. When he reached the bank, he found it as high as a house and steep. There was barely room enough at its base for him to stand; no room for his horse. All the time he sat there he felt unsafe; some one might come along and beat him to death. As he sat there he held to the end of the rope and let his horse swim back and forth. They had started to fight in the middle of the morning. It was just before noon that he swam the Colorado.

As he sat there, wondering how he could get out, he felt that there was no chance of being saved. He saw some small birds coming out of little holes in the bank. They fluttered all about him. Late in the afternoon, he suddenly heard a noise on the bank above him. He did not know what it was, but he could understand it just as plainly as if his own people were talking. As they, the little birds, stood up there, he heard them say, "What shall we do? Shall we take him out or shall we leave him in there?" At the same time he heard an owl hoot. The owl came to the edge of the bank and sang:

maki'lyȧvakȧmi'   xuma'ʀkwȧxω't

At what place   a fine boy
is he crying?

"Where is the fine-looking boy who is crying? The boy's day has come: he is anxious for his day to come." At the end of this song, the little bird said, "No, I am going to save him. I, xŏmkĭ'tĭnya'm (xŏmkĭ' is the name of the birds today; tĭnya'm, dark), will save him." He heard this talking but he could not see anyone. Then the little bird said, "Come!" When he heard this, he turned right around and saw that the bank was now only a foot or so high. So he crawled over it and pulled his horse up. As soon as he got on top he found it was as high as before. The little bird said to the owl, "Now it is your turn to take care of him." So the owl turned around and rubbed himself all over. Then the owl stood in front of him in human form. The owl told the lad that he just wanted to show him what he could do. Then the lad got on his horse and started off. The owl said, "On your way back, it will be just the same as when you came. You will not be alone; you will find some people walking in front and in back of you. You will be all right all the way home." Sure enough he saw some people going before him. He saw several stopping to smoke; he passed them. [The dead seem implied, since this locality, the desert east of the Colorado, was the Maricopa land of the dead.] As he went along the owl flew in front of him. When he caught up with it, it flew ahead again. He rode on until nine or ten at night, when he stopped to rest.

There were twenty Maricopa or fewer who escaped: the Yuma say none. They were badly bruised on head and shoulders; some were shot.

The next morning he rode on and overtook them. They had stopped to rest in the shade at noon. His father and uncle had been saved. On their way back, they had cried, thinking he was killed. These two began to wail again as they sat there; others mourned with them. When at noon he came toward them, someone stood up to see who was coming. He saw the lad on his pinto horse: he described them. His father said, "Be careful; perhaps you are not telling me the truth." When they saw it was really he, they all rose to meet him. They rested there: the whole afternoon they cried for their slain relatives.

Years later two Yuma men told him that they had seen him sitting under the opposite bank. They did not know how he did it, but they saw him jump on his horse, whip it, and climb right up the bank.

When he was older he became a great warrior and was highly honored.

THE FORM OF THE DREAM EXPERIENCE

The dream experience purported to be an adventure of the dreamer during the night. Under the guidance of a spirit, he moved from mountain to mountain, where the specific cures or songs associated with these peaks were revealed to him. Three illustrations will illumine the pattern of all.

One who dreams of Eagle becomes a great singer. In the dream Eagle is high in the sky. He takes the dreamer up there and shows him the various places and mountains, naming them for him. Eagle shows him the whole valley, and tells him how to go about his work curing people.

Any man, even a child, might be asleep. Some bird or animal likes the ways of the sleeper and takes him in his dream way up like the eagle does. He is taken to various places on a string. They think of the buttes as connected by strings, even as far as Needles [i.e., to Avikwame, the sacred mountain of the Mohave]. The dreamer thinks he is moved along the string through the air by the bird. At each butte or mountain the spirit tells him of a different kind of curing. The bird appears in human form.[5]

Papago Foot, the Kohuana, went into the cave in a butte near Tempe (see above). He smoked one of the reeds lying there and fell asleep at once. "He just wanted to do it, because he thought that even if he died it would be better than the way he was living, and perhaps he might become a shaman." He dreamed of a human, whom he did not recognize, who came to him, saying he would help him begin. The spirit tied a cobweb from that butte to Tempe Butte, and thence to Four Peaks, to the San Francisco Mountains ("where he saw the natural bridge"), thence to vikwame' at Needles. He travelled on that cobweb and had various cures revealed to him at each butte. But he spoke of this to someone too early, so the spirit said, "You have gone just halfway [around the circuit]. I intended taking you all the way around until you got back to where you started. But since you have told too soon, you have seen only half of what I had to reveal; you can get along with what little you have seen." So this man cured bowel trouble. Others always twitted him for telling.

The form was generically the same for dreams in which powers other than curing were bestowed.

One who dreams of the mocking bird becomes a great orator: he might make speeches lasting for days and nights. The mocking bird takes him along the [long

[5] Curtis records the dream of a shaman in which instruction in curing is given by various insects, etc., to whom he is conducted by his guardian, Buzzard (II, 84).

ridge of the] Sierra Estrella from east to west, the bird talking all the way without pausing for breath. Then he tries the dreamer. When he too can do this he is ready as an orator.

There is one war leader, the only man who dreams of going after the enemy. When he dies, another takes his place at dreaming this. He dreams of overcoming danger and killing enemies. He dreams only of being successful in his fights. In his dreams he could see certain little flies (kumanyihwi') fighting up in the air. He saw by the way they fought how he should act to be successful in his battles. He also dreams he sees certain cacti (ᵃxu'l), in the form of humans, fighting. When they see he is fitted for his position, the spirit [*sic*] takes him into a large cave inside the mountain in enemy territory. As he enters he sees a club, a shield, and a spear hanging on the walls of the house. Each time he is taken there, they give him a chance to use one of these. He keeps practising until he has used them all. Then he leads his people to war.

The dream was also patterned on the four-fold division of the night; a pattern which was omnipresent in Maricopa thought. It appeared in the conduct of meetings, in the organization of curing by shamans, in orations to the dying, and in songs. These divisions were named "went down," evening; "old night," the middle of the night (its major part); "nearing," before dawn; and "dawn."[6] Significant dreams occurred at any time during the night according to the following statements, but those that were favorable came only in the middle hours.

When they dream of animals, birds, and insects, the night is as clear as daylight. In the first part of the night, it makes the dreamer kind of wild. The animals and other beings will eat each other. Hence a child is kept awake during the early part of the night, until ten o'clock, to avoid this. In the early evening one has bad dreams.

After sunset, the birds, animals, and even the spirits of trees are moving around, so if you go to bed early you will have bad dreams. In the second part of the night, they have settled down to quiet. Then is the time one will not dream of anything bad. They do not say anything about the third part of the night.

There is a saying that there is a person standing in the west and another in the east, who between them swing the whole world so that everybody sleeps, just as a baby is swung to sleep.

At dawn, the larger birds (eagle and hawk) begin to wake and kill the little birds and insects. Blood stains are everywhere. If anybody still sleeps in this atmosphere, he will dream of bad things. So they wake children and young people before the sun rises.

Toward early morning, before dawn, the spirit birds are fighting and eating each other, all with bloodstains. If one dreams of this he will get sick. That is why people always wake their children before sunrise.

[6] See p. 145.

It appears quite probable that the blood referred to here is that blood which was released at the time of creation, which is the embodiment of all disease and is ever present in the world about. Most sickness was said to be caused by contact with this blood in "bad" dreams (p. 280), which are here defined as those of the evening and dawn.

There is no explicit account at hand illustrating the effect of this patterning on the dream narrative, but it is implied in descriptions of the content of several songs.

The song il_yicǎ'c, for example, told "of many different things." It told how the little birds or animals of the air are preparing to go to a celebration already under way; how they got there, and how they behaved. It told how, in the middle hours of the night, they thought they should not spend the whole night there, but decided it better to go home, and accordingly how they left the celebration. The song continued that toward morning, those who stayed all night were worn out and sleepy, and how their husbands and children starved in the morning, but how those who had returned had breakfast prepared for their families.

SPIRITS

The spirits of which they dreamed were primarily birds, with some animals and insects, the mountains, certain stars, lightning and thunder, and possibly the rain. Trees were mentioned as having spirits, but that these were power sources is exceedingly doubtful. The number of spirits seems to have been definitely limited, but the basis of their discrimination from those birds, animals, or natural phenomena which were not spirits remains wholly obscure. The question whether the spirits were single individuals or classes seems to have been of no consequence to the Maricopa, hence unresolved. Thus, whether Buzzard was a particular unitary being, or whether the genus buzzard supplied an unlimited number of spirits which functioned alike, was not made clear. The impression is that they thought of but a single spirit Buzzard, of whom the birds of everyday life were but tangible and earthly representatives. This is clearly the case with Coyote, who is Coyote of the creation tales. In the case of insects, flies, gnats, crickets, and the like, these appeared in dreams as a cloud of insects operating in concert. Their plurality proves nothing, since they never appeared individually.

Birds mentioned as spirits—there may have been others—
were mocking bird, an orange shouldered blackbird, buzzard,
eagle, horned owl, crow, killdeer, "mountain killdeer,"[7] and
duck. Among birds "one does not hear in dreams" were roadrunner, hawks, and crane (heron?). Animals named as spirits
were deer, coyote, jackrabbit, cottontail rabbit, dog, frog, and
possibly bat. Certain spirit coyotes created by Coyote (as recounted in the Coyote tale, p. 355) were also dreamed. The four
insect spirits named are partially identifiable: cricket, gnat (?)
small flies (kumanyihwi'), and xalkwata't. Fish were also
dreamed of. In addition there were the local mountains, thunder
and lightning, rain (?), the morning star, the constellation Orion's Belt, and two spirits of unknown identity, cïly̆aitcuwa'n, and
kukupu'Rȧ.

The powers conferred by these spirits were always specific,
despite the fact that several gave powers of more than one kind.
Some of the powers were obviously more impressive than others,
but why Kutox signaled Eagle and Buzzard as the most important spirit birds is obscure. Last Star stated that Coyote was the
most important: "Every shaman who cures always mentions
Coyote, Buzzard, and Horned Owl. Coyote and Buzzard could
teach the cure for a number of diseases [not specified] and would
select various men for each. Although Eagle is a strong bird,
none of the shamans seem to dream of him; he is never mentioned in their songs."

Curing powers were associated with certain spirits. Horned
Owl alone cured soul loss caused by dreaming of a dead relative.
An insect, xalkwata't,[8] and Coyote gave power to cure any illness.
"Every shaman who dreamed of xalkwata't claimed he was head
of all these animals, the best one living." The power of Coyote
was derived from his having recovered from every known disease
at the time of creation (see p. 351). A shaman with Coyote power was exceptional in that he never sang in public for entertainment. A shaman with this power needed only ride a horse to

[7] Looks like a small killdeer but lacks black stripes on its throat: possibly the
mountain plover.

[8] As large as the thumb, which lives in the ditches.

cure it. One who dreamed of Buzzard became a great shaman, with ability to cure the well-nigh lethal wounds caused by Yavapai poisoned arrows (matàʒau', "poisoned," "bewitched"). Duck and Gnat (? unyïpàwa'pàwa') were mentioned as additional spirit councillors of a shaman who cured such wounds. Further, Buzzard and Coyote conferred clairvoyant power to discover the enemy's position in the mountains and to detect thieves. The power of Jackrabbit and Cottontail was the cure of sickness caused by eating their flesh (jackrabbit at least was forbidden to young people) or of blindness caused by getting their hair in the eyes. They also cured earache. Orange Shouldered Blackbird cured sickness derived from deer,[9] but gave primarily his song, since "the blackbird is a great singer." Similarly, the Deer dreamer was a singer but could cure. Crickets gave the power to cure bewitchment caused by one who dreamed of the constellation Orion's Belt. Shamans who dreamed of crickets used rattles, the sound resembling that of the insect (but see below).

Other spirits bestowed non-curative powers: clairvoyance, bewitching, legerdemain, rain-making, singing, etc. A man who dreamed of Crow became a great thief, of Eagle a great singer. Similarly, the Mountain Killdeer dreamer became a great singer "because the killdeer is a great singer. But Mountain Killdeer is a bad bird. When one who dreamed of him sat down to sing, the whole village was stirred up. Young girls and even married women rushed to this singing, ran off with the singer." Mocking Bird made a man an orator, hence chiefs and battle challengers dreamed of him. A spirit called cïlyaitcuwa'n gave clairvoyant power to see who would win a race. Frog gave power to bewitch and to handle live coals: singing the Frog song brought rain. One "who had dreamed of rain" could cause it to fall, which may mean that rain was a spirit. The morning star was conceived as a spirit: it is the transformed old woman of the Flute Lure tale (p. 396). "A man, when he first dreams to become a great warrior, first describes the morning star. This star has especially to do

---

[9] The meaning of this is obscure, but recalls the Pima belief that animals cause all or nearly all sickness.

with war." He acquires bravery and ability to kill. Again, certain small flies (kumanyihwi') and a thorny cactus (ᵃxu'l) figured as spirits in the preparation of a warrior. "Those who dream of Orion's Belt got power to bewitch at a distance. This was cured by one who dreamed of crickets." It is not clear that this constellation was a spirit. The three stars of the Belt were believed a mountain sheep, a deer, and an antelope, any one of which might have been the spirit involved.

The reason for some of these associations of spirits and powers is patent as founded on natural characteristics of the birds. Thus, the mocking bird as speaker, the crow as thief, blackbird and killdeer as singers. Similarly, the association of the frog with rain is obvious and so possibly clairvoyance (locating the enemy from the sky) with the buzzard's soaring habit.

Other associations depend for comprehension on certain beliefs. Rabbit flesh was believed to cause sickness and its hairs blindness: these were cured by the spirit rabbits on the homeopathic principle. On a similar principle the curing of soul loss by Horned Owl, that is, where the cause was dreaming of dead relatives, seems connected with the belief that a human heart, on cremation, becomes a horned owl and that this owl seen flitting near a dwelling presages death. Certain other associations are founded on beliefs incorporated in the Creation tale (*q.v.*): Coyote, having suffered every kind of sickness, can cure all, and Frog, the first witch of all time, having slain her father, the culture hero, by witchcraft, now gives the power to bewitch.

The mountains as spirits differed from those of birds and animals in that they had no powers to grant. But that they figured as spirits is certified by the way they appear in the clairvoyant act by which the whereabouts of the enemy was discovered. Then the mountain spirits were thought to enter the séance and respond to questions concerning the enemy (see below). The same spiritual quality is implied by the slayer of an enemy turning away from the mountains of the enemy country to avoid their maleficence. Four nearby mountains were thought especially significant for the Maricopa: Pima Butte, Sierra Estrella, Salt River Range, and a butte immediately southwest of the

Salt-Gila junction (but curiously enough called ꭓagȧvĭcȧꝺo', "water divider"; possibly an outlier of the Sierra Estrella). The Salt River Range was known as "greasy mountain" (vikwaꭓa's) as the scene of the incident in the Creation tale where Coyote finished eating the culture hero's heart and wiped his greasy hands. "They thought of these four mountains as their own because they lived between them. They were not safe beyond these limits." However, certain mountains beyond these were selected as of the same nature: ᵃvikatcȧkwi'n_yȧ, "granary basket mountain," the Mohawk Mountains halfway down the Gila; vi'iꝺo', "willow mountain," south of Prescott; another lying northeast of this, called viakȧvȧnau', "ridge pole mountain," because of its level top; and ʻikwĭmkwima'tc, "dancing with horns," somewhat to the east of the last. "The people long ago called these mountains theirs." Four Peaks in Yavapai country, a mountain near Yuma (called vial_yxa", "berdache mountain"), and the sacred mountain of the Mohave (vikwȧme') near Needles also had spirit qualities.

The most significant of these were Pima Butte and the Sierra Estrella. The former (viva'vȧ, "solitary mountain") figures very much like the sacred mountain Avikwame for the Mohave, or the San Francisco Peaks for the Havasupai. "They praise this little butte because when a man begins to dream, the spirits always take him there first.[10] It is famous even among the Mohave and Yuma." This butte and another south of it were thought to fight with Four Peaks and another mountain on its north side. These represented respectively the Maricopa and the Yuma-Mohave-Yavapai. Depending on which pair of mountains wȯn, so it would fare with humans. A better expression of mountains as partisans is the following.

The man who dreams of war says the Sierra Estrella owns the Maricopa, Pima and Papago: Four Peaks owns the Yavapai. These two are always debating. When Four Peaks wins the debate this one (Sierra Estrella) mourns. Then Four Peaks is happy; he sings and dances, for his people will win in battle.

[10] I understood Last Star to state that a shaman was always first taken to a high hill (called matȧu'lgwĭsiꝺe'ʳc, "high dirt that is a shaman") on the north bank of the Gila, opposite Pima Butte. This is an insignificant hill; hence I was presumably mistaken.

Sierra Estrella was thought to have a berdache living in it, hence its name, vial$_y$xa", "berdache mountain." As explained above, this mountain gambled with the similarly named mountain near Yuma to see which should lose a warrior, who became a berdache. Presumably these two mountains also were thought to contend for the success of their people in war, because it was said of the Mohawk Mountains:

> It lies midway between the Yuma and the Kaveltcadom, so that it belongs to both people. It does not take one side, but always agrees with the mountain here or at Yuma as to which people shall die.

In dreams the faunal spirits at least appeared in human guise, or rather, as might be expected, their aspect fluctuated between avian or animal form and the anthropomorphic. "Those who see the coyote, eagle, or buzzard in dreams describe them as a boy or girl going along." "Some people dream of dogs who appear as persons.[11] The dogs tell how they are abused by people and instruct the dreamer to tell this." Dogs are persons; that is why Kutox did not beat his really annoying curs. Again in the vision recounted above: "So the owl turned around and rubbed himself all over. Then the owl stood in front of him in human form." The case is somewhat different with Thunder and Lightning, which were conceived outright as anthropomorphic beings. Such a fluctuating conception of birds and animals would seem an inevitable result of crediting them with human intelligence and speech.

There was no tendency to dream of one's sib totems. This is curious, because some totems, such as buzzard, eagle, and coyote, were repeatedly mentioned as spirits. Perhaps all totems were spirits: this is not clear. The failure to integrate dream experience with the social structure is not surprising, because the totems themselves were left functionless in relation to the sib system. Maricopa thought was accretive, rather than systematizing.

THE SONGS AND SONG CYCLES

The dream experience had its counterpart in song. The Maricopa say that songs were dreamed. They imply that all songs

[11] As exemplified in the tale of the Dog Champion, p. 396.

were originally dreamed, but of some the informants merely remarked that these were revived by individuals who may or may
not have dreamed them in turn. At any rate, they feel that
dreaming, not learning, was the orthodox way of coming by
songs.

Conversely it is doubtful that there were many significant
dream experiences in which songs were not bestowed. Songs were
not mentioned in connection with acquiring oratorical powers:
possibly they were absent from the dreams of the war leader, but
I think not. In describing dreams to me, the song was always
mentioned first, as though that was the most significant element.
The curative powers which the dreamer acquired and the like
were sometimes mentioned as though adjunct to song.

All this is generically true of the Yumans of the lower Colorado. Much, if not all, that Kroeber has written of dreaming and
singing among the Mohave[12] might be transferred bodily to the
Maricopa. But there are real and highly significant differences.

The Maricopa song tells the dream experience. Its burden
might be almost unintelligible by reason of its oblique reference
to the actual happenings of the dream, but its structure was
fixed. Its structure, that is the sequence of events described or
hinted at, duplicated the pattern of the dream itself. The songs
or the clusters of songs that made up the cycles were narratives
of the actual dream. "In his songs a man first tells what the insects or birds did to him in the early evening. They go on to tell
how he went along the strings that connect the mountain tops.
His song tells a story. He refers to the spirits only by nicknames,
but people know what he means." Again, "all songs tell what is
going on at a certain place, or what happened there, or how the
dreamer was taken somewhere."

The songs were not individual verses but clusters or cycles all
carrying forward the same theme. The cycle "tells of his trip, his
experience in dreaming of his spirit." There might be "a hundred or more" songs in a single cycle. The length was such that
they sang the whole night through. Within the cycle the songs
were grouped, but how is not clear. I am not certain whether

[12] Kroeber, *Handbook*, pp. 754 f.

Mrs. Redbird meant that the cycle as a whole was divided into four groups of songs or that the individual songs came in clusters of four. Four major groups was probably meant, since this would then represent the fourfold division of the night and of the dream experience narrated in the song. Yet it is possible that both types of grouping occurred since the pattern of fours was so strong among the Maricopa. The songs in sequence were "in different tunes," she said; illustrating by the contrast of verse and chorus in our own songs. "The sets of songs in any cycle sometimes came in fours, depending on the story the songs told. There would be four different tunes. But there were also sets of twos and threes; not always in fours."

A single song will illustrate the type of all. The song il,icá'c told how the little birds or animals of the air were preparing to go to a celebration that was under way; how they got there and how they behaved. "The middle part of the night," it told how they thought they should not spend the whole night there; how they decided it better to go home, and how they left the celebration. It went on "to tell that toward morning," those who stayed there all night were tired and sleepy; how their husbands and children starved in the morning, and how those who had returned had prepared breakfast for their families. Here is explicitly the quartering of the night: the journey of the early night, the dance of the middle part, the return before morning, and morning itself. There is only doubt whether the rendering of the song through a night's singing did not also conform to this quartering; that "the middle part of the night" does not also refer to the songs sung during that period. But even so, the narrative would conform to pattern.

It is doubtful that there was any element common to all songs other than the experiences of the night. It was said that "they sang about Coyote in every song and mentioned him in every tale." This probably means no more than that Coyote figured frequently in song and story. Similarly, it may be presumed that Pima Butte, with Sierra Estrella a sacred mountain, was commonly sung about since "the spirits always take a man there first" in his dreams.

It is quite clear that the cycles did not recite myths, but were confined to the personal experience of the dreamer. Nor did the dreamer project himself back into the mythological period: dreams and songs referred to the contemporaneous scene alone. Mrs. Redbird was emphatic on these points, contrasting Maricopa songs with the mythological type of the Mohave, with which she was acquainted. In both points they stand in clear distinction to Mohave songs. This is important, for the nature of the songs reinforces the fact that Maricopa dreams were individual experiences of a type more general in North American than the Mohave.

Yet the myth type was not wholly absent. Two songs at least told fragments of the Creation tale. Buzzard song related "all about" the creation; the appearance and actions of the sick culture hero, of his cremation, of the dispersal of the people in the desert and their settling in their historic homes. The song of Frog told how "in the first part of the evening" she left her home (after killing the culture hero); how she was pursued, and how she caused a storm to rise behind her to prevent her enemies following. "It tells all about rain and wind."

Tales also occurred with soliloquies delivered in the form of song, several examples of which are given in the tales at the end of this paper. Herzog also recorded a song incidental to a Maricopa myth.[13] This is a stylistic peculiarity widespread in Southwestern tales. Such songs were not sung apart from the tales.

Not every song was dreamed, at least by its singer. Several instances were cited. It was said, for instance, of the song tcutŏ'-x̣àm, used when a group of boys were set to destroying a bees' nest, that "this song is not dreamed, but a man who knows how sings it." Similarly no mention was made of dreaming in the case of tatuma'npïg, sung during the girls' puberty rites. It may be that ritual songs were not dreamed, although their content was much the same as dreamed songs. But it is more likely that their occurrence was like that of the song Deserted. "This had not been sung for a long time. One man wanted to start it again for a dance. Someone else had dreamed it long ago: this man did

[13] Herzog, *Yuman Musical Style*, pp. 188, 224.

not dream it, he merely danced it again." The probability is that, of the songs in use at any one time, some were recognized as dreamed, others learned, with the assumption that singers of the latter would ultimately dream their songs as well. Obviously the Maricopa were minimizing the actual learning of the highly stylized songs, traditional or borrowed, in favor of their theory of dream origin.

The tribal song repertory must have been fluctuating, due to intertribal diffusion and to death of the singers. Borrowing of songs on a wholesale scale is demonstrable among the Yumans and their neighbors, as Kroeber and Herzog have pointed out.[14] According to my own information various songs of the Maricopa and their guest tribes on the Gila were obtained from sources outside. Songs were dropped on the death of their singers. At the cremation of a singer the mourners sang his songs, "only four of them," and then burned the gourd or basket drum he had used as accompaniment. By doing so they held the songs have been destroyed. The song lay fallow as it were until it was resurrected by a new dreamer. Two instances were given: Eagle was dreamed by a man who sang it once or twice and died. "They sang it no more." Dragonfly was "started again," but sung only a few times: the singer died. Recently they sang a man's favorite songs at his cremation, whether or not he had been a singer, and within a month or two began to sing them again.

Occasions for the use of songs were numerous. Not only were they in use at all social celebrations and dances, but provided incidental entertainment at evening gatherings in the meeting house when topics for discussion were exhausted. At such times shamans, almost without exception, sang their curing songs by way of entertainment. (So stated Kutox, but Last Star declared such songs were held secret for actual curing.) Some of these festivities recurred with annual regularity; for instance, the dances when the wheat came up in February and at the harvest of August–September, or at the sahuaro drinking bout in mid-June. Others were at irregular intervals during the year; at races and games. In times of starvation they went to other tribes

[14] *Loc. cit.*

and sang for them, receiving gifts in return. War and scalp dances, puberty ceremonies for girls, and bee-killing ordeals for boys were other occasions. Songs, of course, were used in curing and at the cremation and mourning rites. The impression is that singing and dancing was very frequent, although ritual dancing was wholly unknown to the Maricopa and their associates.

The list in Table VII embraces all songs known to two informants, Kutox and Last Star. In addition to songs of the local tribes (that is, the mixed group of the Maricopa community), it contains their responses to the names of the Yuman song series noted by Kroeber.[15] They rarely hesitated in ascribing a song to a particular tribe (although they may not always have been correct) and their evidence, obtained independently, was rarely contradictory. It is significant how frequently their identifying remarks duplicated those furnished by Kroeber. I have thought it advisable to give here the song names from Kroeber's list used as cues in order to show what evoked their responses. It should be pointed out that these songs and song-series had recognized names, titles in our sense.

The following notes on songs were recorded.

Blackbird was the proper name of the song about Deer, "because the man who dreamed of the Orange Shouldered Blackbird could cure any sickness derived from the Deer." One who dreamed of Deer would always sing, but he was too shy, "too cowardly," to sing before others. He had several men who sang with him, and would gradually let his voice drop, leaving the others to sing. "He did this because deer is the principal food; hence this man would fear being killed by other shamans." He also cured.

Buzzard told "all about the creation"; how the culture hero appeared and acted when he sickened; of his cremation, and how the people dispersed in the desert and settled in their historic homes. At the war dance, there were formed two opposing lines of men and women alternately, with the singer in the middle of

[15] *Handbook*, pp. 755 f., 786. Kroeber lists as Maricopa songs according to Maricopa information: Salt, Deer, Taris (i.e., Killdeer), Buzzard, and Mockingbird. The last alone was not mentioned by my informants.

TABLE VII

Tribal Identity of Songs

(According to Maricopa Information)

Local Name	Cue Name (from Kroeber's List)	Maricopa	Halchidhoma	Kaveltcadom	Kohuana	Yuma	Mohave	Pima	Kamia	Yavapai	Gourd Rattle	Beat Basket	Scrape Basket	Use
akil	akil								X					
arrowreed (axta')	ahta (cane)										X			
bat (kumpānyākü'c)	bat		X				X							
birds	birds		X				X							
blackbird (xasikwa')	deer													curing
buzzard (ce)	buzzard	X									X			war and scalp dance, and pleasure
catukxo'tás	satukhota					X								
cottontail	rabbit													
crow	raven									X		X		
deserted (vüspo')	sakachara					?						X		frequently danced; war dance
dragonfly (xanavāre')	dragonfly (ahak-wa'ilya)		X									X		involved a performance
eagle (ĕspa')	eagle (ohwera)	X												war and scalp dances
enemy standing (hwici-vau')	————		X											
frog (xanyí')	frog		X			X								for pleasure, but brought rain
grebe (xaltau'p)	halykupa (grebe)	X	X											

TABLE VII—*Continued*

Local Name	Cue Name (from Kroeber's List)	Maricopa	Halchidhoma	Kaveltcadom	Kohuana	Yuma	Mohave	Pima	Kamia	Yavapai	Gourd Rattle	Beat Basket	Scrape Basket	Use
hand game (tatuθulyⁱ'g)..	tudhulva (hand game)	X	X	X	X									"sung by everybody here"
ivaθo' (a fly)...........	avadho (an underground insect or chrysalis)		X										X	the principal war dance song; also when enemy was killed and for pleasure
ilyica'c..............	alysa	X												at mourning rite
kara'uk..............	ohoma					X								
kultě'ckᵃ............	kamtoska						X							
lightning (xuRŎ'vᵃ).....	orup	X				X								war leader's song
morning star (xomáce' ko-vátai'yà).............	—	X						X				X	X	with special war dance performances; and when enemy was killed
mountain killdeer (vitari'c)............	—													
nighthawk (uRu').......	orup	X				X								scalp dance
oxo'mc...............	ohoma													mourning rite
people (pipa').........	pi'ipa	X												war and scalp dance
rat (uxu'lyᵃ)...........	ohulya (rat)		X									X	X	for pleasure

TABLE VII—*Continued*

Local Name	Cue Name (from Kroeber's List)	Maricopa	Halchi-dhoma	Kaveltca-dom	Kohuana	Yuma	Mohave	Pima	Kamia	Yavapai	Accompaniment			Use
											Gourd Rattle	Beat Basket	Scrape Basket	
red ants (cĭmaθuly^á)	chamadhulya	X												scalp dance; occasionally for pleasure
salt (ĕsi'c)	salt	X												war (?) and scalp dance
seal (tuxa'ʀ^á)	tuharl (rattle)	X									X			war and scalp dance (?)
sun (inyă')	nyavadhoka	X		X										"any time for fun",
tatuma'npíg	tumanpa	X												with dance at girls' rite
tcutŏ'xăm	chutaha (crane?)	X	X?	X?	X?			X						probably all local tribes; boys' bee-killing ordeal
tuma'np	tumanpa				X									for pleasure; war dance
tuma'nṕáko'lĭs (long tumanp)	long tumanp	X												for pleasure
turtle (kapĕ't)	turtle				X						X			war (?) and scalp dances
twisting (xĭkwi'ʀĭc)	hayakwira	X	X											curing
vinimulya	vinimulya		X											
wine (xatca')			X				X							sahuaro drinking
xamutcĭ'tc	mat-hamuchicha	X				X		X						
yaxai'k	nyohaiva				X									

one line, supported by a man on each side, all three with rattles. The lines moved backward and forward. It was also sung at the scalp dance, and in general, at times of rejoicing; always with a gourd rattle accompaniment.

The recorded text of one song of this series follows.[16] Below each line of text is given the equivalent in normal speech; other words and elements are meaningless, being inserted merely to carry the song.

xaiĭnyi kŏṇai'yumi'ṇyik_yaviyŏ'nak_yamiyŏm
           miviya'k
           He went crying

Repeat this line twice.

akuṇpiṇyipŏṇ'aiva'	xatcu'ʀkwĭsᵭa'	kumaṇaṇaxai	xima'ṇalyŏṇaxuta
pipa	xatcu'ʀkwĭsᵭa's	maxai	mĭl_yàxo'c
a person	cold weather taking	boy	wing

akuuva'napa'ʀa	anyu	miṇiᵭau	tcaiyă'mavi'ya
kuvàpa'ʀàn		àᵭau	tcaiyĭ'mg viyak
end [of wing]		take	send it on its way
			away

Free rendering: "He went crying. The boy-bird, Taking-cold, sent his wing tip on its way." Taking-cold was the name of an unidentified bird, which arrives in this area about October. He figures here as a person, a boy. Buzzard went along crying, because he was not fast enough to bring back what he desired. (What it was Last Star did not know.) The bird Taking-cold had more power, so Buzzard asked him to go, but Taking-cold had merely to dispatch his wing tip. "Buzzard waṣ like a shaman who cannot bring back a sick man's soul, because he was not swift enough to overtake it. So he might send a quick boy in his place."

Catukxo'tàs was the name of one of the twins of the Flute Lure tale (p. 373). The name of his son, the hero, kwiyăhuma'ʀà, identifies this song with Mohave Kwiya-humara.

Cottontail had been heard among Yavapai visitors. The cottontail and jackrabbit were sung about by shamans who dreamed

---

[16] For the transcription of this and other songs recorded phonographically, see p. 271 f.

of them, but there was no local song named for them. Similarly Fox was the subject of a shaman's song, but there was no song bearing this name.

Deserted referred to a deserted house in which, traditionally, a man was lying when he heard bird spirits gathered there singing this song. These little birds (resembling meadowlarks) were called cikàtca'ʀàk (Mohave sakachieka).[17] For this song men and women sat, beating time with sticks on baskets.

Dragonfly may have been confounded with another song. The native term for the insect, xanavàʀe', also meant king, president (from Spanish *general-a*). A performance named "Moving the king around" is described in the section on dances. The song and performance were given only once, or at most a few times: the singer died.

Eagle was sung once or twice by a man who dreamed it and soon died. The Mohave name Ohwera was not recognized.

Enemy Standing bore the name of the scalp dance, a name taken from the practice of mounting the enemy scalp on a pole. It was used both in war and scalp dances. It was sung by xatisa'-là, an Halchidhoma chief, who dreamed of dead enemies returning to tell how they had been treated by the Maricopa. The song told how a father behaved when someone of his family was taken prisoner or killed.

Frog was sung "by everybody" for pleasure, but it brought rain because it told "all about" rain and wind. "The first part of the evening," she (Frog) told how she left her home (having killed the culture hero): continued how she was pursued and caused a storm to spring up behind her to hamper her pursuers.

Grebe (? "a kind of duck"), xaltau'p, was distinguished from loon (xalyàpu'kc) for which there was no local song (unlike Mohave). Grebe was sung infrequently, "when very happy"; probably not a shaman's song.

Hand Game: the song had the name of the game. Like the Mohave they considered this one of the song series. It was "sung by all the tribes here." They played the game every night. It consisted of only a few songs, indefinitely repeated; telling that

[17] Kroeber, *Handbook*, p. 787, n. 1.

at times one will starve but have plenty at others, referring to losing and winning.

In the single song recorded, the words are wholly meaningless.

wa'xamĕlawe'owĭna hauoyĭk katco'yomĭna awe'owĭna
Repeat this line twice.
xale'ĭpiu iu'ĭna 'iaia 'iaia xa . . . .
xalĭpĭlĭp wiyu'ĭna

Ivaðo' was a small stinging river fly, with gray stripes on its sides. "Just sat around in rings for this song." The cycle told of playing various games and how they went to war. The single song recorded, which follows, tells of the hoop-and-pole game (xutu'ʀᵃ), and "that people here would some day be playing it." The willow poles were scraped, hence referred to as white, straight, and smooth. (Below each line of text appears normal speech.)

tcaiyula'	kwunu'k	wiya'k
tcaiyu'lg	vunu'k	
rolling	they are doing it	[meaningless]

tcaiyula' kwunu'k tcaiyula'k

noṇwi'ya	tcaiyula'k	kwunu'm
		vunu'k
[meaningless]		they are doing it

Repeat all foregoing.

ĭnyṇa'amsa'vi	yŏmsavi'm	'waʀ'wa'ʀà
nᵧĭmasa'vi		'wa'ʀa'wa'ʀà
white		[and] evenly smooth

Repeat whole first phrase.

Free rendering: "They are rolling the hoop. They are doing it. The pole is white and evenly smooth."

Il̯icà'c (meaning unknown) was the song of the birds who attended a celebration lasting through the night (given in detail above). "A Cocopa dreamed ĕlca' (meaning unknown) over here in the old days and the people have taken it up"; presumably the same song.

Kultĕ'ckᵃ was the Maricopa response to Mohave Kamtoska (an unidentified brownish bird). It was described as a bird like a cardinal, but brownish, with a head crest; its habit being to destroy other birds' eggs and corn. There was no song of this name locally.

Morning Star (its name means literally "big star") was the transformed old woman of the Flute Lure tale. Since the morning star "had especially to do with war," a war leader dreamed of it. The song described his warlike deeds.

Mountain Killdeer, with Deserted, was probably the most frequently sung song series, to judge by the manner of reference. This was a Maricopa song also known to the Pima. Two performances which accompanied its singing are described in the section on dances: in one the singer made models of butterflies flutter to his tune; the other was a dance form involving a clown. The song was also used in the war dance and at the time news was received that an enemy had been killed. That night people went to the house of the singer to sing this song, without dancing. On such occasions a woman who wishes to assist him singing seated herself right beside the singer on his east side.

One song of this series was recorded.[18] (Normal speech equivalents are given below each line of text.)

aviaovŏna	kaviovana	aviaovŏna	kaviovam
vovak			
He [Coyote] is here	ditto	ditto	ditto
Repeat this line.			

akupiipanai	kwixatalwaa	ĭnyămosonaa
pipai	xataluwe'	nyĭmasa'và
a human	Coyote	white

siiyàmavii	ikwalacaata	anyumiiϑau
avi	kwalacau'	ϑaug
stone	obsidian	he took

itcŏpyuaak		iyonaamonai	ikŏnakyŏnavĭk
ĭtcĭplyia'kàm		amai'	kĭkya'vĭk
He carried it in his mouth		sky	[He] went around

iyonamat	ikonakyavĭk
amat	kĭkya'vĭk
earth	[He] went around

Repeat first line.

[18] Another song text is given on p. 241.

Free rendering: "Coyote is here. He comes as a white human. He took an obsidian stone. He carried it around the sky in his mouth and he carried it around the earth." The song praises Coyote for his quickness in carrying the stone around the sky and earth; in praise he is described as white.

Oxo'mc (meaning unknown) was volunteered by both Last Star and Kutox as sung by the Yuma together with Kara'uk. This was also Kroeber's information from Mohave sources.

People was sung at war and scalp dances. Its content was ironical: how the enemy fled but were taken captive; how well they were cared for instead of being badly treated; how a father among them shed tears of joy, not sorrow, at this outcome.

Rat was a song without dance used for pleasure of an evening. The accompaniment was with a basket beaten and scraped. The animal referred to (uxu'l$_y$ᵃ) is larger than a packrat, its tail with a bushy tip, and does not build a nest but burrows.[19] The song told about the rat's home and the paths it took.

A song of this series was recorded. (Normal speech is again given below each line of text.)

xaiïca'maⱷi'aiik   ai'icamaⱷi   yïxaiïca'maⱷi'
   cŏmàⱷi'k
   He does not know

Repeat last word four times.

xiyomaxu'l$_y$ maxu'l$_y$ xuma'ʀ
   uxu'l$_y$ᵃ   xuma'ʀᵃ
   rat   boy

hĭcima'txaiï'ta.u'l$_y$ xiaiï'c   ca'maⱷi
   àma't   ta.u'l$_y$ïg   cŏmàⱷi'k
   [his] dirt heaped high   he does not know

Repeat last two words twice.

Free rendering: "He does not know where his home is. The rat is a boy. His dirt pile (i.e., his home) is heaped high. He does not know where it is." It describes how a young (boy) rat did not know where his home was, but implies that he finally reached it. Like all songs the tale was left incomplete: "everybody who dreams tells in his song how someone started for a place, but

[19] This corresponds to the Mohave discrimination ohulya, "rat," from ama'-l$_y$k," "packrat."

never tells how he got there. He always stops telling before that point."

Salt was sung by old men and women "at the time they killed or captured an enemy" (war dance as well as scalp dance?).

Seal (i.e., fasten) was "probably sung when they killed an enemy, because it was not sung for mere amusement." It may refer to sealing the cover on the jar in which scalps were stored.

Tatuma'npig was the name of both dance and song at the Maricopa girls' puberty rite. The song referred to purifying the girl, making her strong and industrious, dignified, kind, gentle, able to withstand thirst, to run well, and the like. The dance form was a line of girls with the menstruant at the middle facing a line of men, both moving backward and forward together. Last Star pointed out that this was not the song *Tuma'np*, a Kohuana song sung for happiness and when going to war by old men and women.

Tuma'npᵃko'lĭs, "long tuma'np," was sung by Maricopa; a wholly different song from tuma'np. It was called "long" (ko'-lĭs) because "it holds," drags. A few old men and women would gather to sit singing this when they were happy, accompanying themselves with a gourd rattle.

A single song of this cycle was recorded as follows:

xikwai	amo'likwai	amo'likwai	amuwa'ṇkol[?]
xikwai	amo'li		
the giver	[an exclamation?]		[meaningless]
xiyai'awi'valĕm			
vawi'm			
he did this			
Repeat all this twice.			

The song was said to relate how a certain bird or animal did something.

Tcutŏ'x̣àm (meaning unknown) was sung by Maricopa, Pima, and "probably all others here." It was sung when they started to look for a nest of bees which young boys were expected to exterminate. "This represents going to war." The song was not dreamed, "but a man who knows how sings it." Its content was a strange combination: it told of plentiful crops and water; then about the bees as enemies; how they were finally exterminated; then how happy they were that the crops were coming up nicely and the enemy all slain.

Turtle was sung "for fun but mostly when they killed an enemy." Its words were "difficult to make out" (because in the Kohuana tongue?). The old man singer had three or four more to help: they called each other by "what was almost a kinship term," ĭnyă'ł (a Kohuana word).

Twisting was a shaman's song among Maricopa and Halchidhoma, used as a last resort in the treatment of a kind of "rheumatism," in which the legs, arms, or body were twisted. The song was called by the same name as the disease, x̣ikwi'ʀĭc (from ȧkwi'ʀȧ, to twist something). It may be significant that the Mohave song name Hayakwira, to which this song was given in response, refers to a twisting animal, a rattlesnake.

Wine, that is the fermented drink made of giant cactus fruit, was sung only at the celebration when this was drunk in mid-June. The Halchidhoma informant said, "The Halchidhoma were the first to sing it, the Pima got it from them, and the Maricopa from the Pima." There was no special dance with the singing. "When they are drunk they think of war." He who first dreamed it heard the dead enemy singing it. It described "red water" (blood), its appearance and how it was made; apparently identifying the sahuaro drink with blood. It told how the enemy joins for the drinking: they had been together in fighting, now they would be together drinking. The name of the song x̣atca' was related to that of the celebration, x̣atca'poŭm, "water mixing." (This song should not be confused with x̣ĭtca', "Pleiades," which although known to Mohave, was not sung locally.)

Yax̣ai'k (meaning unknown) was sung by an old woman or man who stood leaning on a staff. It is identical in this respect with Mohave Nyohaiva, and like it refers to fighting. The song described how the enemy behaved when chased, how he was caught, and how his relatives felt. It declared that they were not crying but dancing for joy because their son was killed: an insult.

The song names shown in Table VIII, also derived from
Kroeber's list, were recognized so far as their possible meaning in
Maricopa was concerned, but they were not known as songs to

TABLE VIII

Cue Name	Maricopa Equivalent	Meaning or Comment
———.................	amŏ's	mountain sheep: "too sacred an animal to describe"
awi-kunchi................	kwiyu'c	meteor
chichohoichva.............	tcuhwĭ'tc	There was a story "called" tcuhwĭ'tc containing songs among the Maricopa, but the songs were not sung independently.
djokwar (speech)..........	tcŭkwe'ʀĭk	speech
hacha (Pleiades)...........	xĭtca'	Pleiades
humahnana (malodorous beetle)...................	xamĭsnŏ'n	malodorous beetle
ichulyuye.................	hasu'lg	a kind of rheumatism
ipam-imicha (person cries)...	ipamĭ'tc	a person crying
halypuka (loon)...........	xalyápu'kc	loon
hikupk (venereal disease)....	tcŏxnu'x	a bad disease (venereal?)
keruk (mourning ceremony)..	kĕʀu'kám (Halchidhoma)	mourning ceremony (cf. Yuma karu'uk above)
nyikwar (crane)...........	nákwe'	crane
nyimi (wild-cat)...........	namĕ's	wild-cat
parhau (fox)..............	xatáluwe'	coyote: saʀámiyo' (meaningless) was its name in myths
sampulyka (mosquito).......	cámpu'lĭg	mosquito
yaroyara.................	kwiya'ʀoya'ʀá	This was the "name" of the songs of the old women with scalps in the tale of Coyote (p. 362).

either of my informants. It is obvious that some of the Maricopa
words brought to mind by these cue names have nothing to do
with the subjects of the named songs.

The following song names illicited no recognition: antelope,
av'alyunu, beaver, chayautai, goose, haykwesa, hehltamataie,
hortloi, kachachwar, mountain, rattlesnake (ave), wellaka.

MARICOPA MUSIC[20]
BY GEORGE HERZOG

The following Maricopa songs recorded by Dr. Leslie Spier share in the traits of the Yuman musical style. These traits are: the absence of strong accents or pulsations, placid flow of the melody, pleasing alternations of two-unit and three-unit rhythmic figures, simplicity of the tonal development and clearly balanced structure.[21] But the outstanding characteristic of the Yuman style, the introduction of a new part, imitating the main motive on a higher tonal level,[22] does not seem to be as common in Maricopa songs as it is in the songs of other Yuman tribes.[23] Among the songs that follow, Nos. 2, 3, and 4 have this "rise" clearly; in No. 6 there is a suggestion of it (in the more emphatic use of *b* in the *g* phrase); in No. 5 only a change of rhythm appears. The fact that this peculiarity is represented somewhat weakly in Maricopa songs may be due to Pima influence but this could be established only on the basis of more material.

No. 1 is in 18/8 (3/2) rhythm. With the change of the text in a³, the triplet-movement is temporarily broken, the phrase has now 20/8 and 17/8 (or 19/8 and 18/8); in the variant 16/8 and 17/8 (or 15/8 and 18/8). The melodic weight is fairly evenly distributed over the two tones of the melody, still *b b* can be con-

[20] These songs were recorded on a phonograph. With the exception of No. 3, they were sung by Last Star (from whom No. 1 was obtained twice): No. 3 was sung by Claude Redbird. Each song is but a single song from the long series of the same name. The texts of the songs, which are printed in the notes above, were obtained independently of the phonograph records. Dr. Herzog has undertaken the awkward task of fitting my texts to the words as heard from the records. He writes: "I did not have much trouble in fitting the text to the music; still at a few places this has not been entirely successful and our texts disagree on a few minor points. I have placed in parentheses a few syllables where I am either not absolutely certain that I am hearing what I ought to, according to the text you sent me, or where I hear something definitely different from the indications of the text. These are, of course, points of minor importance. At one place I have a question-mark in the text since I can not make out the syllable (No. 3, second line)."—L. S.

[21] See *The Yuman Musical Style.*   [22] *Op. cit.*, pp. 196–97.

[23] This is borne out also in the Maricopa songs of the story of Na῾sia, recorded by me from the Pima.

sidered the tonic since it is on the arsis and is also the final tone of the melody. The song has been recorded twice; the two renditions are identical, except for the slight change in a^3 which is given in the last line. The original was sung a half-tone (and an octave) lower.

No. 2 has a somewhat intricate rhythm which is achieved by rather simple means; in place of the 2/8 units with which the song starts out 3/8 units appear at places. In the first, second, fifth, sixth and seventh phrase this unit (taking up the third to fifth eighths) has the value of 5/16 only. The original was sung an augmented seventh lower.

No. 3 is in straight 4/4 rhythm. The hesitant figure marked ♪⌄♩ is approximately between ♪♪ and |≥ ♪. The phrases *ab* are repeated three times before *c* is introduced. The whole of the phrase *c* (until [*a*]) is somewhat lower than noted. The original was sung a minor third (and an octave) lower.

No. 4 is in 9/8 rhythm, except for the first bar of the first phrase which has also the values 11/8 and 10/8. The song ends at ‖. The original was sung an octave lower.

No. 5 has a rhythm that alternates between 3/4 and 6/8 (or 3/8) patterns. In the first two renditions of the song, the second half of the second, third, and fourth bar and the fifth bar have 6/8 or 3/8 rhythm (marked with brackets). In the third rendition (which brings a change in the text) the 3/4 units disappear and the melody is repeated entirely in 6/8 and 3/8 rhythm, but unchanged otherwise. The first three tones may not belong to the song. They are not given in the subsequent renditions and represent perhaps the title of the song, spoken by the singer before commencing to sing. The original was sung a seventh lower.

No. 6 consists of alternating 2/4 and triplet-units of rhythm. At times (as in the second unit of the first bar and in the third unit of the seventh bar) either one of these figures could have been intended by the singer. The song has three parts. The second part is a repetition of the first one, shortened through the omission of the *d* phrase. The third part introduces new phrases, of which *e* resembles *a*, *f* is similar to *c* and *g* is again a modification of *a*. The original was sung an octave lower.

No. 7 has 12/8 for its fundamental rhythmic pattern. In the first two renditions of *a* the first bar is lengthened to 13/8. The phrase *c* consists of a 6/8 and a 12/8 section, the latter being a repetition of the second half of *b*. After two renditions of the verse, the *a* phrase closes the song. The original was sung an octave lower.

Explanation of the signs used in the transcription:

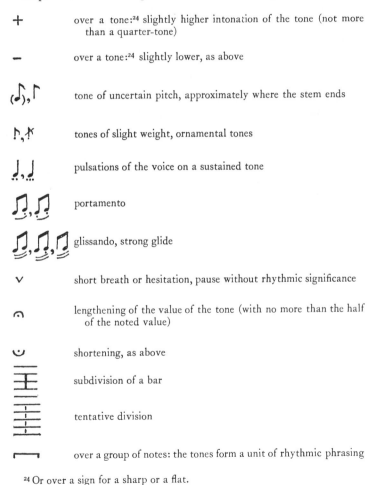

+	over a tone:[24] slightly higher intonation of the tone (not more than a quarter-tone)
−	over a tone:[24] slightly lower, as above
	tone of uncertain pitch, approximately where the stem ends
	tones of slight weight, ornamental tones
	pulsations of the voice on a sustained tone
	portamento
	glissando, strong glide
∨	short breath or hesitation, pause without rhythmic significance
⌒	lengthening of the value of the tone (with no more than the half of the noted value)
⌣	shortening, as above
	subdivision of a bar
	tentative division
	over a group of notes: the tones form a unit of rhythmic phrasing

[24] Or over a sign for a sharp or a flat.

In the scale-schemes, the time-value of a note is symbolic of the melodic weight the tone carries in the melody. A whole tone indicates the tonic, a ⌢ indicating the final tone. Notes within a bracket form a section of the tonal structure; a bracket of broken lines indicates that the section is not a very closely knitted one. A sign in parentheses indicates that the modification is a slight one or that it does not occur in all subsequent renditions of the same place.

I. IVÅΘÓ SONG

(tc)⌐aiyula (kwu) nooŋwiya tcaiyula kwunum   tcaiyula

nooŋwiya tcaiyula kwunum   (wiyak)

(wiyak) (wI)Ynyaŋamsavi 'waᴿwaᴿ (tcaiyula)

Var. of a³:

(wiyak)   Ĭ-Ynyaŋamsavi 'waᴿwaᴿ (tcaiyula)

Scale:

II. MOUNTAIN KILLDEER SONG

III. ILYÁCÁC SONG

IV. LONG TUMANPA SONG

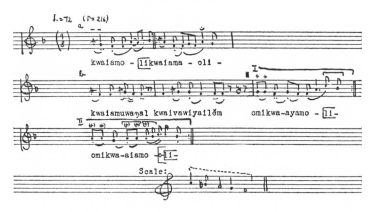

kwaíamo - 11 kwaíama - olí -

kwaíamuwaŋal kwaívawíyaílŏm   omíkwa-ayamo - 11 -

omíkwa-aíamo - 11 -

V. RAT SONG

Scale:

VI. HIDING GAME SONG

wa-mĕ-la - we-yo - wĭ-na - we we-yomĭna a-weowĭ-na

wa-xa-mĕla - we-yo-wĭ-na we we-yo-wĭ-na weyowĭna

wa - mĕ-la - we-yo-wĭ-na - we we-yo-wĭ-na a-weyowĭna

wa-xa-mĕ-la we-yo-wĭ-na

xa-le - ĭ - piu fŷo-u-na ʻi - ya-i - ya xa

xa - lĭ - pĭ - lĭp wi - yu-ĭna - mĭ-tcoi-o- na

Scale:

VII. BUZZARD SONG

CURING AND BEWITCHING

Illness and death were occasioned in four ways: by bad dreams, by the loss of the soul, by the intrusion of a disease object brought about by witchcraft, and by natural causes, old age and violence.[25] The most common cause was bad dreaming: such disorders as bowel complaints, diarrhoea, colds, pains in the chest and side, were attributed to it. Loss of the soul was also common, but less so: this brought fainting spells. Soul loss was due solely to having dreamed of the dead: dead relatives came to persuade the dreamer to join them. Since these two concepts cover practically all cases, Last Star's declaration was justified that "it was always by dreaming that one got sick."

Dreaming wrong meant dreaming of certain things, mostly unspecified, contact with which in the dream brought it about that one acquired an illness. These illnesses were forever afloat in the world around. They were the blood, the sum of all diseases, which gushed from the ground at the time of creation despite Cipas' efforts to stem it (p. 347). Since bad dreams which caused illness were also defined as those of the evening and dawn, when the spirit birds fought and bloodstains were everywhere (p. 248), it seems probable that this ancient heritage of blood-disease was meant. The acquisition of such illness was not in any way due to spirits, whether by the spirits' own activity or a shaman calling on his familiar to inflict disease. Spirits were concerned only in that they had taught each shaman his cures.

The shaman's part in curing was that of one who had the power to draw out the particular illness, because a revelation had been made in his dreams. During the course of the cure he was not possessed, nor did he so much as call on his familiar for aid. He blew, breathed, and sucked on the patient, and brushed with the hand, to allay the fever and pain and to draw the illness from him. But he did not suck out a disease object.

It is doubtful that this should be included with the classical

---

[25] We may remark incidentally that our informants knew of no cases of suicide.

There was no belief comparable to that of the Pima that death was due to Sun and Night (Russell, *Pima Indians*, pp. 193, 251).

cases of "illness by intrusion." The illness was thought of as due to the contamination of the dream. Illnesses were ever present, as we might say of pandemic diseases. They had no concrete form to be sucked out as an object. We can hardly speak here of contrasting theories of disease: soul loss *versus* intrusion.

The loss of the soul was suggested as the cause only when the symptoms were of one kind, fainting spells; when it was assumed the patient had dreamed of the dead. Such a person would be in apparent good health, when suddenly "he thinks he turns around and sees a dead relative coming, and there! he is dead," i.e., faints.

W——, a boy of fourteen, said that whenever he has fainting spells, his dead relatives appear to him; always two or three old men together. They talk to him, saying, "Come on; come along with us." His dead grandfather is the principal visitor. He also said that when a little child, he saw a ghost, dressed in white, seated on the spot where later his uncle was cremated. This ghost kept on nodding her head with its long hair.[26]

Illness and death due to manifest physical causes were regarded as of natural origin, even though the occasion of accident or wounding was held the result of non-physical influences. In answer to the direct question whether natural deaths did not occur, Kutox replied in the affirmative: in old age, but they were very rare (naturally, since few survive to old age). Of them they said "their heart pulls down," 'iwana'l$_y$g.

In all cases it was held that

before a person dies, while he is sick, they say the soul is already gone. During his sickness, his soul wanders in all the places the man has been on his hunting trips. After the soul gets tired, it makes up its mind that it is going to the land of the dead. Then, when the soul goes there, the man dies.

It was not fully specified what things it was dangerous to dream about beyond the conflict of the spirit birds (p. 248), but several plants were mentioned. One called i'icama'c, "root wood," was a vine, which, growing beside a tree, made the tree twist. If one dreamed of this, or went near enough to smell it, he became entirely paralyzed and his body was sensitive to the touch. If this root be placed in the sun, it wiggled; so with the

[26] These "fainting spells" are apparently epileptic seizures. This is the lad who as a child could understand the language of dogs (p. 240).

patient, his limbs twisted. This could be cured by a shaman who dreamed of either Coyote or Buzzard (the informant was uncertain).

Another plant, called i'iuxa's, "scraped wood," caused chills and fever. The shaman never told in this connection of what he himself had dreamed. On diagnosing an illness as due to this cause he secretly dispatched a man of l̯ew'c sib for ironwood (axpa'lg) in the morning. A limb was scraped and fashioned into an image of the patient by this man, who at noon suddenly entered and held it close before the patient's eyes. When the latter saw it, he began to cry aloud. Then the shaman proceeded with his cure.[27]

The most dangerous thing of which to dream was kwaʀao'-kuma'cïc, "iron eater." (kwaʀao' was the name formerly applied to the stone of which knife blades were made, presumably obsidian, now transferred to iron.) The informant knew nothing of this dream object but its name. This disease caused sores, which ate away the flesh and the bone below. A shaman who could cure this had dreamed of a high pile of sand. When a hole is dug into the base of a pile of loose sand, the sand runs in as fast as one removes it. Hence the spirit (what it was is unknown) showed him how to stop it with his hand, which he then knew how to apply to the running sore.

Curing shamans were relatively few; five or six at any time. There is a question whether women were ever shamans. Last Star declared that there were none known among Maricopa and Kaveltcadom, although Mohave, Yuma, and Halchidhoma had them. Kutox's statement that at any one time there were one or two is probably to be interpreted as referring to the mixed community as a whole or to his own Halchidhoma group.[28]

The manner of calling a shaman to cure was stereotyped. An elderly man of the patient's family approached the shaman's house, calling him by the appropriate kinship term. He did not

[27] This is reminiscent of Pima and Papago curing by touching effigies in the Vikita-Navitco complex.

[28] Last Star confirmed Russell's statement that the Pima women shamans specialized on abdominal diseases (*Pima Indians*, p. 261).

hesitate to wake the shaman in this fashion if he went at night. The response was always by the women of the shaman's household, whereon the visitor told at once why he came. He told that the patient "needed help through the night or day, to see how he would get along. 'Whether you know just what the sickness is or not, we want you to take care of our whole family.'" The shaman never left at once with the petitioner, but came some time after.

Curing took place inside the dwelling. It was darkened, the fire put out, but the shaman "could see clearly as though it were daylight." The shaman did not approach the patient at once, but sat apart, while those of the household explained that the patient was very sick. When he seated himself beside the sick man, he felt all over the latter's body to find whether he suffered from fever, headache, or whatever. He never asked the patient for symptoms but discovered the cause of the illness for himself. He then proceeded to relieve him by brushing with his hand, blowing spittle and perhaps smoke on the patient, and sucking his body. He brushed with the side of his hand, back and forth, barely touching the sick man. Most of the brushing was directed toward the feet so as to avoid driving the sickness toward the heart. The sick man always lay with his head to the east, with the shaman south of him so that he could brush and press mostly with his left hand. Shamans maintained that they could always do better with that hand. (Last Star did not know their reason.) He breathed and sprayed with spittle "to give him his hot or cold breath," as needed to relieve chills or fever. He also sucked "to take out the fever," but did not suck out any disease object.[29]

Maricopa shamans used neither feathers for brushing nor a rattle when singing, as the Pima did. Yet the phrase "to sing to

[29] There are several references to sand as a magical curative agent in the myths of the Maricopa and other Yumans. The Anza documents describe its actual use more than once, e.g., Eixarch (1776) related that a Yuman shaman rubbed sand on a sick man's stomach (Bolton, *Anza's California Expeditions*, III, 377). Kroeber recorded it as a Mohave practice (*Handbook*, p. 777). My Maricopa informants had no knowledge of its use.

The Pima use of stone tablets found in ruins for curing was also not Maricopa (Russell, *Pima Indians*, pp. 112, 266). Informants had no knowledge of these objects.

cure" was translated by my interpreter into Maricopa as axna'l-mĭtce'ʳvĭk, "gourd [rattle] singing."[30] This may be because they now call in Pima shamans.

Usually at a cure several old men sat beside the shaman to lend him their strength, but they did not sing.

Before the shaman began, he smoked two or three cigarettes or even four if the patient was very sick. He also stopped from time to time to smoke. "The shaman felt weak without his to-bacco, like a man without food and water. He smoked to make himself feel strong." It is not clear that the shaman blew smoke over the sick man. Last Star did not mention it as part of the procedure and his statement that the shaman stopped to smoke implies otherwise. Kutox, on the other hand, said that he blew smoke over the patient's body, but did not describe it in his own cure, cited below. The tobacco used by shamans did not differ from that of the layman.

The shaman sang two songs or four over the patient when he knew he would recover. Only if the patient was seriously ill did the shaman begin singing from the first. "His songs were like prayers." He sang them to gain strength. These were songs he had learned in dreams and which he used only when curing; otherwise he kept them secret. The songs told how the spirit had taken him to the mountain tops to reveal the cures, but they did not describe this explicitly. In the course of his songs he named the disease and told the patient that "when he heard these songs he might get well."[31]

If, while singing, the shaman mentioned only things that were white (birds or whatever) and called the patient's breath white, the auditors were sure he would get well. But if he changed these references to black, the patient was doomed. On the fourth night (theoretically a shaman was given four nights to effect a cure), if

[30] Forde's Yuma informant, ascribing the use of a rattle to the Maricopa, was presumably mistaken (*Yuma Ethnography*, p. 198).

[31] Informants had never heard of curing by the songs of animals diagnosed as causing the disease, as did the Pima; such causes being foreign to their belief. Possible exceptions were the singing of Blackbird song for sickness "caused by the deer" and the belief that rabbits caused illness and supplied its cure.

the shaman saw the case was hopeless, he sang during the first half of the night to persuade the sick man not to go to the other world. He reminded him that all he owned was here. During the latter half of the night, toward morning, he "pushed him on," telling him that the other world was pleasant; there he would be as happy as were those who had preceded him. All this he told in song, not by oration.

A shaman ordinarily knew the cure for only a single sickness as taught him by one spirit; rarely he would know two or three, having been taught by various spirits. He would try for a day or two, and if he found he did not "know the sickness," he gave way to another. Theoretically he needed four nights to make the cure. Five or six shamans might be called before the patient was cured. A number of sick might gather to be cured at one time by a single shaman.

The fee was a horse, a native woven blanket, a small strip of woven cloth, or a string of beads; in later times a dollar a night. No mention of pay was made before he began: if he did not cure, he received no pay. Kutox stated that if he failed of a cure, he was nevertheless offered half the amount because he had tried, but the shaman would refuse.

One who had failed to cure might be accused of bewitching the patient and be killed. Undoubtedly had he accepted payment when he failed, they would be certain that he had bewitched for his own gain. In these cases the reaction was perhaps as automatic as that of the Mohave in taking vengeance on a shaman who failed: "they would give him no chance at all." Nevertheless, I was assured that the Maricopa did not kill an unsuccessful shaman whose efforts were believed to have been honest.[32]

The only instance of an actual cure I could obtain was unfortunately one in which the shaman was a Pima.

I [Kutox] have been cured several times; that is why I am old. Once I got so sick I did not know myself. I had a bad headache and felt nervous all over. I started off from the field where I was working. My house was a scant quarter mile away, but I could not reach it; I had to lie down. All day I stayed there in the shade, until late in the evening they took me home. They sent for a Pima

[32] This seems also to have been the Mohave attitude (Kroeber, *Handbook*, p. 778).

shaman, named k̯atoi′, the best of his time. When he arrived, he announced that he cured only at night. That night he cured inside the house; there was no fire. He held his long eagle feathers in his left hand: these were four, bound in pairs to a short wooden handle. In his right hand was his gourd rattle. He sat with these and as he sang, everything was made clear to him. We thought it too dark for him to see, but for him it was broad daylight. I lay crosswise just in front of him. Only my wife was present with us.

As I had such a high fever, the shaman fanned me with his feathers to wave it away. When he had reduced the fever, he could see plainly who had bewitched me. He sang his songs as he fanned. I did not understand clearly, since he sang in Pima, but they were about Coyote. Coyote described the one who had bewitched me, told the shaman. When a spirit thus describes the right one, the patient gets well, but if it is wrong, he dies.

He would bend over me, but not touch my body. He took out what was in me, breathing hard as if swallowing something. Suddenly he jerked away and acted as though he was going to vomit. When he took it out of his mouth, it was a little grain of charcoal. Sometimes it is a little pebble, the size of a wheat grain: it depends on what the seizure is. If a fingernail were thrown into one, the sick man would have cramps [probably paralysis]. When he took this out, he switched his feathers back and forth to knock all the sickness away from me. Finally he told me who had bewitched me and why.

Curing for the loss of the soul was obtained as a generalized description. The loss was due to dreaming of the dead; its symptom fainting or dizziness. A person dreams he is in the land of the dead. If he eats anything given him there, he gets sick. He might dream repeatedly of this, join in the games there, and because it gave him pleasure, dream of it every night. Such a one would faint; then they always sent for a shaman who knew how to treat it. The shaman's procedure was to search for indications of the route the soul had taken toward the land of the dead, in order to pursue and capture it. He was one who had dreamed of Horned Owl. Significant of the extent of this type of illness and curing was the informant's statement that "this has often happened and they always tell it this way."

When the shaman neared the patient's home, he stopped from time to time trying to discover which way the soul had been taken, that is, whether by air or along the earth. He circled the locality counterclockwise, which "he says is circling the whole world." The dead were believed to have a path into this world from each of the cardinal directions. But they, the dead, rarely used the east and north roads, which were through the air. South and west roads were along the earth. When the shaman reached the spot where the dead had come and taken the soul, he had chills if they had gone by the south road. He continued circling until by the fourth circuit the patient's house was reached. Should he fail to find signs of the lost soul, he was certain that it must be halfway to the land of the dead. He then quickly rolled his cigarettes and puffed them into the air. By this means, he sent a flame after them. When they, the dead, saw the flame following, "just like blood coming over," they left the soul and ran off. But they always tried to put the patient's soul in front of them, and told it not to look back. If it did so and saw the flames following, the patient recovered consciousness. "Then they [humans] ask him and he tells what happened."

Curing shamans accompanied war parties to exercise their art. One named wantcávaRi' (Juan Chevereah)[33] dreamed how to cure those who were shot, "so they always took him along to war." He dreamed of Buzzard, Duck (a particular species?, ωḳ'ωḳ), and Gnat (? unyĭpáwa'páwa'). When a warrior fell shot, he sang, moving about him with arms and legs stiff. He could cure arrow wounds only. Another Maricopa could cure not only these, but gun, spear, and knife wounds. "He also dreamed of these three spirits, but got more power."

Bewitching was a practice open to shamans, not to everyone. These were shamans, I was told, who had dreamed especially of Frog and Orion's Belt. But a conflicting statement suggests that bewitching was not confined to them. "All shamans could bewitch (matáðau'g). The spirit gives the shaman the choice of curing or bewitching, but the spirit tells him that he will not live long if he chooses the latter." Again, "a man who bewitched others would never try to cure. He would always try to bewitch." The truth seems to be that all shamans made only a partial choice.

The reason assigned for bewitching was jealousy. A handsome person or one who was prosperous was commonly the subject of witchcraft, thought Kutox, who was forever boasting how handsome he had been in his earlier days.

[33] Named as a Maricopa chief by the Mohave and the *Report of the Commissioner of Indian Affairs for 1858*, p. 207.

A man or woman would not bewitch because of a quarrel: it was on account of good looks or being prosperous. In my case it was because I [Kutox] always had good wheat and plenty of horses, and I was the first to get a wagon. That is the reason I always get sick. But I have had this man [the Pima shaman above] to take care of me all these years. The only way to keep from being bewitched is to go about quietly and share things with others; be kind.

But apparently a shaman could also be got to exercise his art in revenge, as the following incident implies.

About twenty-five years ago two Kohuana men were drinking in the Papago country. One was an old man of seventy or more, the other twenty years his junior. They quarreled. The younger pushed the elder flat on his back. Every time he tried to rise, the other kicked him in the stomach. The old man died. When his people heard of it, they decided to kill the murderer. All the Kohuana agreed to this except one man. They thought this man might cause trouble if they killed the murderer, so they did not carry out their intention. Much later, when he was over seventy, the murderer got sick, became paralyzed and died. Because of the partizanship of one man, they could not beat him to death. But it is believed that the shamans accomplished his death.

Bewitchment was greatly feared. "We do not trust one another: that is why we had the Pima shaman. Our people do not like to tell who did the bewitching."

A malevolent shaman was slain if discovered, "but now the law protects them. They are keeping it up, so we are dying out." If they thought that a shaman made people sick, they agreed on killing him. His relatives would not avenge his death, because they knew he had caused the death of others; "they would say it was all right." Apparently such slayings were rather frequent.

The procedure for bewitching was highly stereotyped. A bit of wood was shaped flat and narrow by the malicious person, who notched its edge or scratched lines across it, one for each victim, whom he named as he cut them. Sometimes an owl feather and a bit of charcoal (or recently the head of a match) was tied to it, so that the victim would have fever. Or these were stuffed into a short cane tube. "When he did this, he sat down and talked to the stick just as though talking to a person." He named the number of days until each victim would succumb and how he would sicken. "Sometimes he would say the victim would be sick in two or four days, in a month, or two weeks. On that day the victim knows he is sick." He might also say to the stick that the victim should long for a certain kind of food, but the food would make him worse (as was told in the Creation tale of the dying culture hero bewitched by Frog). He then buried it near the victim's house, or thrust it into a corner of the roof thatch, or in a nearby bush. "Then the victim would soon hear an owl hooting nearby, his dead relatives would come, and he would fall sick." If he buried it quietly the bewitched would simply sicken, but if he whirled it on a cord like a bull-roarer, the victim would feel he was spinning about. The stick might also be planted where there had been a cremation.

In this case the sick man will not complain of feeling sick, but sit about as though sleepy. At night he would see and talk with the one cremated at that place. The bewitched would say he was tired out, overworked. Not until he was about to die would he tell of having seen the dead; that he had made up his mind to leave his relatives. Then they would send for a shaman to cure him. But if he made up his mind to die, he could not be cured. If the sick man was cured, the bewitcher might choose to repeat his act until the victim died.

Somewhat different methods were also recorded. The bewitcher might swallow a morsel of coal from a cremation pyre, and breathe hard at the victim, "shoot him with it" ('ak̯iyă'm, "shooting"). Those who bewitch this way dream of Frog. A man who dreamed of Orion's Belt got power to bewitch at a distance. He would break off a tiny fragment of a stick, or a bit of his own fingernail, and "throw it at a man at a great distance, who would then fall down sick immediately." This was cured by a shaman who had dreamed of Cricket. Hair combings were carefully gathered to be hidden away, lest a shaman use them to bewitch; "make them swallow their own hair."

A few notes were obtained on practical remedies, self-administered for common ailments, such as rheumatism and bowel-complaints. Colds and bowel-complaints were dosed with a boiled decoction of ivusĭ'. The juice of gwĕnmuci'ʀà root (a low plant growing in sandy canyon beds) was used as a cathartic. These were boiled, or simply mashed and soaked in water. The treatment for rheumatism (tao'ʀàm) was to bathe the afflicted part with boiled avĕmàcàðer, "rattlesnake afraid" (an aromatic plant resembling rhubarb, but smaller) or heat it in a pit containing coals on which ivusĭ' was thrown. The patient sat with his legs or arm hanging in the hole, covered with a blanket. When mashed while fresh and boiled, or even chewed dry, this plant served as a specific for colds, headache, and rheumatism. Since it was believed that rattlesnakes were afraid of the plant (hence its name), it was chewed and spat on horses' hoofs when travelling at night so that they would not be bitten. When all else failed for rheumatism, a cautery was used. For this purpose the cottony seed fiber of taci'l, or a pledget of cotton rolled into a ball, was burned on the painful spot. A cautery was called tcĭmȧkω'l like the balls of fiber on this plant. Ordinarily smoking was first tried to stop toothache (iϑωRa'vȧk; iϑω, "teeth"), or they bit on black mesquite bark, or held a mouthful of water, warm or cold. For earache (smalgȧRa'vȧ; smal, "ear"), the sufferer placed his ear over a little hole in the ground into which a few coals were dropped. Blue corn was also mentioned without explanation as a cure for this. A shaman was resorted to for severe tooth- or earaches: for the latter he repeatedly puffed smoke in front of the ear and sucked out "something." The shaman for earaches was one who had dreamed of "small animals, cottontails, jackrabbits, and the like." The root of ipilᵧima'n was used for sores; either mashed and boiled, when the sores were washed with the liquor, or slicing and drying the root to lay on the sores. (The plant resembled rhubarb; its root was chocolate colored and shaped like a sweet potato.)

SHAMANISTIC PERFORMANCES

The primary function of shamans was curing; séances were infrequent, mostly clairvoyant, and these on the whole definitely utilitarian. Shamans also sang curing songs for pure entertainment according to one informant, although a second denied it.

Shamans seem to have performed their tricks to give evidence of their powers only at large gatherings, when dances, races, and games were held. The great dances were those of January and February, when the wheat sprouted, and again at harvest time in late August–September. Another occasion for their display was at the sahurao-drinking celebration in mid-June.

The principal feat was handling live coals; swallowing and

spitting them out again red hot, walking or kneeling on them, or putting them in their pockets. This could be done by those who dreamed of Frog.

When Mountain Killdeer was sung, the shamans all cried "Spread it! spread it!" (kàtàvàta′g) and then performed their tricks. One man who pretended he was one of them went away from the crowd to spread secretly his cotton blanket with dirt. Then he poured hot coals in the middle of it, but he did not notice that dirt was lacking there. He whirled it around until it blazed up, to his discomfiture. They all laughed at him; pushed him about, laughing. This was always alluded to as a joke whenever this song was sung.

Others "who had something around their hearts which gave them power," rubbed themselves on the breast and drew out of their mouths flat tapes, a foot long, which resembled sinew. Sometimes they took from their mouths a hair which seemed alive. There was no stick swallowing trick.

For the rest, shamanistic activities had practical ends: helping fishermen, bringing rain, purifying eagle feathers, and clairvoyance to discover the enemy, foretell the winner of a race, or to detect thieves.

A shaman who had dreamed of fishes would go to a pond or slough when fish could not be caught. He would say, "Wait; I will see what I can do." He threw willow leaves in perhaps more than once, and the fishermen would find these transformed into fish.[34]

When rain was wanted, a shaman who had dreamed of rain would stand and puff four cigarettes toward the sky. "The smoke went up to the clouds." Another shaman might make the rain cease. This was not a public demonstration.

Eagle feathers were considered exceedingly dangerous (muciθe′vĭk or mucàRai′àm), that is, poisonous (xutuRàu′yĭm).[35] They were given to a shaman to purify (xacàvàsu′i). He puffed the smoke of four cigarettes all over the feathers and then sucked each one. "He took all the poison out of it." (There was no singing with this procedure.) The shaman would tie the feather to a

[34] Inquiry on this point was suggested by Mr. E. W. Gifford who understood the Cocopa to say that they used willow leaves to fill up the pond in order to stupefy or poison the fish.

[35] For a myth reference see p. 374.

young man's hair for him. Even then this man would not dare touch a drinking utensil after having touched the feather he wore, else those who used it would get sick. Kutox said he would not touch an eagle feather for anything!

Clairvoyants could reveal the whereabouts of the enemy or forecast his coming. The clairvoyant shaman who accompanied a war party into the mountains, one who dreamed of Buzzard or Coyote, smoked four cigarettes and fell as though dead. His smoking was thought to lift him high into the air. When he recovered he told how Buzzard had taken him to the highest mountain where the location and numbers of the enemy were revealed and how easily they might be slain. The war party then set off following his leadership.

To foretell if enemies were approaching on stormy nights when they might be expected, a shaman performed in the meeting house. His spirit was unknown to the informant. The performance was predicated on the belief that the mountains of the several tribal territories were partisans of their inhabitants. Four piles of dirt were made in the meeting house. This shaman went to each in turn, stooped, and sucked it up, groaning all the while. When he finished the fourth pile, he dropped "dead." They put him with a rattle in a little hut built inside the meeting house. Then the mountains came "in the form of persons": the audience felt the draft as they entered. "The house might be crowded, yet they could hear the mountain talk in there." A mountain would take the rattle, asking "How did they come to kill this man [the shaman]? What is wrong that you killed him?" The mountain spirit would say, "I am tired," and act the part. A man sitting beside the "dead" shaman answered, "Yes, I know you are tired, having come a long way. But this night we fear the enemy; for that reason we called you here." The mountain would reply, "No, the enemy are not thinking of you; perhaps some other time but not now. If you do not believe me, another person [mountain] will tell you." Then it left and immediately another mountain entered. "Even the mountain at Yuma came: it spoke Yuma." Then a mountain of Papago land came in; immediately the other left. The Papago mountain would say,

"What is the matter with you? Were you asleep? Why did you not catch that one, an enemy, so I could club him to death?" The mountains also told if the enemy was on the way and how soon he would arrive. The interlocutor must know how to ask the mountain spirits: if he asked them wrong, the mountain would say, "Well, I do not know about the enemy, but I know that today an important person died," meaning only a lizard or a bug.

Forecasting who would win an inter-tribal race was a similar performance. Kutox described it as he once saw it while camping on the way to race with the Pima. When the shaman sang, he told them he had been instructed by his nȧkï'tc (grandparent's brother or step-father), a spirit called cïl̬yaitcuwa'n.[36] They made only one dirt pile, in which someone secreted potsherds to test him. The shaman sang and rubbed his body, changing the dirt pile into foamy water, which he sucked in without stopping for breath. Again rubbing himself, he took the sherds off his body and flung them away. He fell "dead": everyone had to be quiet. When he recovered he told who would win. If the Maricopa were to win, he told how he had been handed many gifts by the spirit (symbolic of their winnings); otherwise the spirit said, "I was going to give you a certain thing, but now I cannot. I will do so later."

A shaman who had dreamed of Buzzard and Coyote could use his clairvoyant power to discover a thief, as well as the location of the enemy. He never mentioned the name of the thief, names being taboo, but described his clothing or habits.

Two instances were cited. An old woman got a shaman to discover a thief· He sat on the spot where she had last had the money, smoked four cigarettes, and told what she had done. On another occasion, a man left a bead necklace on the bank when he went swimming. It was gone when he returned: there were no footprints. He brought a shaman who made him stand where he had laid it. The shaman went along until he came to a tree, where he said there was a nest. "Sure enough, a crow had taken it there."

PRAYERS, OMENS, AND BELIEFS

Prayers (matyȧxata'l) were not addressed to any spirit in particular, Mrs. Redbird thought. The air was full of spirits who

[36] Meaning unknown to informants, but seems to be based on cïl̬yȧai,' "sand."

would hear any prayer. Last Star also thought that they were
not directed to particular spirits.

Old people think that when the trees begin to bud, their lives have changed,
been renewed; that a spirit has pulled them through the hard winter. They would
then address the various spirits of animals and strong birds [that is, those that
have power]. They did not pray to sun or moon, or dream of them. The sun toward evening says, "I have gone through the whole world watching my children.
They seem all right, so I think I will go down and see how they are getting on in
the other world." The sun claims every living creature as his own: so it seems
queer to Last Star that they do not pray to him. The moon is an old woman who
looks down on little children and protects them. Hence when the moon first appears, the little children are told to call her by a kinship term, cĭnkĭs, grandparent's sister.

Prayer plumes were not used by the Maricopa, although the
Pima usage was known. Nor were other offerings made, as shell,
turquoise; nor sand paintings and fetishes constructed. The
pollen crosses marked on themselves by Yavapai were equally
unknown.

Beliefs in a magical order of events and actions were moderately important in Maricopa thought. At the same time they
gave only lip service to some of these, differentiating rather clearly between sayings and beliefs. Mrs. Redbird, my interpreter,
proved invaluable in this matter, always carefully prefacing her
translation with the observation that the item was one of literal
belief or merely a saying.[37] All beliefs and allied practices not
mentioned elsewhere in this section on religion are resumed here.

Apart from the import of dreams, there were several omens,
almost without exception presaging disaster. If the enemy were
nearing a fishing party, the fish then broiling would shout out
loud from among the coals. Just as soon as the fish were eaten,
the enemy would appear shouting. Sometimes a fish bled from
its side before it was cut: this was a sign someone would be
wounded. If on a journey or to war, a deer joined the party instead of fleeing, it was taken as an omen that one of them would
be killed. But the informant immediately added, that it meant
they would kill an enemy, because to take a deer without having
to hunt for it was lucky!

Death or an epidemic was presaged by a horned owl seen flitting about the houses: when his mouth opened a light was seen

[37] For sayings see p. 331.

in it. When the loon (xalyàpu'kc), flying high in the air, cried out, this also announced the advent of "a terrible disease." It was heard just before the influenza epidemic of 1918 which carried off many of their number. The appearance of a comet also betokened the death of a prominent person or a general disaster.

A young chicken crowing like a rooster was a portent of death in its owner's family. If one's possessions made an unexpected noise, the owner would die. Similarly, if a snake crawled into the house an inmate would die. "The snake says he has come to the funeral."

Before my interpreter's father died, her mother went out one night. She sat down. Suddenly she felt something very cold. Looking down, she saw a little rattlesnake coiled around her ankle. She was too frightened to scream. It uncoiled, crawled a foot or two, and coiled again. She tried to drive it away, but it was dead. Next day a big rattler came to the door and coiled up. It did not rattle before they killed it. Soon after, the man died.

The tale Dog Champion (p. 396) yields several omens: a skull speaks, a pot cries out, a log groans; all presaging disaster to the Yuma at the hands of the Halchidhoma.

It was believed that certain actions would bring on sickness: handling a chickenhawk, or anything it had killed; or a boy eating the game he killed. Similarly, if a father ate the game he killed, his child would sicken. (Surely this conflicts with practice.) Arrowheads (those that were found ?) were dangerous to have: the thunder would be sure to strike one who carried them about.[38] Lightning-struck trees were avoided for fear of sickness. If a turtle shell was put over a child it would grow no more.

In a myth (p. 374) it is noted that killing various desert birds and insects will cause rain to fall: cactus wren, a bird called vitàpana', and tarantula.

The prehistoric ruins were believed to have been occupied by a people, who like themselves, were created by the culture heroes. They were called pipain_yiko'ʀ, "old people."

In the mountains to the northwest were the footprints of a giant, who figures in a tale (p. 409). There was no belief in dwarfs or water-babies in the mountains.

[38] The Papago also associated them with lightning, believing they are to be found where lightning has struck. They were also used for curing (Lumholtz, *New Trails in Mexico*, pp. 111, 180).

Nail parings thrown away would make a noise like a kiss, so they did not like to throw them near where they slept.

SOULS AND LIFE AFTER DEATH

It is clear that concepts of soul were not involved in the dream experience. An individual possessed a plurality of souls: (1) wipai′, the soul proper, the vital principle; (2) ′ĭcĭnyoi′yĭm, "[something that] does not act good," the whirlwind soul, the ghost; (3) iwa′, the heart; (4) iwaǎnŏk̲, "small heart," the pulses. "At death the wipai′ goes to the land of the dead; the ghost stays about [in human guise] as the whirlwind; the heart becomes a horned owl, each pulse a screech owl. The heart is always the last part of the body to burn. It is called 'the horned owl,'" Kutox thinks, because it burns as a black lump. The horned owl was sometimes called kwĭpu′i iwa′c, "the dead people's heart." "The ghost is just the shadow of the dead person," according to Last Star. When illness was said to be occasioned by the loss of the soul, it was the wipai′ which was thought to leave the body. At death, the remaining souls left the body: the whirlwind soul perhaps at the instant of death; more certainly the heart and pulses fled the corpse during its cremation.

The Maricopa believed that the land of the dead lay to the west, in the desert on the lower reaches of the Gila. They called it "the dead people's place" (puĭnyáva′, sing.; hupoi′ĭnyáva′, pl.). Where the Halchidhoma localized their after life while they were still on the Colorado, Kutox had never heard his people mention. As he knew them, living on the Gila with the Maricopa, they said that their own and the Maricopa dead went to the same place in the west. The point is of some interest. The Yumans of the lower Colorado assigned a southerly direction to it, hence this was probably also the original Halchidhoma localization. But the Maricopa have transposed the names of the cardinal points from the normal Yuman order, south becoming west, so that the direction downstream was correctly maintained, and with it, we may presume, the direction in which lay the land of the dead.

When I [Kutox] was young I did not think people who were cremated would be like humans again. But I think I will be dead soon, and now in my dreams I see them in the form of people. I recognize them and talk with them. I have come to believe that there are such people living on the other side of these mountains.

The road taken by the dead was along a low sand hill westward beyond the barrier of the Gila Bend–Maricopa Mountains. Beyond these was a shade under which sat an aged woman. A little farther on the road forked: those who died in war took the branch to the right (i.e., north or west?), those who died of sickness, that to the left (south). An account of recovering a lost soul which had set out for the land of the dead (p. 286) gave a slightly different picture. According to this, the dead have a path into our world by each of the cardinal directions. But the dead never used those on the north or east, only the south and west roads. The latter roads lead along the ground; the first two through the air. But "the dead hardly ever take a person through the air." These south and west roads "lead to [are?] the forked road" described above.

The aged woman was described by Josepha Juan who saw her in dreams. (Josepha, an Halchidhoma, is herself constantly grieving.) This crone dipped her finger into boiled mesquite bark and marked her cheeks with it. She mourned every day. Her tears washed the marks off, so that she continually repeated her action. The stuff was deposited on her breast by her tears. It was so thick that one could thrust a whole finger into it. Under the shade, she kept watermelons. When a dead person (? a soul) arrived, she said, "Eat some for your hunger and go on."

Participating in the life of the dead was hazardous in the extreme for any living soul. "A person dreams he is in the land of the dead. If he eats anything given him there, he gets sick. A person might dream of this repeatedly, join in the games there, and thinking it fun, dream of it every night. Such a person would faint": his soul would be lost and he would die.

There were many people in the land of the dead. "It has become so crowded that they keep on pushing this way [east], until their village extends even west of these mountains." Here is a reflection of the dwindling numbers of Maricopa, fast diminishing under the changed conditions of modern life.

Everything of our world was duplicated in that land, but with its nature reversed. Day and night were interchanged; things bitter here were good food. The dead never stood still; hence the whirlwind with its legs crossed, spinning along on its toes. The dead were constantly at dances and games, so many of them together that there were crowds at the games. They went to war. They were always enjoying themselves, with plenty to eat, "plenty of melons." Even the sole cause of complaint among them reverses real life. When a living person wanted to go somewhere, he had the pleasures of anticipation and fulfillment: he set a day and on that day went off camping enroute for however long it might take him. "But with us," the dead complain, "when we want to go anywhere, we are there before we know. We do not like that."

The aged became young and old things new there. "Old, ragged things burned here go to the land of the dead and are new again." Old people become young again. Kutox said he will again have long thick braids hanging down his back. Even the middle-aged became younger. On the other hand, a baby became a youth of fifteen or so, not a baby. But "the dead have children there" (beget them?). When a man died, he grew old and died again three times in that land. After the fourth death, he became nothing more than a bit of charcoal lying in the desert.

Rebirth and final dissolution as mere charcoal were also described by Last Star, but he thought a series of changes took place other than becoming young again.

When a person dies he becomes a ghost (ı̆cı̆nyoi′ı̆m) and lives there [in the land of the dead]. When the ghost dies again, he is entirely different from all other ghosts, so that they do not like to have him around. They make him bathe in a certain river there to be purified, just as here when a man kills an enemy. Then he can mingle with the other ghosts again. I do not know what he turns into when he dies a third time, but it is some kind of creature. When this creature dies, it turns into a bit of charcoal. They say that these are to be found in the desert down the Gila River. [Questioned on the Yuma belief,[39] he said:] Each

[39] Forde describes the Yuma belief that the soul progresses through four different planes, lingering in each, until it finally reaches the land of the dead (*Yuma Ethnography*, p. 179).

time he comes to life he does not go to a new place to live. I never heard that when they come to life they become young again.

Even modern features were incorporated in their conception of this land. One woman saw a schoolhouse there: she heard its bell. She went to her mother's home there. They told her her children went to school. When she woke, she found everything so lonesome here. There are some white men there, according to Kutox.[40]

A woman was reported as having dreamed of being taken to the top of a mountain, but it was nothing but a hill. A half-sister, who had been dead some time, told her that she should go with her. All their relatives were over there and she (the human) would play the dice game. The dead woman wanted her to join the crowd of dead playing that game. She told her everything was nice there, with everybody present except those left behind, those who had been buried not cremated. The dead say they cannot take in those who are buried, because they smell too badly. Those who were buried live on the north side of the land of the dead. They wander all the time carrying boxes (coffins) on their heads, looking for shades to live under. When they tire, they lay them down and sit on them. The dead think this appalling. The woman who told this died a year after her dream.

There was no belief of the rebirth of ordinary dead in our world, but twins and deformed persons were reborn. They were believed to come from a village of their own, an adjunct of the village of the dead lying to the northwest. Some of the deformed there were without arms, others without noses or mouths; some had an eye in the middle of the forehead. These persons, deformed and twins alike, were born in our world only as visitors. "They say, 'We want to go on a long journey' and they leave there. When others there miss them, they say 'They have gone somewhere to rest under a shade.' These wanderers are born here as deformed babies." This was infrequent "because people do not leave their homes casually." When twins and deformed people died, they returned to their village, not to the land of the dead, until they were reborn. If they were mistreated here they would not stay, but go back where they came from.[41]

[40] When I was leaving at the end of my field trip, Kutox told me that he would be dead before I returned. But I should probably meet him in the land of the dead, for "you are a good white man." If I found my notes insufficient, he would be glad to help me again there. I was to look for a young handsome man.

[41] An instance of the birth of a tiny, delicate baby believed to be one of these, and their reactions to it, is cited in the section on "Birth," p. 314.

CHAPTER X

DEATH CUSTOMS

CREMATION

Like other Colorado River Yumans, the Halchidhoma and
Maricopa cremated their dead and held a mourning ceremony
for them. So far as the details of cremation were concerned the
two tribes did not differ, but the slight Maricopa mourning rite
was incomparable with the ambitious Halchidhoma affair. The
latter closely paralleled that of Yuma and Mohave.

The dead were without exception cremated. This included
those who died while visiting with foreign tribes, warriors killed
in the enemy country, and infants. Those who were not cremated could not enter the land of the dead (see p. 299).

One who died away from home, as in war in the mountains [Yavapai terri-
tory], would be cremated right there. They would be quiet about it; gather logs
at night, set fire to them, and immediately set out for home. If one died while
on a visit to the Mohave, e.g., he was cremated there: if one of their men dies
here, we do the same for him. The ashes were not carried home. But the time
our people were killed at Yuma, we could not attend to them. They died in a
pile in the center of their village. The bones lay scattered about for years. It was
the same with all the Yuma who were killed over here.

Cremation persists to this day: it occurred once while I was
on the reservation. My aged Halchidhoma informant, Kutox,
from whom most of the following description was obtained, was
by common consent director of these affairs.

When a man had a mortal illness, the shaman in attendance
was given four nights in which to cure. On the fourth night,
when he knew his efforts were unavailing, he changed his songs.
Previously he had referred in them only to things that are white;
now he suddenly changed to references to black, and the auditors
knew the patient would die. During the first half of the night, he
sang persuading the sick man not to go to the other world, reminding him that his property was here. During the second half,

toward morning, he "pushed him on," telling him that the other world was pleasant, the people were happy there, and he too would be happy. This was all in song; abruptly changing his text and hurrying on to the end.

The shaman was followed by an orator, who began to talk just before the sick man died. "When an elderly person was dying, he waited until the speaker came to talk to him, before dying." This speech, as well as those he delivers later, were stereotyped and peculiar to each point of the funeral.

The speaker reminded the old man how during the early part of his life he had come to love all people; how he thought his hunting trips were a pleasure to everyone who had gone with him; how he came to think his life all that the world could give him. He went on; that having had all these pleasures, he must now part with them. While he lived he knew how to place all the stars and how the sun and moon appeared. Now everything would change: he might never again see these things. If it was the way they said, he would go to the land of the dead. If it was not true, no one knew where he would go. This made the old man feel badly, too. It was always the case that at the end of the speech, the man was dead.

The speaker then addressed the relatives of the dead, telling them to be happy despite their loss. He encouraged them.

How long the corpse was kept before cremation (hutĭnyĭ′k) depended on the length of the last illness. Ordinarily it was kept but half a day, or if the death occurred at night, cremation followed in the morning. But if the person died suddenly after an illness of only a few days, they kept the corpse longer, a whole night or day.

The corpse was always carefully prepared: washed, dressed in its best, the hair combed, painted and decorated. It was wrapped in a cloth, tied above the head, with another cord tied around the waist and a third below the feet. These duties were performed by some elderly person outside the family, who was not paid, but served out of friendship and pity.

There was one proper method of preparing the pyre (iàϑau′g, "wood pile") and arranging the corpse on it, dictated by practical considerations. A poorly constructed pyre would suddenly fall sidewise and dump out the corpse. Sometimes the pyre was built before the person died. A big post was set into the ground at the eastern end of the spot selected, so that it stood three feet high. Four smaller logs were laid on the ground in an east-west direction with one end touching the post: the inner pair were straight, the outer logs bowed and held in position by two smaller posts on each side of the large post (Fig. 12). Other layers of poles were laid on these until the pile rose to the height of the post at the eastern end. Dry arrowweed was stuffed between these layers on each side for kindling.

Six men were required to carry an adult corpse, three on a side. They took it from the house and laid it on the ground. The pyre was always near the house, perhaps fifty yards distant. Even in

FIG. 12.—Arrangement of cremation pyre

this short distance, they laid the corpse down three times before arriving there. For the fourth time, they laid it beside the pyre, always on the south side. Each of the four times they halted, the speaker delivered an oration. One man then stood on top of the pyre at its north edge. The others then handed the corpse up to him, which he clasped tightly around the shoulders. The corpse was laid with its head to the east and then turned on its right side so as to face the north. (It was never laid on face or back, but always on its side.) Then, reaching in the cloth at the feet, the right foot was drawn back (i.e. south), and thrust between the logs, the left foot was drawn forward and similarly secured. The purpose of this was to hold the corpse firmly on the burning logs, so that it would not drop down between them to burn in a lump. The deceased was placed with his head to the east so that when he "rose," he would face the west and see his dead relatives coming for him.

Clothing and blankets were piled over the whole pyre. These were contributed by every person who attended. If the dead was a man, his favorite horse decorated with paint (or several of them), was staked near by to be killed as soon as the pyre was lighted. The belief was that he could ride one to the land of the dead, packing the clothing, etc., on the others.

While the pyre was burning, an older man (called aume'vȧ, "fire tender") poked with a long pole, running it under the corpse to let in the air, and pushing the blazing logs over the corpse so that it could not be seen. "For the relatives to see any of the corpse would make them sad." The end post was the last to finish burning. The breast and heart were held to be the last parts consumed.

All this time the relatives were about. Children and elders alike were forbidden to eat or drink. When the body was half cremated and again after it was consumed the speaker delivered an oration. After the pyre had burned to coals, everybody left except the fire tender. This would be early the next morning, e.g, if the cremation had begun early in the night.

When the fire had burned out, four holes were dug close to the heap of ashes, two on the south side, two on the north. Then the fire tender, starting at the west end of the heap, scraped the ashes alternately to the north and south of the center line. He then divided these two piles to the west and east, so as to form four piles. Each was put in its respective hole and covered with dirt. Dirt was also scattered over the whole place. "Then the rain obliterated all signs. It is better that way."

At the funeral of a man who was a singer, the Maricopa (but not the Halchidhoma) had singing and dancing; even the relatives rose to dance. They then returned to cry over the dead. The songs were those the dead man "had liked," i.e., those he had dreamed. The same songs and dance were repeated in their mourning ceremony.

Everything within the dead man's dwelling was destroyed. The objects were thrown into a hole dug beside the house, or sometimes within it. The house was then burned down. This was done because the sickness might have been left in the house, and also, if these articles were left about, the dead, returning, might be seen in dreams and the survivors sicken and die too. They moved to a new locality, where a new house was built. This habit seems to have led to a constantly shifting occupation of the Gila valley, much accelerated by the epidemics incident to the coming of the whites.

The relatives would mourn for four days following the death. At the end of the fourth day, they were always visited by an older person who talked to them, admonishing them not to think of their dead relative for fear they might also sicken. He tried to get them to efface it from their minds. For this reason, there was no mourning ceremony, according to my Halchidhoma inform- ant; but he later described the very full rite given below. After four days they resumed their normal occupations.

Purification (mataʀáĕ′k) was necessary for the mourning rel- atives, the speech-maker, and everyone else who had touched or tended the corpse. They threw all the clothing they wore into the pyre and went to bathe. (In fact, everyone who was present threw at least one article into it before leaving the spot.) On reaching home, before going to bed, they built a little fire on which arrowweeds were lain to smoke themselves. For four days they abstained from meat and salt, bathing each morning. Mourning relatives singed their hair short, not close.[1] The length of mourning was not fixed: some widows and widowers remar- ried within a few months, but it was usual to wait a year or two.

I several times observed an old woman walking alone wailing or rather groan- ing for relatives who had died some time before. But when she reached the house of her niece, where I was, she left off abruptly. I was told that she grieved all the time and that she dreamed of the dead.

The objection to naming the dead was very strong, so much so that it was very difficult to obtain genealogical material. This was not an absolute tabu but a strong repugnance. As elsewhere among Indians, mentioning a man's dead relatives (called nĭctcĭm′g) was comparable to cursing him. Kutox, commenting on this, said, "But every time I hurt myself I say, 'I have no grandmother; I have no grandfather.' Soon I will be with my dead relatives so I do not mind speaking of them."

[1] Purification of mourners by bathing and smoking also occurred among the Yuma (Gifford, *Yuma Dreams*, p. 66) and the Mohave purified themselves by smoke in the scalp dance (Kroeber, *Handbook*, p. 752).

HALCHIDHOMA MOURNING CEREMONY

The Halchidhoma had a mourning ceremony like that of the tribes of southern California and the lower Colorado. With the former they shared the construction and burning of images representing the dead, with the latter, a sham combat as well. Consonant with their more easterly position, the Maricopa lacked all but the simplest of mourning rituals.

The Halchidhoma ceremony, called kĕʀu'kàm, was held about the anniversary of a man's death. It seems probable that it was held for all men, but not for women or children, and that it was held but once for a single individual. Its purpose was simply that of remembrance: there was no notion of the return of the dead connected with the image, or the like. The pattern of the proceedings followed in large part that of the actual cremation.

Someone outside the family, a man, went to the relatives of the deceased to inform them that he would undertake the ceremony. They would get the needed clothing and paints ready. Word was sent to the various villages fixing the day and time for the ceremony. Prior to their coming, there had to be constructed the image, a flat-roofed shade, a small oval structure, a woodpile, and a post was erected.

The image[2] was completed before they began to erect the two structures. Four men were selected to make it. They bathed every morning before proceeding to work. Like all the construction connected with the ceremony, work had to proceed very slowly and quietly. (It is not known how long they took to make it.) The image, made of rags, was intended to look exactly like the dead man. It was clothed and its hair dressed exactly as he had worn it. Kutox thought it was as large as a human. The neck was loosely made so that the head would face from side to side when the image wobbled.

When this was completed, a small oval structure was built at some convenient place selected for the ceremony. This, called

[2] The native name was not remembered by Kutox, who had himself never seen the ceremony; hence it fell into disuse before 1847 or the years immediately following.

vaʀau′kᵃ, was designed to house those who took the part of enemies. It was formed of willow branches stuck into the ground with their tops bent over and tied together. Four days were occupied in building this simple structure. At the end of that time, a large number of men gathered to build the shade, called mȧtk_yȧ′l l_yuwe′vȧ, "meeting shade," for the use of the mourning relatives and their friends. This also was worked at very slowly, occupying a second four-day period and being completed on the day of the ceremony. Meanwhile, a selected group built the woodpile and erected a tall post. The shade was placed at the center of the ground where the ceremony was to be held. The oval structure was to the southwest of it, in order to be out of the way of the villagers who later approached from the four cardinal directions. The post was near the eastern side of the shade and the woodpile a little south of this. The clothing they had gathered was placed on the pile of wood. Children were made to keep away from these structures.

The mourners were clustered under the shade before the invited villagers arrived. If the ceremony was to take place in the evening, the latter would have started from their homes in the late afternoon. They halted while yet a hundred yards distant from the shade. Each of the four bodies of villagers,[3] following a leader, moved slowly toward the shade from the four cardinal directions. They each halted four times while the leader made a speech, the fourth time being in the shade. These leaders were the same speechmakers who figured when a man died. The four columns arrived in the shade simultaneously, whereon they all burst out crying. Again their speakers addressed the throng; in order, the one from the south, north, west, and east (*sic*).

The image was next borne out to be erected on the post. Those who carried it made it turn from side to side in time to the measured words of the speakers.[4] It was stood against the post

[3] Only four bodies were mentioned, one for each direction. It may be that villagers from divers places were marshaled in four groups as in the Papago Vikita (Mason, *Papago Harvest Festival*, p. 14).

[4] Note here that the speakers had a jerky, measured delivery, also noted for the Mohave (Kroeber, *Handbook*, p. 750).

with its feet on the ground. It faced the crowd under the shade, that is, looking west like a corpse on the pyre. Everyone wailed when it was carried out, but afterward only a few would help the mourners cry. Others were outside the shade doing what they wished quite freely. Some danced and sang what they pleased, but not in the shade. In fact, there was no singing within the shade as among the Walapai.[5] From time to time the speakers would rise to exhort.

The sham battle followed the erecting of the image. Two parties had been selected; some to represent Halchidhoma, the others enemies. Both were armed: one of the "Halchidhoma" party carried the double-pointed feathered pike (hukwilĭ'c) borne by a leader in battle (see p. 165). It might be carried by the true owner. The "enemy," who occupied the oval shelter, were supposed to be prisoners fighting their way to freedom. They would run out, pretending to escape, while the guards, at a little distance, would chase them back. This sham battle continued until the image was burned. Then all the participants broke their bows and arrows, and threw them into the shelter to be burned with it.

A man ran around making a rattling yell in his throat, followed by women who could run fast. (These were others than relatives of the deceased.) These women carried baskets of various foods. Each time he ended his yell, they scattered a handful of food, repeating this until the baskets were empty. They ran around the post, the woodpile, and the mourners gathered there, sprinkling food on the mourners each time in passing. When all was gone, they shook the last from the baskets and put them on the woodpile.

The image was then carefully taken down, set on the woodpile, and burned. When this was done depended on the time the man had died. If he had died just before dawn, e.g., the ceremony was begun early in the evening so that the image might be burned just before dawn. Hence the ceremony might take place by day or night. At the same time they set fire to the round shelter and the shade. Then everyone wailed and speeches were

[5] Spier, *Havasupai Ethnography*, p. 268.

made. When the woodpile was half burned down, all left except the mourners. The speaker then told them to bear up under their loss, speaking as though the death had just occurred. He then left. The man who tended the cremation also tended this burning. He handled the image carefully as though it were the corpse. He saw that it was wholly consumed, divided the ashes into four parts, and buried them in four holes. Then the mourners left.

Those who made the image and those who took part in the sham fight had to observe the precautions of purification for four days, abstaining from salt, etc., just as at a death.

MARICOPA MOURNING CEREMONY

The Maricopa ceremony, which was much simpler, seems not to have been held for every man, but only for those who were exceptional as singers, orators, or warriors. At this time they sang the songs dreamed by the deceased or enacted a fight in which he had participated, and burned contributions of clothing and belongings. There was no image and no shade built. Further, the ceremony was not on the anniversary but took place within a few days after the death.

Three days after the death of a great man (a warrior, speaker, or singer), some man would arrange this ceremony (called hĭc-pask, "showing"). It occupied an entire day, the burning occurring late in the evening. He selected a place where they made a woodpile as if to cremate. Everyone brought clothing, piled it on the pyre, and burned it. Men yelled and women raced back and forth.

Kutox remembered this done for a man, a war leader who in his day had carried the feathered pike "standard." It took place on the fourth day after his cremation. Word was sent to the Halchidhoma at Sacate and to the Pima. They were invited because this man had always invited these tribes when he went to war. He was always successful. All who came wore their finest clothing and were armed as for war. One carried a feathered pike. When they arrived they rode around the site and then, to one side, enacted a certain battle in which the deceased had fought.

He with the pike took the part of the deceased. Speech making went on all the time the sham fight continued, but there was no singing or dancing. At the end everyone stripped himself of clothing, weapons, etc., to place on the woodpile, which was then burned.

A mourning performance for a singer was described as follows. The Maricopa husband of the sole surviving Kohuana was a man who dreamed of the buzzard and sang Buzzard songs. Although he was ill, he accompanied a large party to Mexico, where he grew worse. His companions went farther, expecting to take him on their return. But a week later, when they returned, they found he had died and been buried (*sic*). The others came home. His relatives gathered at the dead man's house. They mourned two days: on the third day they built a pile of wood, sang and danced until late in the evening, when they burned everything They burned the house and his possessions, threw away food, etc. This man had had four gourd rattles with which he taught, at night, anyone who wanted to learn his songs. Those who knew his songs well (Kutox, my informant, among them) sang at this time. The rattles were burned on the heap of clothing. Although this occurred sixty years ago, these songs were never sung again, until last year (1928) when an old man sang them.

Normally the songs of the deceased singer were used at the cremation, again at the mourning rite, and never again. Of recent years, however, songs have been resurrected only a short time after cremation.

CHAPTER XI

INDIVIDUAL DEVELOPMENT

BIRTH

Birth was preceded and followed by restrictions on the activities of the parents that applied to both to about the same degree. This semi-couvade, as Kroeber styles it, was moderate and of the order that prevailed generally throughout the Southwest and California.

When in the fourth or fifth month of pregnancy, the expectant mother should not lie flat on her back else the embryo would lie crosswise or be born feet first. Neither she nor her husband should look at dead animals or birds, else the child would sicken like the animal, would be paralyzed for weeks. On the whole, it were better that the father did not hunt; if he did, he must not stare at what he killed. Nowadays, neither may look at a picture of any sort; the child will be deformed. Nor could either look at or touch rattlesnakes, else the child would be deformed and never walk: it would seem to lack bones; could not stand.

Food tabus applied to the mother from the sixth month. She must eat no more than she could help and must especially avoid fat. Should she eat fat, the embryo would be covered with it, especially its eyes, nose and mouth (a caul?). The mouth would be filled with fat, so that at its first breath, the child would choke. There was no objection to her eating salt, the common tabu elsewhere. Her husband could eat fat and salt at this time, but he joined her after the birth in eschewing them.

It was known that pregnancy has a duration of nine lunar months. It was, however, not usual to calculate the exact time at which the birth would occur, but some women knew they would give birth at a particular full moon, e.g. Births were rather uniformly distributed through the year.

Birth took place in the menstrual shelter, or a similar structure was built for the purpose near the house by the husband or other relatives. This consisted of a ridgepole supported on two posts, placed east and west, with willow branches thrust into the ground and bent over to it. The whole was covered with arrow-weeds and dirt. It was circular in ground-plan. The lodge had no special name, but like the storehouse was called vana′ʀᵃ. A fire was built within to warm the ground and to heat water.

The expectant mother was helped by her mother and another feminine relative. They would choose a helper whose time of delivery had been brief. If the parturient could not endure the pain, four or five women were called in to assist until the little house was full. They did not sing. Should the case be exceptionally difficult, they thought her bewitched and called in a shaman who could cure this. Then her husband or other male relative would help. There were no internal medicines to accelerate delivery nor for an excessive flow following birth. Some women preferred to give birth unassisted.

A woman of middle age told me that she had borne her five children alone. Her husband, a widower with children of his own, protested that he did not know how to help, but she prevailed on him to heat water, etc., as needed. This was purely a matter of personal preference: she did not like to have the old women fussing over her. She was also aware of the desirability of continuing her domestic labor until the last moment.

It was recognized that births after the first were of shorter duration. In the old days, it was said, a good many women died in childbirth, whereas nowadays not many are lost; which argues for the absence of venereal disease today.

The parturient sat with her back against the western post, because in the tale of the woman who had twins (p. 368), she tried the four directions when her pains began. She said, "A woman who is to give birth should sit against the western post, facing east." A hole made in front of the parturient was filled with sand, which was hollowed a little and covered with a cotton cloth, rabbitskin blanket or other soft thing to receive the baby. She sat with her knees drawn up. A strong woman, standing behind, would put her arms around her, pressing downward and shifting her from side to side. From the time the birth pains began, the parturient was not allowed to drink.

The navel cord was cut after the afterbirth was ejected. Anyone cut it and the stub of the navel was never tied. A delayed afterbirth was considered dangerous not only for the mother but the child. The afterbirth was buried a short distance from the house in a hole waist-deep, filled with stones and rammed earth. Should a dog eat it, the child would become insane.

The newborn child was washed with warm water and tied in the cradle which was prepared before it was born. At this time, a woman who had no relatives to help her look after a crying child, would put her finger in her mouth and press it against the baby's palate, so that it would never cry later. They did not massage or mould the child's features or limbs as elsewhere. Slight occipital flattening, due to lying on the hard cradle, was common and was desired. Warm ashes were put on a cloth placed on the navel and soaked with warm water. They might also place on the navel a salve made of a few crushed castor beans (obtained by trade from northern Mexico) mixed with water. The cord dropped off in two days if well tended, but always within four days. No further attention was given the sloughed-off cord.

Immediately after the delivery of the afterbirth, the mother lay in a pit, extending from armpit to knees, within the house. This was previously lined with warmed flat stones and ashes, with which she was also covered. These were renewed as they cooled.

It was held that the mother should not resume her occupations for eight days. During this period she was washed every morning and given only corn soup without salt. Her husband also washed on these eight days, but refrained from fats, sweets and salt for the first four only. On the first four days the faces of child and mother were anointed with a preparation made by boiling mesquite beans, straining and boiling down the juice to a syrup, which was then mixed with red paint. This was said to take the grease off their faces.

The child was not put to breast for four days. In the meantime it was given drops of warm water. The baby could endure without food, it was held, because the mother had practically starved herself for several months before the birth.

The sex of the child could be predicted: for a boy the pains followed rapidly and were sharper than for a girl. They say that when a woman had borne only sons or daughters and at last one of the opposite sex was born, it would be her last child. An extension of the idea was cited: when the youngest child of I——— walked at an early age, although her elder children had been slow in learning to walk, they said it would be her last child.

Whether one would have a child at all was forecast by a dream. A man or woman might dream of gathering little birds or puppies, of being fond of them. This was an omen that they would have children. Other dreams were interpreted as signs that they would have no children.

Twins and deformed infants, unlike ordinary children, were thought to be reborn. They were in this world merely as visitors, hence if they were mistreated they would return to their home. Their village was believed to lie to the northwest beyond the Hassayampa Mountains. Some of its inhabitants were without arms or mouths or noses; some had a single eye in the middle of their foreheads; others were twins. These people would say, "We want to go on a long journey," and would wander into this world to be born. When their fellows missed them, they would say, "They have gone somewhere to rest under a shade." Their advent was infrequent because people do not leave their homes casually. When twins and deformed persons died, they returned to this village, not to the land of the dead, until they were reborn. It was considered lucky for a mother to have twins.

No physiological reason was assigned for twinning. On the other hand, an albino (hiðà'hwa't, "red eyes") was thought the result of the pregnant mother having eaten something gnawed by a gopher, such as mesquite beans. Albinos were reported to have a reddish iris and be unable to see well in the sunlight, but to have normally pigmented skin and hair.

Twins were both reared, although this was difficult. They were more likely to die than other children. When one sickened or died, the other would also. It was thought that when one died, it had not been well treated, had not been taken up when it cried. The sympathetic bond may well have been thought to apply only to twins as children, for aged Kutox told me he had twin younger brothers, the one surviving being now an old man.

J——, his older sister told me, is said to be from the village of twins. At birth he was so tiny they did not think he would survive. When he was four he was hardly bigger than a baby of six months. His mother took him to all the shamans, who could do nothing. Finally she applied to one married to her mother's sister. He declared he had seen this boy in his dreams. He directed, "Bring the boy, and let him stay a month if he likes me." The old shaman told them to give the boy everything he wanted, which they did. The old man gave him a horse. When the boy wanted a new horse, he would say, "Take the old horse back," which meant that the shaman should give him a colt, which he did. J—— is now a strapping six-footer of thirty.

A curious point was that the first born of twins was called the younger. The reason given was that one always let a child, a younger person, go through a doorway first. The twins called each other in this fashion younger and older brother.[1] It was absolutely necessary that some such decision be made, considering that age distinctions figure at every turn in the kinship system.

Plural births other than twins were unknown to my informants. Mrs. Redbird knew of three cases of twin births among people now living, a number which might have been predicted in a population of less than three hundred. Twins were called xavŏ'kc, "two."

It is difficult to tell how frequently abortion was practiced in the old days: it is common enough today. A cloth was tied tightly around the abdomen, draughts of a boiling hot tea made of iciu' (a plant growing near the river) were taken, and the constricting process repeated until the embryo was killed. (My informant had never heard of pressing the abdomen on a rock.)

The cradle was prepared before the baby was born. Women gathered the materials for it because they knew best what the size should be, but men always put the frame together since they could lash it more tightly. Various women might prepare its several parts, which were assembled by some older woman of the family. It was distinctly preferred not to use a cradle that had belonged to some other woman. A cradle might be kept for the successive use of one's own children, or one gotten from a near

[1] This explains why twins in the myths are called older and younger brother.

PLATE XV

CRADLE AND HOODS
(a, Assembled cradle; b, frame; c, mattress; d, hood; e, girl's hood;
f, g, boy's hoods)

relative. If the older child had been sickly, however, it would be kept for a long time before it was used again. A second, larger cradle, of exactly the same type was made when the first was outgrown after two or three months.

The cradle was the flat carrying-board of the type used on the lower Colorado River: a narrow arch with long parallel sides to which transverse rods were lashed and provided with a broad hood of basketry. The supplemental articles needed to cradle the child were a bark mattress, a pad to go under the shoulders, cloths with which to wrap the infant, and two bands to bind it to the cradle frame (Pl. XV).

The cradle showed the sex of the infant at several points: by the spacing of the cross-pieces of the frame, the decoration of the hood and the objects tied to it, and the design of the upper binding band. As a matter of fact, they used what they pleased in assembling a cradle. A specimen in use for a little girl, which I bought,[2] had been made for an older brother. It had a boy's frame, while the hood and band were those of a girl. But it lacked the extra mattress required for a girl.

The arch of the frame was tough mesquite root, bent into shape and tied until it dried. The transverse rods were arrow-weed, lashed to the arch and wrapped with split small roots of mesquite, chosen because of its strength. These rods were not long enough to rest on the arch, but lay between its side arms. The lashing passed twice around one arm, was wrapped around the rod for its whole length, wound twice around the opposite arm, and the free end tucked under the lashing (Pl. XV, *b*). A man was requested to lash the rods since it took great strength to get the lashings taut. The number of cross pieces depended on the sex of the infant: for a boy these were seven or eight evenly spaced; for a girl one less, leaving a wider space about the middle of the frame, so that the girl would grow up to have fleshy buttocks.

The mattress was made of broad strips of willow bark arranged in three bundles, each bent in an arch and tied (Pl. XV, *c*).

[2] Washington State Museum, No. 2–11913.

Each bundle was wound with bark for some distance at its middle, its long ends falling free. The bent bundles were arranged concentrically and bound to one another only at the sides. This point should lie behind the infant's shoulders. The mattress was placed so that the outer loop did not reach quite to the arch of the frame and the loose ends hung beyond its lower end.

An elongated pad was placed on the mattress behind the baby's shoulders "to keep them straight." This is now made of cloth and probably was in earlier days. It was a wound ring stretched so that its sides met (Pl. XV, a).

Two binding bands were used; the upper broad, woven (see p. 115), and bearing a design to indicate the sex of the baby, the lower narrower and braided of cotton cords or willow bark. The upper band was always fastened by its fringes to the side bar of the frame to the left of the infant between the first and second cross-pieces (Pl. XV, b). The bands were wrapped spirally downward to the left, making a single bundle of baby and frame. The designs of the upper band are shown in Pl. X.

The cradle hood was a broad basketry hoop of twilled weave (Pl. XV, d). The material for warp and weft was the bark of willow twigs, stripped off to the correct width and length. (In winter the twigs had to be boiled to loosen the bark.) Its manufacture was not observed, but it seems that the weft was continuous; the long unwoven portions of warp at each end were lapped, divided into two bundles, and each bound separately. The decoration, varied to show sex, consisted of concentric lozenges containing a central spot, separated by chevrons, diagonal lines, or zigzags. These were produced by twilling. A curious feature is that the design was accentuated by painting with white, yellow, and red, leaving portions of the surface in the natural olive drab (shown diagrammatically in Fig. 13). The hood for a girl had lozenges in the median line, separated by chevrons placed transversely, the ends of which turned back from the margins of the hood (Fig. 13, a).[3] A boy's hood had oblique white lines reaching from one

[3] The specimen illustrated in Plate XV, e, was made incorrectly. It is not quite broad enough, so that the ends of the chevrons do not turn back.

edge to the other: by their intersection the lozenges were set off (Pl. XV, *f* and Fig. 13, *b*).[4] Another hood (Pl. XV, *g* and Fig. 13, *c*), which I obtained from a trader, may be that of a boy. Objects distinctive of sex were also tied to the top of the hood: a tiny bow and arrow for a boy; for a girl a little string of beads fas-

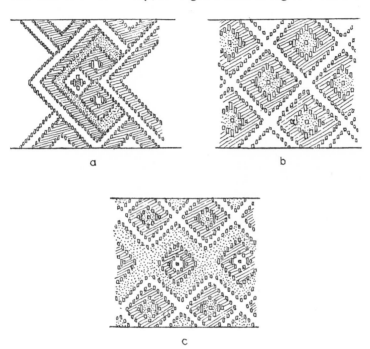

Fig. 13.—Color schemes of cradle hoods (*a*, girl's; *b*, *c*, boys'. Cross-hatching indicates red; stippling, yellow; blank, white; indicated stitches are natural olive drab).

tened along its periphery. The hood was not tied to the frame. It was set on the frame so that the uppermost crosspiece came between the two bound bundles of warp ends, where it was held by the upper end of the mattress resting on them. Since contact with the Mexicans, a red cloth was procured to throw over the

[4] Washington State Museum, No. 2-11915.

hood to shade the baby's face, but in earlier times they relied on the broad hood alone.

To wrap the baby in its cradle, it was assembled as follows: the hood was set in position, the mattress laid on the frame, and the pad placed where the shoulders would come. At least three small cloths were needed to wrap the baby; usually four or five were used. The first cloth was spread over the mattress and pad so that its upper margin would come above the baby's head. Others were wrapped about its body, up to the arm pits, leaving the arms free. The final cloth, spread over the infant, was tucked in at the sides to hold the arms down. The upper band was wound spirally downward to the left around both the baby and the frame, its end being tucked under itself in back of the cradle. The lowermost cloth, lying directly on the mattress, was drawn up between the legs, the cloth and bark on each side was lapped over the top of the legs, and the whole bound by the lower band which passed around the calves and the frame. This band was wound and fastened exactly like the upper band. No absorbent was put in the cradle to take up urine. When the willow mattress was soiled, it was soaked and hung up to dry. A single mattress was used with a boy baby, but two were alternated for a girl.[5]

The cradle was used until the baby was more than a year old. They said that a child strapped in a cradle was more easily carried. Further, that a cradled child would not cry, the reason being that the navel was strapped down: if a child cried the navel would protrude. They tried to ignore crying in order to train the infant. Most of the time the cradle lay flat on the ground or in the swing (to be described shortly), but it was sometimes set upright so the baby could look about. A baby was not allowed to sit up until it was three months old, nor to stand until eight months. If they were allowed to sit up too early, their cheeks would sag below the chin, and if stood up too young, they would become bowlegged. If, when the proper time came, the child did not stand readily, a shaman was called to suck its back and breast so that it would not become feverish.

[5] Which seems the direct contrary of physiological necessity.

The cradle was carried about a great deal, not used as by Zuñi and Havasupai, e.g., primarily as a convenient place for the child to sleep. It was carried lying flat, either balanced on the head or under the arm supported on the hip. For the first two months, it was not carried on the head, because that would make the navel sore, they thought. It was not only customary to balance it on the head without holding, but it was sometimes even perched on top of a load carried on the head, e.g., on an overloaded carrying basket of mesquite beans. Under the arm, the cradle lay flat with the infant's head forward. It was never stood upright on the hip. It was not provided with a carrying-strap, because it was never transported on the back.

Bartlett remarked (1852):

I have seen them [women] in camp with a basket of green corn on their heads, and on top of this the cradle and child. When it gets to be about a year old, it is carried astride on the hip, the mother holding one arm around its body.[6]

Women were seen rocking cradles in a characteristic fashion. The woman, seated on the ground with her legs straight out before her, ankles crossed, laid the cradle crosswise on her lap. She first rocked it end for end with her hands; then continued the motion by slightly lifting the thighs alternately.

At home the baby was kept in a swing, whether in its cradle[7] or not. This was made in the manner of the Pima:[8] a doubled mescal fiber rope was fastened between two posts of the house or shade, with a cloth folded securely over its two halves. Baby or cradle was laid flat on this.

The mattress was always kept under the small of the baby's back, in or out of the cradle, until it was six months old, so that it would not become humpbacked.

When the cradle was outgrown, it was kept for the next child or given to a relative who had need of it. Should the infant die, the cradle was broken up and buried close to the spot where the corpse was cremated. The cradle itself was not burned.

The several parts of the cradle were named as follows: haði'k,

[6] Bartlett, *Personal Narrative*, II, 231, 253.

[7] *Ibid.*, p. 254.   [8] Russell, *Pima Indians*, p. 156.

cradle; tima', the arched frame; hate'ʀĕk, crosspiece; upui', mattress; yaltŏxka'c, shoulder pad; capu'ʀᵃ, hood; xa'a'p or tcuxwĭ'l, the woven upper band; himĕmate'ʀᵃ, the narrow lower band (hime', leg); yăltápai', the outside wrapping cloth (the other cloths having no names).

Children were weaned when more than a year old. They would take the breast even when several years old. There is a little girl today still nursing at six years. No special diet was prescribed for weaning.

An older child was carried on the small of the back supported by a wide cloth tied around the bearer's waist, or astride the hip (without the cloth). I saw an old woman kneeling at work, grinding on her metate, with her twenty-month-old grandchild asleep in a cloth on her back.[9]

CHILDHOOD

The real training of children was naturally largely casual encouragement in learning the tasks of later life. What little conscious training was indulged in was formal, and consisting largely of admonitions, was probably wholly ineffective from a pedagogical viewpoint.

They attempted to ignore a crying child, and probably as individuals with sound nerves, the result of normal healthy lives, succeeded as well as anyone could. It was said that children did not cry much. A boy would be told to be brave, to stand anything. Children were told to behave and to be kind to everyone. They were taught never to answer a scolding and were forbidden to ask questions. They were not spanked, but shaken by the arm until they cried. Should the child still misbehave, the parent would say, "I am going to call So and so (a great warrior) and have him pinch you hard."

The foregoing sounds like our own ideal, but there is this important difference: that the Maricopa, so far as I could judge, actually achieved results. Like all Indians with whom I am acquainted who are still living more or less in the old style, these

---

[9] There was no purification rite for a young child as among the Pima and Papago (Russell, *Pima Indians*, p. 187; Lumholtz, *New Trails*, p. 351).

parents are very indulgent, much given to fondling the younger children, and rarely punish them. But—here is the essential point—they demand implicit obedience and see that they get it.

For all the lavished care normally the lot of children, there were cases to the contrary implying a certain detachment. Children were sometimes abandoned or destroyed.

While the Halchidhoma were still on the Colorado, a woman, whose first husband had sent her away because she bore him no children, had a girl baby by a second husband. His family made them separate because it was a girl. She said it was not right to raise a child who had no father, implying it was a bastard, so she drowned it.

Of a woman now living they say, "She was raised in a coyote's mouth." When she was a newlyborn (?) baby, her mother did not want her and put her off in the bushes. Her children had always died when but a few days or weeks old, so she thought it was no use trying to raise this one. They say a coyote must have kept the baby in his mouth all night, and in the morning opened it so the sun would warm the child. (This was, of course, a saying, not a belief.) Next morning the husband's mother said she did not want the child to die, so she fetched it and brought it up. It was given to various relatives to nurse. The girl, now in middle life, says she is "mean" because she was abandoned to die; that now her mother is old, she expects care from her daughter, but why should she give it? As a matter of fact, it is well known that she takes good care of her mother.

About 1840 a Kohuana widow of Gila Crossing decided that she wanted to rejoin her relatives still on the Colorado. She did not think her children, a boy of six and a girl of two, could make the long journey across the desert, so she abandoned them. Telling them to go to play, she stole away. The children slept in the meeting house and ate with whom they could. They had no relatives there, but people befriended them.

There was a saying: never abuse a child, because the day will come when you too will be a child (childish); which also implies their consideration for the aged.

Captive children, other than those sold immediately, were reared much like one's own. When a capture was made, the child was always turned over to an old man, who had not much longer to live anyway, for a captive might cause its captor to sicken. For sixteen days following the capture, the captive had to bathe, eat and sleep apart like the actual captor until it was purified. The old man's family would usually rear the child kindly, treat it as a son or daughter, especially if their own daughter was fond of her adopted sister. Others than members of this family might abuse them, but after they were grown and married to someone of the Maricopa community, their captive origin was no longer brought up against them.

Admonition was frequently given children. Kutox phrased the ideals of life as follows:

> We would tell a boy to grow up strong and brave, to love his neighbors and to be industrious. When a child was old enough, it was told to treat old people kindly; to share whatever it had with an old woman who could not help herself; never to throw things at an old woman. Boys should try to become famous in war. Girls were told to be industrious and kind to everyone. Girls were looked on as enemies; they were called that (see p. 225).

One thing appeared clearly from discussion, that, unlike ourselves, a parent did not feel that his child should climb to a higher social position than his own, or amass more wealth. "They did not seem to look ahead."

Warfare was an ideal pursuit.

> Fathers told their sons to go to war. It was good to die young: everyone mourned if one was killed in war. But an old man receives scant attention and nobody cares if he dies (said Kutox, himself aged).

Little boys of four to six were trained to withstand pain with this end in view. They were tested by pinching them hard or striking with a stick. The procedure may have been somewhat formalized, for it was said that several boys were tested together by an old man. If they did not cry out when struck, they were next placed on an ant hill to be bitten and finally pushed into a wasps' or bees' nest. It was taken as a sign that they would become brave warriors, if they did not cry. This procedure had no special name and was distinct from the following.

A group of boys of sixteen or eighteen were subjected to a formal test called tcutŏ'xȧm by old warriors. They were admonished to be brave, to withstand starvation, thirst, and fatigue, and were told how to fight. The song tcutŏ'xȧm (p. 268) was sung before the boys were taken to kill a swarm of bees hiving in the ground or in a hollow cottonwood. They were made to sit on the hive and deliberately kill all the bees, one at a time, regardless of their stings. This represented going to war, the bees being the enemy. This was not ostensibly a puberty ceremony.[10]

---

[10] There is an analog in the ant ordeal for boys among Luiseño and Juaneño (Kroeber, *Handbook*, pp. 641, 672).

Boys also played a game, slinging mud at each other, in which they learned to dodge missiles without breaking from the skirmish line (see p. 338).

Girls were trained to carry little burdens balanced on their heads when they were but two years old. Later they assisted their mothers fetching water before sunrise. Girls of four could grind seeds very nicely, it was said: they were wakened when it was barely light and set to work on a basketful. A girl must show her proficiency at grinding such an amount at her marriage. I observed a little girl of five at play making pottery. Working with a ball of mud, she paddled it into form and pinched up the sides to form the vessel with the characteristic motions of an accomplished potter.

Children were not permitted to sleep after dawn. In fact, everyone in the household was roused at dawn, for to sleep after sunrise was to invite bad dreams causing sickness and death. The customs of running toward the dawn and throwing half-roused boys into the water were unknown here.

When children were old enough to understand, all the tales were told them, with a commentary of admonition. (Late youth was not the special time for them to learn as among the Pima.[11]) In winter the boys went into the meeting house when stories were being told. A grandmother would tell them to a group of girls. There was no objection to telling tales in summer, but winter nights were conveniently long. To keep children from having bad dreams early in the night, they were kept awake listening to stories.

Games were played, of course, in imitation of their elders, but not dice, hand game, or cañute, normally gambling games. Some sports were peculiar to children. Boys alone played at hurling darts, slinging mud, arrows; both boys and girls played with tops. Dolls (haʀáoi', "plaything") for girls were made of willow bark: a piece was split and bound to represent head, arms and legs.

Age status terms were few. They turned on the termination of

[11] Russell, *Pima Indians*, p. 191.

infancy, pre-adolescence and puberty, on parenthood, and on reaching the status of grandparenthood or menopause.

For example, Charlie Redbird, newly made a grandfather, was called kwuꞅåŏ'k, to the amusement of his second wife, although he was only in his late forties.

TABLE IX

	Males	Females
Infant of either sex to about 4 years old..	xuma' ꞅå*	
A boy from 4 years to puberty (change of voice); a girl from 4 to 8 years.........	xuma'ꞅåikï'n	xuma'ꞅåxatcï'n
Until a first child was born..............	måxai'	måcåxai'
Adult...............................	ipa'	sïnyåŏ'k
Old age (after a man had a grandchild; a woman reached menopause)..........	kwuꞅåŏ'k	ŏkᵧyoi'

* Cf. xumai', a man's son.

PUBERTY CUSTOMS

Puberty observances concerned girls alone: there was no comparable rite for boys unless the bee-killing ordeal be so considered. Nor, since the vision quest was almost wholly absent, was this an appropriate occasion for obtaining power. The girl's rite aligns with those of southern California in its emphasis on concern for the girl's future physiological well-being, with the "roasting" of the girl an essential. Like the Mohave, the girl was not sung over, but unlike them, and on the other hand like other southern Californians and the upland peoples of Arizona, a dance was held and the girl forced to run at dawn toward the east. On the whole, the impression prevails that here the girl's rite was relatively unimpressive and unimportant.

At her first period, a girl was secluded in a little lodge for eight days. During this period she sat all day long (but did not lie), doing nothing, until late in the evening when she was allowed to sleep. She remained alone, so that she would have no one to talk with and thus would avoid growing garrulous. They did not sing over her at this point in the proceedings, as they knew the Pima did. "We keep her just as quiet as we can. We do not make any noise around her." She was given very little food and then only pinole (a gruel of ground parched wheat); in earlier times mesquite bean gruel. She must particularly avoid meat and salt. She could not touch herself with her fingers: should she use them to touch her head, her hair would fall out. Instead she used a little stick, but could scratch only very lightly. This was prepared by her parents of arrowweed or mesquite. (It was not worn hung about the neck as elsewhere.) This was some six inches long; to the butt was attached by a short willow cord, a bundle of willow bark with which to wipe her face. Her head was plastered all over every night, thinking she might forget and touch her hair. On the first four nights, this was mud mixed with pounded black mesquite bark; on the second four, mud alone. Each morning, as she bathed, she washed this off, so that her hair would be dry before the sun rose. Her face up to the eyes was solidly painted a dark red. This was prepared by mixing red paint with the black liquor obtained by boiling mesquite bark. Her sole garment was a cotton skirt, newly made for the occasion. At the end of the period, it was thrown into the river, never burned. No ornaments were worn.

There is some difference of opinion as to the activities of this period. The old Halchidhoma, Kutox, stated that the girl had to run every morning before sunrise in order that she might learn endurance, to stand the heat, and run tirelessly on long journeys. She was accompanied by two good female runners, one on either side, but not holding her by her arms. For the first four mornings, they ran with her to the river where all three bathed; on the second four, they ran toward the east, returning with her to bathe again. During the second four days, she was subjected to "baking" (pa'vŭg, the word for baking food). She lay in a hollow in the sand outside the hut and was covered with sand. A fire had been previously built in this and the coals raked carefully away. There she lay until the sand cooled. The process began at mid-morning: she emerged about noon, when it was sufficiently warm in the air. The hut itself was kept warm at all times. The crescentic stone of the southern California Indians used in such "baking" was unknown here.[12]

According to an elderly Maricopa woman, Josepha Juan, on the other hand, the running was confined to the second set of four days. When she ran to a distant point in the east and stopped, her companions clapped a hand over her mouth, so that she had to breathe through her nose. Then they ran back. A dance was made on each of these four days. A line of girls faced a line of men, the menstruant taking her position at the middle of the line of girls. The lines moved backward and forward. The song used was peculiar to the rite: both song and dance were called tatuma'np. Last Star, an old Kaveltcadom-Maricopa, said this song was tatuma'npĭg, a Maricopa song contrasting with the Kohuana tuma'np, sung at the scalp dance. Tatuma'n-pĭg referred to purifying the girl, making her strong, industrious, dignified, kind, gentle, able to withstand thirst, run well, etc.[13]

It may well be that we are dealing with a tribal distinction here; the rite devoid of dance, like the Mohave,[14] being Halchidhoma; with the dance, Maricopa.

At the end of the eight-day period, the girl was tattooed.

The whole performance was repeated at subsequent menstruations until the girl married; four, five or six times. Should she not marry for several years the performance was nevertheless continued. Throughout the whole period she remained single, not only during the periodic illnesses, salt and meat continued tabu and the scratcher must be used.

The puberty hut was built expressly for the first rite at some distance from the dwelling. It was kept for later use as a menstrual shelter. This was much like the storage house, but the

---

[12] Kroeber, *Handbook*, p. 865.

[13] Kroeber (*ibid.*, pp. 786–87) records Diegueño Tu-tomunp as the equivalent of Mohave and Cocopa Tumanpa, with Tomanp as an alternative name. His Mohave informants identified it as their "Long Tumanpa," one of the forms of the Tumanpa song-series.

[14] *Ibid.*, p. 748.

wall poles were not so heavy. Long thin willows were selected for these so that they might lap considerably over the ridge. Dirt was banked halfway up the sides, not all over, and the hut lacked the pit of the storage house. The structure was just large enough for a single person to lie.

Throughout their lives, women left their dwellings for these shelters during their monthly illnesses. Meat and salt were again tabu at this time, and the scratching stick, kept in the hut, must be used. They bathed each morning, but did not run to the east. There they worked at their basketry and the like; other women and girls, menstruants and otherwise, joining them in their activities and eating with them there.

A girl at first menstruation was called matavi'ʀᵃ (meaningless?) or macáxai' matavi'ʀᵃ; any menstruant ha'kwĭnyavĭ'g; the menstrual or puberty hut literally ha'kwĭnyavĭnᵧâvâ', "menstruant's house"; the menstrual period and flow, nᵧihwĭ'tk, "red," or by a euphemism xaknᵧivi'k, "living away."

MANNERISMS, CUSTOMARY BEHAVIOR, AND SAYINGS

Like all Indians, these people can sit endlessly saying nothing and looking fixedly into space. It made no difference whether a stranger like myself was present or not. On the other hand, they can become excessively talkative and are at all times ready to joke and laugh. If there is any one noticeable feature, it is their constant spontaneous humor. I observed this before I became aware that Kroeber had recorded exactly the same characteristic of the Mohave.[15] Mr. E. W. Gifford tells me that the Cocopa impressed him as more humorously inclined than the central Californian tribes with whom he is familiar. It may be that this is a lower Colorado Yuman trait.

A humorous incident will illustrate. A group of women once went to gather berries. A man, who had gone hunting early, was returning still early in the day when he met them. Spying a big hole in the ground, he used two knuckles to imitate deer tracks leading to it. He called to them to come look at it. He asked, "You see those tracks? What do you think it is?" They said it looked like deer tracks. He said, "If you are sure, you had better sit around and watch that hole. I will run home to get something to dig with. Your baskets are just the thing to

[15] *Ibid.*, p. 731.

carry home the venison, if we kill this deer." So they all seated themselves around the hole. He ran fast until he got behind the bushes, then sauntered home. The women were left sitting instead of filling their baskets. They waited, watching, until they discovered they had been fooled and reached home late in the day with empty baskets.[16]

Informants knew nothing of puns. Occasional humorous incidents based on unintentional confusion of words occurred, of course.

Two old men, boon companions, always caught quail together. One went away for a time. On his return he asked his companion how quail (axma') catching was. The other replied that he did not know what quantity he had grown, thinking the reference was to black-eyed peas (axma'). This was a current story to poke fun at the one who had confused them.

A very characteristic habit of old women, seated on the ground, was to rest the left elbow on the knee and pass the heel of the left hand upward over the face, running the fingers up the forehead and through the front hair. Women constantly hold the left hand over the mouth or chin while sitting about. I did not observe this as a gesture of embarrassment in either sex.

Women were repeatedly seen idly seated on the ground, pounding the hard crust of ground around them as far as they could reach; all to no useful purpose. I never saw a man do this. Another characteristic trait was for a woman, observing ants crawling near, to brush them away with the back of her fingers, the hand held vertically, not kill them.

Women sat on the ground with their legs crossed "Turk-fashion," the outside edges of the feet flat on the ground, or with their legs drawn back and crossed under them so that they were sitting on their feet rather than on their shins. They also sat with both legs folded back under them and extending to the right. The last two were normal work positions when grinding, making pottery, and the like. Sometimes they sat with their legs stretched out straight in front, ankles crossed (Pueblo-style and also Mohave), even with the feet somewhat raised. This was shifted into one leg straight forward, the other folded back and to one side. I did not have an opportunity to observe the male counterpart of these

[16] Other humorous anecdotes are cited above (p. 46).

habits: the men sat on chairs or if on the ground they were invariably wearing shoes or boots disturbing to the old habits.

Women folded their arms with the palms of the hands flat against the breast under the biceps, fingers extended.

There were characteristic ways a seated person wrapped his robe about him. The robe, thrown over the back, was wrapped over the front, drawn well up under the chin, and the upper right hand corner thrown back over the left shoulder. I saw a number of men and women sitting with their blankets protecting the front of the body, not the back: they were drawn up under the chin, the corners thrown back over the shoulders.

After drinking they wiped the mouth with the heel of the hand.

They shook hands by laying their palms together, not grasping hands, and merely moving them up and down once. At the same time, they uttered the proper kinship term and nothing more, as "My nephew." To a friend the greeting was mata-xavi'k, "my best friend" (lit. "we two" [?]) or more commonly perhaps, kiyi', "friend" (when one of the speakers was a woman, the form was ciyi'). Even a left-handed man shook hands with his right hand. To use the left hand was to imply some deceit. No reason was assigned for left-handedness (kusa'ʀŏk). The left hand was called cŏlkwĭsa'ʀŏk (cŏl, "hand"); the right hand cŏl-gàxa'n, "good hand."

Men meeting on the road would greet each other with ki'lmi-yăm mo', "Where are you going?" A man would greet a woman on the road as freely and in the same terms.

Etiquette on approaching a house was prescribed. The visitor did not go in directly. He would sit or stand by the door until the occupant said, "Come in (kàxa'vŏk)." As he sat down they always said, "Go ahead: help yourself to what [food] I have (kàxa'vŏk kàwi'm)," or the host would say, "Sit down while I get something for you to eat." The host would not wait to hear the visitor's errand before feeding him. They proceeded quite leisurely, smoking together, waiting until the visitor chose to unburden himself. He was never asked directly why he came. The host would ask how the visitor's people were and he would in turn inquire how the host was feeling. An infrequent visitor might tell of the death of a relative, when the host would cry with him in sympathy. (But there was no formal tear salutation such as Russell describes for the Pima.[17]) If a visitor was met outside the house, he was greeted, "Spread your news [gànavŏk, 'talk!']!" If only women were at home, they would invite the guest to eat but would not question him. On leaving, a visitor says, "I came to see you and find your people are well. I feel good to see them well: I am happy. I spent the day well. I am going home now." They shook hands on parting, calling each other again by kinship terms with not another word. (I saw this performance repeatedly and was impressed with the extreme parsimony of the exchange of salutations.)

Carrying habits followed sex-differentiated patterns. A woman invariably carried burdens balanced on her head, usually supported on a ring-shaped pad of cloth. In this fashion, they carried pots of water, baskets of mesquite, or the cradle, the last even perched on top of a basket loaded beyond its brim. On the other hand, a man never carried anything on his head: a log, for instance, rested on the shoulder.[18] Women also carried articles at the small of the back in a cloth tied around the waist, in the fashion of the Pueblos and Havasupai, but men never did so. On journeys a man carried water in a gourd tied to the left side of the belt by a cord tied around its neck, the gourd stoppered with a corn cob. When a man and woman travelled together, "he let her carry everything." Women were, in fact, adept carriers. The carrying net of southern California and the netted frame of the Pima and Papago were unknown.

They never hesitated to draw diagrams on the ground for me and were not concerned to wipe them away, unlike the Havasupai.

A special relation of friendship sometimes united men. "They

[17] *Pima Indians*, p. 200. I think we may doubt that the Pima practice was anything more than what is here described for the Maricopa.

[18] Curiously enough, Garcés' Halchidhoma travelling companion of 1774, who had both hands occupied, carried a jug of water on his head (Bolton, *Anza's California Expeditions*, II, 387).

were more than friends: what one did the other did." When going to war they would take each other's hand, saying, "Let us kill this one or be killed ourselves." There was no rite to establish this bond, which was called mataxcuva′k (compare matàtcu′ig, "married"). Their greeting to each other was mataxavi′k (compare mataxavi′kĭk, co-wife, woman speaking; xavi′k, "two"; xavi′kĭc, the [probably] non-vocative kinship term between siblings).

Some manners of speech were noted. Mrs. Redbird called my attention to the fact that Maricopa said pu′i, "dead," all day long, meaning they were tired. I heard one say, "Look out, you will be dead!" as a warning to children climbing precariously over the house-top. She also pointed out that they say "I and he," not "he and I", mentioning self first, just as they always mention men before women. Women were heard ejaculating da da da da and na na na na in vexation. They have our habit, if they make a slip of the tongue, of repeating the word disparagingly.

A number of sayings were noted by Mrs. Redbird, who distinguished between them and beliefs. So far as I could judge, this was not a distinction peculiar to herself. They had a saying that a woman would give a good-looking daughter to a man who killed a deer. A person who saw a porcupine would never see another. Anyone who said he was never bitten by a snake would immediately be bitten. When one sneezes, they said a woman was thinking of him. He answered her, "All right, I will be there soon." If a child was sickly, they said he would never be sick until he was very old, when only a slight illness would kill him.

Several sayings were playfully told children. They said to the children, speaking of the crane, "Chase that bird! It will fall down: It has been shot by an arrow," so the children ran after it. (The reference was, of course, to the outstretched neck and legs of the flying bird.) It was a saying that if one trod in the tracks of the little river turtle (xaxnaʀàxna′ʀà), he would ever after have rheumatism. So older people said, when children playfully walked in their elder's sandals, "I am as dangerous as a turtle." Milk teeth were thrown away. The child would say, "That hard rock! Throw your old mano (hand grinding stone) away and get a new one," and then snap it out. The children were told that if they threw it away without saying anything, none would grow in its place.

Tongue-twisters and proverbs were unknown to the informants.

A brief discussion was held with Last Star on the subject of thinking. The Maricopa believed that one thinks with his heart. If they went on a visit, they said, "My heart began thinking of you, so I started off to see you." Last Star believes that he thinks with his heart, because "if a man is sick, his heart beats fast; if it stops, his arteries will not work. Some people now say that one thinks with his head, but my head feels to my hand only like a hard stone. It does not keep working; my heart does. The way my heart beats hard, it must be responsible." It would seem that he was identifying thought with the whole of his bodily states, physiological and emotional, and, I gathered from other observations, dreaming was considered part of this whole, that is, just one aspect which bodily states might take. "Thinking" was al𝓎i'm, kĭln𝓎iðu'ck, or iwa'kĭln𝓎iðu'ck, "heart thinking."

DIVERSIONS

SMOKING

Smoking was an indulgence; its use but moderate. There was in addition considerable ceremonial usage, particularly on the part of shamans. With regard to everyday use, "they did not smoke all the time, but a little when at work, and when they gathered in the evening to converse." Tobacco was carried to the evening gatherings in the meeting house, where each man smoked privately. The chief, when calling them to the meeting, shouted out a warning to bring a sufficient supply for those who might come unprovided. Women hardly ever smoked.

Smoking was also in the nature of a prayer. "When I puff it out, I think of someone I want helped, and I pray that I may linger for some years more." When old Kutox did this, he said, he did not address any particular spirit, but was speaking to his "relatives." (The implication is obscure.)

Cigarettes were the old form in which tobacco was smoked. They were rolled in dried cornhusks (hence called hamǐ'nk, "to roll up"), or less commonly, stuffed in sections of a reed (axta'-kasa'c, "soft reed") softer than common arrowreed (axta'). Both varieties grow near Maricopa Wells. These were never passed from one to another. Kutox had never heard of the use of pipes in ancient days: clay pipes came into use only after his birth in 1847–48. These had turned-up bowls and wooden stems made from a hollow stalk. The straight tubular pipe was unknown. Old men made such pipes (mukwǐ'nyᵃ), baking them like pottery.

No tobacco (u'u'vᵃc) was cultivated by the Maricopa, in which they were one with the lower Colorado Yumans and differed from the Pima. Instead they commonly used a wild tobacco, uvȧana'lyᵃ, "mesquite tobacco," so called because it grows on sandy hills in the desert beneath the mesquite trees. It is available in the early spring. When the plants were a foot tall, the leaves were plucked and dried in the shade. When they were double that height, they were no longer considered usable, and called in derision xataluwe'nyicǐu'vᵃ, "Coyote's tobacco." Another tobacco was gotten from the Akwa'ala (akwa'ł) by trade through the Cocopa, not from the Cahuilla (xakwi'tc), as noted below. This was called uvȧsa'kc, "rotted tobacco." They were also glad to get tobacco from the Pima, who cultivated uvȧxa'n, "real tobacco."[19]

According to Kutox, however, the Maricopa cultivated one variety of tobacco (uvᵃ); the Halchidhoma raised uvȧxa'n, "real tobacco," while still on the Colorado. Apparently the Maricopa did not raise the plant from their own seeds, for "it was said that they always got the seeds from the Mission [Cahuilla] Indians"; and again that they got them from the Halchidhoma on visits to the Colorado. The latter is much more probable since the Maricopa probably had no direct contact with the Cahuilla. The reason for the association with this tribe is probably implied in the statement that "at the time of the creation, there was one tobacco plant standing there, ever growing. The people around took that. This is where the seed [all seed] comes from." The Cahuilla were named as the first tribe created at that time. It may well be that the Halchidhoma were merely intermediaries, for most of, if not all, the lower Colorado tribes did not cultivate tobacco.

The informant had heard of another variety, growing wild, "Coyote's tobac-

[19] The first and third are said to have yellow blossoms; specimens were unavailable.

co" (hatȧluwĕ′nĭtcȧu′v), which was gathered when there was no more of the cultivated plant available.

Very little tobacco was grown; "in little patches," "a few plants." It was planted in the spring after the rains; digging little holes, hoeing and weeding by hand. The informant had never heard of planting the seeds in ashes. As the leaves ripened, were large enough, they were plucked; other leaves matured, until the plant shriveled in the summer heat. Leaves were used, rarely the stems. They were dried, broken up, and stored in little pots, covered with a sherd that just fitted. Tobacco was usually carried about in a little deerskin sack or, since cattle were introduced, in a cow horn. (Mountain sheep horns were not used prior to this.)

Kutox may have been referring to Pima cultivation or to some slight imitation by the Maricopa.

GAMES AND SPORTS

Like the Pueblos, kicking races and gambling games were considered the most important contests and were bet on heavily. Kicking races at least figured intertribally. There was the usual unequal division of games and sports between the sexes, with the preponderance in favor of men. While this was perhaps predictable in the matter of sports, it was certainly arbitrary that men had more games. They played at hoop and pole, at ball, and raced, and for sedentary games had dice, cañute, and the hand game. Only double-ball shinny and their own form of the dice game were peculiar to women. The same disparity appears in boys' sports *versus* girls', but here there is every reason to think that children's sports are badly represented in what follows, although I made specific inquiries for them. The hidden ball game, ring and pin, and string figures were pastimes for everyone. All other adult games were inseparable from betting, with the possible exception of the ball game, i.e., the men's form of shinny, which, as a matter of fact, was a lackadaisical, unorganized affair. Basket dice, which might have been expected among the Maricopa, was missing.

The pattern of a race, as elsewhere in the Southwest, was to a given point and return. This appeared, for instance, in kicking races and relays.

In the kicking race (huĭnya′vȧ) they made use of a ball, not a stick. This, called sȧ'a′n, was manufactured by dipping a stone, an inch and a half in diameter, repeatedly into melted gum until it grew to the size of our baseballs. For this purpose they used the red gum of a medicinal plant and that which exudes at the base of arrowweeds, melting it in a potsherd. Two runners would stand, and at a signal, would each kick off their balls, racing with them to a selected point and back. It was thrown with the foot; the toes shoveled under it in the manner of the Pueblo kicking-stick, not kicked along the ground.

Kicking race contests with the Pima were frequent: several of them were noted in the annals (p. 141). Each tribe selected its best runner and bet heavily on him. Each was assisted by a good runner who was sent ahead, armed with a stick, before they started. The ball might be kicked off into the bushes, when the helper, who ran ahead of the racer, could strike it back into the path. These helpers would run only halfway to the distant point, rarely the whole distance. The losing tribe would always be the challenger to the next race, which was held at the victors' village.

Magic was freely used to thwart the opposing racer: as they said, this was the time people found out who were shamans.

The Pima shamans would do things to our racer. For instance, one of them would secretly sprinkle a reed full of water on the Maricopa racer before the race started "in order to drown him" so that he could not run. Or they would run ahead of him and draw a line across his path, so that he would imagine it a deep canyon which he could not cross. One of our men would clear it away by pulling a string across the line as though making a bridge. Both sides did this sort of thing to the other.

Recently a Maricopa shaman, Buffalo Bill, drew a line before the runners: "he dragged that mountain [Sierra Estrella] across there." The Maricopa racer got by, but when the Pima came up, he stood stock still: he did not know what to do. The Pima took him around the "mountain," i.e., the line, so he could race on.

A Maricopa racer told what happened to him. He was ahead of the Pima racer. Every time the latter came abreast of him, the Pima racer breathed hard. Then the Maricopa felt out of breath, as though his chest would burst, although he had not run far. A Pima bystander laid a switch lightly against the small of this Maricopa's back. He felt it as a big log: he could hardly move. Then the Pima on horses rode with their runner, while the Maricopa runner, trailing behind, just walked along. When the others saw this, a Maricopa shaman spurred up and switched him twice with a rope, whereon he found he could burst into topspeed. The Pima were so sure that they were winning that they started to take the Maricopa stakes, when the Maricopa runner dashed up and won the race.

Relay races were held, on which they bet. These were called ma'takovàk_yi'wŭm. Runners of each side were posted at two points between which they ran. Maricopa runners did not wear the curious hair ornaments Russell described for the Pima.[20] (Kutox, who had seen many Pima races, said he had never seen these among the Pima.)

The hoop and pole game (hutu'ʀŭm) was played by active men all through the year. They bet on the results. The gaming ground was always at the center of a village or as near it as possible. It was not oriented to the compass points. The hoop (kapȧtcω'ʀĭs) was six inches in diameter, made of a bundle of straw bound with rolled cords of inner willow bark until it was the thickness of a finger. (It was not netted.) The two poles (hutu'ʀĭc) were six feet long, an inch and a quarter thick; one distinguished by two notches encircling the butt. The hoop was rolled along the course, the two players ran after it, and simultaneously cast their poles to slide along the ground so that the hoop would fall resting on one of them. The owner of this pole got a point and rolled the hoop at the next trial. They always returned to the initial point for each cast. In rolling the hoop, it was held vertically, the fingers grasping the lower margin with the back of the hand down, the hoop resting above the wrist. It was then thrown forward and down. To count, the hoop might rest on any part of the pole but the inner edge of one side of the hoop must clear the farther edge of the pole, as among the Havasupai. Should the pole pass entirely or partially through the hoop, it did not score. But if the hoop remained with one side resting on the butt of the pole, it counted two points. The number of points to win was agreed on before the game began: four or three.

A ball game, a modified form of shinny, was played by boys and men at any time of year. Two sides were chosen, as many as ten to a side, who took their places in front of the goal lines they were to defend. These lines were at the eastern and western ends of the field, about fifty yards apart. They played with straight sticks, thirty inches long by one and a half diameter, and a ball carved from a cottonwood limb, two and a half inches in diameter. The game was called sȧ'a'ntcuta'cĭg, "breaking a ball in two"; the ball, sȧ'a'n; a stick, tȧkuʀo'. Those on one side threw

[20] Russell, *Pima Indians*, p. 163.

the ball or kicked it through the air to their opponents who attempted to hit it back over the opposite goal line. It scored for them if they succeeded, or against them if they missed striking the ball entirely. If they missed, they in turn threw or kicked the ball to the first side. If both sides missed, the ball was half buried at the middle of the field, where two opposing players struck for it as in shinny. Their fellows kept their places at the goal lines when attempting to drive it back, not running after it as in the usual form of shinny. This was a sport, not a betting game, and no definite number of points was set. The usual form of men's shinny was absent.

Double ball shinny (toxcoa'lgĭk) was as usual solely a feminine game. It was played throughout the year, betting strings of beads on the outcome. The "double ball" (xata'p) was in this case a strip of leather or willow bark nine inches long with a heavy knot at each end. The stick (xacta.a'lg) was straight, four feet or more in length, with the lower end somewhat pointed. The goal lines were about two hundred yards apart. Paired opponents stood all over the field. Two at the center twisted their sticks into the leather to get a grip on it. Should they fail to get it from each other, it was thrown between them so they could strike at it in the air. The object was to throw it over the opponents' goal. Any number of women played, but the sides were of equal numerical strength.

A dart game was played by boys. A stick was prepared of a cottonwood limb, ten inches long, one in diameter, with the end split into quarters and allowed to dry so that these four segments would remain apart (Fig. 14, a).[21] The nine or ten boys who played were each provided with an arrowweed dart, the length of an arrow, with a corncob stuck on its point and the butt end feathered to the very tip (unlike an arrow). The split stick was thrown as far as possible. The darts were then slung after it. The owner of the dart that fell nearest the split stick held its split end up as high as he could. All the other boys then pushed the corncobs up the shafts and threw the darts high in the air. The boy with the split stick caught as many as he could in the split

[21] Peabody Museum, Yale University, 19075.

end. Those whose darts were caught retired from the game. The others threw their darts again for him to catch. Again those caught retired. Those who survived this time, then threw the split stick out and the game began again. That boy who caught all (?) their darts was chosen leader for all their games. The

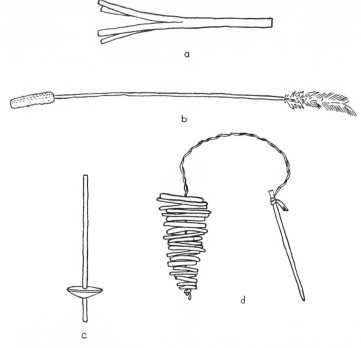

FIG. 14.—Games (*a*, *b*, boy's dart game; *c*, top; *d*, ring and pin game)

game, the dart, and this leader were all called by the same name, tŭmxo′ʀgĭc. The split stick was tcahwa′tc, onomatopoetic for its whirring sound as it was thrown.

Young boys indulged in mimic warfare, slinging mud at each other (called duxwĕcu′m, "whirling"). Two long lines of boys were opposed, each boy provided with a big lump of mud under his arm and a stick a foot long. A bit of mud was pinched off and thrust on the end of the stick so that it could be slung at the opponents. They began at a signal. They must not cry nor run away when hit, but must keep the line intact. They dodged, twisting aside. This was their first training; then when going to war, if shot, they would be able to stand it and hold the line. It trained their arms and taught them to throw straight. The lines moved toward each other until one side broke and ran. This contest was frequent, but was considered very rough. It was played only early in the morning and in the evening.

Boys also used slings for sport. The sling (daθla'p) was not a weapon. It was made of an elliptical piece of leather to each end of which a cord was tied.

They juggled (mai'ȧmtciacu'm, "to swing upward") with little wild gourds, stones, or clay balls. They used two, three, or four. This was played at by anyone. Poles were balanced on end on the hand as a sport. (This was nameless.)

Tops were twirled between the palms by both boys and girls. These, as the name implies (ᵃma'tȧpaiyi'ʀᵃ, "flying clay") were made of a disk of baked clay, an inch to one and a half in diameter, mounted on a slender stick, six inches long (Fig. 14, c). The lower end of the stick being flat, the top travelled in a circle. The boys would use this as a test of good running; each trying to follow his erratic top.

Boys amused themselves by tapping arrows on their bow strings to see who could make the loudest sound. The bow was held vertically, string up, with one end resting between the teeth. This was the only form of musical bow known to the Maricopa.

The bull-roarer (xiuxiu: onomatopoetic) was also merely a plaything. This was a ten-inch length of split and scraped arrow-weed, with a cord fastened in notches near one end.

The hidden ball game (tatu'ᵭulĭk, "hiding") was a pastime, not a gambling game. Two opponents, facing each other, had each a ridge of dirt transversely before him. One ran a small stone repeatedly through his pile, singing kwȧtȧᵭu'n, kwȧtȧᵭu'n, until he left it hidden there. (The dirt was not divided into piles.) The other guessed whether the stone was at the middle or end. If he was correct, it was his turn to hide it; otherwise the first hid it again. (Counters were not used.)

The widely known cañute game (called aχta'mtatuðu'lĭk, "reed hiding") was here as usual a man's game.[22] According to Kutox it was also played by the Halchidhoma before leaving the Colorado, who when playing it, were so intent that they would not heed the enemy approaching. Four sections of arrowreed were obtained, cut so that one end alone was closed by a node. Marks were burned into them; any designs being used so long as they were placed at the proper points. My informant described one as marked for its whole length with transversely encircling lines, the second with such lines only at its open end, the third with a longitudinal wavy line at the middle, and the fourth plain. They were named as shown in Table X.

TABLE X

Marked	Named
Entire length	kwĭʀåŏ'kc, "old man"
Plain	akoi', "old woman"
At center	toχkwĭnyo'ʀc, "middle figures"
At open end	hiya'kwĭnyo'ʀc, "mouth figures"

A tiny length of arrowweed or a pellet of charcoal was hidden in one of these tubes and all four filled with dirt. The hidden object was called n_yåχat, "my dog." Any number of counting sticks were used: each side had a bundle of 75 to 100. Four men played on a side.

To begin the game, each side was provided with a pair of tubes: "old man" and "old woman" *versus* the other pair. Each side hid a pellet in one of the tubes they held and both guessed in which tube their opponents had hidden it. The winners then took all four tubes and hiding a pellet in one of them, while they remained concealed under a cloth drawn over their knees, threw them down before their opponents.

The usual form of the game in the Southwest calls for the

[22] Culin recorded the game under the name ta-thulsh (*Games*, p. 370). His name for one of the tubes kota-aks, "old man," was not recognized by my informants.

guesser to find the pellet in the third tube chosen, when the privilege of hiding passed to him. For each failure to set aside an empty tube, he loses points. My information is that the Maricopa desired to leave the pellet in the fourth tube. This was apparently the usual Pima and Papago objective.[23] If the guesser was mistaken in setting aside the first tube he chose as empty, he lost ten points; for the second tube, six; and for the third, four. If he succeeded in leaving it in the fourth tube, the set of tubes passed to his side, otherwise the privilege of hiding remained with the first side. The markings of the tubes made no difference, only the order of choice counted.

The tubes were not arranged in patterns, as by Pueblo players, with a single exception, in which the Maricopa again resembled Pima and Papago. The guesser might cross one pair of tubes and place the other two side by side pointing toward the cross. This implied that the pellet was in one of the parallel pair. If however, it was actually in the upper of the crossed tubes, he lost ten points; if in the lower, six. Again the markings of tubes did not matter.

An alternative method of scoring depending on which tube was chosen was given by Charlie Redbird. If the guesser erred in the tube he chose, he gave up its face value in counters. The tubes had the values: "old man," 25; "old woman," 10(?); "middle figures," 15; "mouth figures," 6.

The women's dice game was played by two women seated opposite, each with a flat stone before her and a row of small stones on each side of her arranged in a semi-circle from her body to the slab. Four dice were provided. These were split sticks of cottonwood or arrowweed (not made of bone). The flat faces of all four were painted red, their convex faces unpainted or black. One woman began by bouncing the four dice, clenched together in her fist, on her slab. If they fell all red faces up, it counted five for her; if all blacks up, ten; if two of a kind up, two. One of a kind was a miss, the throw then passing to the other woman. My informants did not fully know how points were counted on the rows of stones, but it seems that at least a little stick was laid on the stone representing the number counted off. For example, if

[23] See Spier, *Havasupai Ethnography*, p. 352.

the throw counted five, the stick was advanced to the fifth stone. The number of pebble markers was unknown, but there may have been twelve in each semi-circle. The game was sometimes played without markers, when there would be only a single slab for both women to bounce the dice on. The game was named tatu'ruci̇̆'k for the markers in rows or utci̇̆mpu'm, "bouncing them": the dice, otŏ'xc.

The men's dice game was similar, but it was a betting game played in winter. My informants knew it by no other name than Spanish *quince*, "fifteen," the common name throughout the Southwest. The opposing pair were seated on the ground, each

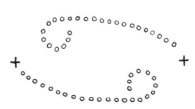

Fig. 15.—Diagram of men's dice game (crosses mark position of players)

with a row of twenty-five shallow pits beginning at his right hand and extending in a curve toward his opponent where it ended in a loop (Fig. 15). A stick or stone served as a marker in the pits: it was called n_yáxa'tk, "my horse (? dog), pet." The four dice were flattened sections of mesquite root, about seven inches long, bearing marks burned into one face (Pl. XIII, *d*). They were known by the numbers they scored; collectively they were called *quinze*. The dice were held clenched in the right hand and struck from below with a stone held in the left. The die with a longitudinal zigzag counted twenty-five; with a mark at the middle, fifteen; that marked at each end with two lines crossed with an oblique line, six; and with simple transverse lines at each end, four. If any marked face alone was up, it scored its face value. But if any two marked faces were up, it scored two; three up, scored three. When all four unmarked faces were up, the set went to the opponent to throw. When the marker had reached the end of one man's twenty-five pits, he made a mark on the ground, and began to amass another twenty-five, since fifty points won.

The hand game was an exciting affair, with much movement and singing. A song series, called tatuðulᵧĭ'g like the game, was sung by way of accompaniment.[24] It consisted of a few songs indefinitely repeated. These told of the players living in plenty or starving as they won or lost. It was played every evening by men alone. They even stripped themselves of clothing to bet on it. Four small sticks were used in the game, so small that they might sometimes be hidden between the fingers (a little more than an inch in length, barely a quarter inch thick). Four men on each side sat facing each other, each of one party having a hiding stick. To start the game, a man of each side played alone. The one with the stick stood up, dancing in place, and singing aonánω' wia aonánω'. He held his arms folded; his tongue stuck out. The opposing party sang "almost the same song." His opponent, on his knees, feinted at finding it, pointing wide of one hand and then the other; then clapping his hands, pointed to the hand in which it was hidden. If he guessed aright, his side took the sticks; if wrong, the original hider's side began the game.

The hiding side had twelve sticks as counters stuck into the ground before them, or these were held by a man sitting between the two parties.

The four hiders proceeded to swing their arms across their bodies and to hold their clenched fists under their armpits. The guessers said, "We will knock them over" (meaning the counters) if they thought all the hiders had their sticks in the same hand. If they guessed correctly, all the twelve counters were thrown to them and the hiding sticks as well. Or each would point to the opposing hider and make his choice. A guesser saying, "I will pierce it," meant that the sticks were in the adjacent hands of the two hiders sitting side by side. For each correct guess, that hider gave up his stick while his companions continued to hide theirs. One counter of the twelve would also be knocked down for each correct guess.[25] The hand game was

[24] See p. 264.   [25] The scoring given here is by no means certain.

called tatu'ϑulĭk, "hiding"; the hand sticks, taϑu'l; while the counters had no special name.

String figures (cat's cradles) were solely for amusement and were made by anyone. They were called ukwo'vtciwŭm, "to make something of string." Their number was legion and were principally moving figures, not stationary forms. A few named to me follow:

wa'a'vkwĭnyu'và, "two rival women fighting over a husband" (little knots met at the center)

xasikwa' tcutcĭ'c, "blackbird's nest"

"metate," which was broken in two trying to move it

"dove," the neck was shown and made to move, then this was transformed into two doves, male and female

xocgĭ'v mĭl$_y$xol$_y$ĭ'c, "dove with a broken wing," was asymmetrical

xocgĭ'v mipukĭ't, "headless dove"

amo'tciu, "making the mountain sheep," showed three knots one above the other which represented the stars of Orion's Belt, called "mountain sheep"

xaiya' gĭcvugŏ'tc, "to meet going for water," represented two girls passing while fetching water

cal$_y$àpi'lk, "hot hand"; the player pulled the string clear of one hand, saying, "My hand is hot!"

The ring and pin game ('uk$_y$a'vĭc, "shooting") was probably played by everyone. This consisted of a stick six inches long to one end of which a string, slightly longer, was tied. Rings of gourd were threaded on the string (Fig. 14, d). As usual, the object was to catch the rings on the point of the stick. Unlike Mohave and Pima, there was no scoring diagram in use with the game.

CHAPTER XII

TALES

There were people living in this world. I do not know whether
they were like me or different, but I have heard that they lived in
this world. All sorts of evil things had taken place. They
thought it was not right that they should live longer, so they
flooded all the land in which they lived. Two of them went under
the sea, the flood waters. The waters rose to the sky so that no
one was saved. These two went under the sea to look for a place
to stay. One had a certain bird (dŭd^{r}iu'c[2]) for a pet, the other another bird (tĭnyă'm kaltcĭ'sk, "dark *Phenopepla*"?). They were
emerging. They wanted to see how far they had come. One sent
his dŭd^{r}iu'c back to see: they heard the sound of it flying all the
way to that place [under the water] and back. Then the other
sent his kaltcĭ'sk ahead. It was so far that they heard the noise of
his going, but the sound faded away before it returned.

These two men were called kukuma't; the other, the older,
isácipa's. Isacipas came out of the water first. As Kukumat was
emerging, he asked the first how he came out of the sea; whether
he haḍ his eyes open or closed. The first man told him that he
had opened his eyes as he came through the sea. Then Kukumat
opened his eyes as he emerged and got them full of salty water, so
he became blind.

They got a big log to sit on, and started floating around the
world. By the time they reached their starting place again, the
sea had gone down somewhat. They went around once again;
then again. When they had gone around the fourth time, the

[1] These tales were told by Kutox and interpreted by Ida Redbird. Curtis and
Culin recorded versions of this tale (Curtis, II, 86; Culin, *Games*, p. 201); the
latter, however, seems to be compounded of Pima and Maricopa versions. There
is a conventional ending to tales: the narrator says n_yupai', "It is gone."

[2] Mrs. Redbird translated this as killdeer, but the killdeer is called tavaʀi'c.

sea had completely subsided and it was dry everywhere. Only sloughs remained all about them. They sat down. One of them dug far down, brought up sand and spread it where they wanted to sit so that spot should be dry.

The whole world was dark. There was no sun, no moon, no stars. Then one, Cipa's [*sic*], took a hair from just below his ear, twisted it, and placed it in the east. That made the sun. For the moon, he took off a fingernail and placed it in the east. But that was not good; it went right down. So he took another fingernail and placed it in the north, but still he did not succeed. Then he tried the same in the south, but again it did not turn out properly. He said that none of these was suitable for the moon: he said the place for the moon should be in the west.

For the stars he dug down deep and took sand from far below. This he spread over the sky to form the stars. Now the whole world was made light. Now they said that the world was light enough to work in, so their work should begin.

As they sat together they kneaded clay. Isacipas faced the east and began to mould people. As he worked, he made the fingers separate just as we have, and the toes just the same. Then Kukumat also mixed clay and began modeling people too. But he made his with webbed feet and hands. He faced the west as he was modeling his people. When they were through, they showed each other how they had made their people. Then they began to dispute about their modeling. The one who made the webbed people said his were better than the other's, because his people, having webbed feet, would not stay at home. Since they were apt to go out at any time and would not carry their drinking cups along, it was handy for them to have webbed hands so they could drink from them. Then the other said that his were better. He said that humans should reason out things: they would hold their fingers together to form a cup when away from home.

They quarreled as to which of their products were best. As the one who faced east modeled, he laid aside the various tribes, each in a group. He gave each tribe its peculiar customs. So he thought his people were better than those with webbed hands and feet. They quarreled about this for some time. Then Kukumat got angry and went back underneath the earth. He broke all his models and threw them into the sea.[3] They became beavers, ducks and all the web-footed things. As Kukumat went down, they heard a thundering noise going down, down until it stopped. There he rested.

As he went down, he pulled the sky down. He left a hole when he went down. Blood came out of it. This blood was intended to be on those people [i.e., cause sickness], and pulling down the sky was to crush the other creator [Cipas].

The other one, Cipas, remained. He knelt down, putting his feet over the hole from which the blood was flowing. Then he put up his right hand to push back the sky. As he was kneeling and pushing, he wondered whether he should stop the blood entirely or let it flow to cause sickness among his people. He said, "If there is no sickness, my people would starve and there would not be enough water for them." So he lifted his foot a little to let a little blood flow out to cause some to be sick. For that reason some people are sick. There are a few stars that rise in the east that still show his finger marks. (The constellation is called cipa' isaʀi's, "Cipa's fingers." They appear in the morning all year round [later information put their appearance in freezing weather, December].)

After he arranged that people should die, he said, "Even after they die, they should have life again." And he said that even after his death, he would have a spirit life.

Then he sat down to wait for all his people to talk. The Mission Indians [xakwĭtc, Cahuilla] were the first to talk. The Maricopa (pipa's) talked next. Then all the tribes spoke in turn. The Chemehuevi talked in the middle of the night, so their language is unintelligible to anybody else. All the tribes here had spoken. The white people were the very last to speak. It was said, that like a younger child, they were cry-babies. So the creator did everything to soothe them, hence they are richer than any of the Indians.

As he did this, he first put blankets over those people who should wear blankets. He put bark [skirts] on the Yuma, and

[3] This and the following sentences of this paragraph were interpolated later.

different costumes on each people that they should wear them. When he had arranged this, he breathed into every one of those people, so that they all alike would reason.

When everybody could speak, that is including rabbits and all other kinds of animals, he built a big house for them. This held all the beings he had created. When morning came they would all go out to play together; all the games of which they could think. Toward evening they would all go into the house. Then he also made a snake. It had no teeth. It was gentle. Its name was kinyama's kàsuʀ, meaning fragile and limp. They would take the snake and hit each other with it. The rabbit always got the snake and played with it. He would bring it out, so that they could play, hitting each other with it until it was half dead. Then they would replace it.

They had no axe nor anything else with which to cut wood. The creator had power to reach out to the north and seize an axe. So they then had an axe to cut wood. As they had fire enough to keep them happy, they were well content in their home.

Early in the morning they all went out to play. The creator was lying right by the door. The snake crawled up to him. The creator asked him what he wanted. The snake said he only crawled up because of his poor condition; he was not being treated right. He had life just like the others: he did not see why he was roughly treated by everyone in that house. The creator told him to sit there and wait for the sun to rise. Then the creator took some coals and chewed them into tiny bits. They both sat there; the snake facing the east as the sun rose. Then the creator told him to open his mouth. This he did. Then the creator put the coal and the sun rays together in it for teeth. The snake now had teeth, so he went back able to protect himself.

Toward evening when everybody returned to the house, they sent the rabbit again to get the snake. As she [*sic*] reached for the snake, she was bitten. She suffered with pain for just a short time and died at midnight.[4] (When a snake really means to bite, it kills at once. If you tread on him accidentally and he

---

[4] The tale was interrupted at this point.

strikes, there is time to be cured. The reason he bit that rabbit first was that rabbits are his food.)

After the rabbit died they felt bad over their great loss. So instead of going out to play, they remained quiet mourning their sister. Then they began to wonder who had put teeth in the snake's mouth. They discovered who it was: their father, who had taken pity on the poor snake. Then they wondered why he did not feel sorry for the rabbit. Then they said they would kill their father, if only someone knew how. They thought he, too, ought to die.

Bullfrog was the one who knew how to do it. The frog sank into the ground and went under a slough where the old man used to swim. If he went swimming again, the frog was to drink up all the water in the slough. He did this. As soon as the old man got out, he felt sick as he was going home.

After four days he was very sick. He told all his children to take him outside to see if he would not feel better. Then he told them to build him a new house to see if that would help. Next, he did not want any bedding; he wanted only pure sand spread to lie on. Last, he said he wanted a travelling shade, but no one knew what he meant, until someone suggested that they cut four willow trees to set in a row. Someone did this and they set them up. Cipas said that was what he meant: it was all right. He said, "I suggested these four [sic] things to see if they would help me, but they do not. Take me inside my own old house." They took him in. He was unable to go out anymore. He wanted things to eat. He wanted cactus to eat—it was during winter— so they sent the cactus wren after some. He brought it but it did Cipas no good: he did not eat it all. Then he sent the mocking bird for wild black berries. Then he sent for some wild red berries. All these were sent for during the winter. Finally he sent the woodchuck for mesquite beans. He sent for these four and tried to eat, but he could not. Then he said, "All these things I have tried in order to recover from my sickness, but they do no good. I have not been with you long enough to tell you all I know. Sickness must come to people just as it did to me." He meant when people live on earth, they will try to raise their children, but they will be likely to sicken and die first. Then he died on the fourth day.

When Cipas died he went under the earth. He lies there yet. Whenever he yawns a little and turns over, an earthquake is caused.[5]

When the frog killed her [sic] father, the children disagreed about it. Some took the father's part: the frog should die in some fashion for her cruelty. They made up their minds to kill her. When she found she was in danger, she crawled under the earth away from the Colorado until she got to the hot springs. Then she came out to hear if there was any noise. She heard a noise following her. Then she knew she was not safe, so she crawled under the earth again. She came up at a spring.[6] Then she went on until she reached Blackwater,[7] where she emerged to listen to any noise following her. She heard nothing, so she remained there free from danger all her life. There is a small mountain there named for her. Because of her cruelty to her father, whoever resembles her will surely kill his father or brother or sister.

When Cipas died, there was one person they were afraid of, Coyote. They were afraid he might eat him. They all thought that they would send him for fire. He could go better than anyone else. They would send him all the way up to the sun to get fire. So he set off as he was told. Then they built a pile of wood to cremate Cipas. They prepared this because they were afraid of this coyote. (This happened somewhere near the coast. When they emerged and made those people, they took a snake from the sky and coiled it all around the land so the water could not encroach on it. From that time, it will be four thousand years until the flood comes again.) When Coyote started for fire, they took the body and cremated it. When he reached the sun and was about to take the fire, he turned around and saw that they had begun cremating. Then Coyote said, "Well, I have been fooled

[5] This paragraph and the following were interpolated later.

[6] A mile and a half east of Gila Crossing.

[7] Two miles east of Sacaton.

this time, when I could have stayed and got a nice big piece of meat for a meal." So he set off home as fast as he could to see if he could not get a piece anyway.

There were four rings of people (animals and birds) all around the pyre. As soon as he got there he acted as though mourning for his father. He saw a place where he could get through; where Opossum, Fox, and all the short animals were in a row. So he jumped over them into the fire and seized his father's heart. (The heart remained because just as when we cremate that is the last portion consumed by the flames. Because Cipas caused himself to be burnt, all our people have done so since.)

He ran off with it in his mouth, everybody chasing him. He ran from the Colorado River to this butte west of here [in the Gila Bend Mountains]. He climbed on top. It was a little higher than the rest, so he could see if they were still following. He set down the heart to cool his teeth. As he set it down, he said, "I had better try it to see if it tastes good." He took a piece and thought it fine. So he finished the rest. Then he gave three names to that butte, so that the new generation might know it by his actions: x̣agȧspĭdⱳ' [meaning unknown]; ixo'ʀȧgwĭsĭnu'k, a kind of willow tree (he spread some on top of the butte to set the heart on); ḳa'ḳȧdȧsȧo'ʀc, Crow's fledglings (Crow had its nest there). Just as he finished he heard all the others coming after him. They chased him again. He ran right by this place [the junction of the Gila and Salt Rivers] to the mountains south of here. ·(We call them the Greasy Mountains, because he rubbed his greasy fingers on them.) Then he went to a mountain south of these, which would be known to all generations as Heart Mountain, because of the father's heart.

He then went to a slough a mile and a half east of Gila Crossing, known as his swimming pool. When he came out from swimming, he sickened. When he acquired one sickness, he had another, and another, until he had all the sicknesses there are in the world, except a few dangerous diseases. He went still farther east, where he caught these too. Then, when he had all the sicknesses of the world, he ate some sort of green grass, some sea weed. He vomited all the sickness and was cured. He was a sorry-looking creature; nothing but bones. That almost killed him. Then he went along the ocean to the south.

When the old father died, everybody was scattered over the country here. Then the white people were sent across the ocean just for their own comfort. They were a fretful, crying people. The Mohave, Yuma, and Cahuilla lingered in their old home. Maricopa, Pima, and Apache [Yavapai] scattered all over the country, because they could not bear the death of their old maker. After they scattered they never took any places for their permanent homes, but hunted about for their food, such as wild berries, mesquite beans, and for game they took deer, jackrabbits, cottontails, quail, whitewing doves and other doves as their principal foods. (Coffee and sugar were unknown to them.) They hunted from one place to another until they settled somewhere unknown to living men. (As long as I can remember I have been living near Sacate east of here.[8]) All this is known only by legend. Things of the olden times never changed until a few years ago when the first whites appeared.

KWISTAMXO[9]

After the culture hero was cremated, the people were thirsty. They thrust a staff into the ground, so that a spring was formed. This is the source of the Colorado River. This was done in the center of their house. The house posts were still standing when the first whites came. They cut them down, but the rocks are still there to show the location. The name of these posts is àxavŭlpo'', "water post."

The people then drifted south until they came to the desert. Kwĭstămxo' went on top of vikwàme' ("high mountain"), a mountain above Needles. He told them how to plant and to clothe themselves. He showed all humans how to think and reason. This mountain is a day and a half journey south of those house posts.

Tcipa' was the culture hero who modeled people. After his death and cremation, he came to life and went on the mountain

---

[8] "Snake Town was the place where the Indians lived."

[9] This was given as an addendum to the creation tale.

to instruct the people. He was then called kwĭstămxo'. This was
after he had talked to Coyote [p. 143].

COYOTE[10]

After the destruction of the big house at the time of the creation, everyone was scattered over the world. Among them were
namĕ't and namĕ't hatagu'lt.[11] They moved but a little way
from their house, and said, "After the destruction of a house
(after a cremation), humans will not move very far. They will go
just a little way and make a new home." So they went a little
distance and stopped. They made a home there. Namet, the
older, stood still. They used his old body for a house: his four
legs were the posts; his backbone was the mainpost that held all
the weight of the house; his mouth was a door. Then he got out
in some fashion so as to leave the old body standing as their
house. The two brothers lived there.

When Coyote recovered from his sickness, he was as thin as
could be. He was going along to the west. The two brothers
wondered where he had gone. Coyote was their younger brother.
They wondered if he had been killed for his behavior. They had
no other way of finding out where he was, so they burnt deer
grease. The wind blew it hard in one direction, south. Then as
Coyote was traveling he caught the odor. (He is also called
saRămiyo'.)[12] He said, "My brothers are wondering where I am.
Sure enough, I caught the smell of it and know where they are.
Then by following the odor, I will get there."

When they were settled there, those two had no food. By their
power they caused rain so that everything would come up: all
kinds of weeds. They used these for food. To make rain, the
older, Namet, took an arrow; stuck it far down in the ground and

[10] This was told, and certainly thought of, as continuing the creation tale.

[11] Both of these are large cats; neither is the jaguar (namĕ't kàtca's). They
may be two subspecies of cougar, possibly the California and Yuma cougars.
Namĕ't was described as as large as the biggest dog, having a long tail and long
sharp claws, solid buff or gray in color; namĕ't hatagu'lt (hatagu'lt, wolf) as exactly like namĕ't but a little taller.

[12] Cf. the Yuma myth name for Coyote, Xuksaraviyö'u (Harrington, *Yuma
Account of Origins*, p. 339) and the Mohave θaRàvi'yo.

pulled it out. He whirled it all around. He whirled it four times and pointed it east. Clouds started up rapidly but finally went down. Then he motioned to the north; again clouds sprang up but finally went down. He did the same thing in the west, and clouds came up as though it would pour, but it did not. Then he said, "No clouds coming from the east, north, or west shall pour down as hard as those that come from the south in smokelike form." Instantly it poured as hard as possible. The rain continued four days and four nights. It flooded the whole country until even Namet and Namet Hatagult were floating on top of the water. Then in four days the water subsided until, on the fourth day, it was dry again. Then weeds came up and everywhere it was green. These they used for food.

But they said, "Greens will not do for us all our lives. We must have some kind of meat." Then for their meat they wanted to make a deer. They took a piece of mesquite to shape into a deer. But it did not live long and could hardly stand: it fell to pieces. Next they took cottonwood and shaped this into a deer, but it also fell to pieces. It had no life. The third time they took willow wood. Then they took sagebrush and shaped this into a deer. It had life, and finally, it could walk around. They put this into a cave. Then in a month's time they had plenty to eat. Namet and Namet Hatagult represent the Apache [Yavapai], so they have deer as their principal food.

While they formed the deer, they sang. At the end of the song, Namet rubbed himself all over, and through his mouth he brought forth a male deer. Then the other did the same and brought out a female. For their legs they took cottonwood, but this was not very good. They then got ironwood roots, which they used for legs, so that their legs were not very straight. So deer are shaped much like an ironwood tree.

After four days Namet went to visit the deer shut in the cave. They knew that they would thereafter have plenty to eat. Then they saw that the deer had fawns. Every fourth day they went to see them and saw that they had young every fourth day. When they visited again, they saw they had a herd in a cave. They decided first to take the oldest deer to butcher to see if it was good to eat. As they had plenty to eat, they wondered how everyone else was getting along.

They wondered what had become of Coyote: he being the youngest, they were concerned where he could be. They said, "We have burnt this fat and sent the odor to the south so that he might catch the scent, and following it, might come to us." They said they would wait for him. They were sure that if he caught the scent, he would surely come to them. Coyote, being hungry, as he went along the ocean, ate all kinds of bugs the waves had cast ashore. Then late in the afternoon he caught the scent. He stopped and said, "Well, what do I smell? It is not anything I have eaten." He said, "It is late in the afternoon, but I will get there."

He went into the sea and bathed. When he came out, he rolled around until he had formed another coyote exactly like himself. He said, "No one shall ever see this coyote. If they see it, it shall jump right into the sea. He shall be known to all generations as the sea-coyote (xatáluwe' xasa.i'l, "salty water coyote")." Then going on in the direction the scent came, he came in this direction [north] until he passed across some large sand hills. Then again he lay down and rolled about until he formed another coyote. He said, "This coyote (xatáluwe' cǐlyáai', "sand coyote") shall never be seen by anyone else, except in their dreams men or women shall come in contact with it, and shall yelp as he did. They shall be praised for their yelping." He ran on until he reached a mountain. Then he rolled around and formed another coyote, which he called the mountain coyote (xatáluwe' avi'). He said, "He is the worst-looking creature, so thin, and his tail is nothing but a dried up stick. People shall never see him except in their dreams, when they may come in contact with him. Whoever does so will have power enough to cure any sort of sickness." Then he ran along until toward evening he reached the place we now are. Then he rolled around until he formed another coyote. He called this the dirt coyote (xatáluwe' áma't). He said, "This coyote shall be the prettiest creature, but he shall be the biggest thief. He shall destroy people's chickens [sic] and all things put away safely. For his mean actions, he shall be called by all the bad names. He shall be known to all humans: whoever comes in contact with him in dreams shall have power to cure whooping cough, pneumonia, small pox, and all kinds of bad diseases."

They were sure he was nearby now. Late in the evening he arrived where his brothers were. As soon as he arrived, he picked up all the bones he could find. When the brothers saw him coming, the younger transformed himself into an old cooking pot (tackĭ'n) and stood close to the fire. He had power enough to do this. So he sat close to the fire waiting for Coyote to come. He felt sure Coyote would come to where they had meat on the fire. Coyote came to the fire to get the meat. Then the old pot seized him by the feet and shouted to the other in the house, "Come out to see what I have caught." Then the older brother in the house shouted to the one outside, "Don't beat him; you might make holes in the hide. Just choke him to death." Coyote cried for help, saying, "I am the youngest brother. Although I have been away only a short time, you have forgotten me." He told them who he was, explaining that they were his older brothers and he the youngest; saying that he was not old enough to take care of himself, hence he was filthy. They finally recognized him and let him free. They received him as their brother.

They took him into the house and fed him. After he had fed well, they mourned over their long separation. They were afraid of his actions, but they said brothers should forgive one another. "All generations shall do as we do." They said, "After our great loss why should we be cruel to each other? If we feel so, all humanity would take after us." After they had a long talk, they took him into the home. He was well cared for after this, so that he forgot what he had done. (There are some songs here.)[13] After they had slept together one night, toward morning they decided what they would do.

In the morning they were going after the deer they kept in a cave, but they did not want Coyote to go with them and find out where they kept them. They told him to go out first. He did so. The two other brothers remained at home until nearly midday. Then they went straight to the cave and got what they wanted

[13] Kutox refused to dictate these, insisting that I could not record them.

to eat. At noon Coyote returned and saw that they had already eaten. The second day he was again told to go. He felt uneasy, but did as he was told. When he returned, he saw that again they had already gotten their deer and had eaten. The third day he was told to go again, but this time he was determined to find out whether they stayed at home or went hunting. He hid in the bushes. He saw that they were still at home. Toward noon they went after their deer and got what they wanted to eat. The fourth day he was told to do as before, but he returned and hid near the house to see in which direction they went for the deer. He waited until they returned and then followed their tracks right to the cave. Then he found they had immense herds of deer in the cave. When he saw this, he said, "People shall hunt their deer and not keep them as pets in caves. All generations shall not have power to keep them penned up." As he said this, he opened the cave and drove out all the deer, scattering them over the mountains. Then he returned home and told his brothers that all the deer had gathered in a cave because of their hunting every day; that they had found a place to hide from the hunters. Then those two felt bad, thinking that now they had to hunt as hard as anyone else.

That night he told them he had a plan and would tell them what he wanted. He said, "You have sent me over rough places, so that I have thorns in my feet and all kinds of hurts like that." He wanted a pair of moccasins (the kind the Apache [Yavapai] wear; this family represents the Apache). So they made them for him. Next morning he went hunting. He climbed far up on top of a mountain where he found a mountain sheep, long dead. He took the bones and skin, and set it up close to the brink of a canyon. When it was set up, he decided to fool Namet [the oldest brother]. So he came running home, saying, "You have had a hard time to hunt. I have found something to kill, but I am not a good shot." He wanted Namet to go with him; he did not want the other. The two (Namet and Coyote) disliked each other somewhat. They started off. When they reached the dead mountain sheep, Namet started to shoot, but Coyote told him he had better go nearer. He made him go still nearer until he arrived at the very brink of the canyon. Then Coyote pushed him over. He fell down, dashed to pieces.

Coyote came home wailing, mourning for the loss of his brother. He told his second brother about the death of the oldest. But Namet Hatagult knew Coyote had done this, so he did not mourn. Coyote cried and cried until he cried himself asleep. Then Namet Hatagult went out, taking an arrow. He thrust it far down into the ground, pulled it out, and whirled it around until rain poured down. It rained as hard as it possibly can. As the rain water flowed down the canyon it brought all the bits of Namet together. By the time the pieces reached the lower end of the canyon, he was reformed. Then he got up, took his bow and arrows, and started shivering with cold. Namet Hatagult knew he was returning, so he built a big fire, by which he sat waiting. When Namet got home, he warmed himself and told what Coyote had done to him. He said that he disliked Coyote for his wickedness; he ought to be killed.

When they told him to go hunting again, Coyote started off. They determined to make everything salty so that he could not eat nor drink anything. Their drinking water, the ponds, and the lakes were all made salty. When Coyote returned from the hunt, he was hungry, so he picked up a pot of mush they had saved for him. This tasted very salty. He got some water to put in it, but it was worse. Again he got water, and put it in, but it was saltier than ever. Then he said he would go all over the world hunting for ponds and rivers, and drink them to quench his thirst. He did this but he found all the rivers and ponds salty. He was dying of thirst and hunger. He came home. He went inside his house; he was half dead. When the brothers did this, they went halfway to the sky and watched him.

Namet Hatagult thought of some excuse to come down to help him, for he liked Coyote better than the other did. He told the oldest brother that he had lost his knife. But the other brother knew that he wanted to come down to help Coyote, so he said, "For his wickedness to me, I want him to die. But it is you who always wanted to help him out of trouble. So it is not for the knife that you were going down: it is to help him." Namet

Hatagult came down. When he entered the house, he found Coyote almost dead. He said, "Poor brother, I shall sing a song for you [i.e., cure you]." At the first song, Coyote could barely open his eyes. At the second song, he moved his feet just a little. At the third song, he began to keep time with the singing: pat, pat. Then, at the fourth song, he rose and danced around: stamp, stamp. Because of this, the Mohave still continue to sing for their sick and dead.[14]

When Namet found the other had stayed so long, he came down to see what was happening. When he reached the ground, he said, "If I had stayed away from my sick brother altogether, humans might do the same. A family may have disputes, but because of sickness they should forgive one another. For this reason, I will forgive my brother, who has done me great wrong."[15]

They all lived together in peace. In the evening Coyote thought of a plan. He said that if they went hunting again, they should take great care of their venison. They should store it in a good place, knowing then that they would have plenty. Coyote said he would go and invite various people to their house for a feast. They wanted to get girls as wives.

The older brothers said they were going again to hunt. They told Coyote to stay near the house, not to go anywhere. They said, "Wherever you go, there is danger. There is an old woman living near by who is very dangerous. Her claws are about three inches long. If she catches you, she will tear you to pieces. She has a pet [n$_y$xat, "my dog"] there who is a great deceiver. No matter who comes, even though he hides, this pet will tell her." The pet was a duck. So Coyote made up his mind he would visit this old woman.[16] He said, "I never heard of a woman being dangerous." He set out to visit her.

When he arrived at the old woman's house, he took ashes and put them into the pet's mouth. Then he asked it some questions, but it was unable to answer. He thought then he was quite safe. Coyote transformed himself into a lizard and lay there waiting for the old woman who was away getting food.

[14] The Maricopa and allied tribes having abandoned the old practices.

[15] Interrupted at this point.   [16] Who is nameless.

The old woman returned at noon. As he lay there in the thatch he thought whether he had better come down and speak to her, or crawl out of the house through a little crack as a lizard. But the old woman was wise enough to kill any little thing she saw. So he thought he had better come down and speak amicably to her. He thought she would not be so cruel as to tear him to pieces. He came down, but he found he was in danger. She stretched her hands toward the doorway. Coyote thought, "Surely I can jump out of danger." He tried this. As he jumped through the door, the old woman split him in two with her claws. Part of the coyote was taken and half his body was left to him, so he went home.

He went into the house and stayed in bed. When the brothers returned, they brought venison. They asked him to come out and prepare his own meals, for they knew already he was in trouble. Coyote told them he was badly hurt. They said, "You can stand all sorts of pains." Then he came out and showed them what had happened. But Namet Hatagult already knew this, so he brought half a deer. Then after they had eaten, they put this half on the coyote. Now Coyote was all right, although part of his body was deer. If one ate coyote, he would find it tasted much like deer.

When they learned the old woman had done it, they made a blood sausage to poison her. Then they told Coyote to take it to the old woman, but to be sure not to go very close to her. Coyote took the sausage to her. The old woman was grinding meal. Coyote went right behind her and gave her the sausage when she was not looking. When she turned around to see who it was, Coyote had run away. She called out to Coyote, asking him to take some of the meal back to his brothers. She said she was sorry for her cruelty and wished to be peaceful with her neighbors. This time Coyote was afraid of the old woman, so he kept away. Then the old woman sat down and began to eat what he had given her. She finished eating it. She felt sleepy. She lay down and went to sleep. So ever since she has been dead.

Then Coyote wondered if she was sound asleep. He went close to her and hit her with a lump of dirt. She did not waken. Then he went still closer and poked her eyes with his finger. When he found she was dead, he decided to stay at her house and eat whatever she had. He stayed there four days. When he was ready to return home, he took off the old woman's finger- and toenails. He bored holes in the center of each and strung them together. He put this on his head as an ornament. He then went home to his brothers.

In the evening he said he was now ready for the feast. Coyote went out to invite four tribes to join the feasting. They were to be present on the fourth day. As he set out, the older brothers saw that they were in danger because of the old woman's claws. The four tribes came on the fourth day as they had been told. They had a feast and danced, having a good time. Coyote got two girls, to whom he tried to talk, but they said his breath was so bad they could not bear it. Then he got two more, older girls, but they said the same and ran away. The third time he got two women and tried to talk to them, but they said the same thing. Then the fourth time he went out and got some older women; they said the same thing and ran away. This made him very angry.

He went out to get his hat decorated with the dangerous old woman's claws. But the hat had disappeared, for the older brothers had known he would take his hat into the dance. They had dug far down under the earth and buried it. He looked everywhere and could not find it. Finally he dug deep beside the fireplace and took his hat out.

He put on his hat and joined the dancing crowd. He too danced. As he danced his hat rattled. Then everyone stopped dancing to watch him. "Well, he has killed the dangerous old woman," they said. Then they all crowded around him and tried to beat him to death. But instead of beating him, they struck each other, so he escaped. Then they rushed to the house and killed Namet and Namet Hatagult. They scalped them (right above the nose, taking all their hair). Then they all went back to their homes taking the scalps.

When Coyote returned he found them dead. He began to cry. He cried for two days. On the third day he decided to go after the people to see if he could not scalp them or die among his enemies. So he started. As he went along he came to where they had camped. He felt their fireplace, but it was cold. Then he went farther until he came to another camp. This time the fireplace was a little warm. He went still farther until he arrived at another camping place. This time the fire was still burning. Then he was sure they had just left.

As he went along he saw an old woman travelling in the same direction. Instead of going up to her, he went far around so as to approach her. The old woman had a bundle on her back. She was singing and dancing. Then he asked why she was so happy. The old woman said, "Well, how is it you did not hear the good news? We were asked to a feast by Coyote. We all started off and in four days we got to their place. And when everybody was happy, feasting and dancing, Coyote tried to have his will of various girls. He became angry and got the dangerous old woman's claws. When he joined the dancers, we all knew what he had done, so we all tried to kill him but he escaped. So instead, we killed his two older brothers. Now I am carrying their scalps." Then Coyote said, "How did it happen that I did not hear the news? I visited the houses and all were vacant." He said, "You told me this good news, but now it is all over. But the songs you were singing sounded so pretty that I would like to learn some." [These songs, which evidently were sung at this point, were called kwiya'ʀoya'ʀȧ.] The old woman said, "Those are the worst songs you heard:" she did not want to sing for him. But Coyote urged her to teach him the two songs she had sung. The old woman taught him these two. Then Coyote said, "As I have learned the two songs, we might sing together as we go along. When the crowd gathers, we might dance around once or twice before they begin." When Coyote learned the two songs, he thought whether to kill the old woman or to take the scalps and run back home. Finally he thought he would kill her. He seized her by the bangs [on her forehead] and dragged her to a big rock. There he pounded all her bones and shook all the fragments out of her mouth. Then he got into her skin.

So he carried her bundle, walking and acting as she had done.

When the people saw her coming, they said, "Get out of the way and let her go around once or twice." They did so. She said she was tired out; as for the scalps, they made her happy, so she wanted to go around once or twice anyway. She held the two scalps in her hand as she circled. She told every one to get out of her way for fear they might get blood stains on them. While she danced around, she whirled the scalps so as to scare everyone away for fear of the blood. He grabbed the old woman's skin by the hair at the top of her head, jerked it off, and threw it into the middle of the crowd. As he did so, he said, "Here, take this and dance all you want." They watched him. He started off, taking the scalps home. A roadrunner,[17] a coyote, and an eagle chased him. He thought he could go faster than they, but he could not. When he realized he was in danger, he stopped. He said, "In my youth I could run faster than this." So he started off to show them how fast he could go. They finally agreed it was no use to chase him. So they all went back while Coyote went home to his brothers.

When he reached home, he found that his brothers were nearly dead. He tried to find a way to replace the scalps. He took mud from the river [to cement them in place]. The scalps stayed on a while: it was pretty good. But as soon as it dried, they fell off their heads. Three other things he tried, but he was unsuccessful. He was tired out by the middle of the night, so he went to sleep. When the brothers saw he was asleep, they rose, dug deep under the ground, and took out some sand. They put it on their heads, put the scalps in place, and were whole again. Then Namet Hata-gult said, "We could not have gone for our scalps, but you see how he risked going after them. He did this for us, so that we are alive again. Always remember this." So he was forgiven the wrongs he had done them.

When they were together again, Coyote thought one night of a plan. He said, "Whether my plan is good or not, it is a shame for us to remain unmarried all our lives." He said he knew of a woman across the mountain. He said, "We might set out in the morning to get her." The two older brothers refused to go. "Why, the

[17] Chapparal cock (*Geococcyx californianus*).

woman belongs to the most dangerous people!" Then Coyote asked who were the most dangerous people. Those two answered that they meant the bears. Coyote said, "Well, I do not see how they can be dangerous for they never risk their lives when I am in danger" [?]. He said, "I always go through danger and I always come through safely." Finally they decided to go get her. As the two older brothers were getting ready, Coyote stood watching them. He said, "Well-dressed men will never be noticed by a woman. A shabby-looking man such as I am will be noticed and will always get some woman to marry him."[18] So they set off. Coyote did not wash or dress up at all.

When they were half way up the mountain, he said, "Now, brothers, stand still until I tell you of a plan. We will not all go together. You can go in different directions killing rabbits and jackrabbits, and then take them to feed her with fresh meat. If we take this woman, and she should happen to die before we reach home, we will have all future generations talking about us: that when but half way home, she died of starvation." So they did as he told them.

Coyote knew where she usually came to get food; wild plants. Then Coyote went directly to her while she was busy gathering them. He threw [shot?] his arrow right in front of her. It was unfamiliar to her: she picked it up wondering whose it could be. As she looked at it, Coyote came close to her. He said, "Don't you think I am the best-looking boy in the world? I have two old brothers coming: you will not know which is which." So she turned around and saw them coming close. They built great fires, roasting rabbits and jackrabbits for her. While they were doing this, Coyote as he went along, killed rattlesnakes, gopher snakes; all kinds of snakes. He also built a fire and threw them all into it: one could hear them rattling. Before they were half cooked, he took them out and ate them. She thought he must be crazy. After they fed the woman well, they took her home.

Her husband waited for her all day. Toward evening he sent someone to see if she was all right. He was afraid something had

[18] There is a Maricopa saying that a handsome man will never get a handsome wife, while an ugly one will marry several women.

happened to her. When he got close he saw that someone had taken her away. Then the bears started after them to fetch her back. Her name was sĭn‚yamu'l, Antelope[19] Woman. When he got halfway, he wanted to see how strong his claws were. When he reached some big rocks, he scratched them, breaking them into little pieces. Having found out that he could break these, he was sure nothing could withstand his claws.

When he reached the doorway, the woman was seated inside the house. He told her to come out and go home with him. (This was the time the first adultery occurred. Since then, men are apt to take someone else's wife.) She said: no, she was not going. She had been badly treated by her first husband. The bear husband said he did not think she had made up her mind to stay with these people. As they were quarreling about taking the woman back, and she was insisting on remaining, a little pup owned by Coyote (called nyĭmĭsava' kwĭcĭtu'l, White Trotter) jumped right at the bear's jaws. Instead of biting a piece off, he was smashed to bits and thrown in back of the house. When Coyote saw what had happened—he had been fast asleep—he turned over, saying, "Who is the old woman visiting us? You had better feed the old woman with what is left and send her home." The oldest brother said, "We are in trouble again through following your plans." Then Coyote jumped up and got his club, thinking he would beat the bear to death. Coyote said, "A man should tend to his business, and not sit about quarreling like an old woman." But instead of winning, he was split in two and thrown in the back of the house.

Namet Hatagult and Namet thought it was not fair to fight only one, so they sent the bear back. Then the bear went home and told. He brought three other bears to help him. As these set out, Namet and Namet Hatagult wondered what they should do to protect themselves. Each had a walking stick. They rubbed them, put them to the top of their heads, and thrust them down through their bodies. Then they tried to see how this was. They

---

[19] While the story indicates clearly enough that the other characters are bears, the word surely means Antelope Woman although it was translated Bear Woman.

scratched their arms: it did not hurt, so they were sure they were safe. They covered the whole house with snow. They were prepared.

When the bears came near, they wondered what they should do. They [the bears] sat down and thought. They thought they would pull the house post down, which would surely kill them. They pulled at it, but they could not budge it. They next thought to bring a heavy stone so as to knock it down. They tried, but failed. The third time they said, "If we should take some little red-headed insects (like grasshoppers) and tear them to pieces, it would start a fire and burn up the house." They tried, but failed. The blaze did start but the fire was quenched by the snow.

They saw it was no use to try a scheme, so they decided to fight with their paws. As Namet and Namet Hatagult came out, the bears began to sing, telling the others what wrong had been done to their wives. [Song here.] They told in their song that they were close relatives. The brothers then said, "We did not think of that. We have done you great wrong. We did not mean to." Now they were going to begin: they were to kill each other four times. Whichever survived the fourth time would win.

The bears first came up to the cats to fight. They scratched and scratched until they killed them. As they lay dead, a wind from the east whirled around and around them until it brought them to life. The second time, the bears were killed. A storm from the east whirled around them and brought them to life. The third time, the cats were killed and the same wind came from the east, whirling around until they were alive again. The fourth time, the bears were killed. This time a black wind came and whirled and whirled until it gradually died away. That was the end of the bears.

Namet and Namet Hatagult went home. At the beginning of the fight, the pup and Coyote had been killed. They took the two, laid them on the ashes, and buried them with ashes. After a while they came back to life. When they got out and smelled the blood stains on the ground, they acted as though they were going to beat someone to death, too. They took their clubs: the dog barked and Coyote ran all around the house.

(If you ever come to a crowd where this story is being told, when they reach the part about the fight, they take sides. If you are not careful they will scratch you to pieces. For the reason that those animals fought over a wife, humans do, too. Indians are likely to kill when they fight over a woman; by their supernatural power, they claim; but whites shoot each other. Every tribe has its own way. In the beginning there was war, so we have wars, too.)

FLUTE LURE

After their father died, at the time of creation, everybody was scattered over the whole world here.

No one has ever said whether her family was living with this girl. She said, "I can not follow these people around. It will be better to make my own home." She said, "There is a body of water, called blue-water (xa'gwavàcu')." She decided to make her home near it, so that she could bathe there. As little girls do to amuse themselves, she made a slide. She put mud on the bank and slid down on it. She saw no one about. For three days she went to slide. On the fourth day she saw a man standing on the opposite bank. She wondered who it could be. She called him Yellow Gopher (ceăkwa's), her father's brother (nàvi'). She said, "Why don't you come and stay with me?" She had the power to make the water deep and swift so that he could not cross. She said this just to mock him. When she slid down again, the man went under the ground and came up in the river as she was swimming it. She felt someone touch her, and as she went down the third time, someone seized her. After the third time, the Gopher decided to show himself or to go back underground. She wanted to slide down a fourth time. She thought that it must have been a root or limb, so she scraped down the bank with her hand, and rubbed mud over it again. Then she slid down a fourth time. Then Gopher stood up as a man right in front of her. As they stood there, Gopher decided he would have intercourse. The girl said, "It is an awful thing for me to have a husband while I am alone, with no one living near." So Gopher decided to go back.

She wondered why she had told Gopher to go back. She said, "I ought to have had sense to take this man home with me, in case trouble comes to me." She climbed up the first hill on her way home. She found it was rather hard to climb. She tried to get up the second hill, but found she could not go over it as easily as she had formerly. Going over the third hill, she found herself creeping. Then, on the fourth, she found she was unable to get over it. She was going to stay there on the fourth hill, but she said, "I will try my best to get home." As she started up it, she said, "If I stay here to give birth, other people (i.e., humans) will do the same. They would never try to get home for confinement, and that would be very hard for them." She got home as well as she could.

Then her first son was born. Yet the pains still came as sharply as ever. She said, "It could not be from walking all the way home, nor from the cold. I don't know just what to do." Then she said, "I know as well as the humans will, these are twin brothers." Then the second son was born. (She sang between each of these occurrences.) She then attended to herself. She had nothing on which to lay the twins. So she sang and at the end of each song, she got an arch for the cradle-frame, cross sticks, the bark placed lengthwise [mattress], a hood, and a woven square of bark [woven bark cloth].

When she had them strapped in her cradle, she said, "What shall I do for wood?" When all the birds and animals heard that the twins had been born to her, they claimed the children [as their sons?], and brought in bundles of wood for them. She threw away these bundles. Then the gopher put his bundle of reeds on the north side inside the house. She accepted his bundles and used them for her fire.

When the children were old enough, she made a swing for them inside the house. (It swung east and west.) She placed the twins so that their heads faced one east, the other west, and with their legs crossed. Then she left them and went out to gather food. She went out each day. (There is a song between each of these incidents, so that the tale takes half a night to tell.) On the fourth day, when she went to gather food, she set out south again. She had ground mesquite beans and thrown the seeds away. This time the children were outside the house in the swing. As quail came to scratch at these seeds, the older brother called to the younger, "You say you have power to do things. If you have the power, kill those quail over here." The younger brother said, "I did say I have power enough to do things. I will try it although I have never tried it before." He rubbed up the dirt in front of his ear and made a pellet of it. He held it to the sun until it was transparent. Then he filliped at the quail and it killed all of them scratching there. Then the children got down, gathered the quail, and piled them under the swing. Then they got into it again. When their mother came home she was so angry that she called all the animals and birds names. She threw the quail away. The children began to cry. She looked to see if they were hurt, but she found nothing. So she tried to nurse them, but the children would not nurse, but cried the harder. Then she thought, "It must have been my children who did this." She hurried and got wood, built a fire, and baked the quail in the ashes. When they were cooked, she ate them. Then she picked up the children again, and they stopped crying.

That night she thought that if they meant to provide for her by hunting, she would not have to go everywhere gathering food herself. She made bows and arrows for them that night. She wanted them to try these on the mice in their house. The children tried and killed them. The next morning she went again to gather food.

That night she told them there was another animal similar to those they had killed in the house. She called it ami'lk [prairie dog?]. She said, "One who was skilled with bow and arrows could kill those, but to little boys like you, I merely tell of them." She said, "They come to me as I gather plants: they come to me like puppies, but suddenly they run off." The children thought, "If older people can kill with their bows and arrows, we can use them as well as they." In the morning they set out. They found the prairie dogs running about in the bushes. But they were afraid: they cried and ran home. Their mother ran toward them, asking "Did a scorpion sting you or a rattlesnake bite you?" The children said, "No, we saw something that looked dangerous." They described it. Their mother said, "That is the thing I spoke of last night." Then the boys went out and killed all the prairie dogs.

Then she told them of another animal that she saw farther away among the mesquite trees. "These are a little larger than the animals you killed," she said. She called them amă'lgĭc, pack rat. "You will never find them running about, but this animal piles up small sticks at the base of a tree. If you do not find it running about, you can see where it goes into its house. Stop up all the holes save one, and wait there. Then the other boy can throw sticks on top of its house to make it come out." The next morning they set out. When they saw the rats filling their burrows with mesquite beans, they thought them horrible creatures, so they went home, crying. When they were halfway, the older brother stopped the younger, saying, "That is the very kind our mother described; let us go hunt them." So they took home big bundles of slain rats.

The next night the woman described another kind of animal. She said, "They are horrible-looking creatures with long ears. When they raise their ears, as they stand in the east, it looks like a pair of fires. No child can hunt these rabbits and come home with two or three of them. A man who can use a bow and arrow well is the only one who can kill these rabbits (xĭlyảau')." They decided to try. They set out the next morning and saw them hopping around through the young, sprouting arrowweeds. When the rabbits saw them, they stopped hopping and raised their ears. The boys thought them awful-looking creatures and turned home crying again. The older brother stopped the younger, saying, "This is the very animal our mother described." So they went back for the rabbits and came home carrying them all around their belts. (They put the heads under their belts.)

(She had three ways of preparing rabbits, so today we have three ways, too. She would boil them, or she would build a fire, rake away the coals, place the rabbits there, and heap ashes, then coals, over them. The third way was to spit them on arrow-weeds to stand over the fire.)

She told them that night, that as she went on farther to the desert, she saw other animals. She described them: she said they have long ears and are much larger than rabbits. She said, "I see these animals every day; as I gather wild plants, they eat beside me. They know I can not harm them. Since you are only children, they might do the same with you." She called them kȧu'l, jackrabbit. The next morning they started off again. When they reached the desert they saw the jackrabbits. They ran home crying again. It was hard for them to kill jackrabbits. The older brother said to the younger, "Now if we don't kill any jack-rabbits, but went home dragging our bows and arrows, humans would cite this against the two brothers who went hunting but came back without a thing." So they tried hard and did kill some jackrabbits. They brought them home. When she prepared these, she ate them but would not feed any to her children. She said, "If a child ate this, it might have a big boil on its neck or body. Such a boil would be incurable. But older people can eat this, yet it may happen to them, too."[20]

(When the boys brought home animals they had killed, they did not eat them. She told them that every time they hunted by themselves, they should not eat what they had killed.)[21]

At night when they were ready to go to bed, she told them of another animal. She said, "This is a fearful thing for young boys like you to hunt. As I go toward the mountain, I see another sort of animal that grazes near where I gather things. These animals look as though they were wearing dry branches on their heads. They are called ᵃgwa'gȧ, deer. But a child could not kill this animal, because he is not strong enough, for it has a tough skin." She told them this during the night. The boys said, "If an old woman can become so well acquainted with this animal, why can not boys, too?" Next morning they started off. They went quite a distance, until they came to the mountains. They saw a num-

---

[20] This tabu conforms with Maricopa practice.

[21] This also is Maricopa practice.

ber of deer grazing. They picked out the biggest and shot it. The younger boy shot first, but the deer staggered on, so the older shot it. This time it fell down. But they did not know what to do with it. It was too heavy for the two little boys to carry home. They said they would make it lighter by singing. When they finished the song, they dragged the deer home. When they brought it to the house, the woman was inside. They called to her to come out and skin the deer. She asked them if they really killed this or if someone had given it to them. She said, "Such an animal will sometimes fool you. He will pretend to be dead, but will suddenly jump up and run away." She sent the boys into the house to eat.

While they were inside, she made up her mind to cure the deer and make it run home. She spat on the ground, mixed it to a dough, and put this mud on the deer's wound. Then she breathed into the deer's mouth. It got right up. As she did this, she called to the boys, "Just as I told you, the deer fooled you. The deer is going to run off: come and help me!" Just as the boys reached the deer, she let it go running off to the desert. Then the boys, standing there, said they would follow it a second time; perhaps it would fall again in the brush. "If we let this go, humans will tell this story and it will be an awful thing against us. Humans will do the same: if they kill something which happens to get up and run off, and they are too tired to follow it, they would say, 'Well, the twins of sĭnᵧuŏ'k ĭnyuxa'và, West Woman (their mother) did this very thing.' It does not matter how tired we are, we must find it."²²

When the boys chased the deer, they went far up toward the mountain. As it was getting late, they turned home. Their mother worried. She said the boys were too young to be out late; so she started after them. When she saw them coming, she stopped and changed herself into a post. When they saw it, the older said to the younger, "We have been through this desert time and again, but we never came across this post. Let us try our arrows on it to see how lucky we are." Their mother heard them, so she called out that it was their mother. Then the boys

²² Interrupted for several days.

said, "Women should not act this way. We were going to fill you with our arrows." Then they all started home.

After she had prepared their supper and they had eaten it, they went to bed. She began to tell them stories again. She said, "There is a mountain peak called vitaxa'. Way up on top is a nest. Each year the eagle has little ones, and I go for them to bring home as pets." She said, "Little boys like you could not find the nest. I have power enough to reach the tip of that high peak." Then the boys said, "If an old woman has power to do these things, why can't boys have just as much power to go get those eaglets?"

The boys started in the morning. They went through the desert. The younger brother was thirsty and tired, so that he trailed far behind the other. The older brother called to him "kwiʀăŏkoĕ'v [meaning unknown; cf. ĕndjĕ'n kuʀăŏk, "older brother"], walk a little faster.[23] There is water nearby." Then the younger ran and caught up with him. But when they were together, there was no water. As they stood there, they sang:

xananyaxauwa   yauwȧxauyanya[24]

When he had finished singing, the older brother said, "I know what it was. It was not a body of water nor a stream running through this desert. On very hot days in the desert, people shall come across the same thing as we have, and they shall call it gulnyuxai', mirage."

They went on, but could not walk farther. They were thirsty and tired. Their mother, even though at home, could see how far they had gone. Seeing them tired and thirsty, she took pity on them. She went out, took an arrowweed, stuck it into the earth, and pulled it out. She whirled it around the sky four times. Then it began to rain. Then the boys were all wet and cold, but they got water. As they were standing by a stream of rain water, the older said to the younger, "I fear you have done something to cause this rain. Mother told us in her stories that there are

[23] A song reference gave the name of one of these twins as catukxo'tȧs.

[24] None of the songs that follow were properly recorded, nor their meanings obtained.

certain kinds of birds and insects that you should not kill, for if you do, it will rain hard so you would freeze to death in winter, or in summer it would turn hot and we would die of thirst." Then he mentioned xan$_y$âvâtci'p, cactus wren [?].[25] He said, "Did you kill this bird or destroy its nest?" The younger answered, "No, I have been right along with you." Then the other mentioned gwac^{a}munyoi', tarantula. He said, "Did you kill that one or destroy the little burrow he lives in?" The younger said, "No, I have been walking beside you all the time." Then he mentioned another little bird, vitâpana'.[26] He asked again if he had killed this little bird. The younger answered, "No, I did not kill anything like that. I have been carrying my bow and arrows in my hands." The older brother said, "I am just saying this. I know who caused the rain. It was our mother who took pity on us because we were tired and thirsty. She sent us the rain."

After they had rested, they went on. When they reached the mountain peak vitaxa', they tried to find the place where the old woman had climbed up. They had reached the cliff on the south side. Then the older went around to the east side, while the younger went to the west. They intended to meet on the north side. They were trying to find how the old woman had climbed: whether she had cut footholds in the cliff or made a ladder. As the older brother went along, he gave no heed to the feathers lying about. But the younger brother picked up every feather he came to. When they met on the north side, the older brother found the younger covered with feathers. They were sticking in his belt and his hair; every place he could put them. The older brother told him to throw the feathers away. The younger asked, "Why should I? Mother said I should pick up every feather I could on our hunting trips and bring them home. These being the strongest, I intend to take them home." The older brother seized him, took all the feathers, and threw them away. He said, "For this reason: West Woman's children started to get her pets,

[25] A little bird that makes a closed nest.

[26] The informant did not know what it was like.

and when they could not climb up, they brought nothing but feathers home. People shall tell this story over and over again."[27]

After they threw the feathers away, they sat together at the foot of the cliff. The older brother said, "kwiʀȧŏkoĕ'v, you are always boasting of your power. If you have power enough, you can climb up and throw the eaglet to me." The younger brother said, "Yes, I did tell you I have power enough to do things, and I am going to try now." He rubbed himself until he was transformed into a certain kind of snake (gwĭtnᵧia'lk). He lay at the foot of the cliff ready to start. Then the older brother sang:

yaĕnya akuyununuṇamin
to climb

At the end of the song the snake started up. He had only a little farther to go to reach the nest, when he stopped. That was as far as he could go. Then the older brother said, 'Well, poor brother, he has no arms or feet. Suppose a storm should come up, he could not hold to the cliff. He might be thrown down and broken to pieces. If that should happen, why should I go back alone? I will kill myself among the cliffs here. That will be the end of us." But as he said this, the snake rolled down. When he reached the ground, he was so worn out that he rolled around half dead. Then he changed himself to a boy again.

As they sat there, the older brother said, "You have boasted of your power, but you have done nothing with it. I have never boasted of my power, but I will try." He rubbed himself until he was transformed into a little piece of cotton. But before he started he sang:

yaĕnya akulyununuṅami pada

Then he went up. The younger brother watched until he could no longer see him. As he sat there thinking, he said, "Poor brother, he has no arms or feet. In case of a storm he could not hold to the cliff. If a storm should rise, it would blow him far up in the sky and I should never again see him. I will call to him to

[27] Maricopa belief was that it was extremely dangerous to touch eagle feathers until they had been purified.

see if he is safe. If he does not answer, I will get up and smash myself on the rocks. Why should I go back alone? For this reason, people shall say 'The twin brothers went off to get their pets; then, when the older died there, the younger came home, and now he is grown.' They will bring up this story every time they tell their children. For this reason, I will kill myself." So he sang:

ĭnyakatcanmei uma uvaṇyatĕn

(Telling him to come down: "What is the use of staying up there?") If at the end of the song, he heard no answer, he was going to get up and smash himself on the rocks. Then the older brother answered him with a song:

yaĕ̤nyaàtcĕ̆'nuṇuṇàmi pada aχane

When he got the answer, the younger said, "My brother is safe." At the end of his song, the older brother came down with two eaglets. When he reached the ground, he was so tired, he rolled around half dead.

The younger brother rose and took the older eaglet that was thrown down. (The younger eaglet had brighter plumage.) Then the older brother rose and told the younger to give back the older eaglet. He refused. The older brother said, "Since I am the older, it is not important that I take the bright-colored pet. This one is a dull creature and just suits me." The younger brother said, "If I took the trouble to go up there and bring these down, I would have chosen the bright one. It is all right for me to take the dull-looking one." So they fought over it, until the older brother took this one away from him.

The older brother said, "Let me tell you how our mother would settle this." He was going to describe how she made their arrows. He said that when she was making a bow for the older boy, she took three strands of sinew and rolled them together. As for arrows, she put two feathers and sometimes three on the arrows for the older boy, while for the younger there were only two feathers to an arrow and one without feathers at all. And when preparing their meals, he said, she ground up meal and put it into a plate for the older. "While for you, as she is still

grinding, she feeds you at the end of the metate." He said, "You
see these things are done. You are not my equal, so you must
take what comes to you;" handing the younger eaglet to his
younger brother.

Then they started homeward. When they were halfway, their
mother saw that they were thirsty again. She made it rain on
them again. This time it rained so hard that the eaglets both
died of cold. The twins felt badly over their loss. So they dug a
hole with their arrows, threw in the pets, broke their bows and
arrows, and threw these pieces in, too. They buried them all and
started home.

When their mother saw they were near, she lit a big fire and
prepared their supper. When they went in, she told them where
she had placed the food. But they did not answer: they went
right to bed. She wondered what had happened; if they had
got hurt. She asked whether they quarreled or fought, but
she could not get them to answer.[28] She was aware that the boys
knew that she was the cause of the eaglet's death. They were
angry at her. Early, before dawn, she went out, took an arrow,
thrust it down into the ground, shook it a little, and pulled it out.
She drew out the two eaglets with it. She said, "I told you that
those eaglets were just like children: they knew in which direction you went, so they followed you all the way." The older
brother said to the younger, "Go out and see if they are there.
Come and tell me. If they are not, call me and I will come out.
Then we will kill her and go somewhere else." They knew she
had killed the eaglets, so they decided to kill her.

The younger brother went out and saw the two eaglets sitting
there. He seized the older one again. The older brother waited
inside the house. The younger was outside so long that the older
thought he would go outside to see. When he came out and saw
what the younger had done, they began to fight again. Their
mother then told them they should yield to each other instead
of fighting. At last the younger brother gave it up. They went
after some willow branches and built a little cage for their pets.
(They were the first to build cages for pets, so we always build

[28] Interrupted at this point.

them the same way.) When it was ready, they went hunting [for meat] for their pets.

As they had broken their good bows and arrows, they made new ones, but they were not good. Their mother told them that their old bows and arrows were made while they were young. She told them of a thicket of arrowreeds. "These," she said, "grow far to the east. They are meant for me to use, although I have never used them." As she told them that night, a visitor came. Coyote had come to stay the night. As she said, "These grow far to the east," Coyote said, "I have run past that place you call the 'far east.' It is not far at all. I have raced there and back before the sun rose." She told Coyote to go after the reeds. He started as early as he could. She sang:

xanyumiya   xamakuʀakuʀaměm

By the end of the song, he brought them. Just before sunrise he brought the bundle of reeds to the old woman. He had picked out very straight ones. She said, "Those are the weakest kind: the least wind will break them." So Coyote went again. He selected crooked ones. When he brought them, she said they were the very ones she meant. Instead of preparing them herself, she pointed to the north and got a red hot stone, which she laid on the ground and straightened the reeds on that. She laid them on the stone to straighten them. When Coyote saw this, he said, "Humans could not all have power enough to do what you are doing, so your way cannot be followed." He said, "This is the way they should prepare their bows and arrows." He built a big fire, raked away all the coals, sprinkled water on the ashes, ran the reed through them, and bent it into shape.[29] While Coyote did this, the old woman continued to reach her hands to the north. She was getting the reeds all feathered and having the arrow painted by doing this. By the time she was half through, Coyote had finished his work. So he said to her, "Having power does not mean that you can finish your work better than one who can do it with his hands."

[29] The Maricopa did not ordinarily use reed arrows, but did straighten shafts in the ashes.

When these were ready, early the next morning she told them to go out to try them. They lined up, with Coyote at the end. She told them to shoot at the end of her song. The boys knew what she would do. She sang:

kisaṇâyedïlyama

At the end of the song, they raised their bows as though to shoot but they did not. But Coyote shot his. He said, "I will try again." Then she sang again:

kivaṇa yomïlyama umyayâsauwas amyutisai

Then the twins shot their arrows, but Coyote shot last.

At night, when they finished practicing, she talked to them again. She said, "I have told you everything. There is another thicket of reeds in the middle of the sea that belongs to me. I could never use them otherwise, but sometimes I get them for firewood. But you can not get them unless you have power enough: they are far down in the bottom of the sea. I have power enough." Then the boys thought, "If an old woman has power enough to go down to the bottom of the sea, why can not we get them?"

They started in the morning to get the reeds. When they reached the ocean, the older brother said, "You say you have power enough to do things: see what you can do to get those reeds." They could just barely see the tops above the surface. Before the younger brother dove, he sang:

hankiya hankiyuwawim hamihata

Then he dove, but before he reached the bottom, he could no longer hold his breath, so he came up. He said he would try again. He tried three times more, but he could not get to the bottom. So he gave up. Then the older brother said he would try. But before he went down the younger brother sang the same song to him. At the end of the song, the older brother dove.

When he reached the bottom, he found a little path. Following this he came to a red beaver, which had spread red sand for a mat, on which he was lying. When the little boy stopped in front of him, the red beaver growled and said, "What right have you to come to my place? No child is supposed to be here." The boy answered, "Since I am a child, I can not be expected to explain why I am here." At these words, the beaver recognized him, calling him his younger brother's son (vĕta'). The boy said, "Father's older brother (nàviya'), move aside and let me pass." So the beaver moved out of the way. The boy went on the path again. A little beyond he came to a white beaver lying on a mat of white sand. This one also growled at him, saying "Why do you go through my place? for a child is not supposed to come this way." The boy answered, "I am only a child and I can not explain why I am here." At these words, the beaver repeated what the red beaver had said. So he told the white beaver to move aside. The beaver moved and he went along the path again until he came to a black beaver. The black beaver growled at him, speaking as the two others had. Then the little boy answered, "Since I am only a little boy, I can not explain plainly enough for you to understand." At this the black beaver knew it was the boy the others had called vĕta'. Then the little boy said to him also, "Father's older brother, move out of my way." The black beaver got out of the way. The boy went on until he came to a yellow beaver lying on a mat of yellow sand. This also growled at him, saying the boy should not be near his place. The boy answered, "I am only a child and I cannot explain clearly enough for you to understand." Then the yellow beaver knew him as the others had. The boy said, "Move out of my way." The yellow beaver did this and the boy went close to the reeds. He cut off two and came out of the sea. Each boy took one home with him.

When they reached home, they gave the reeds to their mother. She cut them to the proper length and put them away to dry. She worked on them four days. On the fourth day she pointed them to the south: then little holes appeared in them. [They were flutes, or more properly flageolets.] Then she pointed them to the east and they were all painted. The third time she pointed them to the north and they had fine leather tied on the sides in fringes. Then she pointed them to the west and something else was done. [Kutox had forgotten what.] Now they were com-

pleted. She told them to try their song early in the morning.
Then early she picked up the flutes and gave them to the boys.
Then she went behind the house. She said just as the birds began
to sing in the morning, they were to try their flutes. She went behind the house to listen: if their songs were sweeter than the
birds then all would be well. When the birds began to sing, the
boys played on their flutes. They sang:

> taltal   nǎmǎtaciwǎ   wilwil   nǎmǎtciwǎ
> flute   flute[30]

At the end of this song, she ran toward them and told them to try
again. Four times they sang the same song. Then she said it was
better than all the birds and animals that sing in the morning.

An old man living in the mountains near Sacaton had two
daughters. His name was Patǒkcǒ'tuc. These girls rarely saw
anybody: they lived deep in a cave. They used to go swimming
before the sun rose. They would run over to what is now Blackwater to bathe. These girls went. When they were in the water,
the younger dove. The older sister was about to dive when she
heard the boys' flutes. She pulled her sister out by the hair.
Then she too heard the sound. They asked each other if they
knew what the sound was. They did not know, but they said it
came from far to the north. They took a little bath by sprinkling
each other and went home. At home they painted themselves
and set out.

They had gone quite a distance when they saw a house by the
road. A man there called to them, "I am living right by the roadside to feed any strangers who come along." They turned and
went to his house. He said, "Help yourselves." This man had a
pot of prairie dogs stewing, some dried hanging up, others baked
in ashes: of these he told the girls to help themselves. The older
girl answered, "Before the sun rises, ground wheat and tortillas
are the only things I eat." That was all she prepared for her
meals. She asked whether the music she heard was the song of
three strong birds. She said she intended to go where it came
from. The man said, "That was the very music I made." And

---

[30] The latter is the proper word for flute; but cf. Havasupai dalda'l.

the girl said, "If I have come this far to find the music, you might as well make it again!" But the man said, "I do not make music here. I go over in the brush there, where there is a post, and I sit on that to make music." Then as they started, the man went ahead, the younger sister following. The older sister, coming last, asked the younger, "What sort of looking man is he?" The younger sister described him: "He is a big-headed man. He is short and stout. He has long hair colored white at the ends." Then the older sister said, "Never mind about his looks. If he makes sweet music better than he looks, we will stay with him. If he wishes, he can bury us in the ashes, and put fire over us" (which meant, that if he wanted to kill them, he could do that, too). When he heard what they were saying, he thought, "What a lucky man I am to get these two pretty girls to stay with me." At the thought of this, he rolled his eyes and winked.

When he reached the post, he thought, "How shall I make music?" The only sound he could make was whistling. (He was a chickenhawk [?], xomàse'.) Then prairie dogs came. He pounced on them, and caught them until he had a pile. The girls waited for the music, but this was the only sound they heard. So the older asked, "Is that your only music?" and the man answered, "Yes, but if you hear this music just before sunrise, it is the sweetest music you ever heard. But now it is nearly noon; that is why the music is not so pretty." At this, they started away from the old man. The older sister told the younger to show him her knees. When they did this, they started off. As they left the old man fell off his perch, saying, "How foolish I was trying to make such music, when I could have talked with them in such a way as to win their love."

The girls went on until they came to another house. This was owned by a lizard (xandàsei'ly̆ᵃ). He had stored mesquite beans, pounded them, and sifted this for meal. He invited them to this: "Help yourselves." The older girl, describing all kinds of delicious foods, said, "These things I never forget to serve at home. But at the sound of this music, whether or not it is the sound of those three birds, we set out to find where the music comes from." At this the lizard said it was his music they had heard.

Then the older sister said, "If we had to come this far to find it, you might as well make your music for us." But the lizard said, "I never make music here." He pointed, "In that hollow tree; that is where I make music." So the three started off to the tree. The older girl asked again, "What kind of looking man is he?" The other described him: "This man is short, his head resting in his shoulders. He wears a black band around his neck. His eyes are painted red. In front of his neck he wears something shiny and blue. His skin is very rough. On his sides, it is like a saw: I fear if I went close, he would cut me to pieces."[31] At this the lizard was disappointed. But the older sister said, "Never mind. If such a looking man can make such nice music, we will live here with him." When the lizard heard this, he rolled his eyes and winked.

When they reached the hollow tree, he went in. He tried to think of some kind of noise he could make, but he failed. At last he just whirled around four times and then peeped out at the girls. They asked if that was all he could do. He said, "Yes, that is all; but if I start this before the run rises, it is the very music you heard." Then the older sister said, "Why this is worse than before! Let us go on." The lizard thought, "How foolish I was, when I could have talked to them and told them that I own everything around here. I could have won their love."

Then they went along. They came through this valley here [going north]. There was another house by the road. As they passed, a man there called, telling them to visit him. They went to the house. He told them to help themselves to anything he had. The older sister said, "Before the sun rises, I never forget my meals; but this time I heard music which made me leave home." Then the rock squirrel (xumi'ʀ) said, "The music you heard was what I made on my hunting trip." She said, "Since I had to come all this way to find where the music came from, you should make music for us now." The squirrel said, "I do not make music right at my house. I get on top of a pole some distance away." Now they started; the squirrel leading. The older sister asked again, "What kind of looking man is he?"

31 Possibly the horned toad is meant.

The younger said, "He is a short thing, but he is cute. He turns his hair up and ties it in the middle, letting the rest hang down his back [i.e., his tail]." Then the older sister said, "If he is the kind of man you describe, he is the man who makes the nice music. We will live with him." When he heard this he was pleased. When he got on top of the pole, he ran down and up, down and up, four times, making a chirping noise: tcĭlĭlĭl tȧvĭkȧtĭk [meaningless]. Then he stopped and watched the girls. Then the older sister asked, "Is that all the music?" "Yes, that is all; but if I start this early, before the sun rises, it is that sweet music you heard." Then the older girl said, "Well, this is the worst song I have heard yet." Before they left him, the older sister described what a funny-looking creature he was in her song:

yaṇakwĭnawaisohomĭṇ ĭmiya

Then they went on. The squirrel was heart-broken: he fell down. He said, "Why did I not talk to the girls in a nice way and try to win them, instead of trying to make music for them, when I know I can not. Even if I did win the girls, when the old woman [his wife] comes home, she would beat me."[32]

The girls went on farther. Then they came to another house by the roadside. There were people in that house. As these saw them approaching, they shouted to them to come to the house and help themselves to what was there. The older sister said, "Parched wheat and a pot of beans is what I prepare before the sun rises. But on account of the sweet music we heard, we left our home." The little fellows there, screech owls (takŭ'k), said that they had made the sweet music. There were three who belonged to the screech owl family: xᵃpĕ'kwĭsta'c;[33] nᵧihwĕ'-tgwĭtci'c, "blood drinker"; takŭ'k.[34] All three together were called ĭ'mkwĭtaʀuiᵃʀui', because they sat in a row on a log. The older girl said, "Since we had to come all this way from home trying to find where the music comes from, you might start your music now." Then they all started for that pole they sat on. The older sister said to the younger, "What sort of looking fellows are

[32] Interrupted.

[33] Onomatopoetic (?) for pecking on a metate.   [34] Onomatopoetic.

these?" The younger said, "They are the cutest-looking things! They are all about the same height; all look alike." Then the older sister said, "Never mind; if the music is as sweet as their appearance, we will make our home here." When the owls heard her, they said to one another, "How did we ever come to get those two pretty girls!"

When they got to the place, they set up posts and put a log across their tops. They all sat on this. They wondered what kind of music they should make: they looked at each other. Finally the one at the end pushed the one next to him, saying, "Move on!" The next did the same, until they had all pushed each other, crying, "Move on! Move on!" They kept this up. They repeated it again and again four times. Then they stopped and looked at each other. The older sister asked if that was the only music they could make. They said, "That is the only music we can make now, in the middle of the day. But early in the morning this music is the sweetest you ever heard." She told her younger sister, "Pull your dress up to your knees" and the owls all fell to the ground.

They went on again. They came to a cave near the mountain. The horned owl called to them. They walked up to the cave. Owl said to them, "Come in and help yourselves to what I have." This time the older sister said, "We do not want anything to eat." But they wanted to know where that music came from which they had heard way back at their home. The Owl said, "Why, that was just the music I made this morning." The girl said, "If that was the music you made, make it for us again." He thought, "What kind of music shall I make?" He sat in a corner and watched the girls instead of making music. The girl said, "When do you start your music?" Then he said, "In just a little while." Suddenly he hooted, "Hnhn hn hn; hnhn hn hn." He did this four times. At the end of his song, he stopped and stared at the girls. Then the older sister asked again if that was the end of his song. He said, "Yes, that is the end, since it is late in the evening now. But when I make this music early in the morning, it is just as clear and sweet as you heard at home." This time the younger [sic] sister said, "Why, this is worse than ever!" Without saying more, the younger sister pushed the older out of the door, and they walked on to the boys' home.

As they went toward the boys' house, it was evening. When they were halfway, the old woman saw them. She prepared supper early and, after they had eaten, sent her sons into the house. She covered the fireplace where she had cooked. Then, when she went into the house, she covered the doorway. By her power she made a covering, so that it looked as though there was no doorway. When the girls reached the boys' home, they looked around to discover the entrance, but they could find none. As they went around, the younger girl stepped on the buried ashes. She felt they were warm. She put her cold feet and hands under the ashes. The older girl sat there with her.

When the old woman saw what they were doing, she took pity on them. She called them her brother's children (màrĭcpe'r [plural]). She said, "Come right in. The younger son is on the north side, the older on the south." But she did not open the door. So the girls went around to the south side. They felt around for the entrance but could not find it. Then they went to the west side and felt for the doorway. The third time they went to the north side, feeling for the door. As they stood there, the older sister said, "I know where the door is, for every house should have a door on the east side." Then when they reached the east side, she shook the place for the door four times, and the door opened.

Then the younger sister went to the younger brother and the older sister went to the south side to the older brother. The younger pair talked to each other. The older brother had his face turned down. He was lying flat with his face buried in the bedding. The older sister tried to get him to talk, but he would not. She tried every way, but she failed. So she made an ant hill close to his side so he would turn over. She also made a scorpion to crawl over him, so that if it stung him, he would turn over. While she did this, the mother watched to see if some time in the night he would get up. All this time she kept up a huge fire. She was sitting up. Toward morning the younger brother burst a sleeping power (ϑovoω'ʀᵃ sằ'ŭ't, "sleeping kept in a bag") on the old woman. (They do not describe what it was. It was his power, but they always say it was a powder. Because they did it that time, now people do it, and crawl in to steal.) He did this so that he could sleep with the younger girl. He possessed her. But the older brother still lay with his face to the ground. The older sister did everything she could, forming all kinds of insects to sting and bite him so that he would get up. Toward dawn the younger brother took the sleep-producing bag away from the old woman. As she woke and rose, she growled at the boys for causing her to sleep. She sang:

avo'oʀkwĭnyami   awasaumisa

She told in her song which of the brothers burst the sleeping bag on her. She called the younger one paʀáxa′n [meaningless].

Early in the morning, just before sunrise, she told those boys and girls to go out and bathe. The girls, when they came out, went to the north side of the house. The twins went to the south side. The girls were now returning home and the younger brother wanted to go with them. The older brother would not let him: he held on to his arms. The younger sister wanted to stay instead of going home. At this, the older sister grasped her arms and dragged her along. The older brother could not keep the younger from going with them. The older said, "What is the use of going with those girls? Mother tells us that even the prettiest girl might be good-looking yet be diseased [sic]. In describing such girls, she also says that they wander from home [i.e., are wanton]. These are just such girls." Nevertheless the younger brother was determined to go to the girls' home. Then the older sister, trying to take the younger home, spoke like the older brother. She said, "Our father said that in going away from home or playing about, we might meet a handsome boy, but he might be diseased. What is the use of staying with people you do not know?" But the younger sister said she would stay. The older sister said, "In the spring, when everything is turning green, such people take their baths; then they look perfectly well. That is just how these boys are [i.e., they were diseased]." The older brother dragged the younger into the house, while the older sister dragged her sister along toward their home.

Next morning the boys went hunting as usual. The younger brother took no interest in it as he had formerly. He kept talking about going to the girls' home. Instead of using his bow and arrows, he kept putting the tip of his bow between his teeth, making music by tapping on the string with his arrow. Finally the older brother decided that the next day he would go with him. The older brother said, "Mother told us all about that place where the girls live; they are all our enemies (ᵃxwĭ'c). I know that when we go there, we will be killed." But the younger said, "No, you are foolish. A person who sets out to be married would not be killed by the enemy." At last the older brother decided to go with him.

In the evening the older brother told their mother what the younger had been saying. The older said, "My younger brother is always talking of leaving to go to the girls' home. I could let him go alone and I could stay here to take care of you, but we go everywhere together, so it does not seem right for me to let him go alone. I am going with him." In the morning, before they started, they stuck arrows into the ground near the house and wound a string of beads around them. The older brother said, "When we get there—it will take all day but toward evening we will arrive there—if we are killed, a storm will come from the east. It will look much like smoke. You watch these arrows. The beads and arrows will be broken, and you will then know we have been killed." That is what they said before they started.

When they were halfway, they camped. Late in the evening they saw a light approaching as though someone carried a torch. They saw this as they lay one on each side of the fire. The older brother woke the younger, saying, "Let us go back to see the old woman. She is following us." The younger brother said, "Go back; return to her if you wish." As they talked, a horned owl fell into their fire. The older brother said, "She is throwing something at us." The younger said, "Did not Mother tell us, that when a well-known person is going to die, this owl will be seen nearby, and that person will die? This horned owl fell into the fire: one of us is going to die. That is why it happened." They went to sleep.

In the morning the younger woke the older brother. After they had bathed, the older picked out the two brightest stars and inserted them for his eyes. He put smaller stars all over his body. The younger did the same. Then they started toward the girls' home. They were now quite close.

The girls lived a little to the east of the old man. The old man had a home of his own with his daughter's son [by another daughter; not the twin's son]. The girls were inside their house. The twins did not enter the door. The girls had some short, split sticks, with two or three lines notched on them, used for gambling. (This game is called xutcĭmpĭ'ḳ.) They were playing this. The older sister was on the south side of the house, the younger on the north. They were not sitting, but stooped over. The boys, instead of coming through the door, entered by the smoke hole. The older brother went to the older sister and sat beside her. The younger brother did likewise with the younger sister. At this the girls laughed so loud that their father heard them. Their father said to his grandson, "Hnn, well, what is happening to your aunts over there? They laughed out so loud, and that is not usual." He tried to send his crooked grandson, who was very greedy. The boy said, "I would go, but I am too hungry." The grandfather took a handful of pumpkin seed, parched it with coals, and gave them to him. But he had hardly stepped out of the door when he had finished eating them. The grandfather asked him why he did not go. He said, "I was going, but I finished eating them." This time he got two handfuls, mixed corn with it, parched it, and gave it to him. This time he had gone a little way from the door, when he finished consuming it and came back. When the grandfather asked what was going on, he said, "I did not see. I did not get to their house, because I finished eating." This time the grandfather picked out four handfuls of pumpkin seed and corn. The boy finished eating this when he got to the corner of the other house. Again he said he had finished eating: that was why he had not seen what was going on. Then the grandfather picked out eight handfuls of palo verde seeds and parched this.

Just when the boy got to the door and started to peep in, the girls threw a handful of dirt at him. He fell down by the door and cried with all his might. Then the grandfather ran to his grandson, scolding the girls for mistreating him. He said, "Every time he comes over to see you, you abuse him." He picked up his grandson and carried him home. He was anxious to find out what was going on, so he kept asking the boy. But the boy was sobbing and could not reply. When he got him home, the boy said he had seen two creatures in the house all decorated, and by their decoration the whole house sparkled all over. Then the old man said, "Well, grandson, you do not really mean this. You do not mean that you are going to suck their blood [i.e., kill them]."

As he said this, he took out his black paint and put it across his eyes. Then he took out his red paint and painted his bangs red. Then he took his cane and went out. He invited three tribes and for the fourth looked for the coyote and hawk, two great friends. Whatever the coyote did, the hawk did also. As he approached, they were playing the hoop and pole game. They threw the poles at the old man, knocking him down. When he got up, he said, "Despite your cruel actions, I have come all the way to tell you the news. The proud people have come to visit me."[35] He said, "For your cruel actions, I will pursue you." They said, "All right, we will go on. We will see you later."

Coyote carried a club, a round shield, and all his things together. He tied a string to the shield and slung it around his neck so he could use it at once without having to go back for it. Hawk (tcoʀáhuwa′k)[36] did not carry his shield or club. So he told Coyote to stand where he was, saying, "I have my club and shield stored in my storehouse. When I get all my belongings, I will come right past here, and we will go together." As he started off, he said aside, "Do you really think I am coming back the same way? When I get my things, I will go way up in the sky, and from there I will go over to the boys and kill them first, before you get there." When Hawk left him, Coyote said, "Do you think I will stand waiting until you come back? I will go first

[35] Interrupted at this point.

[36] A small hawk; dark grey, with black marks below the eyes: not the falcon.

and kill the two boys before you get there. That will end our friendship." Then Coyote set out.

He got there before Hawk. But instead of beating the boys to death, he sat with the crowd. For when the three tribes came, they all crowded into the house because they admired the beauty of the boys. Then Coyote came in and shook hands with the two brothers. He called them father's older brother (navi′k). Then he sat down with them. As he sat there, Hawk came through the smokehole with his club and shield. He first beat the older brother to death, then the younger. Then he went right out through the same hole. Just as he went out, Coyote got up and beat the younger brother. The people said, "Never mind about beating the younger brother; he is already dead. You could have killed the two, because you were here first." Then Coyote whirled his club around at the people, saying, "When close relatives [i.e., he claimed the boys for his relatives] are killed like this, one is bound to kill someone else." Then the people were afraid, so they called him saʀámiyo′. "Saʀámiyo′ did this." He was happy because they praised him.

When the twins were killed, the arrows and beads they had left at home broke into pieces. The old woman began to cry when she saw the black storm from the east. She sang:

sipꞷ omisatoko anïɳkwïs

She described the appearance of her children. "They were prettily decked out and painted as they started for the east," she sang. She tore down her house and burned everything in sorrow.

A red-shafted flicker (? kŭkxꞷ′c) pecked at the twins' bodies until he got blood stains all over his breast and wings (as he now has). He looked at his feathers and said, "Before I got all these blood stains on me, I should have gone to tell the old woman, my father's sister (nàbi′). But I am going anyhow." So he started. As the old woman was destroying everything at her house, she saw this bird approaching. She shouted to him not to come nearer. "As soon as they were killed, you could have come to tell me all about it, and then you could have gone back to peck their bodies," she said. "You were the principal one that took part in it." He stopped, grasped some dirt, took it into the air, and shook it out. This made the old woman very angry. So she said, "You think you are going back to peck at the bodies again. On your way there you will find a shady place to rest. When you have had enough sleep, you can get up and say, 'I will go back and fill myself again.'" He went off. As he lay there, he was covered with tiny red ants. He brushed the ants away. He smelled and tasted them. They seemed nice to him. He began pecking at the red ants. From that day, he always feeds on these little ants, because the old woman arranged it so.

When everyone left, the old man Patŭkcŭ't went into the house and dragged out the bodies. They got a long post, tied them to it, and set it up.[37] The blood dripped onto the ground. They parched pumpkin seed and pounded it fine. They caught all the dripping blood and mixed it with this. The whole village came and each took a little. They shared it in all the homes. When the bodies had dried, the bones tumbled to the ground. Those two girls went there and gathered the bones. They placed them on a pile of brush and burned them.

The girls still lived by themselves in a separate house. The younger sister was about to be confined. When her time came, the older sister told their father about it. Then he said to her, "Keep your eyes on the baby. When it is born, if it is a girl, we will keep her, but if it is a boy, I will take him while he is still tender." (I guess our people must have been cannibals.) She said she would watch the child. When the younger sister was about to give birth, the older poured water on the fire in which the old man intended baking the baby. This sent the ashes flying everywhere. Then when the baby was born, the old man could not see it for the cloud of ashes. Then when the older sister saw it was a boy, she dressed it so that the old man would think it a girl. She said, "I think it is a girl." He said, "All right; take good care of her. I am going back to bed."

Four days after that the child was big enough to run around. The older sister made a little skirt for the boy, to deceive the old man. She made a little ring to put on the boy's head, to carry a

[37] The Maricopa sometimes treated slain enemies in this fashion.

pot as girls do. But the boy would throw it away: he would rather play with a little bow and arrows. When the old father saw what the baby was doing, he said, "Well, she is only a child: when she is older she will take the head ring and throw the bow and arrows away." So the child was allowed to carry the bow and arrows.

The boy's mother told him to keep away from his grandfather. She said, "He might seize you and bake you alive." He did as he was told. When the boy grew older, the grandfather decided to take the boy with him. He said, "Let us go to get wood." The old man was tired: he lay in the shade to rest. The little boy climbed a tree. The grandfather thought it queer a girl should climb. Then he saw the child was a boy. He blamed his daughters because he had told them that if it was a boy, he would bake it. Before the little boy came down, the old man started off, thinking that if the boy was lost, that would be the end of him. Instead, the little boy reached home before his grandfather.

They went for wood again next day. Again the little boy played. The grandfather pretended he was asleep. As the little boy came near, he tried to seize him but the boy was too quick. Then he said to his grandson, "Come here. Let me see if you have any lice." The boy went to him. The grandfather had already built a fire where he sat. He was sure he pushed the boy into the fire, but the boy jumped over it and stood on the other side. Then the boy started home. The grandfather went home crying all the way. He told his daughters that the boy was lost in the woods. They laughed at him: "Oh, he is home already." At this he wondered how the little boy could have found his way home.

Next morning they started for wood again. The old man said he was tired and it was too hot to go back, so he would wait a while in the shade. As he lay there, the boy kept shooting his arrow far up in the trees. He began to shoot even harder. The arrow came straight down into the grandfather's heart, killing him. The little boy went home crying. He told his mother what he had done. She asked him if he really meant that he had killed his grandfather. He said, "Yes, I did use my bow and arrows on him." The two sisters told the boy that their father was the one who had invited those three tribes to kill the boy's father and his uncle.

When he learned this, the boy made a hole in the ground just large enough to fit his face. He lay there with his face in the hole and cried until his tears filled it. When the first hole was filled, he made another and filled that too. He made a third and filled that too. Then he made a fourth and filled that too. Then he rose, saying, "What is the use of lying here crying, filling all these holes? A woman does this because she can not go anywhere. But I am a boy: if I start out and find my grandmother, I will learn about these happenings from her."

Before he set out, he came to the place where his father and uncle had been cremated. He thrust an arrow far into the ground and moved it around. When he pulled it out, he drew out the twins. When the father saw the little boy, he looked him right in the face; then hung his head. The uncle too looked at him full-face and said, "Poor younger brother's son (vàti'), if they had not set us up on the pole and let the blood drip, we could get up now and look after you. But since our bones are scattered we are too weak to get up. For this reason, we are going back." His uncle told him that his grandmother made her home in the west, but he did not know where she had gone after their death. But she was probably there fixing her old belongings. The boy said he would go, following their tracks to reach his grandmother.

He set out, leaving his mother and aunt. When he came to the place where the house formerly stood, he found the old woman had been there. Then she had gone to the northwest. The boy followed and overtook her. He stood in front of her. The old woman wondered who this little boy could be. They stood looking at each other for a while: then she knew it was her grandson. The boy then sang:

mawa' mawa' na'ma mawau'à[38]

Then the old woman sang too. She recognized him.

[38] Mawa' was said here to mean "grandmother," possibly by license of song from nàmau', father's mother.

They went together to the little boy's maternal uncle (nágwi'). This uncle played the hoop and pole game. They won from him every time he played. He said, "I hope I win this time, for this is my last chance." Then the little boy asked him how they won from him. He answered, "At the west end of our gaming ground there is a huge rattlesnake coiled. As I go close, it seems ready to strike me. In that way, I miss every time. At the east end, there is an enormous rock. As I go close to it, it seems that it is rolling toward me. So I lose again." The little boy said, "Well, the place you play could not be away from the village: it must be right in the center of the village. When you go there in the morning, you must carry me on your back. I will be crying all the way. Then when you get there, throw me down as hard as you can. If you are to win, some of the women will come and try to wipe my tears away. Then they would say, 'Why do you treat the boy so roughly, for someone might win him too?' This is what they will do if you are to win; but if they do not, you will lose." The uncle did as he was told. He threw the little boy down as hard as he could. Then the boy began to cry: some of the women ran to him and wiped his tears in pity. Then the uncle wagered his nephew. The uncle said, "Before we start this game, we will move this snake away. If you can do that, we will play right here." Then the uncle put his pole under the snake and slung it far away. Then they went to the east, where he wanted them to roll the rock away. The others said, "No, that can not be done. We will play here too. That rock has been here for ages." This time the uncle rolled the rock away. Then they played the game. This time he won everything. Then the uncle, instead of going to the boy and telling him to come home with him, packed up all his things and went off without a word.

The boy and his grandmother went off, asking for the uncle. They were told he went home. As they followed him, where the road curved they could just see him go around the turn. The little boy sang:

xorĕm cakwirki'kimai ai ĭn

They tried to find which way the uncle had gone. But since they could not, they started off together a little way, but stopped.

The little boy said, "We have no home of our own and we can not wander together like this. It would make us feel badly to think we had no home. Let us part in such a way that I will know where you are, and you will know I am somewhere else." Now, the little boy was going to change himself into a comet, but he said he was not going to be seen often; only at times when a well-known person was about to die. He said he would also appear when there was going to be sickness all over the world. "Humans shall see this omen, a red streak across the northern heavens, and they will know there will be sickness." Then the old woman said she was going to change herself into the bright morning star. "Since I am an old woman, when an old person is dying, they will say he will be dead when the first morning star appears." (When an old person is dying, he always says, "I am not going to die until the morning star appears.") So the two transformed themselves into these stars. So the morning star is the old woman and the comet is the little boy (kwiya'homaʀᵃ).[39]

THE DOG CHAMPION

When the Halchidhoma lived on the Colorado, the Yuma came to fight. The Halchidhoma lived in various villages. The Yuma attacked one of these villages and killed all the men. So all the survivors moved. They did not cremate the dead because there were too many, so they just piled them up, where they dried. The skulls lay piled up.

The survivors were scattered all through the mountains. What they had planted, the Yuma took. The Yuma moved up to the place they had been living.

A Yuma man passed by the pile of skulls. A skull said, "Hot," meaning it was hot and thirsty; it said it wanted to get under the shade. It said:

[39] Possibly from kwiyu'c, "meteor" and xuma'ʀᵃ, "child, boy," although the informant made it clear that he is identified with a comet (xŏmceaʀŏsŏ'p), not a meteor. Du Bois notes: "The Diegueño identified the being whose name on earth was Cuyahomarr, the wonder-working boy, and whose name in the sky is Chaup or Shiwiw, with the large meteoric fire-ball which is his physical manifestation. . . . . It is said that the Indians believe that if he casts the shadow of a man on the ground in his passage overhead, the man will soon die" (*Religion of Luiseño*, p. 125).

pilya'	mat^aχai'	gwĭcŏ'k	daϑĕ'v daϑĕ'v
hot	thirsty	shade	to get under.

When the Yuma heard this, he went back and told them as they were holding their meeting at night. They thought something was going to happen to them.

Sometime later a woman went after water. She dipped her olla into the water, and as she pulled it out holding it by the rim, the olla said, "My mouth, my mouth, my mouth (iya'ka)!" She carried the olla home and told them what it had said. When the old men heard this, they said, "Well, some of us will be killed."

Sometime later another woman went for water. The river was high. A log was floating on it. As it passed close, it said that the Halchidhoma will eat and drink. Then it rolled about, groaning. When she told them what the log had said, the old people said their whole tribe would be killed.

The Halchidhoma in the mountains had hardly anything to eat. One man had a dog. This dog talked to him at night, saying, "Now, we left our home when we planted everything. We felt sure we would have plenty to eat. But since we were driven here into the mountains, I am going to try to do something to gain my land back. It was my kind who drove us out (i.e., a Yuma who had dreamed of a dog learned how to drive the Halchidhoma out, and since a dog had told the Yuma, this dog would find a way to circumvent them)." Every night they [the man and dog] went to the village now occupied by the Yuma. The Yuma were gathering and cooking the Halchidhoma pumpkins, and putting them on top of shades. This man would take them down and carry them off, and they would eat together out of the same dish. Every night when the Yuma were playing or singing, they would join them. Finally he went into the house where they held the meetings, taking his dog in, too. (It was an old Yuma woman, named ŏkoi'kulxau'p, who had the dog who told her how to kill the Halchidhoma.) Every night he went into the meeting house and listened to the old men.

One night he heard them say they were going over to the mountains to kill all the Halchidhoma. They told the men to make strong bows and arrows, clubs, and long poles to strike with. They named the day they would start.

The next day, when the man went back to his own people, he called the Halchidhoma together. They had a meeting the night before the Yuma were to start. He told them what he would do. He said, "We have been living in our own country for some time, and you would think anyone who lived there so many years would be able to win any battle. But instead we were driven into the mountains here. We are starving here and our pets are starving. It is an awful thing to beat our dogs when they bark because we are afraid of the enemy. We will start the same day as the Yuma, so as to meet them halfway. When the Yuma come, the old woman will come with her dog. I will take my dog along, too. I will carry a basket [kĕʀi′, like a shallow bowl]. When we meet the Yuma we will stop. When the old woman comes forward she will draw a line across in front, and 1 will do the same. Our dogs will begin to fight. You watch: if our dog wins, then we are sure of winning the battle, but if the Yuma dog wins, you will know we will lose. Before we start, I will strike the basket. When I hit it, though it be clear, it will thunder and lighten. Then you start the battle."

They started the same day as the Yuma. When they saw the Yuma coming, they walked as fast as they could to meet them. The Yuma were coming fast. The Halchidhoma called to them to stop. The Halchidhoma men drew a line and stood along it. The old Yuma woman did the same. Then the two dogs began to fight. The Halchidhoma dog got the other down and chewed him. The Yuma dog started to run. The Yuma men said, "That starving dog almost killed our dog." The Halchidhoma man said, "You drove us from our homes, and we have wandered in the mountains. We are going to try to gain our land back this day."[40] As he said this he stopped. A Yuma man came out, saying he had always killed his enemies wherever he went. He was always successful, and this time he was going to kill the whole tribe. The Halchidhoma struck the basket with his hand (he had carried it on his head all the way) and it thundered and lightened. As they started, the Halchidhoma man told them they must pretend that they were going to hit the Yuma, but instead

[40] Interrupted at this point.

of hitting, they were to bend backward while the Yuma struck. As the Yuma bent forward, they were to hit them then. They killed all the Yuma in the line and the old woman, too. At the first blow they killed so many Yuma, that the Yuma fled. As they fled, the pursuing Halchidhoma killed them. They reached their old home and killed all the women and children there. Then the Halchidhoma came back. The Yuma survivors fled to their own country. The Halchidhoma then went back to their old homes.

The man who had the dog died some time after that. He always told the people that if they abused a dog, the dog would come to him and say, "My master does not give me anything to eat, nor does he treat me well. I am cold: on rainy days when I try to get into the house, he kicks me out. When he is eating, I lie beside him: I do not snatch food, but think he will give me a little piece. Instead, he gives me a hard blow. In spite of this treatment, I watch by the house while my master sleeps." So he told them they must treat dogs properly.

It is a saying that if you throw a bone away the dog says, "Why do you throw the liver away?" People now say it when one throws a bone away.

THE VISIT OF THE DEAD

An Halchidhoma family was coming to visit the people at kwa'akàmat [Gila Bend]. They got half way and camped for the night. They built a fire. Late in the evening, they sat around it. As they sat there they saw the dead people gather and talk to them. The dead threw corn to them and brought melons. But the humans did not say anything. They recognized the faces of those long dead. The dead said, "Hurry up and eat your melons. Let us dance; there is a dance going on." The humans were afraid to go to sleep: they kept the fire going all night. Toward morning the woman went to sleep: she died. But the husband held a little baby in his arms. Whenever the baby fell asleep, he pinched it hard to wake it. The reason the baby was saved was because he pinched it all night long. He arrived at kwa'akàmat with only the baby. He told them he had come with the baby alone. It is always said if you go beyond the mountains to that place, and lie there, you will hear all kinds of noises. If you should fall asleep, you will die.

CORN AND TOBACCO

Once the corn and tobacco were visiting each other. They talked about how they provided for men. The corn said, "Humans use corn more than they use tobacco." The tobacco asked, "In what way is corn more used?" The corn said, "Corn is well cared for because it is of most use. When humans prepare to go to war, the first thing they think of is taking corn, parching it on coals, and grinding it into meal. Men going to war carry it for provision. So corn helps a great deal. When they kill an enemy, I feel as though I was killing the enemy, because I feed the people well so they are able to go kill the enemy. I am more useful."

The tobacco said, "You are used only at the time they are going to war, but everyday people use me day and night. And going to war, they take not only corn, but tobacco. As for corn, when they are ready to return, they have eaten all their meal, and they come back without the corn. But tobacco comes back with people. Even when the men are home tobacco is carried every day and night. If corn is more useful, when men are gathered in meeting, why do they not put a bowl of cornmeal right in the middle, and each take some to swallow? Instead they put you aside, take tobacco and use it all night." So tobacco claimed it was more useful than corn. Then tobacco, after saying this, said he was going back to vikami' [the sacred mountain of the Mohave]. Then the corn was left here alone for a while. Finally corn went away to Mexico.

The corn said, "If I am not useful, they will not call me back: humans would do without me. But tobacco will see that people will try to get me back." On account of these two plants quarreling, we do not get good results with our corn and we do not raise tobacco as well as they do to the west.

CLOUD AND WIND

The cloud and the wind were brothers. They were living at the west end of a village. The wind was the younger brother.

The wind would say, "I want to whirl around a little." Then the older brother would let him go. But instead of a soft breeze, it blew so hard it knocked everything about. A second time he asked the older brother the same, but the latter said, "No, I could not let you go. When you start you blow everything around and the villagers call us bad names. They call out our dead relatives' names, our dead father and dead grandmother. That is something I do not like." But the wind kept on begging to be allowed to go. So the older brother said, "All right, just go softly." Then the wind blew a little, but increased until it blew so hard everything was knocked about again. He got home in the evening. The cloud said, "I have not had anything to eat all day. I mourned all day because the people called out my dead relatives' names." But the younger brother said nothing. Next day he wanted to go again. The older brother would not let him go until noon. "You may go for a while, but do not blow hard." Suddenly the wind blew as hard as he could and knocked everything about. The villagers were very angry at this. The wind had not gone far, so the cloud called him back. He said, "Blow as hard as you can now. We have had people call us all kinds of names, mentioning our dead relatives." He told him to blow over a young girl who was coming through the village. So the wind blew harder than ever and blew all her clothing off. She was naked and was so angry she called the wind bad names.

They went up into the sky. There is a little round hole there, called mai'nyàvutcu'lt. They went through this hole into another world exactly like this one. They made their home there. It rained and the wind blew there; everything was green, and they had plenty to eat.

After they left the earth, there was no rain or wind here, so people were dying of hunger and the heat. At last when they found that all would die, they called a meeting to see if anyone knew where the brothers had gone. No one knew, so they asked the coyote to go all around the world to find them. They gave him a downy feather from under the eagle's tail. They told him he must stop once in awhile and hold his feather up, to see if the wind would blow it. He did this as he went along, but found no sign of the wind. He started from the east, went north and west all the way around by the south until he got back. As he was about to return, he thought, "If I tell them I failed, they would tell me to go again the next day. Now I am going to do this to make them believe I found them." He took the feather and blew it himself. Then he brought the feather home and gave it to the men gathered at the meeting house. He said, "I have been all around the world but could not find them, until I came to the place I started. Then I put the feather up again and this time I felt a little breeze." They knew he had tricked them, so they said nothing.

Next day they sent the buzzard, to go high in the air to find them. He went all over the sky but could not find them, until he came to the hole. Standing near that hole, he held the feather up and felt the breeze. So he told them he was sure they were up in the other world. So he was told to go again and see where they were living.

Next morning he went off to find them. He went through the hole. He went a little way and found where they were living. Just as he entered the door, the cloud, in the south side of the house, turned over toward the wall. The wind on the north side did the same. They did not say a word to him. He sat there all day right by the door. Next day he went again. He kept this up for three days. Then on the fourth day, when he went up there again, they got up and asked him what he wanted. He told them the people were dying of heat and hunger. Then they said they would not come down to live any more, because of the bad names they had been called and the mention of their dead relatives. But the buzzard said he would see that people did not call them bad names. The cloud and wind said, "You go back and tell the people that they must repair their old houses. If they think a house is not strong enough, they should build a new one, and put enough dirt on top so it will not rain through. They should cut off all the brush on their land, and on the fourth day, we will come down."

When the buzzard came down he told the people. They did as they were told; they repaired their old houses and cleared off the brush. On the fourth day it rained and the wind blew hard.

It stormed for four days and four nights. After that they went back to the world above. They are living up there, so we do not have any hard storms.

When the sun appears here, it is night in the land above the sky, and when it is night here, it is day there.

COYOTE HUSBAND

At the time of the wars the Halchidhoma were more numerous than any other tribe. When half [i.e., the Kaveltcadom] moved to Gila Bend, the wars continued fiercer than ever. When the Halchidhoma decided to move, the coyotes had a village of their own somewhere. Their chief called all his men together and they said, "Now these people are going to leave their place. We will not know where they are going to settle. They might be travelling about until they all die. We do not like to see this; let us see if we can not do something for them." He sent out two young boys.

A Halchidhoma girl went out to get water. When she reached the river bank, as she was about to fill her olla, she heard some-one coming. The two coyote boys appeared on the other side. They told her to come with them. She went, leaving her olla there. They travelled for a day, and arrived late in the evening. The people were just like humans. She married into the family of the chief. She stayed there almost two years.

When she disappeared, her own people thought she was dead. Her family burned their house and moved to another place to live.

One night as the coyotes held a meeting, they said, "We should take her back to her own people, for they think she is dead, and have destroyed everything." The reason they had taken her was so if she married there and had a baby, the child might grow up to be a good warrior. And if he in turn had children they might be good warriors too. Through that family, they would be able to capture their old place again.

When she had this baby, they gave her certain rules to obey. They told her, "We are going to take you back to your own people. But you must not tell where you have been. If you do not tell, everything we say will come true, and your people will live on in the same place they are living now. Your people will always win their battles. If you win the first battle, no more enemies will come to fight. You wait for your husband: he will come the fourth night after you leave. When he arrives, they must let him alone. He will come to your house four nights. Then, if your child is treated right, on the fifth night when he comes, he will be just like a human being. He will stay there and take care of the child. But if he is abused during those four nights, or if your child is killed by your people, then you too will die and you will come back to stay with us." She promised she would keep all this secret.

Then the two boys brought her back. When they came to the place where they took her away, they pointed at where she lived. They said, "If you do not find your house, go east from there, and the first house you will reach is yours." The child she carried was nothing but a coyote, but she kept it. She took it with her to the place she lived before, but she saw everything had been burned. Someone called that she was coming. Her parents could not believe it; they started to cry. When she reached the house, people crowded about her and mourned over her. Then they asked where she had been, but she would not tell. They kept on coming to her house and asking, but she would not say anything.

On the fourth night the coyote came there. When everyone was in bed, he crept in. To the other people he was a coyote, but when he got in bed with his wife, they talked together like humans. Toward morning he got up and went out. He came thus three times. The third night he came, the woman's brother saw him come in. He got up, and just as the coyote reached the woman, he took a piece of wood from the fire and hit it on the back. Then the coyote ran out.

The fourth morning they made a gruel of wild seeds and gave the woman's brother a bowl of this. He had it in front of him. The little coyote would jump over the fire, and run in and out. He started to run out again and stepped in the bowl. It burnt him, and he kicked it over his uncle. It made the uncle so angry, he caught the little coyote by the legs and beat him to death on the ground.

The fourth night when the coyote came again, he asked where the baby was. She told him how they had killed it. He said he was going away and the fifth night she would be over there with him. He went off. Before going he said she should tell her people what had been told her by the coyotes. She told them what had been said and how she had promised silence. Then she died as she finished speaking.

We think she is back with her busband. In those days, they would never let children go away from their parents, because they think they might be taken that way. Everything went wrong, for the reason that they were too anxious to find out everything, and by killing the little coyote and beating the older one, they had to leave their country.

BLACKBIRD AND TANAGER

The redwing blackbird and the tanager[41] were friends. They were the handsomest boys in the village. They went about and always took home every girl they saw for their wives. Girls would even come to their house to marry them. They had so many wives that they had to build two large houses to hold them.

Two girls were coming over to them, when Coyote was burning down wood near there. When he saw them coming he knew they were going to the two boys. He made up his mind he would fool them. He took the piece of wood that was burning and scorched his shoulders. He took the skin off so it left big red spots on his shoulders. Then he asked the girls where they were going and they said, "Over to the blackbird's house." She called the blackbird, xasikwa'kŭluta'g. Coyote said, "I don't know how they happen to give me that name, but that is what they call me." The girls said, "All right: let us go on home then." So Coyote took the two girls home with him. When he reached home, he went in, fetched out a basket of corn, and told the girls to grind it.

[41] Or oriole: described as yellow with red shoulders.

So he set off to invite the villagers to attend his wedding feast. Everybody came and crowded about the house. The girls prepared four baskets of corn mush. When they set it outside for the people to eat, they went into the house. The people said, "Why is it the two friends do not come over to the feast?" They wondered who it could be who had that name. All of a sudden they saw those two friends coming and they all said, "Well, the two friends are coming to the feast now." As Coyote went along, he told everybody to come and see his winyi (sister- or daughter-in-law). The blackbird and his friend flew over the house and in by the smoke hole. They took the girls, came out by the same hole and went to their own house. When Coyote came back, he stood outside and talked to the people: asked if they had enough to eat. They answered, "Yes, we had enough to eat." The people went home. Coyote sat down and started to eat some mush. Then he called to the girls, "Come on, let us help ourselves." The second time he called, he said, "Now, young girls who are just married are always bashful this way. You will not be bashful all your lives: we will quarrel sometime. Women are always stubborn. Even if I have to pull one of your arms out, I will do it." So he ran inside, but they were not there.

Then he started to cry. Some people passing said, "The coyote is crying because they took his wives away from him." Coyote said, "No, I am not crying: I am singing and whistling. With these songs I draw girls to the house. It happened I did not, so they went away. If I sing and whistle, more girls will come."

He told the cardinal that he should use his tricks on these two friends. Instead of talking to the two, the cardinal flew over and sat on a post near the door. The tanager tried to shoot this bird. He said, "I am not good at this, so I will ask my friend Blackbird to come and shoot this one." The blackbird came and tried to shoot this bird. He used all the arrows he had but could not shoot him. With the last arrow, the bird hopped to the ground. Then he used his bow to beat the bird but it hopped around. Finally it flew up and the blackbird flew after it. They flew up until they got to the sky where there was a little opening.

When the cardinal flew through, the blackbird followed, and
the opening closed. Everything there was strange to him [Black-
bird]. He did not know how to come down, so he stayed there.
Late in the evening he saw smoke toward the east. He went
toward the house where he saw two old men and two girls. Their
house was made of blocks of ice. They had their fire right in the
center of the house. The boy tried to step right in the house to
sit by the door. But as soon as he got down, he slid to the end of
the house where the girls were, so he sat between them.

Then the old man, their father, said, "We have no covers to
keep the boy warm: he is not used to it. He will freeze to death.
The only way is for you girls to lie beside him and keep him
warm." So the boy lay down on the ice and shivered and shivered. Toward morning he almost died. Then the girls dragged
him out and laid him in the sun. Then at noon he got up and
started on a hunt. But everything was strange, so he did not
know where to hunt. The only way they could keep him warm
was to lie beside him. They did this four nights.

Then he started to look about: there were some vacant houses
there. He found pumpkin and watermelon seeds, peas, and
beans. He looked for these, went farther and found a good place
to plant them. He began to plant all the seeds he had gathered.
When he came home, the girls asked what he had been doing. He
would answer, "Oh, I was just looking around: everything is so
strange." Then in four days everything was ripe. He brought
the corn for the girls to try. They did not know what it was. He
said, "Taste it." They did and thought it was fine, so they almost ate the corn cobs. The second time he brought armfuls
back. He did this with every plant he had. Then he hunted rabbits and quail. They did not know what these were, but he
coaxed them and they became fond of them.

The girls told him all they lived on was wild greens. They said
they saw some animals who came to graze on these greens. They
said, "The animals have a certain path that they take and they
come down to graze near us." So he went out with them and hid
behind the bushes near the path. Then the deer came by. He
killed one. He roasted all the venison on hot stones, and tried to

make the girls eat it. They did not know what it was. Finally they tasted it, and they became so fond of it that they almost chewed up the bones.

While he was doing this up there, his wives below were mourning his death. They burned his house and broke the pottery and all their possessions. They singed their hair. His friend, the tanager, shut himself in his house all alone, saying he was dying. Then Coyote came over and lived with the tanager's and the blackbird's wives. He said they (the two birds) were not the men they really wanted to marry: he, Coyote, was the real one. The wives and the friend tried to get all the birds to find where the blackbird was.

Then the buzzard came to the blackbird up there. He had just killed a deer and was about to skin it, when the buzzard flew right at him. He thought it strange, so he tried to shoot the buzzard. The buzzard said, "Let me alone: I have a message for you." Then he came in the form of a man and told him that the tanager was dying for sorrow, and that his wives were continually mourning. If he wanted to go down to see his friend, he should leave the deer there. "Leave the deer here and go back to where you are now living. Early in the morning of the fourth day, come over to this place again."

During those four days at home, he looked sad. The girls asked him why he looked so sad. They asked him whether he was starving or sick. He said, "Everything is all right, but I am wondering how I ever came to this strange land." On the fourth day, the buzzard was there already, eating up the deer. Buzzard said, "How will I ever take you down? You lie on my back and I will try to fly down." He tried this, but Blackbird was too dizzy. Then he tried two other ways but he could not do it. He said, "We will try the last thing: if we do not succeed, I will have to leave you here." The buzzard spread its wings, the boy lay right on his back and put his arms under the buzzard's wings, and his legs curled around the buzzard's legs. He tried this and said it was all right. The boy said later that the buzzard soared up and down four times before they reached the ground.

When he reached home, he did not know which was his house,

because everything had been burned. He was told where to find
his friend. When he entered the house where his friend lay, the
tanager looked up at him. When he saw who it was, he jumped
up. They went arm in arm the whole day, not saying a word to
each other. Late in the evening they built a big fire. He told
them how he had disappeared. Then their wives rushed in and
interfered so they had to take mesquite bark and tie up the door.
At last they found out it was the scheme of Coyote, so they
chased him away. Then they got their wives back again.

For that reason, anybody who dreams of the tanager or blackbird is always after girls. A person who dreams of the coyote
will interfere in someone else's love affairs, and then will loose the
girl or his wife, and pretend not to care, but sometime later he
will make trouble.

BROTHER-SLAYER[42]

The story begins with the brothers living with the old people. One was a
giant, named xavàtca'c mŏkĭḻyàpu'k (meaning man of xavàtca'c who wiggles because he is tall). Another was married. They started across the Colorado. They
stopped in a line standing in a shallow place. As they reached down to get water
in their palms, some spilled. One brother did not take a palmful for himself, but
caught the water his brother's wife spilled. So through jealousy, the brothers
separated and began to fight.

A blind man was one of the enemy. They had a huge house
filled with men. One of them was a good fighter. He killed all the
enemies about his home. He even went among his own people,
killing them. He killed his older brother, too. His name was
matgwĭnàpa' [no meaning]. His father, named djio'tĭc, was married again and lived some distance away from the village. It was
the children of this couple he killed. This family lived in a cave.
They had a younger son, who said he would start off to see if he
could not kill some of the enemy. They said, "No, you must stay
home. You are only a young boy and your half-brother [Mat-
gwĭnàpa'] is older than you." This boy could fly in the air. He
came over and killed some of the men in the village. They would
always try to shoot him when he came over to the village, but
they could not.

[42] Told by Kutox, who professed not to know it well.

The old blind man in the village was very wise. He asked the people why it was they could not shoot the little boy who flew through the air. Then he said, "How does he act when he is up in the air?" Then men would say, "Every time we take our bows and arrows and point at him, we are sure we will get him when he is high. By the time we shoot, he swoops down. And if we shoot while he is low, he flies up again. He does this every time we shoot, so we cannot get him." Then the old man said, "I will try: I think I will get him." He pulled one hair out and put it across the smoke hole of his round house. He said, "If I cut the hair in two, it shows that I am going to kill the boy." So they gave him the bow and arrow. Instead of pointing it at the hole, he pointed it at the north side of the house. He said, "How does this look?" They said, "You are pointing it to the north, not at the hole." Then he pointed it to the west and they told him, "No, you are still away from the hole." Then he pointed it to the south and they told him, "No," so he pointed it to the east. He asked, "Is that close enough?" They said, "No, that is worse than ever." All of a sudden he shot the arrow through the hole and cut the hair in two. The blood ran down. As the old blind man did this, the crowd yelled so that the old man and woman [in the cave] heard the noise, and thought they were coming after them again.

Next morning the boy went over to the village. As he came toward it, they told the old man he must get ready. The old man got ready. He sat upright in the center of the village. Then the old man raised his bow and arrow and pointed at directions different from that the boy was coming. They said, "You are not going to hit the boy. You point in different directions." They would say to him, "Up" and then "Down." When he pointed right at the boy, they said, "Down," but instead of pointing it down, he pointed up and hit the boy. He shot him in the knee. The boy said, "Although I am shot in the knee, I can squeeze out the blood and I will be all right again." The boy was of the sib xavàtca'c. The boy said anyone who has this sib name will die from the slightest sickness, will die very young, although they are prosperous in everything they do, like planting or gathering.

They will be the best warriors. Then he said he would die anyway, although he knew he could get well from the little wound.
He died in the enemies' village.

Before he started, he told his father and mother that if he was
killed they would see a dark cloud coming. Then they would
know. Then the father and mother mourned for him. His mother would not stay home: she wandered all over the desert mourning for him. On the fourth day she decided to go to war herself.
During these four days in the desert, she took the black sappy
bark of the mesquite and brought it home. Another four days
she stayed home. At night she boiled it and mixed it with mud
and put it on her hair. She trimmed her hair off short. The four
nights that she put this on, her hair grew down to her knees.
She told her husband that she had prepared herself to go to war
and that he should dress her up. He said, "A young woman that
wears her hair below the waist does not look well." So he
trimmed off her hair at the waist line in back. Then he put some
beads around her wrist and some around her neck. He got yellow
paint and put it all over her face, body, and arms. Then she went
and stood at some distance. She was to approach, walking like
a young girl. She did as she was told. As she came toward the
old man, he said she was prepared so that he thought she would
win her battles.

Before she started she said that if she was killed by the enemy,
the old man would see a dark cloud coming. The old man gave
her a reed stuffed with tobacco. He smoked a little of it, put it
out and gave it to her. He said, "You take this with you. As
you go along, do not hurry, so you will arrive at the village late
in the evening as the sun is going down. If everything is going
to go well, a berdache will come out to meet you. If he tries to
take you to the village, act as though you did not want to go.
When you get to the house where the old man lives, tell him you
have come to marry their best warrior, Matgwĭnȧpa'." (He was
the old man's son, but not the old woman's son.)

They tried to give her something to eat but she shook her
head, just as her husband had told her. They named different
kinds of foods, but she only shook her head. Then someone else

in the house said, "Dig way down in the middle [of the house] and give her the wild seeds. She will gladly eat that." (This was ĭkca'm.) But instead of parching it, she ground it. Her husband had told her, "When they give you this wild seed, grind it coarsely, mix it with water, and bake it in the ashes. Take it out whether it is done or not. Then wash it and take it in the house. They will tell you where Matgwĭnàpa' sleeps."

Then they told him [Matgwĭnàpa'] a girl had come to live with him. They also told him that she had baked something for him and had taken it into the house. But he said he was tired and would eat it later. Now, when everybody came in the big house to sleep, he ate the baked bread, and went right off to sleep. The old blind man said to her, "It is just his way: he has been all over the country here looking for enemies. He is tired from fighting, so he goes to sleep early." She went out. As she was just coming in, she crept over to her bed. She pretended she found something; it was the reed of tobacco she had brought from home. She said, "I found something." Then the old man said, "My grandchildren are always scattering my things around." He said, "Light it and bring it to me." She lit it and handed it to him. When he took a puff, he went right off to sleep. This made the other people in the house fall asleep, too.

When she went out again, she pointed to the north. As she held out her hand, a very sharp knife came into it. When she went in, she dragged the young man to the center, piled up dirt and put his head on it. She cut off his head. She took the head and went on top of the house. When she cut his head off, the body rolled around and the blood splashed on everybody who was sleeping. Then the old blind man said, when he heard the noise, "Some one wake him up!" He thought the young man was dreaming. He called, "Wake him up quick! For he may take the main thing and throw it on you." (He meant the club he always carried.) When the body rolled to the blind man again, he felt the blood and knew the man was killed. The old man called her name, "Sinᵃkŭmaði (woman of kŭmaði' sib)." He knew who she was. He said, "The biggest enemy we ever had is this old woman. She is standing on top of the house with the head. I was fooled that time." The people in the house woke, seized and beat each other, and yelled inside the house. They kept it up all night until many were killed or hurt. The old blind man tried to stop them. Some that were not wounded started for the door to kill the old woman. She made the wind blow hard, blowing all the thorns from the mountains, until the door was stuffed with thorns. They tried to get them out of the doorway but the thorns stuck into their hands. The more they tried the harder the wind blew. She said she would stand there as long as it was still dark, and would start off as soon as the sun rose.

She waited until just as the sun was rising she said, "I am ready to start now; you can do whatever you wish with me." Then the people began to get out. They crowded around the house in four rings. She said, "I could have sneaked off in the night. But anyone who kills an emeny should remain to see what they do." She said, "I am ready to go." She started down. When she went through the first ring, they thought they had caught her. But instead they caught hold of, and began to beat, each other. When she went through the second ring, they did the same. When she passed through the third ring, they also grabbed and beat each other. When she went through the fourth ring, instead of facing her, they went forward to the inner rings, grabbed them by the hair and clubbed them to death. She went off, carrying the head in her hand. After she went some distance, they chased her.

When the old man, her husband, heard the yells, he started off to meet her. When she reached him, she handed him the head. When he took it, he turned it over and looked at its face. He knew it was his son; he had tatooed his forehead when he was a little boy. He pretended to drop it. She said, "Go back and bring the head along with us. The reason I brought the head was because the young man knew very well he was killing his brothers, and he did not have pity on his old father. For that reason, I brought the head home for you to see." Then he cried over the death. She told him to stop. She said they had shed enough tears for their lost sons. As she said this, the enemies were pretty close. When the old man saw they were in danger, he scratched a big mark on the ground which formed a big canyon. The old woman and the old man went down into it and the canyon closed again, so the enemy had to go home.[43]

ABSTRACTS

CREATION TALE (p. 345)

The world is covered by a flood. Kukamat and Isacipas emerging, send their pet birds to test how far they have come. Kukamat, deceived, opens his eyes and is blinded by the salt water. They float four times around the world while the water subsides. One of them brings up sand for dry land. It is dark. *Isacipas makes the sun of his hair, the moon of his fingernail, and stars of sand.*[44] They model humans of clay. *Isacipas gives his their tribal characters;* Kukamat makes them with webbed hands and feet. They quarrel; Kukumat goes under the earth with a thundering noise. *His products become beavers and web-footed birds.* Kukamat pulls the sky down and leaves a hole in the earth from which blood flows. Cipas kneels on the hole and pushes up the sky. *He lets some blood flow so that there will be sickness. His finger marks show as a constellation. He ordains life after death.* The people speak; Cahuilla first, then Maricopa and others. The Chemehuevi speak at midnight, *hence they are unintelligible.* Whites speak last like babies; the Creator soothes them. *Hence whites complain and are sick. He clothes each people appropriately and breathes reason into them.*

All the animals and people live in one house. The Creator procures an axe so they have firewood. The rabbit plays with the snake, using it for a whip. The snake complains so the Creator makes him teeth of coals and sunrays. The snake bites the rabbit; she dies. *Hence rabbits are snake food.* Holding the Creator responsible, the people decide to kill him. Bullfrog drinks all the water while the Creator is swimming. He sickens. He tries lying in four places and eating four things, but he dies. *Hence people sicken and die.* He goes under the earth; *when he turns over it causes an earthquake.* Some decide to kill Frog, so she flees under-

[43] The story continues, but the informant did not know any more.

[44] Explanatory elements are italicized.

ground. *Those who resemble Frog commit parricide.* (A sky-snake was coiled about the earth to hold back the sea.)

Coyote is suspect and sent for fire. Meanwhile they cremate the Creator. *Hence people now cremate and the heart is the last consumed.* Coyote, discovering the ruse, seizes the Creator's heart and runs east to devour it. *Where he stops he names the buttes.* He swims and gets all diseases. He goes along the southern ocean. *The tribes scatter to their historic locations.*

KWISTAMXO (p. 352)

People form a spring in the Creator's house: *it is the source of the Colorado. The house posts are now rocks.* Kwistamxo goes on top of Avikwame and *instructs the people to plant and reason.* (Kwistamxo is identical with Cipa, the Creator.)

COYOTE (p. 353)

Two mountain lions leave the Creator's house after the cremation to rebuild and ordain that *humans shall do likewise.* They use the body of Namet, the older, for a house. They burn grease so that their brother, Coyote, wandering in the south, discovers their whereabouts. Namet makes rain by plunging an arrow into the ground; whirling it, and pointing it at the cardinal points. *He ordains that heavy rain shall come from the south.* A flood rises and subsides. Living on seeds, they decide to make deer. They try four kinds of wood, succeeding with sagebrush. They bring male and female deer from their mouths, using ironwood for legs, *hence deer-legs are crooked.* They put the deer in a cave to multiply. *Because of this the mountain tribes live on deer.*

Coyote makes four spirit foxes by rolling, *of which humans shall dream to get curing power.* Coyote arrives at his brother's home. Namet Hatagult, transformed into a pot, seizes him. They recognize him, fear his wickedness, but *forgive him as humans should do.* Each day they secretly get deer from the cave, but Coyote discovers and frees the deer, so that *humans shall have to hunt.* Coyote props a dead mountain sheep on a cliff and induces Namet to hunt it. He pushes Namet over the cliff. Namet Hatagult causes a rain which washes the broken bits of

Namet together again. They decide to destroy Coyote. They make everything salty. Coyote cannot relieve his thirst and hunger; he returns home. Namet Hatagult comes down from the sky and restores Coyote by singing. *Hence humans sing for the sick and dead.* Namet also descends and forgives Coyote, so that *humans shall forgive their sick relatives.*

Coyote suggests a feast, so they can get wives. They warn him against visiting a woman who has a pet duck. He silences the duck with ashes and hides in the form of a lizard. As he attempts to escape the woman claws him in two. He returns home. Namet Hatagult replaces Coyote's missing half with half a deer, hence *coyote tastes like deer.* They make a blood sausage to poison her. Coyote gives it to her; she dies. He takes her nails for a head ornament.

Four tribes arrive for the feast. Coyote fails to attract women. Meanwhile the brothers hide his claw ornament. Finding it, Coyote wears it in the dance. The dancers attempt to kill him in revenge for the old woman's death, but fail. They kill the mountain lions and take their scalps. Coyote follows, finding successively fresh fireplaces. He overtakes a woman carrying the scalps. He tricks her into teaching him the songs, kills her, and dons her skin. The disguised Coyote dances for the people with the scalps. He jerks off the skin, revealing himself, and runs off with the scalps. He outruns his pursuers. He fails to replace the scalps to resuscitate his brothers. They do so themselves.

They set out to get Antelope Woman; the two well-dressed, Coyote otherwise. He sends his brothers to kill game. He persuades the woman to join them. *Since then humans commit adultery.* He cooks and eats snakes, the others rabbits. The bears follow. Bear, her husband, shows he can break rocks with his claws. Bear orders his wife home; she refuses. Coyote attempts to kill Bear but is split in two. The mountain lions send Bear home to get his fellows. They strengthen themselves for the fight by thrusting canes down their throats and covering their house with snow. The bears attempt to destroy the house but fail. The mountain lions are killed three times; an east wind restores them. The fourth time the bears are killed; a black wind fails to restore them. The lions revive Coyote and his dog in the ashes. Because animals fought, *humans now wage war*.

FLUTE LURE (p. 367)

A girl (West Woman), living alone, plays at sliding into the water. Gopher comes under water and has intercourse with her. On the way home she finds she is pregnant, but struggles home *else humans will give birth in the open*. Twin sons are born. Animals bring wood, claiming paternity: she accepts only Gopher's. One baby kills quail while she is away. She throws the game away thinking it left by the animals. Finally she eats it realizing the twins will provide food. She makes bows for them. They hunt larger and larger small-game, turning back in fear each time, but killing them. *Since she had three ways of cooking rabbits so have humans. The boys do not eat the game they kill: jackrabbits are poisonous.* They kill a deer, sing to make it small, and carry it home. Their mother brings the deer to life and lets it run off. The twins follow *so humans will recapture escaping game*. The woman transforms herself into a post, the boys are about to shoot it, when she reveals herself.

The twins go to capture eaglets. They are thirsty. They see and name a mirage. Their mother causes a rain to succor them. One boy accuses the other of *killing various birds and insects, causing rain*. They circle the mountain bearing the eagle nest. The younger gathers fallen feathers; the older deprives him of them. The younger transforms himself into a snake and attempts to climb to the nest. He fails and falls down. The older transforms into cotton and floats up. He returns with two eaglets. The younger takes the dull-colored eaglet in modesty. The other takes it from him, citing their mother's treatment to show the younger has no choice. They are thirsty as they journey home. Their mother succors them with rain, but it kills the eaglets. They bury them and destroy their bows in sorrow. The twins are angry with their mother. She thrusts an arrow in the ground and pulls out the eaglets alive. *They build a cage for the eaglets, so humans do.*

Their mother tells of arrow reeds in the east. Coyote boastfully goes for them. The woman refuses straight reeds, making him go again for crooked ones. She reaches to the north for a hot stone on which to straighten them. Coyote shows how *humans will do it with hot ashes*. She reaches to the north to finish the arrows magically. The twins try their arrows against Coyote.

The twins go for reeds at the ocean bottom. The younger dives but fails to get them. The older dives. He finds there a path guarded by four beaver, who let him pass. He gets two reeds and returns. Their mother makes flutes of the reeds by pointing them at the cardinal directions. She has them play these at dawn. Two girls hear the sound and journey north to seek it. They are stopped by various men: chicken hawk, lizard, rock squirrel, screech owls, and horned owl. Each one claims to have made the sound, but failing to reproduce it, is mocked by the sisters. When the girls reach the twins' home, the mother obliterates the doorway. Finally, in pity, the mother invites them to enter. They discover the doorway, *where every house should have its entrance, on the east side*. The old woman is watchful of her sons. The younger twin magically causes her to sleep, *hence people now bewitch in this fashion*. The younger twin has his will of the younger sister. The older sister makes insects to provoke the older twin to respond to her, but fails.

The girls start to return home. The younger twin wants to accompany them, but his brother holds him. The younger girl wants to remain but her elder sister drags her off. The older twin agrees to follow them. They leave a life token: two arrows in the ground supporting beads will break if they are killed; a storm will come from the east. When they camp a horned owl falls into their fire. *This will be an omen of the death of an important person.* The twins cover their bodies with stars. The girls are playing with dice in their house. The twins enter by the smoke hole and sit beside them. The girls' father hears them laugh. He sends his grandson to spy on them; each time the boy's greed prevents him getting there. When the boy does look in their house, the girls throw dirt in his eyes. He reports to his grandfather that there are two sparkling creatures there. The old man decides to kill them and gets the aid of Coyote and Hawk. Coyote is ready for war, Hawk not. They intend forestalling each other in killing the twins. Coyote goes to kill them, but makes friends. Hawk flies through the smokehole and clubs the twins to death. When Coyote then clubs the dead twins, the people twit him, so he turns on them pretending to be the twins' relative. *Relatives should take revenge.*

When the twins are killed, the life token breaks and their mother mourns. *Flicker gets blood spots on his breast* from the twins' bodies. He goes to tell the news to the old woman, but she accuses him. She causes him to *eat ants, which are his food now.* The people catch the twins' blood and eat it. The two girls burn the twins' bows.

When the younger sister is about to give birth, the girl's father says he will kill a boy baby. A boy is born but the older sister disguises it as a girl. But the boy plays with bow and arrows. The child climbs a tree: the old man discovers its sex. The old man attempts to roast his grandson, but he escapes. The boy shoots arrows, which fall and kill the old man. When he grieves, his mother and aunt inform him that his grandfather was responsible for slaying the twins, his father and uncle. The boy mourns for the twins, filling holes with his tears. He decides to see his grandmother. He thrusts an arrow in the ground and brings out the twins. But they are too weak to live. The boy finds his grandmother. She recognizes him.

The boy's maternal uncle is playing hoop and pole, but losing because he fears a rattlesnake and a rock. The uncle wagers the boy in the game. Women wipe away the boy's tears, which is an omen that the uncle will win. The uncle removes the snake and rock, and wins. He goes off with his winnings.

The boy and his grandmother try to follow the uncle, but fail. The pair have no home, so the boy decides to become *a comet, which will be an omen to humans of impending death.* The old woman becomes *the morning star to mark the time of an old person's death.*

THE DOG CHAMPION (p. 396)

The Yuma drive the Halchidhoma into the mountains. The Yuma hear omens of disaster; a skull, pot, and log which speak.

An Halchidhoma dreams his dog will help them (as an old Yuma woman had dreamed of hers). Secretly visiting the Yuma, this man hears them plan to attack the Halchidhoma. The dog champions fight; the Yuman dog is worsted. The man strikes his basket to cause a storm. The Halchidhoma slay all the Yuma. The dog told his master how they felt when abused, so *people must never abuse dogs.*

THE VISIT OF THE DEAD (p. 399)

A family cross the desert east of the Colorado (the land of the dead). The dead come, offering food. The wife falls asleep: she dies. The husband keeps himself and their baby awake: they escape. *If one falls asleep in this place he will die.*

CORN AND TOBACCO (p. 400)

Corn and Tobacco quarrel over which is most useful. Corn boasts of feeding warriors, but Tobacco boasts of being used by everyone as well. In anger, Tobacco goes to the west and Corn to Mexico, *hence corn and tobacco do not grow well here.*

CLOUD AND WIND (p. 400)

Cloud and Wind are brothers. Wind blows too hard; people curse the brothers. In anger, Cloud and Wind go up through a hole in the sky. There is a drought on earth. Coyote is sent to discover the pair. He is given down to test the wind. Failing to find them he blows the down: they discover the trickery. Buzzard searches and at the sky-hole his down is blown. He goes to their house, but both turn away from him in anger. They finally tell Buzzard to instruct the people to repair their houses and prepare their fields. Cloud and Wind descend and make a storm. *Now they live in the sky so that there are no longer any hard storms.*

COYOTE HUSBAND (p. 403)

The coyotes decide to help the Halchidhoma. Two coyotes entice an Halchidhoma girl. She marries a coyote: her people think she is dead. Her coyote-child is to be a great warrior. The coyotes decide to take her back. She is warned not to disclose where she has been and to await her coyote-husband. The coyote visits his wife. Her brother discovers it and hits him. The baby-coyote kicks over this brother's gruel: the brother kills him. The coyote-husband returns and says she will die. She dies. *Parents take their children with them. Because the coyote-child was killed, the Halchidhoma were forced from their country.*

BLACKBIRD AND TANAGER (p. 405)

Blackbird and Tanager attract all the girls for their wives. Two girls are going to them. Coyote burns his shoulders raw so as to pretend to be Blackbird. The deceived girls join him in his house. He invites everyone to a feast outside. Blackbird and Tanager fly in through the smoke hole and take the girls away. Coyote discovers they are gone and cries. He pretends he is not weeping, but whistling to attract girls. He sends Cardinal to the two birds, who fail to shoot Cardinal. Cardinal, pursued by Blackbird, flies through the sky-hole, which closes. Blackbird finds a house of ice in the sky. He slides in between two girls who lie with him to keep him warm. He finds seeds to plant. He brings the plants and game, and persuades the girls to eat these. Meanwhile his wives and Tanager mourn: Coyote appropriates the wives. Buzzard locates Blackbird in the sky and persuades him to return to earth. He carries Blackbird down on his back. Blackbird recovers his friend, Tanager, and his wives. *Anyone who dreams of these birds will pursue women; those who dream of Coyote will meddle in and spoil love affairs and cause trouble.*

BROTHER-SLAYER (p. 409)

Brothers are crossing the Colorado. One drinks water spilled by his brother's wife. The married brother (Matgwinapa) fights with the first [and kills him]. He kills his older brother. Their father lives in a cave with a second family (of xavatcac sib). Among them is a boy who flies over the village to take vengeance. People fail to shoot him because of his erratic flight. A blind man tests himself to shoot the boy: he puts a hair across the smoke hole, feints at shooting it, and hits it. When the boy comes, the blind man shoots him in the knee. He dies. *Hence xavatcac people, although successful in all else, die from the slightest cause*. His parents see a dark cloud as token of his death. His mother mourns and decides on vengeance. His father dresses her as a young girl. She goes to marry Matgwinapa. She gives him bread which causes him to sleep. She causes the blind man to sleep with a special cigarette. She holds her hand to the north and gets a knife. She cuts off Matgwinapa's head. The body rolls about, waking everyone. They kill each other. They pursue her but she causes a wind to choke the doorway with thorns. She is on top of the house. They form rings around it. She eludes them, carrying the head, while they club one another. She gives the head to her husband, who mourns. When the enemy pursue, he scratches a cleft in the ground, into which they escape.

THE DOG PIMA (p. 7)

Two men have a dog. While they hunt, she turns into a girl and cooks for them. They discover her and persuade her to remain human. *Their children become the Dog Pima, a tribe.*

THE CALENDAR (p. 143)

Kukamat, the creator, returns to *name the months and when to plant.* He speaks like thunder. Coyote alone remains awake: he tells the people.

MOON (p. 146)

Coyote wishes to marry the moon. He goes close, opening his mouth.

Coyote steals something, tries to jump over the moon, and *can now be seen in the moon.*

BIBLIOGRAPHY

The following abbreviations are used:

AA   American Anthropologist
BBAE   Bulletin of the Bureau of American Ethnology
JAFL   Journal of American Folk-Lore
PaAMNH Anthropological Papers of the American Museum of
        Natural History
RBAE   Annual Report of the Bureau of American Ethnology
UCPAAE University of California Publications in American
        Archaeology and Ethnology

ABBE, CLEVELAND. Report on the Solar Eclipse of July, 1878 (Professional Papers of the Signal Service, War Department, No. 1, 1881).

BARTLETT, JOHN RUSSELL. Personal Narrative of Explorations and Incidents in Texas, New Mexico, California, Sonora, Chihuahua, etc. (New York, 1856, 2 vols.).

BOLTON, HERBERT EUGENE. Kino's Historical Memoir of Pimería Alta (Cleveland, 1919, 2 vols.).

———. Anza's California Expeditions (Berkeley, 1930, 5 vols.).

BROWNE, J. ROSS. Adventures in the Apache Country, etc. (New York, 1869).

CLIMATOLOGICAL DATA: Arizona Section (U.S. Department of Agriculture, Weather Bureau, Phoenix, Arizona, 34, 1930, No. 13, 51–56).

CORBUSIER, WILLIAM F. The Apache-Yumas and Apache-Mojaves (American Antiquarian, 8, 1886, 276–84, 325–39).

COUES, ELLIOTT. On the Trail of a Spanish Pioneer. The Diary and Itinerary of Francisco Garcés, etc. (New York, 1900, 2 vols.).

CREMONY, JOHN C. Life among the Apaches (San Francisco, 1877).

CULIN, STEWART. Games of the North American Indians (RBAE, 24, 1907, 3–809).

CURTIS, EDWARD S. The North American Indian (Cambridge, Mass., 2, 1908).

DAVIS, EDWARD H. The Papago Ceremony of Vikita (Indian Notes and Monographs, 3, 1920, No. 4).

[DIXON, ROLAND B.] Indian Population in the United States and Alaska, 1910 (Washington, 1915).

DORSEY, GEORGE A. Indians of the Southwest (no place, 1903).

DU BOIS, CONSTANCE GODDARD. The Religion of the Luiseño Indians of Southern California (UCPAAE, 8, 1908, No. 3).

EMORY, W. H. Notes of a Military Reconnoissance from Fort Leavenworth, in Missouri, to San Diego, in California, etc. (Ex. Doc. No. 41, 30th Congress, 1st Session, Washington, 1848).

FORDE, C. DARYLL. Ethnography of the Yuma Indians (UCPAAE, 28, 1931, No. 4).

GIFFORD, EDWARD WINSLOW. Clans and Moities in Southern California (UCPAAE, 14, 1918, No. 2).
———. Californian Kinship Terminologies (UCPAAE, 18, 1922).
———. Yuma Dreams and Omens (JAFL, 39, 1926, 58–69).
———. The Kamia of Imperial Valley (BBAE, 97, 1931).
———. The Southeastern Yavapai (UCPAAE, 29, 1932, No. 3).
———. Cocopa MS.
HARRINGTON, JOHN PEABODY. Yuma Account of Origins (JAFL, 21, 1908, 324–48).
HAWLEY, FLORENCE M. Prehistory Pottery and Culture Relations in the Middle Gila (AA, n.s., 34, 1932, 548–50).
HECK, N. H. Earthquake History of the United States Exclusive of the Pacific Region (U.S. Coast and Geodetic Survey, Special Publication No. 149, 1928).
HEINTZELMAN, S. P. In Indian Affairs on the Pacific (House Ex. Doc. 76, 34th Congress, 3d Session, Washington, 1857, 34–53).
HERZOG, GEORGE. The Yuman Musical Style (JAFL, 41, 1928, 183–231).
HRDLIČKA, ALEŠ. Maricopa Weaving (AA, n.s., 7, 1905, 361).
IVES, JOSEPH C. Report upon the Colorado River of the West (House Ex. Doc. 90, 36th Congress, 1st Session, Washington, 1861).
KISSELL, MARY LOIS. Basketry of the Papago and Pima (PaAMNH, 17, 1916, 115–264).
KROEBER, A. L. A Preliminary Sketch of the Mohave Indians (AA, n.s., 4, 1902, 276–85).
———. Shoshonean Dialects of California (UCPAAE, 4, 1907, No. 3).
———. Phonetic Elements of the Mohave Language (UCPAAE, 10, 1911, No. 3).
———. California Kinship Systems (UCPAAE, 12, 1917, No. 9).
———. Yuman Tribes of the Lower Colorado (UCPAAE, 16, 1920, No. 8).
———. Handbook of the Indians of California (BBAE, 78, 1925).
———. Arrow Release Distributions (UCPAAE, 23, 1927, No. 4).
———. The Seri (Southwest Museum Papers, No. 6, 1931).
———. Walapai field notes, MS.
LAUFER, BERTHOLD. The Early History of Felt (AA, n.s., 32, 1930, 1–18).
LLOYD, J. WILLIAM. Aw-aw-tam Indian Nights (Westfield, N.J., 1911).
LOWIE, ROBERT H. Social Life of the Crow Indians (PaAMNH, 9, 1912, part 2).
———. Notes on Shoshonean Ethnography (PaAMNH, 20, 1924, 185–314).
LUMHOLTZ, CARL. New Trails in Mexico (New York, 1912).
MASON, J. ALDEN. The Papago Harvest Festival (AA, n.s., 22, 1920, 13–25).
NORDENSKIÖLD, ERLAND. An Ethno-geographical Analysis of the Material Culture of Two Indian Tribes in the Gran Chaco (Comparative Ethnographical Studies, 1, Göteborg, 1919).
———. The Ethnography of South America Seen from Mojos in Bolivia (Comparative Ethnographical Studies, 3, Göteborg, 1924).
OPPOLZER, THEODOR VON. Canon der Finsternisse (Akademie der Wissenschaften. Math.-naturwissen. Classe. Denkschriften, 52, Vienna, 1887).
PARSONS, ELSIE CLEWS. Notes on the Pima, 1926 (AA, n.s., 30, 1928, 445–64).
Report of the Commissioner of Indian Affairs . . . . for the Year 1857; Ibid. for the year 1858 (Washington, 1858).

425

Ross, Clyde P. The Lower Gila Region, Arizona (U.S. Geological Survey, Water-Supply Paper No. 498, Washington, 1923).

Russell, Frank. The Pima Indians (RBAE, 26, 1908, 3–389).

Sapir, Edward. Song Recitative in Paiute Mythology (JAFL, 23, 1910, 455–72).

[Sedelmair, Jacobo.] Relación que hizo el Padre Jacobo Sedelmair, etc. (Documentos para la Historia de Mexico, series 3, v. 4, Mexico, 1853–57, 843–59).

Spier, Leslie. Southern Diegueño Customs (UCPAAE, 20, 1923, 297–358).

———. Zuñi Weaving Technique (AA, n.s., 26, 1924, 64–85).

———. Havasupai Ethnography (PaAMNH, 29, 1928, part 3).

———. Klamath Ethnography (UCPAAE, 30, 1930).

Stratton, R. B. Captivity of the Oatman Girls (Salem, Ore., 1909).

Trippel, Eugene J. The Yuma Indians (Overland Monthly, 2d series, 13, 1889, 561–84; 14, 1889, 1–11).

Velasco, [José] Francisco. Sonora: Its Extent, etc. (trans. by Wm. F. Nye. San Francisco, 1861).

Waterman, T. T. The Religious Practices of the Diegueño Indians (UCPAAE, 8, 1910, No. 6).

Winship, George Parker. The Coronado Expedition, 1540–1542 (RBAE, 14, 1896, part 1).

INDEX

Abortion, 314
Age distinctions, 209-16, 314, 323
Agriculture; see Cultivation
Akwa'ala: location of, 11; trade with, 333
Alakwisa, 11
Alarcon, 11, 12, 16, 94
Albinos, 313
Animal foods, 65, 71
Antelope hunting, 69
Anvils, pottery, 107-8
Anza, 3, 24, 28, 30-37, 183
Apache, 7, 9, 58, 72, 103, 132, 183, 189; attacks, 18, 39-40, 160-78, 184; location of, 1, 8
Apron, woman's, 95
Armament, 166, 175-76
Armor, 131, 137, 164
Arrows, 133-35, 378; heads, 103, 134, 150, 295; release, 133; straightener, 137
Awatobi, 110
Awl, 123
Axes, stone, 130

Bags, woven, 126
Bahacechas, 10
Balls, 334, 336
Bartlett, J. R., 9, 22, 319; on cultivation, 48, 59; on dress, 94-96, 99, 103, 163; on houses, 83, 86, 90; on implements, 123-24; on location of Maricopa, 25, 37-40; on population, 4, 17, 20; on warfare, 161, 163, 176; on weaving, 111, 114
Baskets, 43, 78, 89, 90, 122-25, 307, 316, 327
Bathing; see Swimming
Beals, Ralph, xiii, 15, 113, 158
Beans, 64
Beard, 101
Beauty, concepts of, 219, 232, 315
Bee-killing ordeal, 262, 268, 322

Bees, classification of, 73
Beliefs, 103, 108, 135, 150, 186, 243, 248, 294-96, 303, 324-26; about children, 196, 315, 318; birth, 310-14; concerning xavàtca'c sib, 410; see Sayings, Tabus
Berdache, 6, 242, 254
Berries, first gathered, 53
Bewitching, 239, 251, 285-89, 387, 412
Birds eaten, 71
Birth customs, 222, 243, 310-14; hut, 91
Blankets: for doors, 87; rabbit-skin, 93, 96; repaired, 121; robes, 93, 96, 163; traded, 43; willow bark, 125; woven, 111, 125
Bolton, H. E., 13, 35
Boundaries, 23, 60
Bowguard, 135
Bowls, 105, 131
Bows, 132
Breechclout, 94
Broom, 131
Browne, J. R., 184
Buff ware, ancient, 110
Bull-roarer, 339
Butchering, 125

Cacti used, 54, 56, 64, 131
Cages, 74
Cahuilla, 9, 42, 172, 333
Calendar, 61, 142-45, 189; sticks, 138-42
Cannibalism, Yavapai, 177
Cañute game, 340
Cape; see Robes
Captives, 17, 45, 182-84, 267, 321
Carrying frame, 123; net, 126
Carrying habits, 78, 126, 135, 318-20, 330
Carson, Kit, 38
Cautery, 290

Fishing, 38, 48, 65, 74-77, 294
Flageolet, 131, 380-81
Floods, 49, 58, 60, 75
Font, 6, 23, 32-37, 43, 45, 59, 93, 96, 99, 101, 103, 183
Food quest, 48-49
Forde, C. D., 23, 165, 205, 298
Friendships: intertribal, 41-42, 57, 334; personal, 330, 409

Games, 200, 323, 334-44
Garcés, 3, 13, 14, 16, 23, 33-37, 42, 43, 59, 82, 93, 130, 183, 330
Giant cactus, 56-58, 146, 162, 258, 262, 269; jars for, 105
Gifford, E. W., xiii, 8, 11, 137, 177, 205; on Cocopa, 44, 179, 291, 327
Granary, basket, 90, 124
Griddle, 63, 106

Hairbrush, 100
Hairdress, 98-100, 164, 165, 181, 291, 298, 304, 336; for scalps, 184
Halchidhoma: dreaming, 236; flight of, 14; games, 340; kinship system, 216; location of, 2, 10, 12; Maricopa attitude toward, 46, 174; mourning ceremony, 305-8; in myths, 396, 403; name, 4, 6; sibs, 186-96; tobacco,333; weaving,110; women shamans, 282
Halyikwamai, 82, 155; dreaming, 236; incorporated by Kohuana, 10, 14; location of, 2, 14, 16, 18; sibs, 186-96
Hand game, 264, 343
Harrington, J. P., 6, 205
Hats, 93, 100
Havasupai, 95, 104, 130, 151, 158, 221, 229, 230, 336; carrying habits, 319, 330; dances, 229, 230; tribal names, 9, 45
Hawley, F. M., 141
Headband, 98-99, 111
Headring, 105, 330
Head-scratcher, 180, 325, 327
Herzog, George, xiii, 257-58; on Maricopa music, 271-79
Hidden ball game, 339

Hoe, side-scraper, 62
Honey, 73
Hood, cradle, 316
Hoop and pole game, 265, 336
Hopi, 8, 43, 93, 110, 169, 189, 226
Household arrangement, 88, 226
Hrdlička, Aleš, 112-13
Humor, 46, 97, 174, 179, 220, 228, 327, 328
Hunting, 48, 65-72, 310

Images, used in mourning, 305, 308
Informants, xii, 9, 12, 25, 98, 139, 271
Inheritance, 60, 156, 240
Irrigation, 24, 59

Jalchidunes; see Halchidhoma
Jimsonweed, 243
Juaneño, 322
Juggling, 339

Kamia, 45, 209, 214; location of, 2 ,11
Kaveltcadom: coiffure, 99; facial painting, 101; in myth, 403; location of, 1, 2, 9, 12, 14, 25-41; name, 9; necklaces, 103; settlements, 23-25; weaving by, 110
Kicking-stick, 334
Kino, 14, 27-30, 75
Kinship terms, 194, 208-19, 228, 329
Kissell, M. L., 90, 124
Knives, 130
Kohuana: as allies, 161; dreaming, 236, 309; location of, 2, 10, 14, 16-18, 140; in Maricopa community, 82, 155, 206, 225, 227, 288, 321; sibs, 186-96; songs, 185, 268-69
Kroeber, A. L., xiii; cited, 92, 155, 156, 177, 258, 259-62, 267-70; on Maricopa sibs, 190; on Mohave, 6, 16, 62, 158, 187, 255, 283, 327; opinions, 4, 10, 12, 151

Labor, sex division of, 73, 77-81, 83, 90, 96, 98, 102, 103, 104, 112, 125, 158, 242, 314, 330, 334
Ladles: pottery, 106; wooden, 130
Land of dead, 286, 296-99, 301, 303
Laufer, Berthold, 114